Feet First: Jules Vallès

Walter Redfern

UNIVERSITY OF GLASGOW FRENCH AND GERMAN PUBLICATIONS
1992

University of Glasgow French and German Publications

Series Editors: Mark G. Ward (German)
                   Geoff Woollen (French)

Consultant Editors : Colin Smethurst
                     Kenneth Varty

Modern Languages Building, University of Glasgow,
Glasgow G12 8QL, Scotland.

1000332867

0852613156 T

First published 1992.

Cover engraving by André Gill (published 14 July 1867) reproduced by
kind permission of Glasgow University Special Collections.

Typed by Jay Wild of Hypertype WP Services, Glasgow.

Printed by Castle Cary Press, Somerset BA7 7AN.

ISBN   0 85261 315 6

Gustave Courbet: Portrait de Jules Vallès

(Musée Carnavalet, Paris)

cliché

Contents

Acknowledgments

First among equals: Roger Bellet, who latched on to the key word in Vallès's vocabulary, *coller*. Sticking to it: Bellet has embodied this principle in decades of critical devotion to Vallès. He has been of enormous help to me.

At differing stages of my research, I have been very grateful for advice, materials, and encouragement from: Pierre Pillu, Émilien Carassus, Silvia Disegni, Federico Montanari, Bernard Gallina, Charles Stivale, Pamela Moores and Theodore Zeldin.

Sussex University Library was very helpful in supplying material on the Commune, and Glasgow University Library gave permission to reproduce the portrait of the artist as a young dog that graces the front cover. I am grateful to Tim Hobbs, Keeper of Special Collections, for his help with this latter, and also to the Musée Carnavalet and its *Conservateur des Peintures*, Christophe Leribault, for permission to reproduce the frontispiece painting of Vallès by Courbet.

The significance of the title of this book lies, unsurprisingly, in the *œuvre* of Jules Vallès himself. Intrigued or impatient readers may turn without delay to page 124.

For all the rest, I am grateful beyond words to my wife, Angela, and in particular for her insistence that I put in more flags.

I wish to express my thanks to the British Academy for a research grant.

Walter Redfern   Reading, March 1992

Abbreviations

Full details of these works are given in the Bibliography. The frequent references to volumes I and II of Roger Bellet's Pléiade edition of the *Œuvres* are given thus: (I, 935), followed by (p. 937), etc., for ones to the same volume following *closely* after in the English text until there is a change of cited source. It has not been reiterated between brackets that all page references to *L'Enfant*, *Le Bachelier*, and *L'Insurgé* are to Pléiade volume II.

Enf.	*L'Enfant*
Bach.	*Le Bachelier*
Ins.	*L'Insurgé*
RL	*La Rue à Londres*
EFR	*Œuvres complètes* (Éditeurs français réunis edition)
Corr. A	*Correspondance avec Arnould*
Corr. M	*Correspondance avec Malot*
Corr. S	*Correspondance avec Séverine*
TP	*Le Tableau de Paris*
SEP	*Souvenirs d'un étudiant pauvre*
CP	*Le Candidat des pauvres*
LCD	*Œuvres complètes* (Livre Club Diderot edition)
JVJR	Roger Bellet: *Jules Vallès, journalisme et révolution*
AJV	*Les Amis de Jules Vallès*
Cri P	*Le Cri du peuple*

Quoi qu'on fasse, c'est toujours
le portrait de l'artiste par lui-même qu'on fait.
Cézanne, c'était une pomme de Cézanne.

(JEAN GIONO)

Vous y trouverez, sinon la valeur d'un livre,
au moins, j'espère, la griffe d'un homme,
et vous devinerez quelqu'un sous cet amas de miettes.

(VALLÈS)

Prolusion

Son œuvre peut se passer d'exégèse
(MAX-POL FOUCHET)

The fact that Jules Vallès has only recently begun to be justly evaluated stems from three main factors: his lifelong immersion in journalism, which disqualifies him in many eyes from serious interest; his whole-hearted involvement in the Paris Commune of 1871, which for some virtually disbars him from the status of human being; and the difficulty of pigeonholing him (though, as Valéry said, nobody gets drunk on the labels of wine-bottles). Vallès has long been a writer in a critical limbo, often dismissed, or barely tolerated, as a joker, a wrecker, a *mystificateur*. In 1987 the primary École Jules-Vallès at La Seyne-sur-mer was debaptised and rechristened with the far safer name of Marcel Pagnol. In 1913, Vallès's bust in Le Puy was knocked over by vandals, and lately another was detached from his grave in Père-Lachaise, but dropped because of its weight. Among the most festive of French writers, Vallès was also *un empêcheur de danser en rond, un trouble-fête*. As a local councillor said at La Seyne: 'Des générations de Seynois seront marqués à vie parce qu'ils ont fréquenté une école qui s'appelait Jules Vallès'.[1] You can take that either way.

The negative pole of Vallès's deepest conviction was his hostility to authority in all its forms: parental,scholastic, governmental, ideological, cultural. And the positive pole: an unkillable urge for justice, on behalf both of the the self and others, for 'la vie des autres est un morceau de la vie de chacun'.[2] Common humanity, in the fullest sense. He kept up a very direct connexion, of anger as well as of enthusiasm, with his times. He sought, not the ivory tower, but the scrum. Much of his life was not high spots, nor even keel, but troughs, of despair or frustration; large sections of it he lived hand-to-mouth. At different points of his childhood and youth, he wanted to be a peasant, a cobbler, a printer, a clown, a sailor, and a Negro. Luckily, he stayed himself, through thick and thin. This self-fidelity housed much approximation, many near-misses. His first book, *L'Argent,* was partly aimed at catapulting him from the have-nots to the moneybags. He missed death by the absence of his beard in the Commune. His very style is often hit-or-miss, a matter of lunges. One of the names in French for his cherished mode, the pun, is *l'à-peu-près*. One of his favoured adverbs was *presque*. Not out of caution, for the proverb says: 'Presque et quasiment empêchent de mentir' (the more brutal Anglo-Saxon counterpart: 'Almost was never hanged'). As Vallès once said: 'Ceci étant tiré en l'air comme un coup de fusil par un aveugle (s'il attrape un oiseau tant mieux)'.[3]

I see Vallès as an in-between — between novel and memoir, literal and figurative, country and city, the bourgeoisie and the lower classes. Yet not passively caught: he plays between. In *L'Enfant,* Jacques Vingtras wears 'un costume de demi-saison' (p. 295). Despite his loathing for intermediaries, his taste for direct action and straightforward living, Vallès consistently offered himself as a bridge between *les blouses* and *les redingotes,* workers and bourgeois. As a writer, he is neither truly popular (Sue), nor high literary (Flaubert). Metaphors bridge gaps. The highly metaphorical Vallès worked, and played, to do just that.

I see Vallès also as 'un ours mal léché'. Deprived of affection as a child; as a result, bearish, moody, spoiling for a fight. Like the bear (on whom he wrote an article in a collective work on animals),[4] Vallès is both cuddlable and dangerous. He is always ready to perform, to put on a show, but he remains wild. In *Le Bachelier,* newly weaned from his gaoler parents in his minuscule garret, he feels like a caged bear about to break loose (p. 465). In *L'Insurgé,* stuffing himself for once in his life, 'je trouve une volupté d'ours dans une treille à pommader de sauce chaude mes boyaux secs' (p. 877). In between, a more depressing kind of *ours* was his often daily bread: a manuscript touted vainly around.

The words that come most readily to mind are negatives: disrespect, demystification, derision, but how positively he charges them. He starts thinking in polarities, but does not often conclude in black and white. He has doubts, he records ambivalences, he relents, he stresses overlap or interchange. 'J'adore les convaincus qui sont doublés d'un bon vivant, les martyrs qui sont rigolos à leur moment', he wrote of Gounod in 1881 (II, 437). What Vallès strove to join together, however, many critics try to put asunder. Dumesnil: 'En dépit des idées, la prose de Vallès demeure magnifique.'[5] This mild schizophrenia is typical of many would-be sane readers of Vallès.

The fair imperative of declaring an interest makes me come clean about my approach. Vallès, this anti-pedant, has attracted motley pedants. Yet he is impossible to vapourise as an author. Perhaps that part-time Stakhanovite, Max Gallo, author of several dozen books and Vallès's most recent biographer, is right. Perhaps only some kind of *vie romancée* is possible, interweaving between the written, published self and the known facts. Vallès did indeed pour himself into his works. *(Requiescat in) pace* Barthes, Vallès is neither dead nor absent, and reports of his death are (and were, in reality, during the Commune) much exaggerated. Anti-empiricists are, strangely enough, and in the old sense, empirics: that is, charlatans. Taxonomic critics have had no more success than the venal asylum doctors at Nantes in confining Vallès to a straitjacket of ready-made schemes and labels. In his childhood, he escaped home and school on country holidays. He escaped imaginatively via *Robinson Crusoe.* He escaped being shot in the Commune. This escapologist does not coyly wriggle, à la Gide, out of definition. He naturally eludes capture. He was too much of an awkward customer to fit the Procrustean bed of some over-sophisticated critics. He makes a monkey of them.

Vallès is not a suitable case for treatment. His unusual ability to laugh at himself I take as sign of psychic health amid the unhealthily solemn and pedantically ludic culture of his day. He would have abominated neo-Freudian analysis especially. This is yet another attempted take-over, that wants to appropriate his subconscious. Vallès spent his life fighting back against annexation and imprisonments of all kinds. Take the scene in L'Enfant where, forced to wear an apron, Jacques is busy scrubbing the house when outsiders pass. 'On ne sait pas si je suis un garçon ou une fille' (p. 217). This scene is what it says: embarrassing. It seems excessive to speak, like Béatrice Didier, of 'une mère castratrice' or, in a later ablutions scene, of an ogre-mother raping a feminised son.[6] No doubt humour, palpably at work in both these scenes, can serve to disguise deep psychic wounds, but it can also dress them to aid recovery. Freud himself had a far better sense of humour than most of his neophytes. In such scenes, it is almost as if Vallès were prophetically forestalling future analysts. 'I know what you're thinking, so I will feign to play along with you. But who will laugh last?' The nearest Vallès gets to a 'family-romance' is when, in La Dompteuse, he states: 'C'est lourd, ces romans que d'autres ont écrits pour vous',[7] which puts the onus on the off-loading parents rather than the fabricating child. Vallès knew in his marrow whose son he was. No danger that he would erect a myth of the bastard, the lost-and-found child. When he moved his eyes beyond his parents, it was to the social determinants (school, employers, government) that had helped to mould and distort both him and them, and not to some fanciful realm of alternative genitors. We cannot, honestly, make a Freudful mess of Vallès.

If, as his Freudian scholiasts maintain, Vallès had a castration-complex, it was because he felt in his flesh over many years the enforced political impotence of his fellow-men and himself. He knew the fate of rebels in the censoring, scissoring France of his day. If he has such a complex, it was surely a sign of sanity. He would have been ill-at-ease on the couch, because there was so little he repressed, and no doubt he would have remembered that, in Roman times, the couch was the antechamber to the vomitorium. We have got so used to burrowing beneath a text that we have almost forgotten how to trust the teller. Beneath his often pieced-together clothing, Vallès is, like the lot of us, stark naked.

My approach is to counter one kind of obvious reading (i.e. obvious to academic readers who are, to use Vallès's key category, 'victimes du livre') and to offer another: what seems to me obvious from the text, patent. Even when devious or hypocritical, Vallès means what he says, and says what he means. All authors play games with the reader; Vallès 'joue franc jeu'.

Let us, one and all, listen to Vallès's plea: 'Ne serons-nous jamais débarrassés de ces gens qui ne marchent qu'escortés de précautions rhétoriciennes?' (I, 954). Nobody can, or should even desire to, evade rhetoric: it is the stuff of all communication. But let it be more freelance, and less praetorian guard.

The structure of this book will, in the main, be thematic, because Vallès is the least linearly systematic, the most associative of writers.

Chapter One

Bandwaggoning and Outsiders

L'Argent is several things at once, a phrase which can denote riches or dubiousness. In 1857, Vallès was uncomfortably caught between continuing to be an unoriginal Bohemian drop-out and becoming a drop-in, or bandwaggoner. The borderline between real and imaginary desires is unmanned. Money, notoriously, talks. In *L'Argent*, Vallès aims to say, indeed to sing, money. In *Le Candidat des pauvres*, reconstruing this period, Vallès writes, as so often in the graphic present: 'Cela me flatte de remuer des millions du bout de la langue' (p. 410). Savouring finance, smacking his chops. He was prophetic, if hardly mint-fresh, in seeing the Stock Market as *the* modern phenomenon, more powerful than governments, legislatures or judiciaries. Though *L'Argent* celebrates the outsize financial personalities of the day, Vallès himself chose anonymity, as a calculated risk. After all, in *romans à clef*, non-names like La Marquise de ***, which make the dark lady sound like a bottle of non-vintage cognac, arouse curiosity. The title-page states 'par un homme de lettres devenu homme de Bourse.' Fittingly, as the Stock Exchange lives like a leech on the body public, Vallès's text is parasitic. The bulk is recopied from notes assembled by an insider, and the only unalloyed Vallès is the introductory *Lettre à Monsieur Jules Mirès*.

Mirès was a dubious model. After the standard rapid rise, he was almost ruined when charged with financial malpractice. Admittedly, this was after the publication of *L'Argent*, but in any case this text lauds the heroic riskiness of speculation. Mirès understood how the press and the financial world could profitably feed off and benefit each other. He bought a string of newspapers, and sold advertising space, disguised as 'City' pages, to banks and other institutions. Thus share prices could be boosted and fortunes made. Mirès was Jewish. While there are flickers of traditional, unthinking antisemitism in Vallès's letter—though these are far fewer than in Proudhon's *Manuel du spéculateur à la Bourse* (1853)—, Vallès cannot resist a joke about 'le petit juif': the funny-bone, the site of excruciating comedy and pain, and, as such, a fitting comment on a text that swivels constantly between hilarity, anger and frustration. Why the address to Mirès? Vallès was, in effect, aping the magnate, for his text is *un boniment*, a puff for his own (nominally hidden) self, as a means to making a reputation and money. He wanted to bull the Vallès stock. Whether poor or, as here, rich, it is *irréguliers* that attract Vallès's interest. It is piratical, lone-wolf capitalism (cf. Ferral in Malraux's *La Condition humaine*) that excites the author's imagination. 'Je me fais le Diogène et l'Aristophane des millionnaires classiques, au nom des irréguliers de la fortune et de la misère' (p. 411).

In claiming to renounce literature, Vallès still parades, as in this quotation, the wealth of classical allusion dinned into him at school. From the start of the letter, Vallès utters continuous barker's patter about abandoning the world of letters. Afterwards the multiple ironies rarely let up. He clearly sees the need to grab the attention, to practise the come-on. Even the examples of the so-called 'poet-martyrs' of the Romantic Bohemian tradition are invoked undeceivedly as 'mes Christs de contrebande' (I, 3). He poses as a former idealist recovered from such delusions, though he knows that loud-mouthed converts are often suspect, and that he will be dismissed as being simply 'paradoxical': shooting a line (p. 10). Clearly, however, he speaks from the heart, and the seat of his trousers, when he talks about clothes and how shamefully difficult life is made by ragged apparel. There are practical, honourable reasons for wanting more money. Above all, it makes you unbeholden, whereas the poor have to compromise. Vallès quotes one of his favourite protest-slogans, Lamennais's sardonic 'Silence au pauvre!', which attacked the *cautionnement* which effectively muted financially weak newspaper-editors: a fact of life Vallès would have to struggle with throughout the 1860s.

Vallès was never a cultural pessimist, a Cassandra of civilisation à la Schopenhauer (so palatable to so many nineteenth-century French writers). If he talks of big social changes in this letter to Mirès, it is not to bemoan the end of a world but to register a dynamic transformation. He pens, then, a hymn of praise to the Bourse as a hive of activity, and he cannot stop himself dramatising the financial world. With his native genius for fiasco, he weighs the catastrophes against the success-stories. Moreover, his lifelong hostility to the cult of the past helps him to adhere to the present: 'Il faut marcher avec son temps, vivre en prose' (p. 10). In his three-quarter ignorance, he stresses the need to study political economy, although later in life he could never quite get round to reading Marx. However greedy the tone, Vallès even here is not selfish; he wants the goodies shared out. Even when ostensibly belittling literature for missing the main chance, he cannot resist calling in prestigious literary predecessors who never sneezed at amassing lucre: Voltaire and Beaumarchais. At the other extreme, Rousseau's peevishness was, for Vallès, a product of his *misère* (pp. 4-5). 'La misère a fait son temps, je passe du côté des riches' (p. 6). He concludes ringingly, and with a sting in the tail: 'Faisons de l'argent, morbleu! gagnons de quoi venger le passé triste, de quoi faire le lendemain joyeux, de quoi acheter de l'amour, des chevaux et des hommes' (p. 10).

Vallès and his parents had saved up throughout his childhood to 'buy a man', that is, to pay for a replacement that would excuse the lad military service. In this letter, while willing the end (material comfort), was Vallès with equal vigour willing the means (possible sell-out)? Convinced always of the inescapability of budgets, of the price to be paid for everything, Vallès was also aware of the related possibility: that everyone has his or her price. This is a strained text, a shotgun marriage between eulogy and ironic mockery. Mirès's capitalist publicity is here transmuted to what Norman Mailer called 'Advertisements for Myself'. The irony helps to sabotage Vallès's worst instincts towards *arrivisme*. While he, nakedly, lusts to arrive, it is rather, in this instance, like a grinning death's head at a party. It is a mock-suicidal text, like Swift's mock-infanticidal text on the starving Irish. One of the meanings of *blague* is: saying what you don't really mean in order to raise a laugh—which has always been easier than raising a loan. But it has, too, blacker connotations of reprisal. The irony here is so over-determined that it secretes, as so often in Vallès's work, bitterness. Sympathy for poverty is conspicuous by its absence, and so, terribly present. The praise of riches is an *amplificatio ad absurdum.*

Vallès said in a letter, addressed possibly to a henchman in the enterprise: 'Ce livre est un grelot' (I, 1162). This suggests both belling the cat, and ringing a bell to attract attention. Vallès paid part of the production costs himself, and so this book was a form of vanity publishing. In *Le Candidat des pauvres,* Vallès reports a newspaper owner advising him to write knocking copy against his own book, so as to distance himself from it and make his name that way. He did not, but the *Lettre à Mirès* is scrupulous only in a roundabout fashion. While boasting of his improvements to his leg-man's documentation, Vallès has to admit his plagiarism: 'Je laisse les épithètes pâles et je mets des adjectifs écarlates, je renforce les phrases molles, je dramatise les passages plats, j'arrive à être empoigné par le sujet et je sens un revenez-y de Proudhon me trotter dans la tête' (*CP*, pp. 413-14). Note how spirited the borrowing is made to be: it canters through his head. *Un revenez-y* is also an appetising dish, which makes you feel more-ish. So, while the phrase does recognise parasitic behaviour, it is of the non-pejorative, convivial kind. He is in good company with Proudhon. He parts company with him in his much greater reluctance to indict stock-market speculation as a phenomenon. After a childhood, adolescence and young manhood of enforced economising, Vallès here envisions expenditure, and moves even further away from Freudian anal fixation. There was a fashion in the 1850s (and 1860s) for plays decrying the corrupting powers of money. Vallès writes against the grain, against such 'bons sentiments'. In 'Victimes du livre', he dwells on the dream of *Robinsonnades:* '...les finances à *désorganiser*—tout est là' (I, 233). Huysmans responded to this subversive side of Vallès's effort: 'La démonomanie qui fait sourire les modernes, n'est-elle pas dans ces deux choses—l'argent—l'amour. Ce serait l'histoire de l'Humanité si on écrivait ce que cette brute de Vallès a intitulé l'*Argent.*' [1] In suggesting as much, Vallès here again oscillates between swimming with or against the current.

His market-venture paid off, in that it won him employment on *Le Figaro*, writing a series of articles, short-lived as was usual for Vallès, on 'Figaro à la Bourse'. In them, Vallès shows that he knows the jargon, but seems less equipped to understand the operations of the Stock Exchange. He offers himself as a language-tutor, an expert in thieves' cant: 'Je vous apprendrai l'argot de ces coulisses, le javanais du lieu' (I, 122). He reiterates the theme of *L'Argent:* every citizen is affected by the Bourse, and so it is an integral part of democracy. In defending it, he admits his fascination with the 'frenetic dance' of money. Bellet is right to claim that 'la Bourse est avant tout, pour Vallès, une fête du mot' (p. 1232). Again Vallès agrees that there is no incompatibility between making money and maintaining a polemical stance, and he puns nicely on Voltaire's activities: 'Il ne travaillait pas toujours pour le roi de Prusse, le vieux malin!' (p. 120). He confesses frankly to his own appetite, and that of others: 'Ma foi! je comprends trop la vie, le besoin d'agir, de lutter, d'essayer des plaisirs ou des joies; j'ai les cheveux trop noirs et les dents trop aiguës pour en vouloir à ces chasseurs de leur robuste appétit!' (*ibid.*) (I am reminded of the liberal Austrian journalist who said that some of his impoverished compatriots joined the Blackshirts, not because they were black but because they were shirts). Vallès's version: 'Combien changeraient de langage s'ils pouvaient changer de chemise' (quoted *JVJR*, p. 321).

Many of Vallès's early writings centred on people who had often neither shirts, nor *la niche et la pâtée*. Much of it is devoted to the marginals of society. *L'Argent* had already reacted violently against the still potent Romantic myth of 'la Bohème', associated principally with Henry Murger, in his *Scènes de la vie de Bohème:* the cult of gay-cum-poignant poverty among garret-artists and their mistresses. Bohemia was (and is) a no-man's-land between the ensconced bourgeoisie and the working masses. For Vallès, it was never an innocent golden age, but 'la bohème dédorée' (*TP*, p. 367). Murger himself seems to have been fully aware that the Bohemia he evoked was not all rosy. Vallès undoubtedly simplifies his target for the sake of the cause. He refuses what he sees as a political quiescence which scarcely contemplated incriminating society for such misfortunes. Vallès wanted to turn bohemianism into a more contestatory way of life. In 1859, Murger, like Flaubert later, accepted the Légion d'Honneur. Vallès is certainly right to detect a feyness in Murger's prose, and to see the non-conformism as essentially apolitical. Murger tends to apologise for the gloomier episodes, and even these are only operatically sad. Louis Veuillot's verdict on the whole phenomenon is harshly plausible: 'Le bourgeois adopta Murger parce qu'il trouvait en lui [...] l'objet perpétuel de son étonnement, de son admiration et de son mépris, ce mélange du maniaque, du bouffon, de l'affamé et de l'inspiré qu'il appelle *l'artiste*, et qui constitue le véritable fou de la démocratie'.[2] Such licensed fools obviously represent no danger to the dominant culture.

As Louis Guilloux said of Vallès: 'La misère n'est pas pour lui un thème à exploiter mais une réalité contre laquelle il faut se battre *joyeusement*.'[3] He could be as *misérabiliste* as the next man, but he consistently attacked those who unprotestingly wrote up their woes, 'les pseudo-souffrants' (I, 463). One genuine sufferer to whose memory Vallès remained loyal was the minor poet Hégésippe Moreau, whose life of twenty-eight years consisted of extreme poverty, writing unrewarded poetry about his home province and indictments against Society, fighting on the barricades in 1830, and dying in a work-house. Most Vallès-like of all was his finding his unsold poems being used as packaging by a grocer. Vallès's fondness for this *réfractaire* was as near as he got to swallowing the topos of 'le poète maudit'.

As little is reliably known of Vallès's own Bohemian daze as of Diderot's (and he resembles Diderot in his fragmentation of output, his vivacity yet his strong awareness of automatisms, his loathing for imprisoning systems of belief, his love of 'la vie d'échange'). His friend, the caricaturist André Gill, offers this high-toned account of Vallès's stage-presence:

> Avec tout son masque heurté, aux plans durs, qui semble avoir été martelé par quelque tailleur de fer, en son pays d'Auvergne; avec, surtout, sa voix de cuivre, amoureuse de tempête et le roulis farouche de son allure, il s'est fait, autrefois, une renommée de casse-cou, d'exalté violent, dur à cuire. C'est son premier succès, son succès de jeunesse; il y tient. Et, soigneusement toujours, il a défendu, de la retouche et de l'altération, cette extravagante contrefaçon de sa propre physionomie, où, depuis vingt ans, le public le voit grinçant de la mâchoire, et rageusement campé devant la société. Moi-même, pour complaire à sa manie, ne l'ai-je pas caricaturé en chien crotté, lugubre, traînant à la queue une casserole bossuée et retentissante? [...] Quand je le rencontrai pour la première fois, il fendait l'espace [...]; les pans d'une redingote allongée démesurément sur commande flottaient derrière lui; un chapeau vertigineux, élancé de sa tête, menaçait le ciel.[4]

This suggests a studied, flamboyant pose, and obviously dates from a time when he had some money; when, having put behind him the monstrous clothes foisted on him by his mother, he could freely choose to distinguish himself strikingly and less ridiculously. Yet, despite such extravagances, and these were more lastingly of voice and ideas than of dress, his deepest urge was to be a working writer, not a misunderstood genius. Far less than Nerval or Baudelaire, who both came from more comfortable social origins, was Vallès going slumming when he acquainted himself with the lower depths. Beyond this purely Parisian sub-world, besides, he was deeply conscious of the

ancient peasant tradition of 'le Bonhomme Misère', from the popular
almanacs of the 'Bibliothèque bleue' and the *images d'Épinal,* which
always spoke strongly to his imagination. As Bellet points out, this is a
very ambiguous myth, as it enthrones the 'misérable, affamé de justice,
incorruptible lui aussi, et si fort sur sa terre! Sa Majesté la Misère et sa
Majesté le Misérable' (*JVJR,* p. 138). Later in life, Vallès would preface
a new *Histoire du Bonhomme Misère* with these words: 'Il y a là-dedans
une fleur de naïveté et un grain de révolte comme on n'en trouve que
dans la terre de France'. Always seeking not only contrasts but links
between capital and provinces, Vallès would near the end of his life cite
the *complainte* of an inner-city Jean Misère 'en blouse', who both
embraces and goes beyond the ancient, peasant Bonhomme Misère (II,
428).

Another link between city and countryside are travelling people, *les
saltimbanques,* nomadic entertainers. These contain elements far more
troubling than Murger's bohemians. Since *La Rue* and *Les
Réfractaires,* published in 1866 and 1865 respectively, contain a good
deal of overlap, indeed interchangeability, and as the general movement
of Vallès's commitment goes from eccentrics to more militant forms of
non-conformism, I will concentrate first on the *saltimbanques* sections
of *La Rue.* As well as harking back to the ancient commonplace, 'All the
world's a stage', Vallès adds a different dimension: 'We are all on or in
the same trestle-theatre'. Already his home life, as we will see in
L'Enfant, had much of the clown: outlandish clothes, physical fiascoes.
Indeed, the trio of son and parents often, collectively, provide
bystanders with unintentional, impromptu vaudeville routines. Vallès
was cut out to sympathise with entertainers.

First of all, some definitions. *Saltimbanque,* like the Italian
montambanco and the England *mountebank,* refers in part to a vendor
of quack medicines, a horse-doctor, at fairs, attracting crowds and
sometimes purchasers by his patter, tricks and antics. The term thus
bears elements of the charlatan or impostor, but also of the performer
or actor. *Quack,* from *quacksalver,* links prattling and fake remedies—
an early instance, perhaps, of the 'talking cure'. The *bank* or *banque*
was the counter on which such merchants displayed their wares, and
which they often mounted to promote them vociferously. By extension,
it denoted trestle-theatre generally (and of course survives today not
only in this form, but also in that of political hucksters' platforms).
Vallès was specially taken with the verbal come-on: *la parade.* This is a
suitably polysemous word, for it betokens the knockabout show of
saltimbanques, the verbal parrying, as in fencing, and likewise a medley
of defence and aggression, and repartee. Other related terms are spiel,
pitch (a good old English word), *boniment, les bagatelles de la porte,*
barker *(aboyeur).* P.T. Barnum gave currency to the term 'humbug' for
his inventive forms of illusion-making. The whole operation is

designed, varying soft soap and loud pedal, for the hard sell. In terms of
registers, *saltimbanques* used a curious mixture of the high-falutin'
(classical allusions, long words) and the coarsely colloquial. In mid-
nineteenth century British demotic, 'to climb the slang-tree' meant to
perform, to make an exhibition of oneself (in both senses). Among the
several meanings of 'slang' is fetters, and, in all his celebration of the
world of *saltimbanques,* Vallès is always sharply aware how much these
free spirits are imprisoned: by dependence on the generosity of their
audiences, or by confinement within a set role.

Nonetheless, the cacophony, the violently garish colours magnetise
him, and his reportage enacts the *parade,* onomatopoeically:

> En parade! Sur les tréteaux: Dzing, dzing, boum, boum! *Le voilà! Le
> voilà! On va lui couper la tête!* Et les cymbales sifflent, la caisse gronde,
> c'est un vacarme à casser le tympan, tout frémit, tout tremble. [...] tout
> appelle l'œil en blessant la rétine, attire l'oreille en la déchirant: on s'arrête,
> comme saisi, pour assister à la bacchanale... (I, 528-9)

The whole spectacle is a kind of corporeal anarchism, frenzied and
staccato: 'La parade n'a ni queue ni tête, elle a des tics et des hoquets, va
à l'aventure par soubresauts et par saccades, et danse en riant la Saint-
Guy' (*ibid.*). Classical decorum, one of Vallès's choicest black beasts,
could not be further removed from this deafening, sense-assaulting
chaos. Apart from discordant music, words per se are individually less
important than grimaces. Here, if not in political oratory, Vallès equates
hamminess with authenticity and naturalness. The travelling
showpeople's world lacks harmony in another respect. Each group
competes against the next, noisily, in the 'CONTRE-CARRE' (p. 530).
Vallès's reportage is a sort of *boniment,* or blarney, itself, and he lends
himself to the general mystification: 'On dit que ses animaux mettaient
l'oreille au barreau de leur cage [...] quand le dompteur racontait les
drames apocryphes dont ils avaient été, suivant lui, les héros dans le
désert' (p. 532). He is a willing, half-open-eyed, dupe, a streetwise
sucker.

Although the full-blown circus (Cf. *L'Enfant*) had its many charms
for Vallès, especially during childhood, it was street fairs and street
theatre that attracted him most. Punch and Judy more than that white-
faced clown so dear to what we can call the symbolist or pseudo-
metaphysical tradition (Banville, Laforgue, Apollinaire) of
Pierrotarians. As Bellet notes, 'Vallès aime mieux les clowns de la vie
que les clowns du cirque, [...] les clowneries du corps, du vêtement dans
la vie' (*JVJR*, p. 218). One particular feature of the clown's repertoire
would speak above all to him: the desperate clawing for dignity when all
around conspires against it, the pratfall on would-be solemn occasions.
This is tightly connected with the clown's outlandish clothes, to which so
often Vallès's closely approximated; for example, the 'gibbous' overcoat

which transmogrified him into a circus hunchback or a one-man band
(see *ibid.*, p. 321). It is such practical concerns that help to keep Vallès's
version of the *saltimbanque* resolutely on and of this earth. He is,
however, frank enough to admit that he does exploit the phenomenon
for his own ends, as well as championing it: 'Ces saltimbanques que
j'aime comme vous [i.e. Banville], ils viennent, témoins bizarres, en
bottines à peau de lapin, servir à la défense de mes doctrines comme ils
ont servi à poétiser ma jeunesse' (*TP*, p. 88). Even myths, however, are
always *costed* by Vallès: he gives detailed budgets for the daily life of
the denizens of *les foires* (*ibid.*, pp. 93 ff.).

After the marginals, the more truly ousted: freaks. In the lead-in to
his story, 'Le Bachelier géant', Vallès confesses proudly: 'J'ai eu de tout
temps l'amour du *monstre* . Il est peu de têtes d'aztèque ou
d'hydrocéphale, de cyclope ou d'Argus, plate ou carrée, en gourde ou
en table de jeu, que je n'aie tâtée, mesurée, sur laquelle je n'aie fait toc-
toc, pour savoir ce qu'il y avait dedans.' He refutes the putative
rejoinder that his fascination is unhealthy: 'Non que j'aime l'horrible!
mais je voulais savoir ce que Dieu avait laissé d'âme dans ces corps mal
faits, ce qu'il pouvait tenir d'HOMME dans un monstre.' (I, 264). Just
as he often caricatures normal people, he wants to naturalise as best he
can freaks. Note the stress on *heads* . He sees them as minds, and
emotional systems, as well as misshapen bodies. Now, like prowling
journalists, desk-bound academics can get over-excited about monsters,
and transform deviation, mere difference, into transgression (of natural,
divine, or social law). The hard thing is to accept freaks in the general
run of things, a part of life (diversity) and not apart from life. Vallès
was aided in this direction by the monstrification—imposed or self-
induced—visited on him during his life: his mother's choice of
grotesque clothes for him, his father's having him locked away as a
dangerous mental defective, his own pose at times as a would-be
monstre sacré. The frequently hybrid nature of freaks is parallelled in
the confessedly heterogeneous nature of Vallès's style. Their incongruity
chimes, discordantly but troublingly, with his sense of being generally
ill-fitting, out of place. We should remember, too, the literary model, as
present for Vallès as for most writers, those experts in productive
plagiarism: Léonidas Requin, *l'homme-poisson*, or merman, in Eugène
Sue's *Les Misères des enfants trouvés*, which Vallès read under the desk
at school.

Now to etymology. It is well known that monster/*monstre* derives
from the Latin *monēre*, to warn, and not from *monstrare*, to show. But
to show can be to warn: object-lessons, ill-omens; spectacles can be
didactic. Freaks, like lunatics, have often been put on show as dire
cautionary tales about the dangers of vice, miscegenation or folly. Their
core is ambiguity. They can be an artificially created creature, or an
excessively natural one—nature toying with itself, proliferating,

overdoing things. As with many underlings, freaks are often denied a voice; they are, like children (often treated by adults as little monsters) to be seen and not heard; like nude showgirls in earlier days, they are supposed to be unmoving. Vallès gives his *monstres* a voice, a full life, an intrinsic value. He was aware how the French word *prodiges*, even more than its English counterpart, slides over the boundary line between prodigies and monsters.[5] At the very least, the abnormal defines normality, as Diderot repeatedly argued.

Vallès was on the whole, and this backs up his rejection of the charge of morbidity, less drawn to the 'Gothic' kind of freak. As Christopher Lloyd has pointed out, Vallès would have found loathsome Huysmans's 'mystical, dolorist Catholicism', as shown in *Les Foules de Lourdes*, with its public parade of hideous deformities in a hospital.[6] Similarly, I feel sure he would not have deemed it worth a detour to respond on the vast American prairies to the seduction of those three-headed sheep and six-legged cows with which desperately boastful small communities hope to lure travellers off the beaten highway to their otherwise unmagnetic hamlets. It is people, however excessive and over-the-top, 'les incomplets ou les surabondants'—three arms or no legs—that draw Vallès (I, 293). He seems more sympathetic to giants, preferably gentle, than to dwarfs (probably malignant). A less dwarfist reason is that, in the age-old topos of Ancients versus Moderns, the Moderns (Vallès's chosen camp) are the dwarfs on the shoulders of giants. Yet he knows how much fakery (special effects) goes on in the world of *saltimbanques:* many so-called giants, like undersized folk, wear elevator shoes (p. 729). In the face of such trickery, Vallès is nearer to the willing 'mark' than to the heckler. His suspect obsession with hydrocephalous children is explained by Bellet by reference to scarred memories of 'l'enfant à tête gavée', and the resulting top-heavy body, at school (*JVJR*, p. 221). Vallès, in fact, detects school everywhere. Even the magnificent 'Vénus au râble', the beautiful, sexy, legless woman, opens up a monstrous vision of the school she longs to start for 'les enfants mal venus'—perhaps the only school, for misfits, which Vallès could regard with any affection.

> Quel pensionnat que celui-là, où l'une aurait eu des bras à revendre, l'autre à peine un nez pour se moucher; où tous les disgraciés du monde seraient venus chercher dans le tas la difformité qui aurait suppléé ou diminué la leur: un garçon sans mains épousant une quadrupède; un argus jetant ses trois yeux sur une borgne. (I, 720)

Different readers will find this callous, or heart-warming in its faith in the possibility of reunification, a homeland, for the displaced, disjoined ones. The Vénus herself is a dynamic testimony to the erotic tug of abnormality (Cf. Beauty and the Beast). The very practice of 'l'entre-sort', the quick viewing, in a tent, of freaks,—'on entre, on sort,

voilà'—makes it sound the most natural thing in the world, a rather
telescoped form of sexual congress (p. 727).

Naturally, too, the peepshow is unnatural, possibly perverted, a
spectator sport encouraging voyeurs, and the word sideshow emphasises
the marginality. As Fiedler reminds us, viewers of freaks sometimes
snigger. The response is ambiguous: frank enjoyment and sinister
delectation. Rather like the response often to puns that make us squirm,
titter or laugh on the other side of our face. It is, incidentally, not
specious to link monsters and puns. Puns, too, mingle, cross-breed,
overlap. To many, the pun is outrageous, a freak of language to avert
one's ears and eyes from. The origins of 'pun' and 'freak' are likewise
unknown. Whatever the moral dubiousness of an interest in freaks,
Vallès is keen to show his fellow-feeling. He knew as well as Malraux
(or better, because of his much greater comic sense) that each of us, to
ourself, is 'un monstre incomparable'.[7] Metaphorically, it is easy to
accuse or to be accused of being a monster of (especially filial)
ingratitude. Freakishness is not confined to fairgrounds; it infiltrates
medical science. Vallès was fascinated by the new-found science of
rhinoplasty (nose-jobs), as if he sensed the grotesque element in the very
term (the outsize bestial hooter). I would indeed call Vallès's interest in
the monstrous essentially healthy, for his main life effort was devoted to
the preservation of normality in a society hell-bent, like all, on serious
imbalance and its resultant deformation of individuals. Besides, though
deceivers themselves often, such show-people are frequently exploited:
fakers and fakirs. They gull, and suffer, and sometimes doctor that
suffering, to turn a penny. Above all, monstrosity is a sign of life's
freedom to experiment, to digress. Vallès is again close to Diderot here.
Freaks, for them, are less moral portents than variant humanity, as
shown in the terms 'sports' or *lusus naturae*. The same determinisms
govern their eccentric existences. They, too, can be past it, as seen
pathetically in the strong man whose teeth are now too rickety to lift
weights (p. 717). As so often, Vallès sums up what he sparks to in such
people by reanimated idiom: 'La nouvelle parade, où défilent déjà les
filles en maillot, les musiciens, le sorcier, l'hercule, *tout le
tremblement!*' (p. 710, my italics). Vallès is entitled to speak of his
'curiosité courageuse' (see p. 723).

'Le Bachelier géant' is a résumé of Vallès's variations on the subject
of *saltimbanques* and freaks. It is a real, extended narrative, not just a
sketch, and the earliest true fiction Vallès penned. Though the gatherer
of the giant's story is close to his subject in terms of humour (the giant
is relieved to be confiding for once in 'un homme qui n'a qu'une tête'
(I, 267), Vallès tries hard in this tale to give fiction its head, to escape
for a time from his own direct experience. He even engineers his own
defeat, in a contest of knowledge of 'dead' languages, with the
bachelier géant (who is six foot five inches, more impressive then than

in today's welfare state). He is a performing dog (*chien savant:* it sounds nobler in French). He makes an honest confession of his earlier experience as *un pion,* savagely mocked by his juvenile charges. He is too big for any given space; he cannot fit in. His millstone glory is that his heart is oversized too. Despite women's curiosity, often barbed, about this gentle freak, he was starved of love until the erotically charged arrival on his scene of Rosita Ferrani, leader of a troupe of *saltimbanques* specialising in contortionism. When this artiste begins to dance,

> les seins gonflés et les bras nus, sourire aux lèvres, cheveux au vent, mon sang ne fit qu'un tour; il courut sur mon front une bouffée u'air chaud, ma poitrine s'élargit, et tout mon être tressaillit dans sa longueur devant cette statue vivante de la volupté et de la jeunesse. (p. 270)

His excitement is total, whole-body, but embarrassment handicaps any direct approach. Eventually, his love is revealed, at a remove, by the clever pointing hooves of a performing horse. Vallès remains discreet on the eventual sexual consummation, with a nice hint of Dante's ' ...and they read no more.'

Despite lovers' tiffs, the giant is now enslaved, shrivelling; he joins the travellers.[8] As always, Vallès displays his close familiarity with the daily facts of life of such communities. The group's poverty is such that the *bachelier géant,* despite his paper honours, must turn himself into an earning curiosity. When Rosita becomes pregnant, unlike normal folk, the company hopes for *un monstre (un enfant de la balle,* in fact), but the baby is delectably whole and well-formed. The troupe undergo many ups and downs, including a fire, in their life of 'misère comique' (p. 286). Abandoning his dead languages, the giant (never named, only titled) starts inventing tongues, to mystify the public, generally seen by the performers as dupes. As befits contortionists, his companions and he are ready to turn their hands, and indeed their whole bodies, to anything that will pay off. They twist to survive. They work alongside more extreme freaks and hybrids: 'Quels échanges entre le bipède et le quadrumane, le crustacé et le mammifère! série de plagiats et d'emprunts barbares! enfer pavé d'intentions horribles!' (pp. 293-4). Vallès records the unconscious black humour of one such, 'la Râble mystérieuse', legless, who had two sons of whom she says proudly: 'J'ai deux fils bien portants et *conformés comme vous et MOI* ' (p. 254). Some of these companions are malevolent. The crafty clown always outwits the naïve strong man. The giant is deceived by Rosita for *un paillasse.* Vallès resorts to belligerent sentimentality: 'Que celui qui n'a jamais été fou et lâche devant les femmes me jette la première pierre!' (p. 302). Increasingly desperate, he switches to lion-taming, which thus sets up the unabashedly melodramatic finale: 'C'est ma nature à moi de plonger au cœur du danger, tout d'abord; par lâcheté peut-être, pour en

finir d'un coup, mourir ou vaincre' (p. 304). This admixture of fear
and foolhardiness sounds remarkably like Vallès himself faced by
political choices. When the giant takes his little girl Violette with him
into the cage, she is of course mauled to death by the lion, which he then
kills.

Countering the view of *saltimbanques* as radical heroes, a critic such
as Marotin stresses the amount of satire and criticism of the show-world
by Vallès. Furthermore, 'se réfugier dans un autre monde que la société,
c'est chercher à fuir et c'est aussi refuser de lutter pour la
transformation de la Société bourgeoise. [...] Le cirque est une image de
défaite, non pas d'espoir révolutionnaire'.[9] For Pillu, too, most of these
creatures are failures: 'Il y perçoit, ou y projette, plus ou moins
obscurément, le conflit entre la volonté d'agir, de réaliser, et le
sentiment de son impuissance'.[10] It is certainly true that, already in the
1860s, Vallès was noting the decline of the whole phenomenon, 'cette
race d'irréguliers qui disparaît noyée dans le flot de la civilisation' (I,
528). In the 1880s, although he still warmed to them as the pariahs, the
scapegoats suspect to all sedentary folk, he disliked their increasing
regimentation, for instance their banding together in *syndicats,* and their
multiplying corruption by capitalism. The *banquistes* were becoming
banquiers. Despite such decline, Vallès never lost his love of the general
atmosphere—the crowds, noises, lights and smells—of this popular
entertainment for people off duty and seeking a good time.[11]

While the views of Marotin and Pillu are unarguably correct, they
leave out the more permanent and positive value of the world of
saltimbanques for Vallès. Bellet describes this astutely: 'En vérité, Vallès
n'est pas attiré par les saltimbanques comme par un monde séparé de la
vie ordinaire: il est fasciné par le lien ambigu, souvent parodique, qui le
relie précisément à cette vie' (*JVJR,* p. 217). In other words, they are a
distorting, but telling, reflection of the 'real' world. 'Les lois de la
société juridiques et esthétiques n'y sont certes pas bafouées, subverties,
main à coup sûr secouées' (*ibid.,* pp. 237-8). Like humour, they
question the norm, the accepted; and, like it, they suggest that the world
can be made different, that it does not have to be the way it is.
According to Bellet: 'pour Vallès, le passionnant est la rencontre, la
contradiction, le hasard objectif' (p. 218). *Rencontre,* earlier in life,
meant 'pun', which is also 'un hasard objectif'. The world of show
business helped Vallès to open up to other possibilities. Apart from this
incipiently political lesson, Vallès also learned from such exposure to a
different world a fuller awareness of the beast (often caged and
maltreated) in man; and to a subtler view of art: the great deceiver, the
sweet cheat, a necessary counterbalance to his cult of literary realism.
As Sartre, and many before him, recognised, literature has to 'mentir
pour être vrai'. And this generous lie takes the form of an alternative
reality.

After the outsiders, in their alternative milieu, the strugglers in the midst; after *les saltimbanques* and freaks, *réfractaires* (or *irréguliers*). A keen blender himself, Vallès might have relished the portmanteau-word 'hobobohemians',[12] for his chosen people are hybrids, straddlers, while resolutely, even eccentrically, individualistic. They are, said Vallès, answering paridoxically a charge of being paradoxical , not 'l'exception, mais la règle' (I, 922). They take exception to being ruled. Yet they remain rebels in only a problematic sense, for they are in-betweens, non-conforming outsiders who wish to get in on the comforts of those inside, the ensconced. *Saltimbanques* are even less obviously rebellious, for they rely on a paying public. One of Vallès's many reasons for championing travelling showpeople is that, like gypsies, they have served as reach-me-down scapegoats for local crimes, disasters and mysteries. After all, they lack *un état:* a steady job and an assured civil status. On the other hand, writers (like Vallès) busying themselves with such picturesque subjects quite suited the authorities of his day, for it seemed a safish activity, marginal to the mainstream of national life. Vallès struggled against and within the widespread commonplace of his era: the representation of Society, the Stock Exchange and Parliament as varieties of spectacle, show business. The real showpeople could be used, Vallès believed, to show up the posing, fake show-offs who rule the social roost. *Réfractaires* could perform a similar function, but with a greater outward display of *non serviam.*

Réfractaire houses several meanings. It can refer to peasants taking to the woods or hills to avoid conscription; to priests resisting the French Revolution; to rebellious soldiers under the First Empire. It can also, when attached to appropriate nouns, signify fire-proof, acid-proof, etc. In Bellet's persuasive view, the word, for Vallès, had little ideological content, even Proudhonian. He had a regard of a kind for republican or Jacobin *réfractaires,* but equally for *les Chouans*. In all these cases it was the hostility to the over-centralised state that most appealed to him. Bellet further points out that the word was quite commonly used, in the Parisian context, for non-conformist artists (*JVJR*, p. 53). One of the most flamboyant of these, Courbet, when young, drew up a six-point programme against religion, schools, conventional poetry, etc., which he called 'le programme des réfractaires' (I, 1265).

In the texts of *Les Réfractaires,* the exemplars of this tendency are, as befits the term which Vallès exploits with more metaphorical verve than historical accuracy, a motley group, or rather conglomeration. True, he recognises himself the fairly tenuous thread linking the factual rebels and his own oddball dissenters. In fact, he begins with a non-comparison, a negation of gainsaying, for, after evoking the former, he adds: 'Ce n'est point de ceux-là que je veux parler' (I, 138). *His* version 's'en [va] battant la campagne le long des ruisseaux de Paris' (*ibid.*). A

nice play on words, for they both scour the urban countryside, and are
frequently, through psychic make-up or hunger, delirious.[13] 'Ils vont
vivre une vie à part, étrange et douloureuse' (p. 139). Proudly, they
make a feature of their physical, indeed existential, abjection. Vallès's
distinguo is a thin but tenacious one: 'Entre eux et le pauvre banal existe
la différence de l'esclave au vaincu' (p. 140).

Hunger dominates their days and nights. There are passages worthy
of Hamsun's monochordal masterpiece, *Hunger* —'des rêvasseries
d'halluciné, les oreilles tintent, la tête tourne, le délire commence' (p.
160)—and a foreshadowing of Jacques Vingtras's own experiences in
this area in *Le Bachelier*. Vallès expresses his interest in a startling way:
'J'ai le vertige à descendre dans ces estomacs vides' (p. 141): empathy of
a high, or deep, order. He works an ingenious twist on that frightening
idiom, 'tromper la faim', to conquer or beguile away hunger: 'Ils
prennent leur demi-tasse avant dîner, puis ils ne dînent pas; le public s'y
trompe, leur estomac aussi' (p. 149). He records their artful dodges,
with which he was fully conversant from his own garret days; for
example, hanging around outside schools to pick up the crusts thrown
away by the children (p. 165). When one, such as M. Chaque, manages
to procure some food, his clothes become a portable larder. It is a real
economy, this 'bœuf à la mode dans un bas de laine' (p. 187). The
réfractaires are mainly, like Diderot's great Nephew of Rameau, 'pique-
assiettes'. Their clothes are in keeping with their state (though, *sans
état*, they are close to being stateless refugees): rags and tatters, gaping
holes. Vallès's refrain of holes in the seat of trousers is here made a
two-way optical contest: eyes staring at, or staring out: 'Les pantalons
écarquillent, derrière, des yeux étonnés' (p. 145). Life is expedients,
living from hand to mouth, and a pretty wretched life it sounds to the
comfortable reader; not only defeated, but self-defeating and self-
punishing. Although Vallès honours *réfractaires* as a kind of
freemasonry (p. 141), each one seems very much on his own in the
quest for survival. Although he abominated political turncoats, he seems
ready here to justify any makeshift (e.g. trumped-up religiosity) (pp.
148-9).

The knee-jerk response is to wonder why they do not get a regular
job. Vallès answers on their behalf that, in their state of distress and
disarray, with no obviously bankable qualifications, how could they,
even to feed their desperately growling stomach, equally *en chômage?*
(p. 146) He lists the jobs they occasionally land: low teaching posts,
hack-writing for ephemerals or compilations, acting as stand-ins
(*passeurs*) for *baccalauréat* candidates (pp. 147-8). He was personally
familiar with the dilemma of where to pluck up and maintain the will to
go on in such conditions: 'Combien de demi-volontés, d'intentions
presque courageuses' (p. 149). They talk big because they are so low.
The desolate end of many is *l'hôpital*, not far off a knacker's yard.

As if realising he was skirting sentimentalism, Vallès at times strikes a more militant pose, ostensibly inspired by the small number of *irréguliers* who actually went off to become adventurers, mercenaries and the like:

> Donnez-moi trois cents de ces hommes, quelque chose comme un drapeau, jetez-moi sur une terre où il faille faire honneur à la France, dans les rues de Venise [i.e. Garibaldi's efforts at reunification of Italy], si vous voulez, jetez-moi là sous la mitraille, en face des régiments, et vous verrez ce que j'en fais et des canons et des artilleurs, à la tête de mes réfractaires! (p. 153)

We cannot ignore that some of Vallès's *réfractaires* hardly had the strength to stand up, that the tone is falsely jingoistic, and that Vallès normally shows little lust for leadership. This passage is out of step with the rest of *Les Réfractaires*. Vallès is generally more convincing when he shifts from resounding generalisations to closely-observed particular cases: Fontan-Crusoé, Poupelin, Chaque, Cressot, Gustave Planche. No doubt when Vallès tells other people's stories, as here, he basks in their reflected eccentricity and pathos, but he is also doing them a service by ordering and articulating their patchwork existences. It seems unlikely that he took copious notes in his interviews. When interested, his memory was faithful. I feel, however, that in these portraits he was part elaborating and part inventing.

A *déclassé*, Fontan-Crusoé rejects envy of more fortunate ones as unworthy and against his grain. 'Je ne crois pas être séditieux' (p. 166); he presents a picture of philosophical *clochards, misères savantes*—this last word retaining its hint of circus performance. His gentle gaiety, his uncomplaining tone, his never entertaining thoughts of suicide, his asking for so little—all of this, in contrast and in compensation, makes Vallès feel the urge to revolt on his behalf. Poupelin, nicknamed 'Mes papiers', is much more of a clown. 'Les bouffons m'attirent', even a Bonapartist one like Poupelin (p. 177). He is reminiscent of Rameau's Nephew, for in telling his story he becomes a pantomimic one-man-band. Like Fontan, he is dwarfish in stature. Vallès is drawn to both extremes, these two stunted men and the *Bachelier géant* . Poupelin is a jumped-up gnome. Unfazed by repeated fiascoes, he lives on unkillable great expectations. Like Jacques Vingtras in *Le Bachelier*, he places excessive trust in paper credentials, but fails to see that others will testify only to unmarketable qualities: 'Je certifie que M. Poupelin jouit d'un excellent appétit' (p. 181). Another guarantees that Poupelin wept on seeing a wretched prisoner. Not so much a 'victime du livre', then, but, closely related, a 'victime des papiers'. Anyone accustomed to the amount of paperwork involved in the successful prosecution of daily living in France will sympathise with as well as laugh at Poupelin's touching, harmless, but, to the badgered officials concerned, irritating mania.

Throughout, Vallès maintains his lively curiosity about other people's modes of life, their 'existences hétéroclites' (p. 188). He allows for the possibility that some of them, Chaque for example, are pulling his leg, gulling their captive audience (*ibid.*). Chaque has splendid non-qualifications. He does not know Persian, Manchurian or Hindustani, 'mais il aurait pu les savoir. Voilà pourquoi on l'appelle l'orientaliste'. Unlike Poupelin or Fontan, he has never had to go without food or lodging. He ends up, in some gender-confusion, as *une pleureuse* at Montparnasse Cemetery, a one-person funeral *claque* (p. 196). The most hard-hitting of the *réfractaires* is the critic Gustave Planche, for whom Vallès served as a sort of secretary around 1855-1857. Literary critic on *La Revue des Deux Mondes,* this physically clumsy man was often thought of as being gratuitously savage in his articles. It is significant that Vallès deems such knocking jobs an integral part of renegade politics.

The rag-tailed 'army' of Vallès's *réfractaires,* as he is fully aware, 'compte dans ses rangs moins de fils du peuple que d'enfants de la bourgeoisie' (p. 201). One reason why his tactics are so metaphorical and so little programmatic is that, all his life, a constant in his thinking was that all systems of belief secrete sclerosis, 'l'impiété de la veille la religion d'aujourd'hui, l'athée d'une génération le dieu d'une autre' (p. 202). Even avowed revolutionaries like the Blanquists, with their cult of commemoration, do not inspire him: 'Je ne viens donc point faire de leur tombe une tribune et haranguer du fond d'un cimetière' (p. 198, in a section on 'Les Morts'). Chaque's rent-a-tear at least had the excuse of keening for his supper. Even so, at this early date, Vallès was already hoping for *alliances,* between dissident writers and at least the more thinking members of the middle classes (p. 203).

The section 'Le Dimanche d'un jeune homme pauvre' moves somewhat away from eccentrics to the odd-day-out: Sunday. While Vallès was all for difference—'vive la différence!', whether that between the sexes, or competing political choices, or the style of singular lives—Sunday was too different, too unlike weekdays. This article studies dodges 'pour égorger l'ennui' of endless Sundays (p. 249). It is a generous text, for, apart from his subjective woes, Vallès recognises that not he alone was left out of the general festivity of others on this day. It is a foretaste of the cheerless, colourless English Sunday anatomised in *La Rue à Londres.*

Any reader soon spots that Vallès's *réfractaires* are still caught up in the values of the marketplace; writing as much as any other activity depends on buyers and consumers. As Bellet suggests, *Vaincus,* or *Victimes,* would have made an apter title than *Les Réfractaires* (I, 1251-2). Bellet quotes a letter to the critic Paul de Saint-Victor in 1866: 'J'ai peint une vie de bohème difforme comme l'*Enfer* de Dante' (p. 1256). Vallès is talking through his outsize hat. Whatever the sufferings of his dropouts, they are hardly of that depth. Bellet also quotes the Goncourts' for once warm response to this collection, in a letter probably of late November 1865:

> Vous avez l'observation qui va au cœur; vous avez le superbe mot cru de la vérité nouvelle et moderne. Il passe, dans toutes vos pages, cette amertume généreuse et mélancolique que donne aux âmes tendres et hautes le spectacle des misères sociales. Vous montrez des coins de martyrs dans des grotesques de la bohème. Vous devinez cette grande danse des morts de Paris qui s'en va à la fosse commune. Vous avez le souffle et la fièvre de ce temps-ci. Nous aimons ce que vous écrivez pour tout cela, et encore pour la forme, le tour rare, l'épithète qui peint, le coup de pouce vivant qu'on sent dans votre phrase. (pp. 1252-3)

Other critical reactions of the day were more hostile. Pontmartin complained about: 'Ce récit, pétrolisé de communisme'.[14] Or again: 'Ce sont des phénomènes, rien de moins, rien de plus, et l'on ne raisonne pas d'après des phénomènes'. Diderot would vehemently disagree. But Pontmartin also asks the extremely awkward question: how *could* society have aided such oddballs?[15] Barbey d'Aurevilly, for whom Vallès had high regard despite the *Connétable*'s reactionary politics, achieves in his over-the-top way a more balanced view than do Pontmartin or the Goncourts:

> Il ne peint que ce qu'il a vu. Il a mis dans sa peinture ses souvenirs personnels, et il a eu raison. [...] Seulement, ce que je lui reproche c'est de n'avoir pas assez de souvenirs, [...] c'est de ne traîner jamais que le boulet, trop lourd et trop rivé, d'un *seul* souvenir personnel. [...] Un ombilic à regarder n'est pas le tour du monde.

More positively:

> Il a la verve sombre, le feu noir, le nerf, le mordant, le trait brutal, qui viole, mais féconde, et l'amertume de la caricature, s'il n'en a pas toujours la gaieté. [...] Ce meurt-de-faim d'hier [...] a dans son livre peut-être trop de cris d'estomac, mais il a aussi des cris de cœur. Les intestins n'empêchent pas les entrailles.[16]

In examining the lower depths, Vallès was not slumming nor adopting the 'mucker-pose'. He had shared much of what he recorded. His simplest plea is that *saltimbanques, réfractaires* or *irréguliers* have a right to a place in the sun (however watery), that ordered society should make room for and afford its deviants, those who shuffle offbeat steps. In picking out such picturesque nonpareils, Vallès was seeking to rescue them from oblivion and memorialise them, and so doing, to pacify his own fears of living and dying unnoticed. They are not run-of-the-mill paupers, the bag-people of cardboard cities—though Vallès had no racist scorn for these—but a kind of élite of the dregs. If they protest at all, it is *per absurdum*. They underline their generally sorry fates, they accentuate their hardships by persisting in their self-depriving choices. Vallès detected so much restriction in the society of his day that he turned for relief to all those who tried to escape stereotyping, even if there was no other point (political, for instance) to their option. It is, I imagine, a kind of inverted snobbery on his part, but one of generous imagination. Most importantly, these sketches, together with 'Le Bachelier géant' are Vallès's first stabs at creative fiction: if not the invention at least the elaboration of characters who are first and foremost singular beings and only secondarily symbolic representations of wider postures.

A step nearer to true rebels of the pen are those Vallès calls *les francs-parleurs* (Cf. *francs-tireurs*, in the military world). Planche was one such. Some of his other selections for the accolade are surprising. Edmond About, a *Normalien*, for his 'scepticisme joyeux en ce temps de philosophasses ennuyeux et de providentialistes majestueux!' (I, 902). Francisque Sarcey, who would later reveal his true despicable colours during the Commune. Despite his taste for polar opposites, Vallès was never a black-and-white demonologist, for he could recognise honesty, courage, free thought, even in writers and critics who, politically or socially, were far distant from himself. What he valued in such men was that 'leur critique est expéditive; ils affirment plus qu'ils ne discutent, vont droit au but' (p. 898). Vallès always tended towards blatancy, cards on the table: 'Je crois peu à cette guerre d'allusions voilées. [...] Il est arrivé bien souvent qu'on se méprenait sur des sous-entendus. [...] Ce sont plaisirs de grands seigneurs, desserts fins de lettrés' (p. 722). For his own part, he boastfully confessed 'je ne sais pas glisser les serpents sous les fleurs, quand l'ennemi passe, entonner la cloche; je ferais de la polémique plutôt en corsaire qu'en contrebandier' (*ibid.*). He exaggerates. Irony, double meanings, euphemisms, litotes, as we will see, are all frequently part of Vallès's weaponry. But he does aim to be readable, user-friendly, accessible. 'Ayons à notre service une langue franche et claire que tous pourront comprendre, les gens de la foule comme les petits conspirateurs d'écritoire' (p. 956). As the less-deceived Bellet notes, Vallès was prone to striking, and being seduced by, attitudes, surprisingly for a man so hostile to statuary (*JVJR*, p. 293). Certainly, precise political affiliation was of lesser concern to Vallès than the uses the particular mind was put to.

Much superior as a critic to About or Sarcey, Sainte-Beuve represented for Vallès another instance of misleading appearances. Not, it should be stated, in the pejorative mode as with Gambetta (a bogus rhetorician, in Vallès's eyes), but rather in the meliorative, as a fine if unlikely example of independence of mind. 'Un esprit libre. [...] Je préfère ce sceptique clairvoyant au troupeau des convaincus aveugles' (pp. 612-13). It needs a kind of cinematic double-take to see such a free spirit in the Sainte-Beuve so at home in imperial circles. Even more provocatively, Vallès selects vehement Catholics (admittedly of the more heretical persuasion), like Veuillot or Barbey d'Aurevilly, for acclaim. Veuillot, like Proudhon, belongs to 'les nets et les vise-droit' (see *JVJR*, p. 434, quoting a letter). These are, for Vallès, 'cette famille d'enfants terribles de l'Église'. Vallès salutes 'toute cette race de saltimbanques catholiques, honnêtes mais bizarres, dont Veuillot est l'hercule, d'Aurevilly le clown, et Gounod le trombone' (II, 410). He does not hesitate to appropriate even their minds: Pontmartin 'est un de ces gentilshommes qui, ayant le cœur royaliste, ont l'esprit républicain' (I, 899). But to call any of these 'l'avant-garde de la révolution' requires considerable naivety (p. 898).

Vallès admitted regretfully, to having once tried, in a *chahut*, to abort a lecture by Sainte-Beuve before he had begun to speak. Love of free speech beds ill with censorship. Believing that the public should be the judge, Vallès was so hostile to censorship that he fought shy, for instance, of subsidies for writers, which he saw as a demeaning charity, and of infinitely smaller urgency than freedom of expression and of association. Having studied in great depth the press of the Second Empire period, Bellet can claim that Vallès was truly audacious in this area (see I, pp. 396-7 and 1375). As a writer, Vallès was always ready to be knocked by readers, but not to be silenced, by them or the authorities (p. 773). He was fully aware that in that age of widespread censorship and surveillance, 'le difficile [...] n'est pas de dire, mais de ne pas dire' (p. 772). The result was that 'De peur de ne pouvoir rien dire, on dit avec précaution, timidité, détour: [...] on cache les armes sous la fanfreluche des phrases, on n'ose aller droit et jusqu'au bout!' (p. 836). He believed in a dialectical exchange of opinion, a *quid pro quo* (not a quiproquo!), a ding-dong: 'Quand on aura dit sur moi des infamies, on me laissera peut-être le droit de dire la vérité sur d'autres' (p. 1045). He believed in a genuine two-way process, for 'où serait la joie, s'il n'y avait pas de péril? [...] J'aimerais peut-être mieux, tant j'ai l'esprit mal fait, être attaqué qu'applaudi' (p. 920). Presumably because he would know that such hostility is possibly franker than a facile consensus; he would have struck home. He was convinced that obscurantism opened no one's eyes: 'Je suis contre tous les mystères. Je crois que la publicité ne tue rien pas plus que la cachotterie ne sauve rien' (II, 121). He was never averse to noisy, heckling audiences, but was dead against would-be silencers, even those inspired by leftist passions: 'Je commence à avoir une peur furieuse de la vertu!' (I, 589). Such purism permanently appalled him. Later, in the Commune, he would persist courageously in arguing against censorship, even in a war situation, just as he was in the minority resisting the setting-up of a Committee of Public Safety.

Self-censorship is, of course, another story, and one that I will come back to often, for example in relation to *L'Insurgé*, which offers a wilfully partial picture of the Commune (though by the time this novel was written, it was safer to be more outspoken). He had his good reasons, as we will see, but self-censors always do.

Chapter Two

Politics

This chapter on politics, in its more conventional senses, will be even more bitty than the previous one on nonconformists, just as Vallès's relationship to the political life in his age was fragmented and fluctuating. It partook more of resistance than involvement. Vallès remained himself a *réfractaire*. Bellet's account of the three main, interconnected, phases in Vallès's political evolution makes good sense: the social *réfractaire*, the cultural rebel, and thirdly the Communard, for whom the idea of revolution was made flesh.[1]

As we saw in the last chapter, Vallès was very catholic in his valuation of cultural rebels. All who react against clichés, or have flamboyant styles, who are ironists, polemicists or realists—no matter what their overt political opinions,—are on Vallès's side of the pale. I am reminded of Michel Tournier's statement that all writers who care for and about their mother tongue are the true guardians of the nation.[2] No more than Vallès did he have in mind crusty anti-immigration *passéistes*, hostile to borrowings or neologisms. Indeed, a draughtsman like Daumier or a light opera composer like Offenbach found favour with Vallès precisely because of their mockery of classical models, the official idols of the governing classes.

A supreme hinge-figure in Western culture, and central to Vallès's whole response to politics, is Jean-Jacques Rousseau. It might seem odd for a writer of the left to be so unremittingly hostile to such a precursor. There was, indeed, much to link them. Rousseau made great efforts to establish the child as someone precious, special, and not just a grown-up writ small. Neither Rousseau or Vallès allowed much room for Original Sin: environment and nurture (or mis-nurture) are the true moulders of the individual. In *Les Confessions,* Rousseau confesses his early bookishness, much more chosen than Vallès's, but *Émile* and other texts feature strong attacks on book-learning, the tyranny of print; and Rousseau appears to rejoin Vallès in the resistance to being a *victime du livre.* Only *Robinson Crusoe,* also one of Vallès's favourites, would be allowed into Rousseau's educational utopia. On the other side of this medal, however, the *cabinets de lecture,* in which Vallès and Jacques Vingtras sought warmth and reading matter as impoverished *bacheliers*, were 'largely a consequence of the vast popular demand for Rousseau's *Nouvelle Héloïse'.*[3] Rousseau's ideas inspired the whole progressive wing of educational thought in the nineteenth, and on into our own, century. Much, then, links the two men. Yet, despite Rousseau's preference for self-restraint rather than externally imposed regulation, his backing of the tyranny of public opinion in *Le Contrat social* could only alienate Vallès.

Vallès chose to see Rousseau as a peevish, melancholic philosopher, who bred a like-minded following, the Jacobins. Rousseau was adopted and perverted by Robespierre and Saint-Just, who were in turn mythified by the revolutionary tradition. Vallès is clearly at several removes from the original. For Bellet, Vallès 'connaît Rousseau à partir de Proudhon: du moins le Rousseau idéologique qu'il critique âprement et ne comprend pas; car, de l'autre, de Jean-Jacques, il est plus proche qu'il ne croit' (*JVJR*, p. 302). Not that Vallès was ever nervous about seeming biased. 'Je ne trouve au monde rien de plus lâche que de mentir à sa conviction par crainte d'un préjugé' (*ibid.*, p. 306). Vallès's loaded legend about Rousseau was one important way of animating and exemplifying his own political options, or more accurately aversions. Another aspect of this was his youthful preference for Rousseau over Voltaire, in the classical polarisation; but he grew out of this: 'Je préfère aujourd'hui le rire libre d'Arouet au sanglotement étudié de Rousseau, le scepticisme de *Candide* à l'enthousiasme du *Vicaire* ' (I, 381). Vallès associated Rousseau with the eighteenth-century cult of a deity, culminating in the 'Être suprême' of Robespierre, who thereby achieved his own apotheosis, for this had merely swapped one god for another: 'C'était changer d'eau bénite simplement' (*ibid.*).

Vallès accused Robespierre and the Montagnards of crushing the Girondins. Robespierre, son of Rousseau, 'étouffa la voix gênante de Desmoulins' (p. 430). The Jacobin clubs were 'a cross between a church and a school' (two objects of intense hatred by Vallès); 'they consciously set themselves up as the moral guardians of revolutionary principles'. [4] Along with many others, Vallès deemed the neo-Jacobins of his own day backward-turned, taking all their references and precedents from the French Revolution, suitably rewritten 'pour les besoins de la cause'. The Jacobins in the revolutionary period themselves looked backward. Their cult of *Romanité* was fostered to give them glory, cachet, corroboration. In Schama's words: 'these lessons in moral earnestness Robespierre had learned from his lawyer father, from devotion to the precepts and life of Jean-Jacques Rousseau and from the passion for Latin history and oratory that earned him annual prizes at the Lycée Louis-le-Grand in Paris as well as the nickname "the Roman" '. [5] Robespierre's view of himself as 'a messianic schoolmaster, wielding a very big stick to inculcate virtue', [6] could only be anathema to Vallès, though he had to fight against his youthful infatuation with such head-banging oratory ('Moi, bourré de jacobinisme, sentant malgré moi Rousseau et Robespierre'—letter to É. Gautier, p. 481). Always more bolshy than bolshevik, Vallès was to spend his activist's life caught in the crossfire of conservative right and authoritarian left: an in-between.

Indeed, his first direct involvement in political action in 1848 at Nantes saw Vallès frequently as much at odds with his student coevals as with society at large. Looking back from the mid-1860s on those heady days, Vallès claims (and he was not alone) not to know what the battle cry of 'La Sociale' meant. Naturally, he mocks his adolescent idealism: 'Je disais, moi, dans mon style de rhétoricien féroce, que le trou de la guillotine avait encore la forme d'une couronne. —Oh mon Dieu! Je ne puis songer sans rire à ce temps-la' (I, 809). He and his fellow (would-be) conspirators were, in one of his favourite oxymorons, 'cocassement tragiques'. Yet he cannot altogether help admiring this youthful fervour and panache. As so often, he marries rhetoric with clothes. He brandished in those days an outsize hat with a huge cocade:

> J'exaspérai tout le monde, j'en rendis sourds quelques-uns. Les tièdes me maudirent, les convaincus reconnurent ma supériorité, et ma tournure légendaire, ma musique vocale sans précédent, me désignèrent à l'attention. Pendant quatre mois, de février à juin, je fus chef de groupe dans l'armée des conscrits révolutionnaires. (pp. 809-10)

Vallès never reneged on his hopes of that time. Nor did he join the anvil-chorus of those who, like Flaubert, chose only to mock the insufficient support provided by the workers. Vallès knew in 1848 and recognised on all later occasions that bourgeois radicals not only expected too much of the workers, but also had no real contact with them. Indeed, as Zeldin indicates, 'the intellectual [in 1848] could be more of a stranger to the worker than his employer, with whom he lived and worked'. [7] Flaubert, in L'Éducation sentimentale, relishes displaying ideological clichés of stereotyped characters frantically engaged in remouthing the famous words of past great names. Given his obsession with cliché and plagiarism, secondhand living, Flaubert presents 1848 as a take-off of 1789. Revolution, for him, bears its mechanical meaning: spinning wheels, historical cycles. Vallès's stark difference from Flaubert is that he did not believe that all revolutions had to be replays of this failed one.

However ill-acquainted Vallès was with Marx's writings, they met on common ground in this area of historical repetition:

> The tradition of the dead generations weighs like a nightmare on the minds of the living. And, just when they appear to be engaged in the revolutionary transformation of themselves and their material surroundings, in the creation of something which does not yet exist, precisely in such epochs of revolutionary crisis they timidly conjure up the spirits of the past to help them; they borrow their names, slogans and costumes so as to stage the new world-historical scene in this venerable disguise and borrowed language. Luther put on the mask of the apostle Paul; the Revolution of 1789-1814 draped itself alternately as the Roman republic and the Roman empire; and the revolution of 1848 knew no better than to parody at some points 1789 and at others the revolutionary traditions of 1793-5.

Marx admitted that certain repetitions, e.g. Cromwell's revolution modelled on 'the language, passions and illusions of the Old Testament', can be valid. Essentially, however, Marx held that it was to the future, not to the past, that revolutionaries should turn. Vallès would be in agreement with this open-ended outlook which refuses to preconstruct the future state.

In all this, Marx was building on Engels's rewriting of Hegel, about history being 'unrolled twice over, once as a great tragedy and once as a wretched farce'. Less dialectical and more taken with coexistence, Vallès would run tragedy and farce closer together. He would no doubt have enjoyed Marx's depiction of Louis-Napoléon as a 'serious buffoon'. [8] Though thoroughly naïve about practical politics in multiple ways, Vallès did foresee Louis-Napoléon's *coup d'état* more clearly than many supposedly professional commentators or even politicians themselves. This coup was aimed principally against a conservative bourgeois National Assembly. Not many workers were keen on taking to the streets to resist this take-over. Despite his insight, Vallès was out of touch with public submissiveness in 1851. His own small-scale failure to incite local insurrection could have been traumatic, as it was for Paul Nizan's Antoine Bloyé, who never again took a risk.

His instinct was never to trust the vested interest, the professional. Politics is not a specialism. We are all, loathe it or not, political animals, because we are, love it or not, social creatures. We have a say; we have to have a say. That Vallès was allergic to theory, as Bellet amply demonstrates, is patent to any reader (*JVJR*, p. 130). He played hookey from all schools of thought. He mocks all authority-figures, including that major source of the pompous: the precious self. He struggled all life through against all forms of corseting, and even in his stock-market journalism he wrote ironically of speculation in whalebone (I, 124-5). Although he retained real fondness for certain pleasurable aspects of religion (e.g. Christmas festivities), and although he habitually uses religious metaphors, he was permanently hostile to the Church as a socio-political force. He detested even more the very idea of substitute-religions, though prone himself to endorsing selected myths, especially that of 'le Peuple'.

In truth, Vallès enjoyed little prolonged contact with manual workers, except in the more expert and independent form of artisans, such as the shoemakers he knew as a child, or the 'compagnons du Devoir' in his own extended family. As the century wore on, the latter, of course, began to seem increasingly archaic as a social and political phenomenon, though artisans figured considerably in the ranks of anarchists and anarcho-syndicalists into the first decade of this century. There were few large factories in the France of his day for him to visit, but he did go down a mine. Even if his report includes no political or economic dimension, the freshness of his response was undoubtedly news from foreign parts to his readers in *Le Figaro*. Largely he lets the facts, the hideous conditions of work, speak for themselves. (Near the end of his life, together with Guesde, Lafargue and others, Vallès attended a meeting in support of striking miners at Anzin, but was much too ill to address them). He keeps his good humour: 'Nous avions, mon ami et moi, l'air de deux mottes de beurre tombées dans une écritoire' (I, 912). Bellet remarks on the near-total absence of reference to the numerous mines of the Saint-Étienne region in *L'Enfant* (I, 1641). Vallès, besides, likes swinging between extremes. As well as going down a mine, a few months later he went up in a balloon (see p. 960). Apart from these excursions, his main leg-work as a journalist was around the streets of Paris. Naturally, as a widely-experienced pressman he was thoroughly familiar with the *détours* of this particular *sérail*.

Though he was often accused, and sometimes accused himself, of laziness, his most constant plea was for the right to work. That is, the right to earn enough on which to live decently, rather than any puritanical work ethic. This right embraced the request for radical intellectuals (the word had not yet been invented), such as writers and journalists, to be considered also as workers. He once wrote to his friend Arnould that 'les ouvriers trouvent le travail infériorisant. Je tiendrais, moi, à l'universaliser et à l'anoblir' (*Corr. A.*, pp. 233-4). Vallès seems not to have known Denis Poulot's *Le Sublime, ou le travailleur comme il est en 1870 et ce qu'il peut être,* published a year before the Commune (and raided by Zola for his *L'Assommoir*). A foreman turned employer in 'la mécanique' (mechanical engineering), Poulot's stance, despite his denunciation of the indiscipline he saw spreading throughout the work-force, is not inflexibly anti-employee. 'Sublime' was the sardonic title given by workers themselves to workmates hostile to authority. Almost despite himself, Poulot reveals widespread instances of resistance to the boss and his underlings. If he had known of this study, Vallès would have relished the way humour was used as a weapon of stonewalling or retaliation. (In *L'Enfant*, the child is in a comparable position in the familial factory, which is likewise aiming to manufacture a predesigned product).

In the absence of direct contact with workers, Vallès relied on myths and convictions. Yeats's lines would not have moved him: 'The best lack all conviction, while the worst / Are full of passionate intensity'.[9] Vallès always had the courage of his convictions, and went to prison, fought duels and exposed his life in the Commune to prove it. 'Conviction', of course, can be ethical, or penal. Vallès himself recognised that he was often prisoner of his own beliefs. While he accepted that their active presence can confine or mislead, their absence, in his eyes, would greatly diminish full human being.

The myths he adhered to were likewise convictions, hopes pious or otherwise, crossed fingers. The principal myth is that of 'le Peuple'.

Vallès defines it elastically: 'La Rue représente le peuple, le peuple qui n'est pas un ramassis d'émeutiers ou d'ivrognes—chair à barricades—le peuple où se mêlent et se coudoient tous les déplacés: gentilshommes qui sont descendus, bourgeois ruinés, travailleurs qui montent' (*La Rue*, 14 septembre 1867). A heterogeneous collection, marked by vigorous aspirations or dynamic grievances, and overspilling all class boundaries. His target-audience in *La Rue* was younger men of lower-class origin but bourgeois by education. Despite this motley, Vallès habitually refers to *le peuple* as *les blouses* (a very rough equivalent would be 'cloth caps'). No doubt he clung to this (disappearing) emblem of the working class because it offered a link—there were not too many others, except poverty itself—between the Parisian proletariat and the peasantry, between city and country. For all his naïve optimism, his cataracted vision of *le peuple* at least never backtracked. Many sympathisers with the have-nots respect or even love them as long as they are victimised without protest, but recoil once the sufferers become self-assertive. Zola is a good example of this seasonal humanitarianism.

Vallès never lost faith. In his exaltation of *le peuple*, he at least avoided the singular personality cults of his times. It seems saner to put trust in a large body of people than in one leader. The fact remains that he is utopian in outlook: 'Or il s'agit moins d'expliquer une idée que de lancer les questions, et il suffit qu'un problème soit posé pour qu'il soit résolu; il sera résolu par l'effet simple et fatal du travail souterrain qui s'accomplit sans cesse dans l'esprit d'un peuple' (I, 822). The lyrical rumblings of Michelet can be heard in these sentences. Rather closer to likelihood is this later, post-Commune view of the crowd:

> Ils ont tort, ceux qui croient que tel ou tel homme peut soulever ou enchaîner la Ville. Non! c'est de toutes parts que vient la force, absolument comme les inventions sont trouvées, grain par grain, goutte par goutte, dans des tamis ou des cornues placés on ne sait où! Un beau matin, un homme donne la matrice d'une formule à tous ces éléments dispersés,—et l'on dit qu'il a du génie! Il n'a fait qu'accoucher le peuple en travail! (*TP*, p. 114)

Here, a kind of interdependence is imagined. The crowd is not totally illegible and a law unto itself; it needs to be channelled. As we will see, there are fluctuations, in Vallès's thinking, between fatalism and voluntarism. A mystery remains at the heart, not Rousseau's general will, but some power more elemental and uninflected by reason:

> Il faut être indulgent pour la brutalité des foules. Quand les êtres humains sont serrés par centaines, autour de n'importe quoi, qui a l'air d'un clocher du régiment, chaque cervelle et chaque cœur abdique aux mains d'une force invisible et aveugle qui conduit le troupeau commun on ne sait où. (*ibid.*, p. 310)

This, of course, is the extreme case, but it shows Vallès more tolerant of collective violence than of solo terrorism. He never quite distances himself nor plunges in. As Bellet argues, Vallès was on the whole a very down-to-earth mythifier. What he refused is as important as what he swallowed, and he certainly did inherit some of his attitudes towards *le peuple:* 'Le forgeron préfigurant l'alchimiste ne le touche pas plus que le mineur se muant en démiurge chtonien' (*JVJR*, p. 257). Vallès's favourite working image is that of the shoemaker: on close terms with his clients, transforming raw materials into an impressive finished object, unbeholden to any master, and gaining true satisfaction from his labours.

Son of a printer (one of the trades Vallès often hungered to acquire), Michelet could claim, with somewhat more accuracy than Vallès: 'Je suis né peuple, j'avais le peuple dans le cœur' (these two sentences have no necessary logical link). Elsewhere, Michelet admitted that the common man's tongue was inaccessible to him, and he frequently stressed how wide was the chasm between the idiolects of the different classes and their cultures in France. Vallès's native suspicions, which coexisted with genuine admiration, on the subject of Michelet were well-founded, for he is a notoriously unreliable historian. Still, as Bellet points out, Vallès values Michelet more than Hugo as an annalist (not so strange a conjunction, for Michelet was a very novelistic historian), 'parce que son peuple est celui d'une histoire et d'une géographie précises, terriennes, rocailleuses' (*JVJR*, p. 454). To put it another way, the more mystical aspects of Michelet's writing and oratory were more grounded and closer to Vallès's obsessions than those of Hugo were.

Though, like Vallès, critical of the harsh discipline practised in schools, Michelet in general lauds the teaching profession, in which he spent over two decades. In his 1848 lectures, he proclaimed that students could act as intermediaries, hyphens, between the people and the supposedly thinking classes, translating the messages from one to the other. Though this idea appealed to Vallès, in its linking, barrier-breaking, aspects, its top-down approach was essentially foreign to him. In terms of revolutionary history, Michelet was, like Vallès, hostile to the Jacobins, similarly viewing them as a negative force working against revolutionary dynamics, pursuing power and relying on police-methods, like surveillance. Yet Michelet recognised that Robespierre remained his companion and yardstick throughout the writing of his *Histoire de la Révolution française.* Two later writers who acknowledge their debt to Michelet are C.L.R. James, in *The Black Jacobins,* and Edmund Wilson, in *To the Finland Station:* 'Michelet went on teaching long after his death'.[10]

Vallès and Michelet met most in the idea of *le peuple* as the principal actor in history. Though aware of the mystical elements in his concept, Michelet thought he offset them with an alternative mysticism: the man of genius, who, in some fantastic way, subsumes the masses. Even though he was fully conscious of Michelet's ham-acting when on a platform, Vallès did relish his anticlerical lectures. But even then there were days when 'nous applaudissions M. Michelet de confiance', (I, 611). A chapter in *Le Bachelier* records this sceptical trust. Michelet in old age, after suffering two strokes on learning of the outbreak and the outcome of the Commune, struck Vallès as 'solennel et féminin, éloquent et bizarre' (*Ins.*, p. 978). Before agreeing to sign a petition against a death sentence on two radicals, Michelet left the room twice to consult his wife, which both amuses and touches Vallès (*ibid.*). The more macho side of Michelet's attitude to women, however, which made him, like Hugo, keep a sexual score-card, would have struck Vallès, if he had known of it, as pedantically climaxiomatic. For all his reservations, nonetheless, Vallès could never have murmured, like Jules Renard: 'Il faudrait un Michelet rapetissé'.[11] I cannot understand, either, how Gille can maintain that it was jealousy that prevented Vallès from being totally bowled over by Michelet's lectures.[12]

Among admirers of Michelet was Proudhon, whom Vallès valued highly, and who, like Michelet, was trained in type-setting. Proudhon had no more success than Vallès in the arena of practical politics, and there was in his scheme of values a higher dose of conservatism alongside the undoubted radicalism. Despite his famous dictum that property is theft, Proudhon had no desire to abolish property. What he meant was that profit exacted without labour (e.g. by landlords) was theft. He wanted a 'balanced society of small peasant proprietors', and 'communal ownership was anathema to him'.[13] Like Vallès, he was keen to reconcile the middle-classes to his proposed social changes, especially the loose federation of autonomous communes, intended to replace the over-centralised state. Considered dangerous both by the right and by republicans, he suffered exile and repeated imprisonments. Unlike Vallès, he was a virulent critic of universal suffrage and of violent revolution, and far more systematically anticlerical.

Bellet resumes Vallès's debt to Proudhon in these terms:

> Vallès a pris de Proudhon, d'un Proudhon plutôt polémiste qu'idéologue, ce qui lui convenait: quelques invocations, quelques imprécations, quelques formules contre le jacobinisme, contre Rousseau, histoire de se décaper soi-même. Vallès ne cherche qu'à être Vallès: il n'est pas homme à subir des influences idéologiques, à s'imbiber d'une pensée, à se pénétrer de philosophies. (I, 1470)

It seems likely that he read little of *Le Manuel du spéculateur* or *L'Idée générale de la Révolution*, though he did read *Les Confessions d'un révolutionnaire* (*JVJR*, p. 304). Their biggest area of coincidence was clearly the concept of authority in all its governmental forms. On patriarchal authority, however, they would part company. In *La Pornocratie*, Proudhon declared there were only two possible roles for women: housekeepers or prostitutes; he calculated their intellectual and moral worth as one-third that of men. He listed six cases, including immodesty, drunkenness, theft and wanton spending, in which the husband is entitled to kill his wife in strict marital justice. Though only partially, and quite late in life, pro-feminist, Vallès would have found such views totally repellent.

Vallès found Proudhon readable, when skimmed. 'Point n'est besoin d'éplucher ses livres. — Sont ouvrages médiocres ou qu'il ne faut pas lire tous ceux qu'on est forcé d'éplucher' (I, 1591). Vallès had had a bellyful of swotting at school. In *L'Insurgé,* he claims he had to read Proudhon at the gallop, but 'lorsque j'avais avalé une gorgée de Proudhon—il en restait des gouttes toutes rouges sur mon papier' (p. 938). This passage gives an interesting slant on the commonplace images of absorption and regurgitation. Ingestion, here, is seen as revivifying, not suffocating; an overspill of verve; an osmosis between two writers. Indeed, it was probably Proudhon's style and his irony that most magnetised Vallès. As Marx detected: 'Just as Peter the Great defeated Russian barbarism by barbarity, Proudhon did his best to defeat French phrase-making by phrases'. [14] Irony was Proudhon's 'compagne robuste' (I, 800). Vallès would have echoed and applied to Proudhon himself Proudhon's hymn to Voltairean irony:

> Ironie, vraie liberté! c'est toi qui me délivres de l'ambition du pouvoir, de la servitude des partis, du respect de la routine, du pédantisme de la science, de l'admiration des grands personnages, des mystifications de la politique, du fanatisme des réformateurs, de la superstition de ce grand univers et de l'adoration de moi-même! (Quoted *ibid.,* p. 1572)

Proudhon is, for many, an honoured ancestor of anarchism. The preference for the word 'social' over the word 'political' is a profoundly anarchist impulse (as it is for would-be apolitical people). To that extent, Vallès was an anarchist. By definition, an anarchist seeks to sidestep definition. By nature he jibs at being corralled. Indeed, such attempts to confine and tame him are exactly what he judges to be wrong with presently constituted society. More thinkingly responsible anarchists want to be a law unto themselves, and so do not pursue anarchy. Vallès wanted to abolish neither the right to vote, nor parliament, nor armies. He did not even plead for school hierarchies to be turned topsy-turvy, for it was the programme of (largely classical) studies, repressive teaching methods, and excessive reverence for authority, that angered him most in educational practice. Though Vallès rarely used the term 'anarchiste', because that too was a straitjacket (like atheism), he did believe that everything emanating from the state, even handouts to the arts, was suspect. As Bellet concludes: 'Tout corps établi, constitué, représente fatalement ce qui est. Il est le gardien du *statu quo'* (p. 887). If, then, an anarchist at all, Vallès would be more at home on the generous, and not the selfishly elitist, wing of anarchism.

Although he mocks them comprehensively in *Le Bachelier,* Vallès was always closer to the tradition, or rather the spirit, of secret societies than to above-ground, organised political parties. He met, and admired with reservations, the prime French exemplar of this tradition, Auguste Blanqui. Held to be the most implacable revolutionary of his period, Blanqui in fact had limited direct impact on historical events,—the main incident was a failed attempt to overthrow the July Monarchy in 1839. It has been computed that Blanqui spent forty-three of his seventy-six years in prison or under strict surveillance. [15] As a result, most of his life was a dull routine, which seemed to suit this ascetic man, altogether too Spartan for Vallès's deeper tastes. It should be stressed, however, that Blanqui cannot be held responsible for his legend, 'L'Enfermé', which 'acquired connotations of sentimentality altogether foreign to the studied pessimism with which he accepted his ordeal'. [16]

What separated Vallès most from Blanquism was death, and the uses made of it. In 1881, when it was proposed to erect a statue to Proudhon, Vallès made clear his refusal: 'Mais non, passant, ne t'arrête pas! Va de l'avant sans te détourner pour saluer le passé. Droit en face! Et ne perds pas de temps dans les cimetières, à moins qu'il n'y ait à y percer des meutrières pour s'y défendre, comme au Père-Lachaise, à la fin de la semaine sanglante' (II, 735). Vallès's instinct was always to take off from rather than commemorate the past. When workers' associations adopted dates of religious festivals for their own militant purposes, Vallès commented that he disliked 'cette centralisation des regrets' (*TP*, p. 219). More customary cemetery-visits, while he still used them to make a political point, he regarded as normal outlets for popular emotions. He argued that they were not of Christian inspiration, lugubrious and terrorised like provincial outings to gravesides, but pagan, festive and joyful: 'C'est plutôt une visite à un ami endormi qu'un pèlerinage funèbre'. [17]

Blanquism was marked by an obsession with ritual, frequently centred on cemeteries: 'Pilgrimages to the cemeteries where fallen heroes of the revolutionary cause were buried, erection of monuments to honor the most celebrated martyrs of the cause'. [18] This cult of the dead recalls ancestor-worship. 'The Blanquists' emphasis upon precedent and repetition was deeply rooted in an archaic mentality which understood revolution as a resurrection of an unchanging primal state of mind'. [19] Blanqui himself, when he appears in *L'Insurgé,* is physically a wreck, but the eyes persist in gleaming; the appearance and the spirit are at odds. Though Vallès calls Blanqui, with a distant admiration, 'le mathématicien froid de la révolte', he rather strangely goes on to talk of the feminine appeal of true revolutionary leaders to a crowd seen as essentially male (*Ins.*, pp. 987 ff. and 1901). In the 1860s, Vallès could say of him: 'Auguste Blanqui est, je l'avoue, un de ceux que j'admire tout bas et que j'ai défendu et défendrai tout haut, car il a, celui-là au moins, la logique terrible de ses convictions' (I, 811). Apart from the differences about the use of the past, and of commemoration, Vallès also was too much of a spontaneist to agree with Blanqui's lifelong championing of organised military squads to initiate and control the *coup de force*.

Hutton detects strong traces of Blanquist attitudes in Third World national liberation movements of our day, despite the essentially backward-looking stance of its tenets:

> The past, the Blanquists believed, could be relived as well as remembered. The task was to reenter the passions, hopes and anxieties of revolutionaries who had gone before. To the extent that these emotions could be recaptured, timebound experience could be transcended. More than a method for fomenting popular insurrection, Blanquism was a commitment to revolutionary struggle as a means of consciousness-raising to this timeless plane. [20]

Mainly after his death, Vallès's *Le Cri du peuple* went heavily in for such commemoration. Vallès's own attitude to revolution, while strongly influenced by precedents, was much more dynamic in outlook. The fact that it fluctuated proves that it was alive, and not ossified.

Despite such disagreement with Blanquist thinking, Vallès, like many another radical, saw revolt as meaning the recapture of a lost or stolen past quite as much as, or even more than, building a precast future. In fact, the latter could have no solid foundations lacking the former. The stance is thus retrospective as well as prospective. More importantly, however, Vallès always seemed to be *awaiting* a revolution. That is, a spontaneous uprising of the lower classes. He paid much less attention to organised agitation (except in the form of written polemics), propaganda or the formation of *cadres*. As such, and his fictional name no doubt had a say in this, the model was the *jacquerie*. His lifelong capacity for surprise, his immunity to the blasé, make him think of revolution as something that happens (Cf. the intransitive verb *survenir*). Only thus, perhaps, could genuine, unprogrammed volition have its expression. We have seen earlier how scornful he was of 'inkhorn conspirators'.

It is difficult to ignore the view of even the most sympathetic of Vallès's commentators, summed up in Sandy Petrey's '[Vallès's novels] could not proceed beyond demystification to suggest an alternative to the ideology they so stridently refused'. [21] Difficult, but not totally impossible. If what Petrey avers is true, was it by instinctive choice or by inability? Was this Vallès at his most anarchist: sweep away the dead past, but do not chain the future by dictating its shape and contents? Sartre, for one, would understand this well. Brupbacher states: 'De positif en lui, il n'y a, pour ainsi dire, que l'élément négateur, belliqueux, révolutionnaire. Mais cet élément-là, lui non plus, n'avait pas encore trouvé sa forme historiquement valable'. [22] So the leftish rodomontades were not entirely Vallès's fault; he was born too soon? The negating burden is indisputably weighty, but I remain convinced that Vallès was more of a gainsayer than a nay-sayer. Bellet has a comparable view, expressed with his customary intricate clarity. For Vallès, Revolution, as imagined by his contemporaries, was most often puritanical flummery or pomposity. His own version 'ne cesse de se définir contre cette idée; une négation éperdue et passionnée, une négation toujours plus "idéale" puisqu'elle s'oppose, la plupart du temps, aux révolutions réelles inspirées de l'Idée de Révolution' (*JVJR*, p. 123). In fact, so sick did he get of the fake revolutions clamoured for in his time that for part of the 1860s, as Bellet demonstrates, Vallès in effect repudiated Revolution. It needed to be 'desacralised' (*ibid.*).

Indeed, in the 1860s, Vallès's politics could be viewed as 'plutôt un individualisme libéral teinté de saint-simonisme qu'un "socialisme"; aucune idée des "contradictions économiques" dont parlait Proudhon; aucune idée de force ouvrière. [...] Vallès est fort proche encore du romantisme et de Victor Hugo' (Bellet, I, 1375). Certainly he had grave doubts about the desirability or feasibility of insurrectionism. It would take the Franco-Prussian war, and the Commune, to turn him into a revolutionary. Until then, though he habitually used military images of battles and barricades, he had not experienced these in the streets of Paris. When finally they became a reality, he discovered a strong moderating urge. Perhaps he was truest to his own instincts when he declared, in 1865: 'J'aime mieux, après tout, la littérature qui refait les moeurs que la politique qui fait les lois' (p. 435). Even here, however, he views literature as a social, and therefore a political weapon. It must alter, awaken those it touches, never leave them indifferent.

With his own deep experience of fiascoes, in private or public life, and his ineradicable sense of humour, Vallès often talks of revolt as an unbroken spectrum going, both ways, from buffoonish to tragic (cf. his account of Rigault in the Commune: 'Il leur offrira sa poitrine comme il leur montrerait son derrière—héroïque ou ignoble suivant que la situation sera tragique ou bouffonne' (*Ins.*, p. 960). What matters most to Vallès is the oscillation between defeatism and victorism. Having suffered is his main criterion, yet he rarely sounds like our contemporary proponents of 'political correctness', who take pride in purloining membership of a putatively or authentically oppressed minority. For one thing, Vallès's criterion is wider: his sympathy for sufferers embraces his enemies. He puts it in a typical oxymoron: 'le bonheur d'être malheureux', which was denied, in his eyes, to Vermersch (II, 117). This is well away from masochism. However Romantic Vallès could remain on occasion, the word 'martyr' rarely springs to mind, or even 'victims', in the sense of the defeated. [23]

Martyrs do not survive. Vallès was a survivor. 'Nous sommes nés pour être dupes et victimes, nous qui sommes de tempérament, d'allure, de coeur, avec les blousiers. Seulement, nous le savons, et nous ne sommes pas des gobe-mouches' (*Corr. A.,* p. 174). If, for Vallès, most people are indeed always victims, political, or 'victimes du livre'—suckers for false expectations—he strove hard to show how to fight back. The tyranny of print culture, or governments, inspires his revolt. Unusually for a Frenchman, he exalts the heroism of defeat—the plucky loser and his moral victory: terms that sit ill, in their French counterparts, on Gallic lips. 'Mes vaincus sont certains d'avoir leur heure dans mon œuvre' (*Corr. M.,* p. 208). More positively, his negation is sustained by hope, even if it is often whistling in the dark, as it must for anyone who has any intention of changing things for the better.

Politics are mostly less extreme. Much of Vallès's efforts went into mocking the middle-of-the-roaders, the Joseph Prudhommes (whom Vallès tended to conflate with the opportunist Jérôme Paturot), who populated many an office, theatre seat and political gathering (see *JVJR,* p. 259). If never censorious about adultery, Vallès loathed adulteration. When Jules Favre (to whom, like Jules Ferry or Thiers, Vallès was presciently hostile before they showed their true reactionary colours) entered the Académie Française, Vallès spoke of 'ce *panachage* opportuniste'.[24] Republicanism, the official opposition under the Second Empire, never failed to excite his scorn, and no republican more than Léon Gambetta. Vallès was impervious to the widely acknowledged charm of this ugly, glass-eyed, untidy, semi-bohemian speechifier. His banal, repetitious speeches went down well with mass audiences by the impression they gave of sincerity. A *parvenu* himself, he was the self-appointed champion of 'les nouvelles couches sociales' (he disliked the term 'class').[25] For Vallès, he would remain 'le Danton de pacotille' (*Ins.,* p. 985), unforgivable, despite his moments of dubious glory during the Franco-Prussian war.

Vallès's own experience of practical politics (apart from in the Commune, to be discussed later) was limited. In 1869 he stood in the eighth district of Paris, in the legislative elections, against the moderate republican Jules Simon and the leading barrister Lachaud, under the polyglot title of 'revolutionary socialist democrat'. Vallès had serious misgivings about his speechmaking talents and his appeal for voters. It seems that he found the whole episode an exhausting chore and was much relieved when it was over. His own score was buried in the 600-odd votes gained by the *divers* (also-rans); Simon polled 30,000. Vallès had none of the mechanical doggedness nor the expedient manoeuvrability essential for a candidate. His manifesto to the electors put the stress on poverty and defeat, and was vague about the legitimate demands of the oppressed. It was, as a critic has said, an appeal to sentiments, not a programme.[26] Vallès's appearance on the hustings was greatly mocked at the time, and gave birth to republican slanders about his dipping into slush funds, which he always indignantly and plausibly denied.

This candidacy came at one of Vallès's lowest points of political morale. Bitter and largely disappointing ventures into running his own newspapers in the later 1860s, a sense of the impotence of opposition, doubts, too, about the general lack of direction or clear success in his own career, all of these depressed him in the period running, or slouching, up to the Franco-Prussian War and the Commune. A constant part, anyway, of his view of politics was the need for a warrior's rest. However vital and exciting politics can be, no reasonable person should or could be totally immersed in it. Arms have to be laid down, rest taken, and refreshments. So many demagogues assume that people have nothing else to do but militate. In curiously classical terms, he sums up his belief on this score: 'Après la bataille, le partisan ou le soldat, le bourreau ou la victime, dépose son fouet ou dépose sa chaîne, ôte son masque, défait sa cuirasse, il redevient *homme,* reprend sa liberté, et alors nous savons le secret de son âme, ce que vaut sa gaieté publique, son courage au soleil' (I, 551). As well as judging people by how they perform in action (the existentialist approach), we must use the yardstick of the private person (the essentialist approach) in order to illuminate the public activist. Here, as in so much else, Vallès's outlook is that of a heroic, sane ordinariness.

I wonder what he would have made of Paul Lafargue's *Le Droit à la paresse.* Despite his own belief in the need for rest, his own splendid comic gifts, his anti-puritanism and his love of exaggeration, I imagine that Vallès's down-to-earth demand for the right to work would have jibbed at Lafargue's wilfully paradoxical plea for the right to idleness. The 'Auvergnat' Vallès would dislike Lafargue's attack on 'les races pour qui le travail est une nécessité organique. Les Auvergnats; les Ecossais, ces Auvergnats des Iles britanniques...' Lafargue's conclusion is: 'Il faut que le Prolétariat [...] retourne à ses instincts naturels, qu'il proclame les *Droits de la paresse,* mille et mille fois plus nobles et plus sacrés que les phtisiques *Droits de l'homme,* concoctés par les avocats métaphysiciens de la révolution bourgeoise; qu'il se contraigne à ne travailler que trois heures par jour, à fainéanter et bombancer le reste de la journée et de la nuit'. [27] Vallès knew too well that, even in dreamland, life could not be all beer and skittles.

In general, Vallès is too political for the would-be 'pure artists', and not politicised enough for ideologues: *à cheval,* caught in the crossfire. He was often separated from his fellow student militants by his verbal extremism as a youth, and divorced from other revolutionaries by his moderation as an elder. His sharp awareness of (and indeed his proneness to) clichés made him refuse to take much for granted; he rarely sprang to worshipful attention to anything. If it is true that most people stick by the politics of their formative years, then Vallès's could only be an approximate socialism, as socialism in the 1840s and 1850s was vague, dispersed, splintered and utopian. His effort to motivate and excuse his 'criminal' parents spills over into his political attitudes, where, likewise, he could never be a demonologist, a Manichaean. The 'logic' of his parents, however painful its application to him, had to be given its say. When contested or rejected by workers, Vallès did not rush to the opposite extreme and become a scornful mandarin.

Despite his multiple negations—freedom is basically the power to gainsay—he was never *un casseur*. He wanted better conditions and relationships, improvements, not a *tabula rasa*. In his preference for 'social' questions, he was closer than most French intellectuals (strange how badly this hat fits on his leonine head) to down-to-earth matters: the price of bread or coal or accommodation. If, like Gallo, [28] we term Vallès's political vision elementary, because it was not sophisticated, nor, at times, even realistic, we neglect the fact that it is elemental things that matter primarily. And is tolerance a non-platform? He was not anti-utilitarian. The growing machine-age held out the promise of help to humanity. He was not even automatically bourgeoisophobic. The middle-classes must be won over to the cause they shared with *le peuple*, not alienated beyond the pale.

He came to equate all forms of injustice, and to believe that, if you protest against one, you protest against them all: in the family, at school, in the work-place, or in the nation at large. He always mistrusted party-apparatus and party-lines. He detested pundits and system-builders, who to him were but variations on the hated pedagogue. In general, he was as afraid of state violence becoming institutionalised, programmed, as he was of revolutionary passion yielding to authoritarianism.

Chapter Three

Society and Press

Society

In a society increasingly caught up in centripetal forces, Vallès refused to think of diversity, cussed difference, as a shortcoming, an impediment to progress, or an evil. Whereas the Second Empire is stereotypically marked by *faste* — parade, surface glitter, conspicuous consumption (and not the galloping kind afflicting garret dwellers) — Vallès gives us the below-stairs view of society and its daily history. It was an age of industrial and economic expansion, of vivacious living for a privileged minority, and it underwent a large rural exodus to the cities. Much of this Vallès barely refers to in his journalism or fiction. Paris was becoming a major industrial city, even if most industry was still confined to small-scale *artisanat*. It had seen the spectacular phenomenon of big department stores (which Zola was to chronicle in *Au Bonheur des Dames*). New systems of communication, such as the telegraph, came into operation. Though he was intimately familiar with another modernism, the rapid growth of the popular press, he omits much else. It is as if, even while gradually becoming *un parisien parisiennant,* his eyes still focussed in Paris on the vestiges of other ways of life, the provinces-in-the-city, which, to be sure, did not altogether disappear until this century. At times, rather desperately, he tries to argue that decadent, chaotic periods can generate great changes. He emitted such 'paradoxes' under the 'moral order' of the Second Empire, which enjoyed its own brands of frivolity (the *opéra-bouffe*, for one), but prided itself principally on its 'virtue'. If he praised corruption, it was as the lesser of two evils. He was much more averse to purism (whether bourgeois or Jacobin).

His social panorama, then, is very partial, but focussed with vehemence. Though a keen observer, his metaphorical mode of expression, and his proneness to discuss in terms of myths, make it inevitable that he operates figuratively more often than factually. Certain dominants surface. He sees society largely as a set of interconnecting prisons (school, barracks, political regimes), and, more widely, the constricting mind-sets created by fashions, fear or laziness. The danger of such over-arching images, such generalisations, is that of self-cancelling, for a universal prison would be normalcy. He can sound at times very neurotic. Of an outwardly weak library assistant he says:

'Il a eu des échappées de colère ou d'ironie dans les coins. Les coins ont des oreilles'. Every profession, for Vallès, breeds informers and betrayals. Or a city man watched by small-town eyes: 'Se sentir *sans défense*, dans l'impossibilité de remuer et d'agir, enfermé dans un cercle de défiance, de cruauté, d'ignorance... qui n'a qu'à se rétrécir pour vous déshonorer ou vous tuer' (*CP*, pp. 231; 429). In reality, Vallès was surveilled by family watchdogs, by police-spies in Paris, and again in London and Brussels, by doctors and nurses during his stay in the asylum, by guards in prison, and by official censors in his journalism. He had good reasons to feel spied upon.

Vallès spent one month in Mazas prison in 1853 for plotting to kill Louis-Napoleon: a mild sanction, but, like his father's decision to incarcerate him earlier, a way of invalidating his choices. In 1868, he was given two different stretches of one and two months in Sainte-Pélagie: firstly for insulting the police, and secondly for 'incitation à la haine et au mépris du Gouvernement'. Admittedly, jails for this kind of prisoner, in 1868, were not horrible. Prisoners enjoyed congenial company, adequately furnished cells, and tastier food could be bought in. Vallès even edited a prison news-sheet in Sainte-Pélagie. In several ways, Vallès could be said to enjoy prisons more than carceral schools, where he felt the force of punishment and deprivation of freedom more acutely. Naturally, age made a difference; and he was in jail for positive, willed acts, whereas he had been locked up in school through no fault or choice of his own. The fact remains that imprisonment scars you: 'La pensée a horreur du vide. On subit la nécessité de l'échange dans le monde des idées comme dans le monde des faits' (II, 1127). Unlike Camus's Meursault, Vallès would never have contemplated with a calm mind living alone in a tree trunk. His recognition of the terrible effect of sensory deprivation and enforced solitude shows him striving to think more widely than his own experience, to that of longer-term and less 'privileged' prisoners.

He knew, too, that not all prisoners are in jail. He was obsessed by the great number of convicts (*galériens, forçats*) in French society: all those people trapped by poverty, by the censorious regime, by the past encrusted on the present, and even those leaders snared by their own earlier or current reputations or achievements. The gamut runs from hypochondriacs to the governmental press. Vallès is hardly indulgent in his survey of human weakness, or victimisation-proneness, but he puts most of us, including himself, in the same boat: 'Nous traînons tous une chaîne que nous avons forgée de nos mains ou qu'a accrochée le hasard' (I, 808). He knows what he talks of; for many years he remained himself in thrall to his own image (his own pose, said his enemies) as a fireball.

Pleasure, too, is a tyrant. Vallès takes care to distinguish between different kinds of collective amusement and horseplay, for anything smacking of the regimented—one of the reasons for his aversion from onions was that they call forth mechanical tears—chilled him. As for actual criminal behaviour, he was, already in childhood, sympathetic to jailbirds, in his native town. Late in life, he would propose that district juries should decide, on the basis of their knowledge of the accused, whether there was any valid case to answer. His innate urge to decentralise functioned here as elsewhere (See *TP*, p. 324). On the question of responsibility, Vallès did not share the later nineteenth-century view, promulgated mainly by Lombroso and his cheerleaders, of individuals predestined to criminality. Environmentalist, Vallès places a heavy stress on upbringing and socio-economic conditions; melodramatist, he fancied the fatalistic idea of people doomed to commit crime by inner determinisms; voluntarist, he knew how much each of us chooses and wills what we do. No more could he be a party to the post-1870 topos of the moral and physical degeneracy of the French people. His view was essentially liberal. Poulot conceded that there was no higher proportion of criminals in the workforce than anywhere else, but those there were he saw in pathological terms (as did most of their work-mates) as 'born' criminals. [1]

All such problems really came home to roost with the issue of the death penalty. Vallès's accounts of witnessing two executions reveal his honesty. He recognises how expecting a heavily programmed event can suck you into obscenity, so that a last-minute reprieve would anger the watchers and waiters. As with his descent down a mine, he draws no overt lesson, and lets facts be their own spokesperson (I, pp. 933 ff.). In another *reportage,* he keeps up a running sardonic play on the phraseology of legal murder. The executioner wears a scarf ('il avait bien soin de sa tête'), watches his smoke rings expire, and thinks of his country property 'large comme un cimetière de village'. The bystanders wonder how to 'tuer la nuit [...], assassiner le temps'. This is truly pointed gallows humour, and it has for its punchline: 'Le cocher, pour troquer les sous du picotin contre un beau verre de vin rouge, fera peut-être déjeuner la bête avec le son du panier' (II, pp. 1351 ff.). The black humour does not detract from but underlines the seriousness of the account, which bears comparison with Orwell's 'A Hanging'. A further text brings home the element of lethal statistical gaming involved in capital punishment: 'Mieux vaudrait ne couper que trois têtes sur dix et ne se tromper qu'une fois sur mille!' (I, 1019). Even in war situations like the Commune, Vallès did his level best to abort summary executions by fellow Communards.

There are other ways of being alienated, temporarily or permanently, from normal society: the label or millstone of madness, for one. Already in his writings on showpeople, Vallès was nervous about the possible contagiousness of madness. It takes the form of a literalisation of the parental warning: 'If you pull that face, it'll stay like that!'. It concerns a *grimacier* who has lost control of his knack: 'Cet homme avait commencé par faire des grimaces pour rire, il les faisait maintenent pour tout de bon et malgré lui; sa tête jouait toute seule. Il n'était plus maître de son visage, qui était devenu fou en singeant la folie' (p. 723). If I keep stressing Vallès's sanity, I must also record his natural or induced fears of madness. They break in, sometimes as asides, as when he mentions the harmless eccentric 'L'Homme orange': 'Le voisinage des fous laisse fous ceux qui le sont et peut rendre fous ceux qui ne le sont pas' (p. 660).

Under the *Code civil,* a French father's rights included that of having his offspring arrested and held in a state prison; the formalities were fairly minimal. The law of 1838 merely extended and made explicit this basic provision. Vallès's father had his son committed to the Saint-Jacques asylum in Nantes from 31 December 1851 to 2 March 1852. The family doctor certified that Jules was so exalted that violence was to be expected, either against others or self. Two asylum doctors diagnosed 'aliénation mentale' characterised by a belief in imaginary torments, suicidal tendencies and 'une faiblesse d'intelligence avec lésion organique du cerveau'. [2] The whole sick and sorry business was a concerted cop-out by a father terrified that his son's recent militancy would in some way threaten his own admittedly hard-won position in the educational hierarchy. It was clearly a way of embodying Jules' non-responsibility for his actions, and thereby invalidating his choices. Charitable interpretations, such as the father's putative wish to protect his aberrant son from even worse legal sanctions, or his fear that madness ran in the family (the other surviving child died insane at the age of sixteen) barely hold water. The doctors ended by decreeing, in effect, that Vallès had recovered as miraculously as he had originally succumbed. There is something obscene about medical practitioners prostituting their talents to the dirty work of family discipline. Getting Jules locked up alienated him in several senses; it robbed him of his freedom and rights, and sought to derealise him.

Being shut away for his subversive potentialities is an early example of the politically repressive exploitation of such imprisonment. Certainly, the equation dissident militancy = psychic disarray is common to many regimes, totalitarian or liberal. Vallès himself believed the opposite: that political commitment preserves from madness. He felt sadly that André Gill's and Vermersch's madness resulted from a lack of thoroughgoing involvement—dissident minds spinning unproductively in a void. The supreme irony was that it was at least in part his son's championing of the rights of children that alarmed his father enough to have his son banged up. In the 1880s, Vallès visited Sainte-Anne asylum, and felt both pity and horror at the fate of its wretched, suffering inmates, on the production line of this factory of madness (as he called it in *La Dompteuse*—see *TP,* pp. 58-75). He loathed the awful euphemism, 'les innocents' (I, 326).

Vallès's love of eccentrics ensures that a *fou littéraire* like Paulin Gagne appealed to him. A believer in a universal language, the author of an epic *L'Unitéide* in sixty acts, the founder of 'satanic' newspapers and a 'supernatural' candidate in the 1863 elections, Gagne elicited this testimonial from Vallès: 'Nous ne croyons pas qu'on ait bien compris jusqu'ici le célèbre et supercoquentieux auteur de *l'Unitéide*. Nous pensons qu'il y a en lui plus que l'âme affolée d'un toqué vulgaire, et que M. Gagne pourrait bien être quelque chose comme le Juvénal de Bicêtre. [...] Allons, il n'est peut-être pas si fou qu'il en a l'air' (*La Parodie*, 12 décembre 1869). For all his preference for the quick over the dead, Vallès could never have risen to the giddy heights of Gagne's 'philanthropophagie', by which he offered his corpse to his fellow-beings: 'J'aime mieux devenir l'aliment sacré de mes semblables, qui me vénéreront, que d'être la stupide, l'ignoble pâture des vers'.[3] It must be good to have such a sense of your own intrinsic, and nutritional, value. Vallès also met comparable loonies, denizens of libraries:

> Les vieux se divisent en deux classes. Il y a les chercheurs de systèmes et les faiseurs de Franciades. Ce sont les heureux, ceux-là. Ils ont leur manie et leur dada, folie douce et presque sainte, qui donne à leurs crânes fêlés un bout d'auréole et leur met un éclair dans les yeux. Ils vivent de rien, en cherchant leur étoile à l'horizon. J'ai fait connaissance, à la travée près du bureau, d'un fondateur de religion et d'un découvreur de mouvement perpétuel (*CP,* p. 234).

Vallès was ever able to respond generously to the sheer variousness of other people.

Hostile to labels, Vallès would no doubt have shrugged off that of antisemite that some feel tempted to pin on him. Much antiSemitism is traditional, the product of centuries-old loathing of usurers. Much was fomented by the Catholic Church. Any traces of it in Vallès were unoriginal. In the 1850s and 1860s, several of his very long-suffering and hounding suppliers of clothes, etc., were Jewish. During his exile in London, Petticoat Lane afforded him several references to Jewish clothes-dealers. He adds, distinguishing them from their more prosaic Gentile counterparts: 'Le juif a du sang de maudit dans les veines', which leaves open whether this endears or estranges them from him (*RL*, II, pp. 1280-2). One of his first love affairs on arriving in Paris was with a Jewess (see II, 1703). A good part of Vallès's humour, as we will see later, is 'Jewish': stoical, self-wounding, hyperbolic. The mother/son routine in *L'Enfant* is a kind of 'Jewish' vaudeville double-act. No doubt, like many another, Vallès read Toussenel: *Les Juifs, rois de l'époque, histoire de la féodalité financière* (1847—see *Corr. A.,* p. 26). We have already discussed his Letter to the Jewish financier, Mirès. Many people want to practise *l'amalgame*. Drumont's libertarian leanings, rather than his more notorious antiSemite harpings, might explain why the right-wing Thierry Maulnier in 1937 founded a weekly, *L'Insurgé*, claiming allegiance both to Drumont and Vallès. [4] What these disparate elements add up to, I cannot decide, but I think the label will not stick well.

No doubt, as a man of the left, Vallès was largely antimilitarist. Yet, as a child, like the young Céline and myriad others, he was dazzled by the parade past of a regiment of mounted *chasseurs*, and, like many a lad hardened by street-battles, he thought he wanted to be a soldier. When older, he felt more forgiving to the Jacobin national armies than to the later state version (see I, pp. 672; 1511). He accepted, probably with no choice in the matter, his parents' recourse to the practice of 'buying a man', that is a substitute for military service. Weber points out that, in the relevant period, about a quarter of all conscripts were such stand-ins, and so it was a common occurrence, rarely frowned upon. It made, besides, economic sense for farmers' sons not to serve, for such departures would have deprived the fathers of cheap labour. [5] What was the motivation for Vallès's landless parents? Perhaps it was the vestigial peasant in them. It is hard to imagine Vallès in the army. He would have been, willy-nilly, the awkward member of the squad or, more provocatively, the barrack-room lawyer. The fact remains that a great deal of his vocabulary is, very tritely, military: flags, cannons, blood, smoke, rifles, wounds. When it came to real war, in his first *Cri du peuple* during the Commune, Vallès put his faith, in the event of invasion, in last-ditch fighting by common citizens: *francs-tireurs*, snipers. A possible premonition of twentieth-century urban guerrilla combats, and a sign that Vallès thought most commonly in terms of *defensive* fighting. As so often, Bellet sums up with empathy Vallès's complex feelings on military matters:

> La continuité est intime et parfait entre la tirelire enfantine [where the family saved up the money for the substitute], l'achat d'un homme, le marchand d'hommes, le cochon vendu, le défilé d'un régiment dans les rues de Saint-Étienne, la lecture d'Erckmann-Chatrian. [...] C'est une continuité affective: pas de hiatus; le vêtement est ravaudé ici et là, mais il tient, il colle encore à la peau. (*JVJR*, p. 287)

And, more poetically and more incisively:

> Il appelle au clairon contre le clairon: à un clairon nouveau et abstrait, individuel, individualiste, désacralisé, ni politique ni lugubre, un peu clairon sans régiment: clairon introuvable. (*ibid.*, p. 288)

Not a Platonic trumpet, exactly, but one that has not yet sounded on this earth.

Press

The reference above to 'cochon vendu' is to the idiomatic term for military replacements. In one of his most percussive articles, with this title Vallès widens out the specialised use to embrace all traffickers, whether in others' lives or one's own, other sellers-out: politicians, teachers, journalists, 'Cochon vendu, quiconque vit de flatteries au pouvoir ou de complaisance à l'opposition' (I, 1014 ff.). The venality of large areas of the French press in the nineteenth century was obvious. While it is impertinent double duty to re-cover the question of Vallès the journalist already treated comprehensively by Bellet, it is such an important part of the total Vallès that I must do precisely that, *in parvo*.

The more excusable fraction of that generalised venality resulted from the politico-financial facts of life for the press at that time. Any paper in the 1860s aiming at an identifiable political content had to pay considerable caution money. It was a very effective form of official censorship, or gelding. Vallès quoted frequently the famous conclusion of Lamennais's article of July 1848, when his paper *Le Peuple constituant* was seized: 'Il faut aujourd'hui de l'or, beaucoup d'or, pour jouer du droit de parler: nous ne sommes pas assez riches. Silence au pauvre!' This last issue was bordered in black. Vallès used the same lay-out to frame the same formula in his short-lived *Le Peuple* of 1869 (I, 1176).

On another level, it was common practice in that period for writers to think of journalism as a stopgap source of income and publicity, to be abandoned for the ostensibly higher good of writing novels, poetry or plays, as soon as practicable. This continued the tradition chronicled in Balzac's *Illusions perdues*, and was decried lugubriously by the Goncourts as 'l'écrasement de l'homme de lettres par le journalisme de lettres'. [6] Even if he often complained bitterly of the many servitudes and few grandeurs of journalism, Vallès did not at heart share this snobbish opportunism. All of his work (essays and fiction) appeared first, with the exception of the mongrel-origined *L'Argent*, in newspapers.

In his early 'Chroniques' (*Le Présent*, 1857), Vallès relies very much on ready-made social types of the more 'literary' variety, though even there the odd sighting, for instance of a country girl who excites his sensuality, seems fresh. The fact remains that he is largely aping a part. *L'Argent* confirms this facility for impersonation and pastiche. Much of the early prose is clichéd and arse-licking in intention (if he could have got his tongue near enough to the targets): Vallès crooning with the wolves. Even when he became more assured and more recognisably individual in the early to middle 1860s, there remains something both energetic and iffish about his journalistic spread, as Bellet recognises:

'On ne peut qu'être frappé de cette pluralité et, souvent, de cette simultanéité des collaborations vallésiennes: comme si, à elle seule, elle assurait plus de liberté à un Vallès contradictoire, à ses propres simultanéités intérieures' (*JVJR,* p. 85). Before he became a frankly militant journalist, Vallès had periodically to slough off the skin of licensed entertainer, the joker in the pack, to which others, even admirers, sought to confine him, in order to utter unwelcome truths.

He needed to distinguish himself from 'les boulevardiers', of whom he said in retrospect: 'Ce n'est pas qu'ils manquaient de courage!' C'est bien pis; ils manquaient d'idées et de conviction' (II, 400). Rather as the polemical and therefore endangered *Encyclopédie* of Diderot and D'Alembert cultivated irony, allusiveness and other roundabout tactics, so the repressive Second Empire regime begat in journalists verbal quick-wittedness, though speeded up in tune with the age of industrialisation. Of course, this acceleration and pressure produced in turn its own casualties (Cf. Vallès's term, 'les forçats du bon mot'). A prime example was Henri de Rochefort, whom Vallès warned: 'Votre talent peut s'user à aiguiser toujours les épigrammes, comme la meule du rémouleur s'use à appointer des aiguilles' (I, 1052). As his biographer, R.L. Williams puts it, by 1868 'Rochefort blossomed into the most notorious of the imperial enemies—not the most dangerous of them certainly, but the noisiest'.[7] A decibel *esprit.* Reading Rochefort, you feel that he would say anything to make a joke, where Vallès's humour arises from what he is discussing; it is not imported and superimposed. He sees the joke *in* the material, the fishy disparity that needs to be highlighted and mocked. In some ways, Rochefort embodies what Vallès might have become—a swashbuckler, who fought twenty duels. Despite his often immense popularity, he lacked roots or any real contact with the masses; there was, for Bellet, something essentially solitary about his adventurism. A *vaudevilliste* for a good many years, he developed a brittle, dry, *boulevardier* wit. 'Il brandit un stylet: on peut à peine parler d'un style de Rochefort'.[8] His later career justifies Vallès's doubts. Rochefort was morally and politically adrift during the siege of Paris and the Commune; he followed General Boulanger; he was anti-Dreyfus. He died extremely alone.

Vallès called this kind of journalist 'allusionnistes', and claimed he was unfitted for such devious strategies: 'Je me trouve inhabile à ce métier; je ne sais pas glisser les serpents sous les fleurs' (*L'Époque,* 27 juillet 1865). It is true that Vallès favours more direct methods of address, and the conjunction of a barker and an allusionist is unlikely. But he clearly had to watch his tongue constantly, or he would have spent even more time in prison, or, just as bad, seen even more newspaper doors closed to him. In an epoch discovering the powers of advertising (Cf. *L'Argent*), Vallès did indeed frequently *bark* his own offerings. It was only after he finally made a name for himself that he could write on rejoining *Le Figaro* in 1868: 'J'y rentre, sans tracer de programme ni faire une profession de foi. On me connaît: je suis un irrégulier' (I, 1044). Though in colloquial French the very phrase *faire l'article* means to puff, as if selling an image were central to journalism, there was little room in Vallès's articles for that buried publicity, that hidden persuasion, that graphic *claque*, which was so prevalent in the nineteenth-century French press. He had less fishy things to fry.

Contrasting his own trade with the profession of Taine as a *lycée* professor, reciting lessons learned off by heart, Vallès uses ironic self-belittlement (i.e. self-boosting): 'Je ne suis qu'un journaliste qui dit sa pensée au lieu de débiter la pensée des autres' (I, 442). Consistently he upheld the freedom of the press, in which, with some naivety, he foresaw no danger: 'Je suis convaincu que si l'on rendait à notre pays le droit de parler et d'écrire, d'avoir comme il voudrait des journaux, de planter où il lui plairait des chaires et des tribunes, il ne profiterait point de ces libertés pour dépaver les rues' (*L'Époque*, 28 septembre 1865—shortly after his first visit to England). He saw far more danger in the *officieux* (semi-official) dependence of the bulk of the press. The word 'hand-outs', which is common currency today, combines ready copy provided by the agencies of power, and financial inducements.

Bellet notes the curious coinciding of 'le libéralisme pragmatiste et financier de Girardin et le libertarisme individualiste de Vallès' on the subject of total freedom of the press (I, 1386-7).[9] In an article on this issue, Vallès contrasts Girardin with another magnate, Prévost-Paradol, who favoured the establishment of a jury to regulate such freedom: that is, post-hoc censorship to replace the anticipatory muzzling practised by the government. Possibly because of his traumatic memories of the *baccalauréat* tribunal, Vallès was hostile to such arbitrarily selected panels. In the world of journalism, as in that of family upbringing, he was convinced that repressive authority breeds only revolt, whereas openness of dealing disarms the potential rebel. He trusted in free speech to be self-regulating. With limitless optimism, he held that the unlimited freedom of the press would mean the death of slander (pp. 428-35). In the Commune, when it mattered most urgently, Vallès re-declared—in *Le Cri du peuple*—his position: 'J'ai écrit bien longtemps, et je répète aujourd'hui, que je suis pour la liberté de presse absolue et illimitée. Je regrette donc profondément qu'on ait empêché *Le Gaulois* et *Le Figaro* de paraître, eussent-ils dû encore rire de nos canons et nous appeler des pillards! La liberté sans rivages' (II, 454).

Such freedom entails a readiness to operate *ad hominem*—which is, after all, one way of respecting your opponent, granting him independence, and not reducing him to a pawn. Though on the right occasion Vallès is perfectly capable of seeing the institution behind the man (e.g. the *Université* looming behind and perverting his father), it is generally true to say, with Bellet: 'Vallès a besoin de personnaliser ce qu'il attaque'(I, p. xxiv). He needs to focus and make concrete his aversions. Even here, his own zest often prevents mere biliousness, as in this description, during the Commune, of Thiers: 'Vautour à tête de perroquet, taupe à lunettes, polichinelle tricolore!' (II, 9). Clichés + twists: a household vulture, a bespectacled mole, and a patriotic Punch. He was fully aware of the possibly comfortable nature of critical writing: 'Beaucoup de gens affichent des opinions boudeuses comme on élève des lapins, pour s'en faire des rentes' (*L'Époque*, 29 juin 1865).

The dominant cliché attached to the nineteenth-century press was that it was a whore (Cf. 'Don't tell my mother I'm a journalist. She thinks I play the piano in a brothel'). Vallès was one of the few writers of his time not to fall into this knee-jerk response. He called himself, with pride, a journalist to the end of his days. The Press was in fact much closer to his ideal of 'la vie d'échange' than literature could ever be. You are far more likely to see and hear a citizen discussing your paper than your novel. When he criticises the press, he does so as an insider, and most of his complaints would have been satisfied by greater press freedom. Of course, in his defence of journalism, Vallès had also an eye to self-justification. It took him so long to become a novelist that he needed to justify his journalistic production, to make it honourable. Naturally, he had his doubts, especially about the ephemerality of newspapers. [10] Anyone as concerned as he was with responding to and capturing the present accepted this risk.

As Bellet sees very astutely, print culture, attacked by Vallès in his 'Victimes du livre', needed to be desacralised, exorcised. 'La continuité et l'unité, le pouvoir d'identification et d'hypnotisme du Livre, devaient céder la place au discontinu de la production et de la lecture du journal' (*JVJR*, p. 328). Vallès wanted to give the printed newspaper page something of the mobility of daily life. It was 'une esthétique de la rupture et de la "barbarie" dont le cirque offrait précisément dans la ville moderne un modèle irremplaçable et, hélas! condamné: contrastes de couleurs, sonorités criardes' (*ibid.*). None of this implies an unkempt prose, for any reader of Vallès's journalism soon registers how correct his French is by formal standards. There is much exaggeration and repetition, but these are permanent and central features of his general rhetoric. Just as the notion of a warrior's rest is built into his political outlook, so in his journalism there is a constant shuttle, between current polemics and backward-turned evocations of the provinces. In Bellet's words: 'Des "paresses"; de la chronique épanchée, il bondit à l'attaque des mœurs, de la culture et des institutions' (*ibid.*, p. 162). Whatever the subject matter, the approach is substantially the same. Journalistic prose should be sharply focussed. Above all, the layout matters intensely. There must be plentiful gaps, markers: an 'aerated' text. This is partly the result of the fear of boredom induced by over-dense pages (picture the eye-boggling monolithism of most nineteenth-century sheets). More physically, Vallès needed oxygen to combat asphyxiation. He wanted the readers' eyes to keep on the move, skip about, not plod dolefully through a morass of characters. [11] It was of course easier for Vallès to push this line as an editor than as a paid hack.

The word *journal* does double duty: a public newspaper and a private diary. Vallès always oscillated between these two possibilities, and at times combined them. The press is itself an intermediate zone, somewhere between literature and speech, and thus cut out for the overlapping Vallès. He assumed he was substantially the same man, indeed the same writer, in both domains. His professional advice to the less experienced journalist Émile Gautier included these points:

> C'est vous qui devez faire votre monde, ou plutôt c'est votre pensée qui créera le moule de la rédaction. Donc, avant d'écrire un article quelconque, cherchez *l'idée-mère,* précisez-vous à vous-même le *coup principal* que vous voulez porter, la résultante que vous tenez à obtenir et à faire jaillir sous les yeux de la foule.

Sound, practical advice. Because Vallès sees journalism as a weapon, he tends to favour hard images to describe it: 'Il serait dommage que *l'éparpillage* et le *clinquant* couvrissent vos feuillets, quand vous pouvez y graver des médailles'. The goal is 'l'allure ferme, sobre, *sans bavures.* [...] Chaque paragraphe doit contenir sa balle propre'. [12] Not wholly unkindly, Bellet wonders whether Vallès himself always practised in journalism what he here preaches: 'Ne serait-ce pas plutôt le romancier de *L'Enfant* qui les appliqua ou, mieux, les expérimenta?' (*JVJR,* p. 435).

Any reader of both areas of Vallès's writing notices that his journalistic style carries over into the fiction, and helps to energise, individualise and modernise it: the often telegraphic structures, the jolting headlines and subtitles, the typographically isolated and thus foregrounded segments of language, the punchy, short sentences, the bloating of often minor details, and, in general, the urge to find drama in the supposedly humdrum (Cf. the idiom 'faire tableau'). In much present-day journalism, the emphasis on 'house style' and 'rewriting' militates against overt militancy, or even individualism. Of course, a journalistic training can also lead to meretricious devices: short cuts, cheapness of effects, unsubstantiated innuendoes, as well as advantages like sharp focus, tension and immediacy. Vallès accepted the rough with the smooth.

Chapter Four

Education and the Mind

Schools

For Vallès, as we saw in the quotation about Taine, even partly gagged hacks are freer than teachers. The press not only deserves freedom; it can help to promote it. Vallès clearly sees an educational role for the press; it can mould opinion, teach the art of criticism. It is educational, but anti-school.

In his determined and repeated attacks on the phenomenon of pedagogy, Vallès was singing an old refrain. Montaigne (a less controversial opinionator): 'Fâcheuse suffisance, qu'une suffisance pure livresque!' [1] Vallès is so consistently hostile to his schooling that he seems to forget what literacy has meant for countless millions. Yet he was closer, in this hostility, to the common people of his times, who often saw schools as superfluous and distracting from the real business of earning a living from an early age.

For Vallès, the shades of the prison-house were all around the growing boy. School meant prison, or barracks. Teachers were disciplinarians, *bourreaux;* and his schoolmaster father suffered as much from colleagues as his pupil son. So as to put his undoubted exaggerations into perspective, I start with the historical facts. French secondary schools in Vallès's day were dark, damp, ill-ventilated, and Spartan in equipment. [2] Many inspectors complained of classrooms like Siberia (not only the temperature, but also the atmosphere). The serious underfunding of education until late in the century led to economising on every level. In boarding establishments, junior teachers often virtually starved; the heads were known familiarly as 'marchands de soupe'. *L'Enfant* records, memorably, such *pensions*. Even after the drum-roll was replaced by the bell in 1815, the whole style of *lycées* and *collèges* was a mixture of the military and the monklike. The system of unannounced descents by inspectors, their often unjust secret reports and omnipresent political favouritism produced general insecurity for teachers. French state education was a variant commerce, with principals making a profit or, at times, going bankrupt. It was a venal profession which instilled timorousness, especially in the frequently poor-quality *maîtres d'étude* (or *pions*), the pariahs of *l'Université* (i.e. the total educational system) in their own and everyone else's eyes. Recruitment was often difficult, and so Vallès-Vingtras was not alone in his reluctance to join the profession; few sons followed in their fathers' footsteps. It was a highly hierarchised and compartmentalised system, riddled with tensions, jealousies, betrayals. Personal advancement, and not teamwork, was at the core of the ethos. In 1846, French teachers were the worst paid in Europe, and especially badly off were those, like Vallès's father, who lived at home and had a family to support. Many had to give private tuition to make ends meet ('courir le cachet'). Their lives were highly regulated. Vetoes were placed on journalism or political activities. All teachers had to swear fidelity to the state. They were easily sacked or forced to move. Yet teachers have always been more (they could hardly be less) valued in France than in England. Hence, perversely, the corsets strapped around them: they were a precious corporation to be held in check. When Sarcey decreed: 'Rien ne crétinise comme l'enseignement', he was speaking from the mentally fatigued teacher's standpoint.[3]

As for their charges, while there was little use of corporal punishment (a practice flogged to death in Britain), teachers and administrators made wide use of extra *devoirs,* impositions and detentions (which increased the sense of being a convict). The stress fell on academic competition between pupils, (carrots and sticks for good and bad donkeys), who had a seventeen-hour day, with two hours' recreation. The only excursions into the fresh air were crocodile-walks *en masse,* one afternoon a week. As for teaching-methods, the *professeur* perpetuated the ancient tradition of lecturing, dictating (in every sense) from *la chaire* (which in French is applied indiscriminately to pulpit, lectern or desk). It was truly *ex cathedra:* one-way traffic, no dialogue; the pupils as passive receivers and largely mechanical reproducers. Like university lecturers today, school-teachers were not trained; they usually reapplied what and how they had been taught. The proportion of hours for French and for classics under the July Monarchy was 1:16. In the *philosophie* class of 1830-48, the abstract, moralising eclecticism of Victor Cousin was the official *doxa*. Only about 3% of secondary pupils gained the *baccalauréat* in Vallès's time at school, and so his long-winded attempts to pass do not indicate unusual thickness or lack of application. The *bachot* was held to be so desirable that a whole industry of crammers grew up, which encouraged much fraud and febrile swotting. Then as now, the favoured image for educational success was: 'it is a lottery'.

This meritocratic pedagogy was 'too generalising', said a child psychologist, 'too vague, too literary, too moralising, too verbalistic, too preaching [...]. It solves the gravest problems by literary quotations from Quintilian and Bossuet; it replaces facts by exhortations and sermons; the word which characterises it best is *verbiage'*.[4] The centre of the system was *le discours*. It was based on the model of writers from Antiquity, in which noble-sounding and predeterminedly fitting words were placed by pupils in the mouths of famous men. It was, in effect, inbred ventriloquism. Psittacosis is a communicable disease. The kind of sententious prose most rewarded by teachers of rhetoric was abstract, or conventionally metaphorical, and strewn with maxims. French public oratory, today, still bows to this tradition. Teenage French schoolboys in Vallès's era were taught formal rhetoric before they had had enough direct experience to wax rhetorical about. Back-to-front: words came first, thoughts and feelings tagged along, except for the blatant inculcation of civic duties and virtues. No real love of Antiquity was fostered, no real curiosity about other cultures (and official France jibbed at borrowing foreign educational practices as much as at importing loan-words). Everything was annexed to xenophobic purposes; hence the pedantic veto on *barbarismes* and *solécismes*. This distaste for the foreign and the new betrays a distrust of life itself. Invention or imagination were scowled upon. What was demanded was amplification (window-dressing); the padding out of pre-ingurgitated material disgorged orally or on paper. Teachers did not realise, to coin an idiom, that 'péroraison n'est pas raison'. All of this rhetorical and stylistic indoctrination had precious little to do with the encouragement of critical intelligence or initiative, and everything to do with set-pieces (French military strategy was similar), and with the production of stereotyped members of the liberal professions and state servants schooled to operate by the letter of the law. Anyone with any spirit kicked hard against such straitjacketing, though the tradition of the *chahut* could be neutralised, with only brief bother, within the overall blanket system.

At Nantes, Vallès publicly and vociferously proclaimed the urgency of abolishing the *baccalauréat,* and indeed all examinations and diplomas, as they worked divisively against egalitarianism. These were, at the age of sixteen, his first political strides, his first and lasting commitment to the cause of the manipulated and the robbed. The counter-insurgency measures of June 1848 started and finished before he could get to Paris. His father intended him to prepare for the *baccalauréat* and the *École Normale* in Paris in order to qualify as a *lycée* teacher. High hopes for his career were at several points entertained by his parents, his teachers, and some of his fellow pupils. He was *un espoir*, un *fort en thème*. He disappointed all of them, and was very much at odds with his co-students at the Lycée Bonaparte, whom he found stuffy, unrebellious, old before their time: *bêtes à concours* ('ces concours de pacotille. [...] Une composition où se fâchait en latin héroïque ou en français médiocre quelque Thémistocle de convention' (I, 871)). He eventually got his *bachot* in 1852, after three unsuccessful tries (largely because of weak maths and eccentric views on philosophy, where it was essential to toe the official line). It seems likely that a friend's father, an academic, leant on the scales the fourth time.

Given his total disrespect for the system, Vallès would be untroubled by such finagling. He writes with much conniving sympathy of 'les passeurs', proxy examinees (II, pp. 578 ff.). He could hardly be sniffy about private-enterprise fraud when he viewed the education system itself as a colossal mystification. (On different premises, the Japanese today indulge in comparable practices). Vallès spent much of his energy extricating himself from compromise. In the winter of 1862-1863, against all his oaths and principles, but desperate for money, Vallès became a *pion* at the *lycée* of Caen. He was doubly guilty. He was consorting with the loathed educational establishment, and as a teacher, albeit a junior one, he was a state *fonctionnaire*, and thus colluding also with the regime. A *pion* is also a pawn in chess, the lowest-ranking piece on the board, easily removed. In function, the *pion* was an in-between: a warder/spy, the butt of those under surveillance (the pupils) and of the senior staff. *L'Insurgé* relates with great comic verve how he got himself sacked.

As regards his specific grievances against education as he knew it, Vallès was, surely, at least arithmetically right to complain of the predominance of Latin and Greek at a time when French itself was insecurely implanted over much of the territory. 'French was a foreign language for half the citizens'. [5] The system was fixated on the erection and worshipping of classical role models, linguistic or biographical. Apart from any intrinsic pedagogical value they thought classical study had in forming the mind, opinion-shapers clearly believed in it as a mark of distinction, a barge-pole separating the elect from the great unwashed. French culture provided additional classical gods. Napoleon, expectedly, lauded the reverent teaching of Corneille and Bossuet: 'Ceux-là ne font pas de révolutions; ils n'en inspirent pas. Ils entrent, à pleines voiles d'obéissance, dans l'ordre établi de leur temps; ils le fortifient, ils le décorent'. [6] A lovely, telling, image: full sail ahead into submission. Pupils were compelled to become expert in mosaic, patching, working to a pattern, using cribs. Back in the seventeenth century, Charles Sorel in his *Francion* describes the *capilotade* (a potpourri or ragout) of selected passages from canonised authors, which dissuaded the boys from developing their own thoughts and expression. [7] Force-feeding is well-known to French geese. In his school (as later in his journalism or his dealings with publishers), Vallès would never get away from *la copie* (original text/imitation). *La copie* is what you have to submit. Yet, in protesting stereotyped exemplarity in a spirit of serious play, in addressing the dangers inherent in not having a style or voice or indeed mind to call your own, Vallès ended up inventing a self and a style that are unmistakable and inimitable. Partly this was because pastiche can be knowing as well as unconscious. 'A dix-sept ans je pouvais faire aussi *vieux* qu'un académicien' (*SEP*, p. 97). Vallès's resistance was partly cussedness, and partly a wilful denial of the obvious: at home then at school, all of us are drilled. We repeat our scripts for future performances. Until very recently in human history, education consisted very largely in the impressing of models on waxy young minds, rote-learning, sometimes decorated by borrowed plumes (cf. quotations in academic books). Realistically, we have to acquire conventional knowledge and standard discourse, both to survive and to give us lift-off. Vallès knew this, but rarely admitted it.

Whether half-education (so little attention paid to the real and contemporary world), or over-education (human beings transmogrified into performing animals), education as practised was, for Vallès, bad education. Bellet captures exquisitely the position for Vallès of the child trapped in all the dimensions of time: 'On y a écrasé le présent pur d'une jeunesse pour lui faire un passé au nom d'un avenir illusoire: un futur antérieur mutile le présent!' (*JVJR*, p. 301). Vallès felt both pity and anger for those who pull down 'sur les oreilles et sur les yeux le bonnet d'âne de l'éducation classique' (*Cri P.*, p. 326). Despite his hammering, he is never permanently monochrome. He celebrates, for example, more than one teacher he found more bolshy, more fun to be with, than their stodgy, conformist pupils (*SEP*, p. 61). Extending to some teachers the sorrow he feels sporadically for his schoolmaster father, he recognises that, like him, they are victims of the system. He is very alert to the various pecking orders in schools: the official hierarchy; that between stronger or richer pupils or teachers and poorer or weaker ones; and that between parents of different social classes. Preferring decentralisation in all things, Vallès must criticise the metropolitan hegemony over education. The monopolistic *Université* was an extension of the authoritarian state, and he loves knocking its eggheads together. Schools, in fact, are society in miniature: a similar kowtowing to superiors, a profound mistrust of children, which matches or apes the fear of the lower classes exhibited by their governors (and both pupils and workers seen as animals to be broken).

Vallès can never remain unrelievedly gloomy. As well as seeing a prison or a forcing-house, Vallès also saw the comic side of all that earnest effort: school was circus, as well. Travelling showpeople borrow from school in their use of trestles, and, as we saw with 'Le Bachelier géant', barkers often speak several languages, including the dead ones. Are pupils so different from seals and dogs, those *animaux savants* ? Prize-givings, above all, are platform rituals, like side-shows, involving rewards and inflated language (See *JVJR*, pp. 230-3). *L'Enfant* features a splendid knockabout routine at one such ceremony.

Although Vallès's version is strongly prejudiced by his own dispiriting experiences, he lent his lusty voice to the mounting chorus of mainly justified complaint throughout the nineteenth century about the many stultifying practices of French secondary education. For his own very different reasons (the intellect was to be distrusted, as it made the undeserving think), Barrès also attacked the excessively cerebral nature of French pedagogy, in *Les Déracinés*. Vallès would appreciate the nice irony of the widespread criticism, after the French defeat of 1870, about 'disincarnated teaching', useless for training soldiers; about the lack of geography teaching (armies find maps useful), of modern languages (how can monolinguals spy efficiently?), and of phys. ed. (retreats are taxing). Nearly a century after him, Céline's beefs ran along similar lines: French *lycéens* 'n'ont jamais eu d'émotions... Ils n'ont jamais épouvé que des émotions lycéennes, des émotions livresques... le rafistolage d'emprunts'. [8]

Until his death, Vallès himself did not relent. In 1884 he writes: 'La Révolution française n'eût pas été lycurguée par Robespierre et césarisée par Napoléon, si les cerveaux de ce temps-là n'avaient pas été hantés par les ombres glorieuses de Sparte et de Rome!' (II, 1342). But he also notes a welcome change. The days of Quinet and Michelet are over. The best lectures at the Collège de France in 1884 were given by an economist: 'Il touche aux questions qui brûlent' (p. 1345). *Le Cri du peuple* campaigned to improve teachers' pay and to grant them greater freedom from political interference. Much of past abuse hung on, all the same. He uses an image from *les fêtes foraines* to express his scorn of the play-safe republican anticlericals: 'L'Église qu'on imite et qu'on salue même quand il faut, après avoir ri d'elle, à l'instar du singe qui fait des grimaces au joueur d'orgue et l'agace et l'irrite, mais dans le poitrail duquel il va se blottir quand il a froid ou qu'il a peur' (p. 743). The eggheads are more truly ignorant than many manual workers. Set a real-life question to a group of each, and it is 'à la Sorbonne qu'il faudra mettre le bonnet d'âne' (*ibid.*). For Vallès, *les fruits secs* are not (as in Flaubert's *L'Éducation sentimentale*) the candidates, but rather scholastic honours: the ashy-tasting apples of the Dead Sea (see I, 852).

So much of what Vallès indicts is still rife in secondary, further or higher education today: *gavage* and regurgitation, government spokes in teachers' wheels, manuals on how to pass exams, plagiarism (encouraged or punished), answers that play up to examiners' computed idiosyncrasies, etc. [9] Vallès had strong pedagogic urges, for all his distaste for schools, but his aim was always to enlarge, to deliver, not to narrow or incarcerate. He hoped his criticism would help to be a prophylactic, a *cordon sanitaire* against a social disease; for him, the well of learning was poisoned, and needed a thorough clean-out.

Books and their Victims

Not only at school are we on the receiving end of brainwashing, but ever afterwards, at the hands (so to speak) of books. It starts pre-school:

'On me fait apprendre à lire dans un livre où il y a écrit, en grosses lettres, qu'il faut obéir à ses père et mère' (*Enf.*, p. 143). From the age of literacy, Vallès was in danger of becoming a 'victime du livre'. Filial duties were impressed on his brain alongside the weals on his skin. He could not thereafter logically ignore, in attacking social tyrannies, that of the printed word.

His essay, 'Les Victimes du livre' (in *Les Réfractaires*), is a theme with umpteen variations. As Bellet notes, it is unusually classificatory (*JVJR*, p. 174): a sign of dutifulness rather than thoroughness. There is, after all, an in-built inertia in the essay form: you set yourself up to go through your own chosen hoops. Like our contemporary polemics about pornography and violence on television or cinema screens, Vallès's piece exaggerates and melodramatises the issues, though some of the hyperbole is surely comic, as in the tall story of a whole family, after reading Walter Scott, packing their bags for Scotland (I, 238). He starts ringingly, plangently: 'Pas une de nos émotions n'est franche. Joies, douleurs, amours, vengeances, nos sanglots, nos rires, les passions, les crimes; tout est copié, tout!' (p. 230). We are seduced by the 'comic tyranny' of book-culture, whose effects on us can be lethal or risible. It is (blackly) comical because of the gaps and disproportions involved.

Vallès does not claim to know why books hold so much sway over our imaginations and behaviour, but he felt sure that they do, and that many readers do not register that they have taken over, or been taken over by, the writer's fiction. (He does not interest himself here in non-fictional, or less fictional, take-overs: political or religious tracts, how-to manuals, etc.). He is no analyst. To disclose the terrorism of the printed word will open eyes. In his eyes, we seek in reading to escape ourselves. He includes himself in this escapist urge, especially as regards the special world of Robinson Crusoe, perhaps because that mythical hero freed himself from dependency and achieved self-reliance. Certainly the Robinson temptation is made to sound charming, unthreatening, pleasurable. That legendary isle can even be inland. You can come home refreshed, 'tout crotté de votre naufrage' (I, 233). The whole essay, indeed, is a testimony, part skewed, to Vallès's own projection of self into fictional locales, his enthusiastically lived readings. Of course, if, as Vallès seems to suggest, all reading is escapist, then this is a definition more than a critique.

Apart from such benign effects as those offered by *robinsonnades*, Romantic literature holds out more dangerous temptations. You can no longer be sure 'qu'on en reviendra' (I, 239). The willing suspension of disbelief can set hard. Chateaubriand, Byron, Musset (who was, however, one of Vallès's all-time favourites), Murger, all mislead, abstract you from society, give you inflated ideas of your precious self (pp. 240-3). Balzac is a pivotal figure: 'Il résume la grandeur du livre et ses dangers' (p. 245). Balzac, who often hypnotised himself with the fictional spell he cast, invented figures like Rastignac, the conqueror arising from petty origins, and as such a great inspirer and an even greater misleading model. Whether the literature is 'high' or 'low'—and Vallès does not care to distinguish in this way—it gives us excessive and wrong expectations. It is not just words that take us in, win us over. As Bellet stresses, often Vallès responds as much to illustrations as to text: gestures, poses, tableaux (p. 1308, and see p. 238). The assault on our gullibility is thus multiple.

In the eighteenth century, Voltaire was already warning paradoxically that the flood of books was making us ignorant. Rousseau, much loathed by Vallès, harped on the denaturing, perverting effect of reading. Flaubert: 'Tant qu'on n'aura pas détruit le respect pour ce qui est imprimé, on n'aura rien fait!' [10] *Madame Bovary, L'Éducation sentimentale, La Tentation de saint Antoine* and *Bouvard et Pécuchet* are increasingly apocalyptic cautionary tales about the mistakes and the chaos caused by reading. Vallès understood, and empathised with, Emma Bovary's desperate shuttling between a book-inspired lust for metropolitan glamour and romance and a misty nostalgia for an already bookish provincial adolescence. Yet, for him, books should be an aid to living more authentically and not a form of proxy existence. He would have responded sympathetically to Clamence's despairing cry in *La Chute:* 'Ai-je lu cela ou l'ai-je pensé?' [11] Who does our thinking for us?

Ironically, Vallès's text against books provided a rare instance of the written word having a measurable social impact. 'Victimes du livre' was cited in a murder trial, and proved instrumental in saving the two accused from the scaffold, because their lawyer argued that they had been led astray by their reading. Vallès was under no illusions on the score of their actual guilt, for he sniffed out that they were opportunists. Given his hostility to the death penalty, he could hardly bear them a grudge (see I, pp. 618-21).

There are other tyrannies in democracies than that of the printed word—public opinion, for one, championed by Rousseau. What is wrong with Vallès's isolating of this particular one? Firstly, he leaves out of the indictment, as inconvenient evidence, the consolatory, therapeutic effect of books; their ability to release from, or at least ease, bondage; their near-unavoidability as learning materials for would-be writers; and of course, the whole area of books as sources of factual information, stretching and enriching minds. The hugest irony is that enormous numbers could not, and still cannot read; a vast proportion of the literate rarely read, beyond the obligatory stage at school; and yet we have this anti-literary literary topos. The privileged knock their privilege. Tallis argues that the average reader (that mythical creature whom all who would talk of must invent) is not such a sucker for novels as many critics imagine; it is the latter who are hexed:

> Reading books is one thing [the common reader] does among many. [...]
> Since she is not paid for exaggerating the value or impact (pernicious or
> otherwise), of books in her life, she will recognise that a book—fiction or
> non-fiction, realistic or anti-realistic—is a book and not some irresistible
> force operating upon her. [...] It is grand theorists, not common readers,
> who are *terribles simplificateurs.* [12]

Vallès is definitely not 'a grand theorist', but Tallis's charge still hits
home. And yet Vallès is in tune with common-or-garden readers (that
is, everybody, at some time), especially on the score of identification
with characters (that usefully overlapping word: personages/printed
marks). We all know, too, the undoubted effect of putting anything
down in black-and-white, whether legal niceties, diplomatic treaties,
school-reports, or love-letters. Print creates a pact more substantial than
any devised by Philippe Lejeune.

Yet the whole essay *is* confused, and keeps changing its ground:
Vallès glides from the painful imposition of scholastic primers to the
literature of wish-fulfilment. The first begets aversion, the second
escapism: there is a clear difference. Bellet encapsulates the whole
situation more lucidly and plausibly: 'Toute lecture est une mauvaise
lecture, toute lecture est une erreur de lecture; toute lecture est, à la
fois, mortelle et salvatrice: nécessairement, donc, peau et chair,
vêtement et nature' (I, 1245). Vallès,—and it might have been his saving
grace,—probably read much less than most comparable fellow-writers.
He is very un-French in the near-immunity to intellectual incest (echoes,
klang-effects); if very French in his argument, outside this essay, that
cultural debunking might seriously shake society. Whether, in this view,
books can have good effects, or mainly, as the essay proposes,
deleterious ones, either way they are powerful forces. He could have
chosen fashions, for instance (vestimentary, behavioural or intellectual)
as his example of how we seek to add cachet to, and at the same time to
flee, our run-of-the-mill selves.

Here, as elsewhere, Vallès mocks and inflates as an antidote to the
danger. He did not seriously wish to abolish books; he wanted to fight
bad, enervating books with better, inspiriting books. As Bellet sees so
clearly, the battle is within words:

> Le mot punisseur, le mot damnateur, familial ou scolaire, qui enfonce; le
> mot 'classique', la citation, qui enferme; la répétition, qui crée *sa* vérité, à
> partir de 'rien'; les surnoms de collège.

But also:

> Le mot polémique, la caricature, et même le mot convenu du boulevard
> traînant ses propres galériens, et appelant son contraire, le mot libre, ou
> libéré, ou libérateur, au moins pour un temps. Il faut combattre et tirer avec
> des mots, pour ne pas être tiré par eux (*JVJR*, p. 195).

Plagiarism is the real subject: 'Nous préférerons toujours l'original à la copie' (I, 485). The problem, of course, is how to tell the difference. Vallès knew that over-deliberate attempts at originality can engender fakery. He saw this both in Baudelaire, and in a study of the 'petit romantique', Pétrus Borel: 'Il souffre de la douleur qu'il feint et se trouve du même coup galérien et plagiaire. M. Clarétie l'appelle un original' (p. 521). Vallès was particularly harsh on the lesser lights of Romanticism who hung on to the coat-tails of brighter ones. Yet he surely was aware that *signer* (to authenticate) and *singer* (to ape) are a readily available source of misprints, and their proximity a fact of life. All writers worth their salt are derivative. Even if existential plagiarism is to be deplored, the artistic version is unavoidable. One of the many ironies about Vallès is that he was forever projecting novels à la Dickens, Sue, Balzac, etc., but that those he finally wrote are *sui generis*. He describes such projects in terms of pre-existing books at least partly because that makes it easier for his confidant to understand his intentions, but much more so because he knew it was impossible to be brand new. Like many a writer, he practised also self-plagiarism, recycling earlier work. Talking of his style at school, when he confesses to stitching together filched gobbets, he knew he was going along with the system, playing ball, for unoriginality was the criterion. But it is a vicious circle, in which the petty larcenist robs himself, of a personal voice. He had to struggle, to learn to shed borrowed plumes, to doff the fancy dress of others. Much plagiarism stems from a lack of self-confidence. At least he knew what he was doing. When he puns on *qualité/quantité* in avowing his artificial construction of Latin hexameters, he illustrates perfectly the mechanical nature of copying: the inertia of rhythm, the fillings for gaps falling pat into place—inspiration equated with *passe-partout* (*Enf.*, p. 320). He was not always so self-critical; in his *feuilletons* (e.g. *Un Gentilhomme*), Vallès was often himself a *victime du livre*, a rehasher of others' fiction.

From his childhood, Vallès experienced life itself as deeply plagiaristic, a constant making-over. For Bellet (*JVJR*, p. 312):

> La vie scolaire, familiale, sociale [...] est toujours 'traduction', donc trahison: traduction de textes grecs et latins, traduction du langage quotidien en beau style, traduction des places et des prix scolaires en pièces blanches, traduction des pièces, par la tirelire-gouffre, en libération militaire et en achat d'Homme, traduction de la vie immédiate en vie seconde et bourgeoise.

Vallès had a very strong sense of the impediments to true living, the constant deviation of effort. Another of the ironies of his life was that this firm opponent of dependence, the second-hand, should have been constrained for much of it to rely on grudged handouts from parents, cadging from friends, or exploiting them in the very bourgeois fashion of 'personne interposée'.

Philosophy and Religion

In discussing Vallès's political options, we saw how he resisted systematic politics, ideologies. Such resistance also applied to philosophy. Sartre said that 'une technique romanesque renvoie toujours à la métaphysique du romancier'.[13] I suspect that, whenever he heard the word 'metaphysics', Vallès reached for his scatter-pun (that loaded weapon). In a variant of *L'Insurgé*, he plays on the slang meaning of *philosophes:* second-hand shoes (II, 1858). He was simply not cut out for abstract thought—a desirable handicap, in many ways, for a French writer. 'Victimes du livre' revealed a Vallès inexpert in analysis. In Bellet's words, Vallès 'n'est guère expert en causalité, en enchaînements, et en conclusions; toute genèse copie la Genèse' (*JVJR*, p. 448). His thinking tended to the explosive (all those exclamation-marks!), the spontaneous, and, inevitably, at times the lubberly. 'Il y a en Vallès un refus passionné du "mystère", de l'ombre, du souterrain: crainte de s'y perdre ou de s'y laisser happer' (p. 282). You do not need to be a mystic to think that this refusal, while heroic, is also troubling and limiting. In more technical philosophical terms, which the well-trained Bellet handles like a second mother tongue, Vallès wards off those capitalised abstractions (which a Barthes indulged in so delightedly): 'Cette critique des majuscules exprime, sans philosophie, le refus d'une Raison ou Logos mystique, cultivée par un homme, Sujet intemporel ou Conscience absolue: Vallès aime le singulier, le divers, le différent, le contradictoire vivant, la lutte contre le principe d'identité' (p. 282). There is virtually no teleological override either in his journalism, his correspondence, or his fiction.

He had in school a bellyful of 'the oracle of banality, Victor Cousin, who memorably pontificated that "the individual by himself is a miserable and petty fact. [...] Humanity has not got the time and cannot bother to concern itself with individuals who are nothing but individuals"'.[14] Vallès rewrites Descartes's founding premise to his own ends: 'Je lutte, je souffre, j'aime, je hais, donc je suis. J'avais trouvé ça, moi, sans avoir lu Descartes' (*SEP*, p. 65). He took especial objection to the lazy use of 'philosophical' to mean 'fatalistic'. The whole jargonautical circumnavigations of so much literary-philosophical French has been aptly termed 'cet espéranto-pour-intellectuels'.[15] He had a particular aversion to sermonising novels (see I, 335). For all his hostility to systems, there is, as we have begun by now to see, a coherence, a backbone, in Vallès's writings; and criticism of abstract reason does not rule out intuitions. His rejection of metaphysics is not solely negative. He shifts the emphasis to useful, applied knowledge. It sounds limiting, but it is a sound enough basis: 'Je ne crois qu'à ce que je touche, et je n'aime que ce qui remue' (see p. 919).

If Vallès rejects metaphysics, it is likely, if not inevitable, that he will give short shrift to religion. 'Il lui manque—et c'est dommage—le sens du divin', said the brutal Catholic critic, Léon Daudet. [16] Vallès himself said that, despite the moral terrorism being practised by ranks of *bien-pensants* on children, 'le bon Dieu n'avait pas mordu sur moi', as if God were an acid corroding solid metals (II, 744). Of course his childhood was suffused with Catholic faith and practices. At six, 'j'avais toutes les innocences alors, la naïveté, la foi; je croyais aux revenants, je priais Dieu' (I, 669). Once past this uncritical stage, and though unreligious by nature, he remained quite tender to the more simple-minded observances (music, flowers, the ingenuous trust in a kindly, fatherly God). His mother's values were more social than religious: appearance, economy. There is no evidence that his parents interpreted their son's 'madness' as the result of divine retribution (an ancient but still current reflex), but rather as a state likely to bring social sanctions on their heads. The Vallès family were mainly a down-to-earth lot: in effect, Jules sidestepped religion as well as military service: *le noir et le rouge.*

A man like Vallès, hopeful of assisting social improvements, has little time for Original Sin, which harks back instead of forwards. It is environment and upbringing, both of which can be either changed or fought against, that matter. When he declares 'je plains les mystiques, je crains l'extase' (I, 339), not only is he showing towards religion the same aversion from depths as in philosophy, he also fears loss of control, as in madness. His natural irreverence makes him an enemy of 'toutes les apothéoses' (cultural, political or religious—II, 426). 'Eh bien! je ne suis rien, ni janséniste, ni moliniste, ni panthéiste, ni déiste, rien, pas même athée.—L'athéisme est encore une religion' (I, 1048). Not a few people shrug off labels in this way, not because they refuse to stand up and be counted,—Vallès never ran away,—but because they believe that such labels have no *raison d'être,* no ground in being. Though he had sympathy for protestants because of their history of being persecuted in France, he thought them killjoy. In England, he found them tyrannical.

As for France, 'nous ne sommes que d'affreux religiosistes, [...] tout en nous vantant d'être des sceptiques et des gouailleurs!' (quoted *JVJR,* p. 278). Yet he often underestimated the clerical threat to education because of his unshakable belief in the freedom of expression. He always preferred equal rights and open conflict to silencing the enemy (see I, pp. 411-12). Indeed, he was rather more relaxed about anticlericalism than many of his thinking coevals. [17] About the clergy, he was more in the line of Diderot and Rabelais, ready to laugh but considering them a much lesser danger than politicians. He was more concerned about the infiltration of religiosity into avowedly republican attitudes: Jules Simon, for instance, 'qui s'est inventé un Dieu de poche facile à porter en voyage' (p. 1013). In general, Vallès displays the unbeliever's idea of faith: it must be total and sincere, non-profitmaking, unworldly. Watching the converted Liszt hamming it up in public, Vallès felt moved to comment: 'L'église modeste de village, avec ses chandeliers de cuivre, ses saints de plâtre, son Christ en carton doré, était plus pleine de Dieu, entre ses murs de planches, que Saint-Eustache sous ses arceaux de pierre avec ce compositeur en prière et ces artistes au lutrin!'(p. 847).

What are we to make of the incidence of Biblical analogies and references, in particular, Christic imagery, in Vallès's work? Is it just another source, like ancient Greece, Rome, mythology or history, which Vallès believed he could count on to be recognised by his readers? I wonder how many of the tens of thousands of readers of *Le Cri du peuple* in 1871 would understand the allusion to 'les fourches Caudines' (II, 14)? Many references no doubt derive from childhood instruction. We should never forget that for every image of bread, wine, cross or blood, there are even more references to polarities like ground/air, earth/sky, humanity/gods, in which the former come off best. When, in the Commune, Courbet threatened to suppress God by decree, Vallès replied drily: 'Je voterai contre. [...] Dieu ne me gêne pas. Il n'y a que Jésus-Christ que je ne peux pas souffrir, comme toutes les réputations surfaites'. [18] A look at a specific example of a Christic image shows how Vallès operates. 'Briosne: un Christ qui louche—avec le chapeau de Barabbas! Mais point résigné, s'arrachant la lance du flanc, et se déchirant les mains à casser les épines qui restent sur son front d'ancien supplicié de ces Calvaires qu'on nomme les centrales' (*Ins.*, p. 950). The reference is contested, recycled, improved upon: Briosne refuses the eternal posture of Christ. It is, in effect, an inverted comparison, or an exploded one, which pulls apart instead of bridging a gap. It is as if Vallès were urging us to resist the facility of the Christic icon. Critics who try to make a meal out of the undoubted frequency of references to Christ are yet another instance of outsiders wanting to go one better than insiders. They miss the antireligious militancy, as when Vallès remarks of the politically committed: 'Les coups de lance qu'on leur porte les clouent à la vie au lieu de les pousser dans la mort' (II, 722). They also miss the humour, as in the 'Le Christ au saucisson' episode in *Le Bachelier* (pp. 617 ff.). Vallès was more interested in salami than *salamalecs*. Huysmans, who remained faithful to his admiration for Vallès, replied to a priest asking him his opinion of Chateaubriand: 'Pas des masses, l'abbé; je préfère Jules Vallès'. [19]

Culture, Classics and the Past

What of other gods, lay gods? Even before the Commune, Vallès was regarded as an iconoclast. He provoked the charge. In 1867, he wrote:

'On mettrait le feu aux bibliothèques et aux musées, qu'il y aurait, pour
l'humanité, non pas perte, mais profit et gloire' (I, 922). In 1884: 'On a
écrit que j'avais voulu brûler les Musées. J'avais dit simplement que,
pendant le combat, j'aurais fait une barricade avec la Vénus de Milo, si
elle avait dû aider à arrêter l'artillerie de Versailles. Je serais homme
encore aujourd'hui [...] à laisser les gelés et les grelottants se chauffer
avec les chefs d'œuvre plutôt de les voir mourir de froid' (quoted
JVJR, p. 471). Books, of course, exist in multiple copies; there is only
one Venus de Milo. There is a counter-hyperbole. Mallarmé: 'Ne
vaudrait-il pas mieux que la Pologne succombât que de voir cet éternel
hymne de marbre à la Beauté brisé?' [20] Tolstoy claimed that, to a
peasant, all Shakespeare was not worth a pair of boots, and Sartre that,
beside a dying child, his *La Nausée* did not pull its weight. For Vallès,
high art was an insult to the deprived or those denied a privileged
education; he claimed that, in so thinking, 'j'exprime le sentiment de la
foule' (I, 923). Possibly the only honest defence of high culture, in this
whole perspective, is to admit that it is a luxury, but to argue that it is a
necessary luxury. Vallès certainly sounds dangerously close to
philistinism, but we need to examine his motives. For Camus, '"l'art
pour le progrès" est un lieu commun qui a couru dans tout le siècle et
que Hugo a repris, sans réussir à le rendre convaincant. Seul, Vallès
apporte dans la malédiction de l'art un ton d'imprécation qui
l'authentifie'. [21] Can this defence be substantiated?

First of all, Vallès was not a lone voice. Artists and writers as
variegated as Daumier, Offenbach, Baudelaire, the Goncourts, all
contributed to the mockery of the classics. It was, besides, virtually *de
rigueur* for post-Romantics. It was self-evidently a sophisticated, non-
popular reaction; you needed to be saturated in the classics to want to
shake them off. Bellet defines a certain French cast of mind when he
comments: 'Pour Vallès, ces dévaluations culturelles sont le signe d'une
société ébranlée' (*JVJR*, p. 270). The wishful thinking of an élite, a kind
of 'si Homère n'existe point, tout est permis'. With the strong classical
overhang in the French Revolution in mind, I should add a further
political dimension to such cultural backlash: in the nineteenth century
there were a good many right-wing attacks on classical antiquity for
implanting in unstable young heads exalted republican ideas. The past
still dominated, as Vallès repeatedly warned, whether as model or pet
aversion. It was a poisoned gift. Vallès underlined the material
foundation of the elitist individualism for which a Plutarch had so long
been a template: the slavery of the many underpinning the glorious
emancipation of the few (I, 380).

It was on Homer that Vallès focussed all his wrath. He had a double
grievance, for it was over his father's prize copy of Homer that Vallès
had to sweat so many hours. He objected more truly to the uses to which
Homer was put rather than to the poetry itself. This reaction may well

be short-sighted, but it does not justify seeing Vallès as a cultural
Luddite. 'Ah! ils me fatiguent avec leur vieil Homère! Ils sont toujours
à nous parler de cet aveugle, et l'on passe pour une mauvaise nature si
l'on ne se signe pas et si l'on n'ôte pas son chapeau devant cet immortel
Patachon!' (I, 829—a *Patachon* is a rollicking driver of a clapped-out
vehicle—an ambivalent insult). Of course, Vallès had a bellyful of
Homer at school, along with thousands of other boys, and he retains the
adolescent response: 'Pourquoi respecter ce qui nous ennuie?' (*ibid.*). It
is a kind of guilt by association. Vallès orders him to a hospice for the
blind: 'Et toi, "vieil Homère", aux Quinze-Vingts!' (p. 831). He
compares Homer and company to a head-cold: 'Ma mémoire prend ça
comme mon nez prend l'eau [fills up with mucus], et je renifle des
chants entiers de l'Iliade et des choeurs d'Eschyle, du Virgile et du
Bossuet—mais ça part comme c'est venu' (*Enf.*, p. 323). But it did not
go away, and Vallès knew it. When a friend ventured that Vallès's style
was of the same ilk as Homer's, Vallès was not displeased and burst out
laughing. [22] Vallès spoke of his novel-project as 'Mon Iliade du peuple'
(*Corr. A.*, p. 94). The Homeric term 'asbestos gelos'—the unquenchable
laughter (of the gods)—was applied to the lame Hephaestus. Vallès
would find this figure, so adept at turning fiascoes to his own advantage,
sympathetic; and his own laughter was similarly inextinguishable. Some
imitation of classical models is acceptable. For instance, young Scythians
went bare-headed in winter. Making a virtue of necessity, the
impoverished student is proud to emulate them (*SEP*, p. 92). All in all,
Vallès's mockery of Homer—a sacred cow, for Vallès, is just bull—is a
way of wounding the smug and much more authentic philistines who
pay lip-service to the great tradition.

Talking earlier of Blanquism, we saw Vallès's aversion form the
French national sport of grave-robbing. Where does he stand more
generally on the question of remembrance of things past? As so often,
the bag is very mixed. A frequently unhappy childhood, but with oases
of joy; a greatly resented schooling; gratefulness for the French
Revolution, but deep concern about the uses it has been put to; a partly
joky but always serious onslaught on the hegemony of the classics; a
profound respect for peasant forebears, especially *réfractaires*. And,
globally, a true fidelity to (some would say fixation on) his own
previous experience, miserable or happy.

So keen on keeping faith with his provincial roots and earlier life,
Vallès would have favoured mass amnesia as regards the paralysing role
models of the French Revolution. Like the *émigrés* of that period,
Vallès's fellow-radicals seemed to have forgotten nothing and learned
nothing. It was a chain-gang: neo-Jacobins moulding themselves on the
revolutionary ancestors, who in turn invoked classical predecessors. At
school, too, the Past was God. Back-reference, back-formation: so many
take themselves for etymologists. Vallès derided 'le néant des mausolées.

Décidément, il ne faut aux grands hommes pour Panthéon que le coeur vivant de l'humanité' (I, 564). Statues are cold and lifeless. 'Elles vous regardent de leur oeil stupide et sans prunelles' (p. 892). The ancients suffered from 'the mania for serenity' (*ibid.*). Statues are 'marble scarecrows' (p. 895). Whereas most people go to museums to feel reverential, Vallès went to feel as offended as Sartre's Roquentin at all this monumentalisation of mere or mediocre men. A moving target like Vallès would obviously loathe stasis. (Ironically, Vallès's head, at its most august, appeared on a French stamp in 1982). Even when he approved of the subject, as with Dumas *père,* he hated 'cette pétrification en pied d'une renommée [...], cet Hercule de la fécondité, Bamboula de la gloire, Michel-Ange du débraillé' (II, pp. 1094-6). Possibly the myth of the Gorgon—the passing of unarguable judgments—was behind this hostility to 'les pétrifications de la reconnaissance' (p. 734). Vallès would prefer death-masks to statues, for they adhere more lifelikely to a human reality (*ibid.*). Iconoclasts, such as Proudhon, do not deserve the indignity of marble or bronze. Bellet also detects the 'statue du Commandeur' (in the film *Amadeus,* an avenging father-figure): 'Il "se dresse" tout à coup devant vous, il vous tire et vous attire, il vous pétrifie de son regard regardé' (*JVJR*, p. 275), coining the blend 'statufictions' to describe these false erections of authority (p. 272). And yet, hating statues, Vallès admired 'natures tout d'une pièce', like Courbet, but these were living monoliths (I, 826).

The Past is death. Vallès often alludes to the Vestals, who were the priestesses of death, serving its memory, and themselves the living dead (I, 1001). Vallès was obsessed by the continuing influence of the past, which he compared to grafting. He refers to the new technique of *rhinoplastie* —nose-jobs—a funny term in itself, a caricatural *mot savant,* for it reminds of the link between the human hooter and the rhinoceros' dangerous and grotesque horn: 'Dangereuse et terrible pour l'humanité, cette école de rhinoplastie qui veut qu'on couse à la page neuve des lambeaux de peau morte' (p. 818). Above all, it was the rigidity of statues, of Roman 'vertu', even 'la raideur anglaise', that appalled him. He knew in his bones, or loins, that only one area of a man needs to be rigid, and then only on the right occasion. The pose of or the aspiration towards permanent rigidity is a rush to *rigor mortis.* Bellet adds to the equation Vallès's 'hantise du vêtement figé et figeant' (*JVJR*, p. 272). Living backwards is always an uphill struggle: 'Remonter! toujours remonter! Je ne fais que remonter depuis le collège—et ça fatigue à la fin' (II, 1675). The whole backward-looking movement leads to plagiarism; even the much-loved capacity for enthusiasm can be a copy. 'Le mort saisit le vif', says the French adage that Marx was fond of quoting. Vallès's version: 'Le présent traîne le passé collé à ses flancs comme un cadavre dont le poids l'entraîne' (I, 882). Either way, it is an incubus.

Totally lacking the Peter Pan urge never to grow up, Vallès is nonetheless a frequent nostalgic for his own past. Even as a child he was as bitten by homesickness (when he moved on from town to town) as he was puffed up with great expectations. As an adult, he judged severely those who wilfully bury their origins, their fundamental self, or their erstwhile companions or revolts. Despite his fidelity to his own past, however, Jacques Vingtras mistrusts his mother's apparently comparable cult of relics, 'miettes du passé' (*Bach.*, p. 659). His own memories are not pawky crumbs, conditioned reverence, but healthy, voracious mouthfuls (e.g. the sustaining images of planturous country girls). While never a stick-in-the-mud, Vallès was singularly adhesive: the key Vallésian verb, as Bellet amply demonstrates, is *coller*. He was never a turncoat, weather-vane, time-server, trimmer or backslider (so many words for this supremely human activity). Indeed, he often acted as a remembrancer, for the civil dead (the mad, the disgraced, the imprisoned); whether they were once famous or always obscure, Vallès makes room for them, reminds us of them (I, pp. 1001-1002). He resembles in this his debtor Guilloux, for whom forgetfulness and oblivion (*oubli* covers both meanings, active and passive) are as criminal and as pitiable as the *oubliettes* of the Ancien Régime. Even those who were startlers in their time can become forgettable. Yet, if Vallès were fully a conservationist of the emotions, he would want the past reborn as it was. He wanted it reborn better than it was, a new start.

'Ce n'est point que j'aie la manie du nouveau ni de l'excentrique; rien n'est nouveau dans ce que j'aime' (I, 883). No neophiliac, he exaggerates his hostility to the Past because he feels sure that it suffocates the present and shackles the future: amplified disrespect versus hyperbolic respect; tit-for-tat. When he relives the past, as in the Trilogy and much of his journalism, he is not copying; he is reinvesting, indeed, often, reinventing it. It is not just, either, a distinction he makes between public past and private yesteryear, for he saw in his parents aspects of the past mummified. 'Those who do not remember the past', said Santayana, 'are condemned to relive it'. That is, to reinvent the wheel. Even when looking back on the Commune, Vallès is thinking less of commemoration than of invigoration for future effort (see II, 1368). The past helps to explain, warp and create the present; it can be used as starting-blocks. For all his derision of classical discourse, Vallès never coddles himself with the delusion that it can be eradicated. You cannot unlearn. You can only overlay, recycle, compete.

In the age-old conflict of Moderns and Ancients, Vallès is a modern, but not, finally, an iconoclast:

> Le culte même des statues. Ne les brisons pas sur leur socle; mais n'essayons pas de singer l'attitude et de prendre la pose. On ne peut que

copier les plis. Il faut être soi, jeter au loin les livres et les drapeaux lourds,
affirmer, faible ou forte, sa personnalité et ne sacrifier le caractère et les
droits de l'individu ni au besoin de gloire, ni aux raisons d'Etat. Ne soyons
pas esclaves de la tradition! Le siècle, dont on est le fils, est toujours le plus
grand, parce qu'il est le dernier. Il a profité, malgré lui, des grandeurs et des
fautes de tous ceux qui l'ont précédé. Pourquoi demander aux aînés son
chemin? (I, 385)

This incremental view is his profession of faith.

Popular Culture and Poetry

It is of course impossible to calculate exactly how much Vallès read.
At school he was forced to read the largely classical syllabus, but he also
read to his own taste under the desk, in detention, or, in small measure,
at home. He swotted in libraries when a student and again when a hack
contributor to works of compilation. Otherwise he seems to have relied
heavily on free books: authors' copies, review-copies, library books, or
only partly cut books squinted at in paying reading-rooms when he
could not afford the fee (see *Bach.*, p. 682). I imagine that he owned
few books, and that, in general, he read less than many writers. I
reported earlier that Vallès largely 'read' Rousseau via Proudhon. I
suspect that much of his reading (and of how many of us is this also
true?) was mediated in this way, a matter of hear-say, and read-write.
If we turn from high culture to popular culture, we might wonder
how many of the almanacs and the products of the 'Bibliothèque bleue'
were read by Vallès, despite the fact that, in accordance with his
political preferences, he defended them. A historian of this popular
literature, Nisard, condemned it; Louis-Sébastien Mercier and Nodier
were fascinated by it and pleaded for its continuance. Champfleury, the
champion of literary realism, while criticising the archaeological
approach, believed that such literature could provide a source of
renewal. Michelet, ambivalently dear to Vallès, both recorded its demise
and dreamed of resuscitating it and exploiting it for politico-educational
ends. Many of the themes in the almanacs came from oral traditions,
especially medieval romances of chivalry. Typical stories featured the
Wandering Jew, Gargantua, le Bonhomme Misère. These *livres de
colportage* (the more genial English equivalent is 'chapbooks') were also
full of practical advice (medical, agricultural) and calendars (dates of
observance). Because they contained pictures as well as texts, the viewer
did not need to be even semi-literate (through Bollème wonders whether
more could read than write, only the second being measured in
records). [23] Astrological predictions figured prominently, but, whether
the text was practical or fanciful, the recourse to narration, linear
division of time, clearly involves a shaping. The separate bits add up to

a world-view. By reason of its popular clientèle, this literature was regularly regarded with suspicion and fear by the authorities and their lettered supporters, as a fount of possible subversion. Bollème queries the dismissive term 'escapism', and asks who can know what readers, or viewers, take from a book and what they make of it. The easiest temptation for well-educated commentators is condescension, but I think that Vallès largely avoided this trap, for many of his values overlap with those present in the popular literature described above. For Bellet, 'Vallès eût aimé voir le journal, création industrielle et urbaine, aspirer les valeurs "agraires" de l'almanach: c'eût été réconcilier, dans l'écrit cher à son cœur, le temps cursif du journal et le temps agraire' (*JVJR*, p. 310). Certainly, time is of the essence. For all the forward march of society, which Vallès rarely damned, he knew there were different, more ageless, rhythms to accommodate and indeed to learn from. Besides, some combination of the benefits of city and countryside, as we will see later, always appealed to Vallès.

On the more recent urban variety of popular culture, he was typically unsnobbish. 'On voit l'aristocratie qui baisse, le peuple qui monte. [...] Je ne vois pas là un signe de décadence,mais plutôt l'avènement d'un art populaire auquel il ne faut pas faire un crime, dès le début, de ses sympathies précipitées et de son enthousiasme irréfléchi' (I, pp. 604-605). Culture must be part of such social brews. Yet some innate reserve makes him tack on to his praise of the popular, demotic-speaking entertainer, Thérésa: 'On pourrait vulgariser sans être aussi souvent vulgaire' (p. 609). It is not entirely clear whether he places total trust in untutored responses—'Votre art de convention, accessible seulement aux échappés de collège, ne peut distraire ceux qui, n'ayant point appris, ne savent rien et n'ont, pour juger une œuvre, que la spontanéité de leur sensation'—for he writes further on: 'Nous avons à lui faire [au peuple] des mœurs et une éducation' (pp. 605; 610). I should add that the dictatorial benevolence of this last quotation is rare in Vallès. With his deep hostility to schools and to didactic literature, he more usually does not pose as an imposer, but as a respondent.

Popular poetry: Vallès's head, like many another, was full of snippets, echoes, refrains, jingles, *scies*; he hummed along (see *JVJR*, p. 245). He remained attached by various fibres even to the highly successful *chansonnier*, Béranger (to whom his father was devoted), despite attacking him frequently for his political compromises, and despite the common view of his verses as anaesthetic and marshmallow-centred.[24] From a very different political standpoint, Flaubert dismissed him: 'Béranger est le bouilli de la poésie moderne'.[25] In an essay, *Des mots*, Vallès keeps up a running contrast between big names (Hugo) and smaller fry (Eugène Pottier, or Vallès himself, referred to as 'un bon ami à moi'). The contrast is between grandiloquent Romantic poetry and humbler verses; between grand, warlike themes and street-level sufferings and longings. Talking anonymously of himself, he recycles Musset's 'Son verre n'est pas grand, mais il boit dans son verre', yet he admits that 'dès qu'il voulut hémisticher, le malheureux, il devint, comme les autres, poncif, plagiaire et déclamatoire!' Quoting his own younger poetry, 'Bas les cœurs', about the trauma of 1851, he belittles it firmly for its succumbing to inertia: 'Par le balancement des rimes on arrivait à ces balançoires de désespéré'. He is even more self-critical about his lines on the *Semaine sanglante:* 'Pourquoi cette afféterie et ces vantardises d'héroïsme? Parce que le récitatif le veut'. The drug and drag of words. The rest of the essay is devoted to staking the claims of Pottier against those of Hugo—truly David and Goliath. For Vallès, Hugo talks too big ('Hugo s'est attardé sur les sommets'). Vallès is not an enemy of Romantic poetry, but a new kind is needed. Pottier is on the level with ordinary people and their concerns: work, food, warmth. Quoting from Pottier's 'Le Chômage', Vallès allows that lovers of phrasemaking will say that it is 'terne et sombre', but this is the colour of working-class life. [26] As well as a poet, Pottier was a talented industrial draughtsman, and so entitled to play a part on the artists' committee in the Commune, alongside Courbet.

The belittlement of Hugo is part of a wider attack on the epic mode: 'Notre littérature sent toujours *l'héroïsme* par quelque coin' (I, 548). Converting the giant/dwarf topos, he asks belligerently: 'Il n'y aurait plus que des nains parce qu'il y a eu quelques géants!' (p. 992). All idealisation, whether angelism or demonology, is epic, and untruthful. He admits that to escape such habits of mind entails self-violence: 'C'est arracher une part de soi-même, tant l'imitation s'est intériorisée' (*JVJR*, p. 281). Vallès's refusal of the epic centred on Hugo, but he did not spare Hugo's more intimate poetry. On *Les Chansons des rues et des bois*, Vallès charges that Hugo speaks of love like a *voyeur*, 'sa gaieté est fausse, sa caresse est triste'. Above all, he objects to the mysticism: 'Je ne prends pas le vide pour la profondeur et le creux pour l'abîme. C'est la tactique de tous ceux qui ont le cerveau épuisé ou vide de se draper ainsi dans des pans d'ombre et de se perdre dans les nuages. Ils veulent avoir l'attrait du mystère et le prestige de l'élévation'(I, pp. 569-72). This outspokenness is no doubt globally unfair, but surely many readers of Hugo have felt something similar without daring to strip the emperor. Vallès did value some of Hugo's prose works, e.g. *Quatre-Vingt-Treize* and *Les Misérables* for their warmth towards *le peuple*, but it took him a long time to forgive Hugo's self-admitted turncoatism: that of the tricolour—red with the reds, white with the whites, blue with the blues. [27] Vallès never mentions *Les Châtiments*. During the siege of Paris, Hugo went in for the kind of paper sabre-rattling bombast that Louis Aragon would later commit in the Second World War. Hugo's subsequent generous offer of asylum to Communard exiles in his Brussels home in 1871 repaired some of the damage. But, all in all, 'M. Victor Hugo n'est qu'un superbe monstre' (p. 951). A major distance between them is that Hugo's *mélange des genres* is principally an alternation, but Vallès's a coexistence, or an internecine struggle, like cats in a sack.

Feuilletons

The great contribution of the nineteenth century to popular culture was the *roman-feuilleton*. Before looking at Vallès's own efforts (some of them out of chronological order, for the writing of the Trilogy did not improve his post-1880 *feuilletons*), I must stress that he never conceals nor disparages what he got from such popular fiction, which was of course not marginal, not 'paraliterature', but, in terms of readers and cultural effects, the true centre of literary production. For Vallès, never a partisan of minority art for art's sake, Mallarmé might well not have existed. We have already remarked on the interchanges of journalism and literature in the nineteenth century. As sales of volumes remained in general quite low, novelists depended on serialisation in newspapers for a paying outlet and, conversely, editors looked to popular serials to increase their readership. The phenomenon thrives still today in soap-operas and numbered films. Serialised literature then was usually printed at the bottom of the page: 'le rez-de-chaussée', ground-floor fiction. One of its most successful practitioners was Eugène Sue, whose example influenced Vallès much more than the contemporary classics Balzac, Stendhal, Hugo or Flaubert. Nor was it a matter only of plot, or style, but also of political persuasion: Sue's sincere socialism, for which he had to pay by fleeing to Annecy. The author of 'Victimes du livre' was more influenced by writers like Sue than by political theorists, even Proudhon (*JVJR*, pp. 136-7).

For all their faults, often howling, Vallès's *feuilletons* make up, or over-compensate, for what he was accused of lacking in his major fiction: inventivity. The first, *Jean Delbenne* (1865) features the Romantic topos of a dark hero eaten by some secret. As Bellet points out, it meshes conflicting elements from Stendhal and Dumas père's *Antony* (I, 1732). Jean Delbenne, a blasé 'nature incomplète' (*LCD 4*, p. 300), gets involved in a one-sided liaison. Born poor but proud, he suffers humiliations until, driven to distraction, he goes mad and dies after an attempted rape. The tale is totally lacking in humour, badly amputated and hardly recognisable Vallès. It tells, it does not show. It relies on, and makes no attempt at fruitful subversion of, the popular mode of melodrama (as, for example, Darien does in *Le Voleur*).

Un Gentilhomme (1869) houses more Vallésian constants, without forming a satisfying whole. He sets up a contrast of gloomy château and zestful farm, dark rooms and sunlit fields. He satirises the effects of religiosity, though showing some sympathy for the young woman trapped by its vetoes. Yet when Augustine tries to escape this trap by reading novels, she exchanges one form of misleading for another. The parents are cold and vengeful. A still 'feudal' relationship subsists between landowners and field-workers; though these labour hard, their skills are appreciated, and both sides consort for meals; they enjoy a good working relationship. Such peasants are capable of revolt if pushed too far, and they march on the château and its murderess *châtelaine* at the end. In fact, there is a regular holocaust of rape, murder, suicide and poetic justice in the finale. Despite this accelerando, there are several stalled and clumsy sections, where Vallès resorts to flashback, potted biographies and the pluperfect. There is a monster, a country Quasimodo (Babassou), though Vallès tries to suggest a pathetic man in the heap of misshapen flesh. Changes are too well-lubricated. As Bellet comments: 'Maurice change de peau quand il change de vêtement' (I, 1734). He detects that Vallès's parents are disguised—in the dead father, domineering mother and good uncle of *Un Gentilhomme* (pp. 1734-5). The parents crop up again, more sadistic than in the Trilogy, in *Pierre Moras* (1870), written in haste and in dire financial need. It is essentially a satire of Vallès's experiences in the period 1854-1865 in offices, in journalism, among literary cliques, and bohemian café-life. Significantly, Vallès in 1879 refused permission to reprint either *Un Gentilhomme* or *Pierre Moras,* on which the journalist Gustave Puissant collaborated, when Vallès discovered that he had been a police-informer. With somewhat more dubious justification, Vallès explained that *Un Gentilhomme* had been a rush job, and *Pierre Moras* too much inflected by Puissant's taste for sombre effects (see p. 1736).

Les Blouses (1880) is the most interesting of the *feuilletons.* It is a novel about grain-riots (hunger and bread are constants in all of Vallès's work) in Buzançais (Indre) in 1847, a year of widespread famine. The historical small-scale *jacquerie* is inflated and deviated by Vallès into an essentially townee's view of provincial political confrontations. He imports revolutionary theory and secret societies, and tries on his habitual conjunction of *blouse* and *redingote:* middle-class plotters trying simultaneously to respect and to exacerbate popular grievances ('ennoblir leur fureur et les enrégimenter pour la Révolution!' (*Blouses,* p. 156). Vallès remains surprisingly neutral over the dissensions between ideologues and populace, and within the group of ideologues. He stresses the initial legalism of the wheat-seizers, and acknowledges that not all of the inhabitants, even the poorest, are keen on violent confrontation. Against the later official view, he claims there was no criminal element amongst the rioters. Written after the Commune, *Les Blouses* gives a major role to women as governing the changing moods of the crowd. It was no doubt bad timing on Vallès's part to recall in 1880 past divisions of the left, when it was trying to persuade moderate republicans to support the amnesty of the Communards (See Dautry, preface, p. 144). When publication of the serial in Clemenceau's *La Justice* was broken off, no doubt after pressure from bourgeois readers, Vallès apologised for inadequate documentation (he wrote it while still in exile). *Les Blouses* is historical fiction. Among powerful, if over-insistent motifs, such as that of the 'arrested' wheat, the prisoner of the crowd, or the idea of using a corpse as a rallying-point and a springboard for action, Vallès slumps into falsities of conjunction and polarity like the following: 'On avait étudié ensemble. Le printemps de leur vie avait été imprégné des mêmes parfums, que leurs mains, restées jointes pendant les années d'école, avaient conservés longtemps encore, malgré que l'un eût manié l'encens, l'autre la poudre' (p. 215). This is just one example among many possible of how Vallès fails in his *feuilletons* to observe his own injunction: 'Peindre la vie sans fioritures comme Sieyès demandait la Mort sans phrases' (quoted *JVJR*, p. 350).

Possibly the reason why Vallès seems so often barely identifiable in his *feuilletons* is that he tries too hard to think himself into different shoes, to imagine people not himself. In *La Dompteuse* (1881), this leads to a kind of schizophrenia within the text: 'Il s'en voulut de ce mouvement, et s'empoignant par le habit, comme si c'était un autre: "Ah! ça, Fanjat", dit-il, faisant mine de se brutaliser' (*LCD. 4*, p. 326). In a maladroit, long-winded but more recognisably Vallésian seriocomic twist, Gourmichel, an ex-actor whose stage-villains were genial, runs a home for children off-loaded by parents. He acts the part of a harsh disciplinarian, but in fact treats his charges humanely. 'Il était le crocodile du vice', as Vallès puts it with welcome pungency (p. 377). Whereas the parents expect education to be punitive, he allows his youngsters to 'battre la campagne, courir les champs' (p. 377). Another episode features a punchy, Catch-22 account of a visit to Charenton, where a specialist diagnoses as 'manie raisonnante' a patient making a reasoned request to be set free (p. 418). Earlier a husband had gone instantly mad on learning of his wife's guilty abortion. Nature is here seen for once as anti-natural: 'Où naissaient ces plantes qui ne voulaient pas que les enfants naquissent?' (p. 337). 'La Dompteuse' is finally defined as 'la Misère' (p. 426). Within this melodramatic and sporadically interesting story, a defence is made of the conventions of melodrama, by an appeal to life's coincidences and mysterious networks (p. 486).

Intended as potboilers, nice little earners, these *feuilletons* by Vallès certainly helped his always rocky finances without ever earning him fortune or fame. They reveal an author yielding facilely to plagiarism, clichés: the prefabricated. It is parasitic fiction and, as such, immeasurably inferior to the Trilogy. But his critics can outdo him in melodrama: 'Un monde invivable, impossible, contre lequel on ne peut pas crier: le style mélo, c'est son suicide à lui'. [28] It was a suicide which he survived amazingly intact. The fact remains that Vallès writes far better when he applies his melodramatising urges to comic ends (thus mocking it while preserving some of its emotional impact) than when he plays it straight. Many of his puns, ironies, pointed antitheses are inherently melodramatic, over-the-top. When Bellet sympathetically describes Vallès's 'besoin de sentiment direct, de vision immédiate, d'émotion vive: pas de hiatus, pas de béance où s'insérerait le vide des grandes pensées', he implicitly recognises also that Vallès fails, in his *feuilletons*, to mediate, to distance this 'romantisme de la sensation' (*JVJR*, p. 350).

Realism and the Novel

Vallès championed literary realism, about which he was as confused as everybody else, some time before he got round to enacting it, except in the form, as we have just seen, of largely 'misérabiliste' melodrama. It was in his year (1 February 1864-30 January 1865) as reviewer for *Le Progrès de Lyon*—among the best of liberal provincial papers—that he strengthened his confidence in his taste and judgments. He made clear his ordinary qualifications: 'Je suis fait comme tout le monde, j'ai lu un peu plus que quelques autres, *regardé* sinon *vu* beaucoup' (I, 323). He adds, fairly incoherently: 'Quand on se fait présenter par cette pauvre femme qui s'appelle la Sincérité, il faut bien essayer d'obtenir la confiance pour pouvoir l'inspirer et vanter sa franchise, quand cette franchise-là doit être votre originalité' (p. 325). With his niche in mind, he reminds that most Parisians are of provincial origin: 'C'est en province, après tout, que commencent et finissent toutes les histoires; on y tient toujours par quelque lien, un souvenir d'enfance ou de jeunesse' (*ibid.*). The fluidity of his concept of realism is shown when he calls the story of 'un enfant du pays qui rentre au village natal' 'ce récit à la fois poétique et réaliste' (p. 462).

As the status of the theatre was higher in the 1860s than that of fiction, Vallès sees the novel genre as another of the underdogs, the in-betweens, and in need of championing as the ideal literature for the new age. Comparing it with the drama, he stresses the novel's *demi-jour*, its nuances, with the blatancy of the footlights (I, 324). It is a better medium for evoking inner life, 'cette existence du soir' (*ibid.*). Above all, Vallès is 'avide d'impressions fraîches et vraies' (p. 335), and attaches little value to inventiveness: 'Inventer! mais pour ce qui est des larmes, il n'y a pas de sources à découvrir' (p. 358). What he values especially is personal testimony: 'Ma haine de l'allégorie et mon mépris pour les fictions m'entraînent du côté des études personnelles et véridiques; j'aime à savoir que celui qui écrit a vu ce dont il parle' (p. 455). He believes in the personal hall-mark view of style: 'Regardez de près et vous devinerez la fraude: le poinçon n'y est pas' (p. 465). He thus expects a writer to be striking—albeit tenderly. To this end, he places much more stress on recording his own impressions (sensuous images, scenes) as a reader than on analysis of plot or ideas.

In several ways, his expectations of literature (as of painting) are those of the normal, non-specialist consumer. He demands that a novel or a canvas should appear so real that you feel you could walk into it. *L'Enfant* relates a novel by an obscure writer (a teacher!) which managed to 'faire passer cette rivière dans un coin de chapitre' (*Enf.*, p. 160). Vallès wanted novels to be like homes, or landscapes, with running water. Of course such demands are naïve, but then the most way-out deconstructionist also relies on a kind of mimesis—in her case, a keeping faith with chaos. In case Vallès should appear to prefer the fleeting—moods, water—he favours equally often images borrowed from the plastic arts: engrave, relief, vigorous stroke. The two series come together in his account of a legendary spring in the Auvergne which was reputed to change anyone approaching it to stone, preserved for all eternity. Shades of the Gorgon. He goes on to define genius as the power of moulding and fixing, but animated also by the breath of life. So the analogy spring/art is only, and typically, approximate (I, 890). He likes fictional characters to be monolithic (but not statues), variable, filled with concentrated and contradictory emotions. Not that any old mixture would do. Great works have to prove their worth to each individual reader; and he knew that we all talk of many masterpieces by hearsay. Consonantly with his belief in the total freedom of the press, Vallès held that any work, once published or performed, becomes public property, or that, at least, an open season begins for criticism (p. 514). Conversely, in a largely mystified society, the novel could act as a demystifier, a demisting panel, on the social window. The novelist needs clear eyes and honest emotions. As Victor Serge suggested: 'Listen to your nerves'.[29]

When it came to specific writers, Vallès swears his admiration for Balzac. He delivered a highly controversial public lecture on him in 1865, which suggested, before Engels or Lukács, that Balzac was a critical realist whose picture of society carries a built-in charge against it. Though much response to the lecture was congratulatory, Vallès was banned from further public speaking for daring to attack the régime. Later, when Vallès had moved into a clearer idea of committed literature, he would praise Balzac as a half-way revolutionary because of his focus on money as a social dominant (II, 1339). Vallès always acknowledges that Balzac was not a preacher, but a setter-in-motion, a demiurge, yet he had reservations. Just as Baudelaire felt that even

Balzac's concierges had genius, so Vallès declares that 'Balzac anoblit toujours ses personnages' (I, 549). It is true that Balzac habitually bestows accolades, at either extreme of the ethical gamut. George Sand earns Vallès's criticism for her 'agromane' preaching: 'Je ne voudrais pas que le roman se fît avocat ou tribun, même pour défendre les idées que j'aime' (p. 550). On didacticism in general he believed that 'il faut le reflet et non pas la rengaine' (p. 403). He had had more than enough sententious dinning at school. As it took the Commune to widen Vallès's mind on women, it was mostly Sand's feminist egalitarianism that annoyed him. The bipartite Erckmann-Chatrian gained his praise, but he found them *too* regionalist, their writing too riddled with cliché ('Le procédé crève les yeux') (pp. 330-3).

In line with a general reticence about sex and scatology (though I will later discuss important exceptions), Vallès clearly disfavours the more documentarily anatomical or clinical kind of realism associated with the Goncourts (and later with Zola and Huysmans—I, 358). As Bellet underlines, any 'réalisme du débraillé' is alien to Vallès (*JVJR*, p. 428). About the early theorists of realism, Champfleury and Duranty, Vallès remains largely silent. Indeed so naturally averse to schools of thought, — in literature, philosophy or politics, — was he that he coined his own term, vaguer and putting the stress on response to one's times rather than mirror-images, 'Actualistes' (I, pp. 890-4).

In his literary criticism, Vallès was not purely negative, egotistically clearing the decks for his own future novels. His praise of Dickens was genuine and durable, though based on the reading of only three novels, it would seem (*JVJR*, p. 203). Vallès played him off against Balzac. If Vallès had known more, or anything, about Dickens's biography, his facts of life, he might well have formed a different impression of him, for Vallès was never able nor willing to separate the man from the writer. Dickens, for instance, insisted on 'apple-pie order' in all things in daily life, although his imagination was most powerfully fired by violence and destruction. He was often supercilious about the lower classes and the inmates of jails or asylums. Carey speaks of 'the contempt Dickens felt for those who were not successful, not gentlemen, and not Dickens'. Though, in the feeblest of his articles on Dickens, Vallès tried to refute a French claim that he was a Christian, Carey reports that 'Dickens used to become quite savage, when people suggested he wasn't a Christian'. [30] Dickens's passion for law enforcement, including the death penalty, is a further long step away from Vallès. There is indeed not much common ground between them on the issue of social change and how drastic it need be. Compared with Vallès, Dickens, even at his best, is humanitarian rather than political in outlook. Jacques Vingtras is much more resistant than Pip or David Copperfield to social conditioning. On education, where Vallès protests the abstract, past-orientated nature of the French system, Dickens in

Hard Times protests against the anti-imaginative stress on 'factuality'—a curiously abstract factuality that banishes representations of horses from classroom displays, as horses do not live on walls.

The convergences are, however, powerful. Dickens's bitter experience of factory work and family debt, the street-wisdom he acquired as a journalist, his warm relationship with the reading public that Vallès could only dream of, all of these elicited Vallès's admiration. Where they come closest to each other is in the obsessive theme of brutalised childhood (psychic and emotional as well as physical), and humour. Vallès brings together the two aspects. 'Toujours le grotesque marche à côté du grandiose, le bouffon coudoie la victime, et ce n'est pas seulement le drame, mais c'est aussi la comédie de la souffrance' (I, 556). *L'Enfant* is suffused with such 'tristesses comiques'. Vallès salutes Dickens's ability to 'surprendre le côté douloureux des farces et le côté plaisant des tragédies' (*ibid.*). Dickens's humour was often judged vulgar by anal-retentive French critics, but for Vallès it was his chief glory. Vallès, I suspect, linked this capacity for humour with childlikeness. He quotes from *David Copperfield* a passage about some select people retaining freshly in adulthood the vivacity of childhood impressions. 'Je suis de l'avis de Dickens plus que personne, moi dont les impressions les plus vives datent aussi des premières années' (p. 558). Altogether, what Vallès values in Dickens is 'l'humour dans l'observation, la poésie de l'image dans la réalité des faits: l'émotion arrive sur l'aile humble et fine de la mélancolie, et, à cette émotion se mêle une gaieté tendre qui fait que l'on sourit, parfois qu'on pleure, et qu'après avoir pleuré on rêve' (p. 552).

Dickens, like Vallès, preferred to restrict pictorial art to the lifelike, yet, unlike Vallès, when Millais depicted Christ in a carpenter's shop, Dickens complained that he had failed to 'etherealise' and 'ennoble' his subject. [31] Vallès greatly admired Dickens and Daumier for cutting people down to size and for capturing them at their most salient points. He championed Courbet consistently, though more for his bolshy character than his specifically artistic genius: 'Le plus bel animal que j'ai vu, ce sacré bonhomme-là! Travailleur comme un bœuf, mais gai aussi comme un ourson: bête des champs et bête de foire. On a pu lui appliquer ce que Michelet disait de Dumas père: "qu'il était une *force* de la nature". Mais il en était une *farce* aussi' (II, 1475). Even so, Courbet's concern for closely-observed detail, his many self-portraits (and his fine painting of Vallès), his anti-idealisation of treatment, strongly attracted Vallès as much as the big and noisy ego, the active embroilment in the Commune, the hunger for success and the irascible impatience with discipline. Vallès did not share Courbet's taste for exaggerated patois. Like L.S. Lowry, Courbet tended to claim that he painted what he saw. His frankness of portrayal was considered by many to be ugly, and seditious.

Despite his intense concern with words, Vallès never lost his equally strong fascination with pictorial images. Like many another writer, he envied the immediacy, the simultaneity of pictures, as against the linearity of language. In many ways, if words are the mind's business, pictures are the body's.

Chapter Five

The Body and its Setting

The Body

For Vallès, the body speaks volumes, tells tales, yet he always retains, and expects on his own behalf, a final respect for the private self beneath the corporeal envelope. In the case of enemies, he looks for confirmation that the outer informs reliably on the inner. In general, in his eyes, we are all on show, on stage (or trestles). We are, each for the other, spectacles, solo tribunals, or duellists: on occasion, partners!

In the 1860s, the Goncourts were already warning that furniture was taking over from human beings in novels. Flaubert is often seen as such a *chosiste* a century before the now geriatric New Novelists. Vallès's stance is explicit. On a visit to the *Times* printing press in 1865, he declared: 'Je ne suis pas grandement intéressé par les choses. Il est besoin que l'homme paraisse pour que j'éprouve une émotion' (I, 1563). Workers there, he felt, were truly cogs in a machine. Yet the same year he acknowledged the thinginess of memory:

> Toutes les images de la vie extérieure s'attachent au cerveau, restent dans la prunelle, et le souvenir des choses sera aussi vif un jour que la mémoire des émotions. Quelquefois même l'émotion s'efface, et ce n'est pas la pensée qui jouit ou souffre, c'est seulement l'œil qui voit, l'oreille qui s'ouvre; les condamnés à mort écoutent une mouche qui vole, regardent un caillou qui luit (p. 555).

Thus, Vallès draws no hardline distinction between things and sensations: objects are tokens, relics, giveaways that trumpet or hint. It is what a thing means that matters to him, not objects-in-themselves. [1] And where can sensations come from except the material outside?

'Je n'admets comme sûres que mes sensations, et je respecte mais ne subis pas les idées des autres' (I, 583). If Vallès could hardly be idea-proof, he resists such invasion much more pugnaciously than that of sensations, which he seeks avidly. He often talks of sights, smells, tastes, noises as *irritating* his senses, and he cherishes them for that very reason; he revels in being got at. No doubt, as when he saluted Dickens, he saw this sensory alertness as a key way of keeping faith with the child within. The child, before eyes start to get myopic, before tongues and lungs become coated and dulled by tobacco, unhealthy diets, urban pollution. The child, freer from the conventions which inhibit grown-ups from frank display of or delight in sensuality: touching or smelling eagerly what attracts, or indeed repels, making a shindig, eavesdropping and butting in. 'Il faut que la jeunesse boive la vie par les lèvres, les narines et les prunelles!' (II, 816). A different kind of brainwashing from school: a mental spring-cleaning.

Such attitudes led the prissy Bourget to pronounce: 'Nul écrivain n'a été emprisonné plus que celui-là dans la sensation personnelle et animale des choses'. Unable to transform such brute material on to the higher plane of the intellect, Vallès knuckled under to 'la tyrannie de chaque secousse venue du dehors'. Deliriously, this arch-conservative concludes that 'Vallès fut un exemplaire, et le plus saisissant peut-être, du nihiliste français'. [2] Mistrust of the body could scarcely go further.

Corbin, a historian of smell, sees, or sniffs, straighter, if he too reaches weird conclusions. Starting from the persuasive premise that smell has always been in the pits of the sensory hierarchy, he sets out to give tongue to 'le silence olfactif'. Vallès, who loved noisy smells, championed the underdog and would not turn up his nose at the underarm. Smell is often dismissed as betokening the animal or the barely distinguishable savage, though we all need to smell danger in order to survive, and enjoy the erotic and gustatory pleasures of smells. Vallès is clearly uninterested in the odour of sanctity; that of erect, fallen humankind suffices. In *L'Enfant,* the mother's onslaught of scrubbing aims to purify the *indécrottable* son of all the dirt he loves; in her campaign to 'clarify' his nose, she wants to hose out its grosser residues. Here too she apes the bourgeoisie in its fastidiousness (still relative, as Corbin stresses, until well into the twentieth century). Not only does Jacques Vingtras love to be waist-deep in rivers, he longs, more generally, to be submerged in sense impressions. Even so, Vallès is a world away from the decadent nasal orgies of Flaubert, Baudelaire, the Goncourts or Huysmans. For Corbin, 'Vallès adopte tout ce qui fait suffoquer le bourgeois'.[3] I believe Vallès would have experienced sensory deprivation in our largely deodorised society. He was not perturbed by bad or strong odours (he could take a tannery): it was smells per se that interested him. They are frank; they do not play double games. This is another area in which Vallès went naturally against the grain.

Let us sink to the pungent area of scatology: in *L'Enfant,* Vallès does not succumb to the persistent contemporary link of emanations (e.g. from latrines) as pestiferous. They are, for Jacques, a strong smell, and a reminder of his marginalised position next to them. Scatology is rare in Vallès's writing, but pointed when it occurs. Some pages in *L'Insurgé* mock the more absurd socialist ideas of Pierre Leroux in terms of bowel movements. In the same novel, a mayor locked up in a cupboard by insurgents is taken short; and there is a splendid joke comparing waiting for a watchword to waiting for a diamond to be defecated by a Negro slave miner (pp. 926 ff.; 982). The intention of all three instances is that of levelling. For Vallès as for Montaigne in the parting shot of *De l'expérience*, 'on the loftiest throne in the world, we still have to sit on our arse'. Vallès seems to feel a special affinity with the chamber-pot (*un jules* in the demotic), though ludically. One scene describes sunbeams dancing on one, and in another Jacques bangs on one during a dormitory *chahut* (II, pp. 170 and 883).

The most sustained treatment of sewage comes in *Le Candidat des pauvres*, when the hero is employed to write puffs for a shady enterprise that makes a pumping-machine to extract fertiliser from slimy sea-sand (*la tangue*):[4]

> Cette invention consiste à aspirer un produit avec une pompe, et à expirer (verbe actif) par le derrière de la pompe le produit avalé. Cela ressemble comme deux gouttes d'eau au jeu de la digestion; mais le produit qu'avale la pompe ne change pas de nature en route: il se transplante simplement de la bouche à l'orifice contraire, de la tête à la queue. (*CP*, p.394)

This replacement for human dung excites his verve; he obeys his employer. 'Je prends des notes qui tombent de sa bouche et qui, après avoir passé dans mon tuyau, doivent sortir en phrases sonores. Tout se tient: système de fonctionnement des choses et des hommes' (*ibid.*, p 395). A joky recycling of Marx's theory of reification. Vallès caps this tie-up of writing and metabolism with a splendid twist. Another *publiciste* comments:

> Cet engrais [...] a un tort, celui de ne pas sentir mauvais. Un engrais qui n'a pas d'odeur, et qu'on peut mettre sur la table d'un salon au lieu de l'isoler dans une table de nuit, un engrais qui n'a pas de fumet perd beaucoup aux yeux et au nez du public. (p. 402)

The whole episode displays Vallès's scatological imagination as not coy, but disciplined and joyous.

Women, to Vallès, were never sewers of iniquity, as they often were to other bachelor writers of the nineteenth century. It has been calculated that only a minority of workers actually married throughout that period, so in this at least Vallès was on a par with plebeian (and Bohemian) practice.[5] He may never have met the perfect (available) partner. No outsider, certainly at a century's distance, could dare to speculate how the experience of a wretched marriage enacted before his young eyes might have put him off for life against marrying. Little is in fact known of his relationships with women, of which he had a fair share. We know his printed attitudes. Up to the Commune he seemed to think of women principally as a warrior's rest. Though a confining view, this at least escapes the retrograde, virulent antifeminism of Proudhon. 'Elles n'apparaissent point dans l'arène, attendent à la porte la fin du combat et se contentent de mêler leurs larmes au sang des blessés' (I, 371). This (given Vallès's prejudices) curiously Roman and gladiatorial picture occurs close to a passage where, in an unusually mean-spirited way, he attacks the revolutionary sympathiser Madame Roland for plagiarising Rousseau in her memoirs, and for behaving like a Cornelian Roman heroine: she is a *victime du livre*. Her crime is unyielding stiffness; Vallès prefers pliable, voluptuous women. 'L'on aime, au soir des jours bien combattus, à s'oublier dans les bras faibles de ces anges de grâce ou de dévouement qui essuient d'une main aussi fière, sur les fronts lassés, la sueur du triomphe ou la poussière de la défaite' (p. 776). Win or lose, you want your woman waiting for you, preferably big-breasted, like the lady barber who offered 'à mon cœur d'innocent sa gorge de Percheronne pour oreiller!' (*SEP*, p. 34). A Lesbian bearded woman troubles him, like many another male, no doubt (I, 735). *Pace* feminists, I do not think we should transfer to the man the writer's occasional obsession with rape in plots, in his *feuilletons*, where it seems a commonplace, unthinking accompaniment to other forms of melodrama. And when, discussing public opinion, he urges journalists 'Bravez-la, ou plutôt que de lui céder, violez-la! Après le viol, grosse de vous, elle est capable de vous aimer', he is possibly echoing the elder Dumas's macho attitude to historical exactitude.

The real, frank sensuality of Vallès emerges in the trilogy, notably *L'Enfant* and *Le Bachelier*. *L'Insurgé* records a change of attitude towards the status of women (though ambivalence hangs on). 'Quand les femmes s'en mêlent, quand la ménagère pousse son homme, quand elle arrache le drapeau noir qui flotte sur la marmite pour le planter entre deux pavés, c'est que le soleil se lèvera sur une ville en révolte' (*Ins.*, p. 959). Having seen them in action, he now accepts and values militant, combative women. Yet, late in life, he was still positing for girls a man-centred vocation. Because he believed republicanism to be riddled with its own religiosity, he disapproved of girls' *lycées*. If girls are locked up in separation, they will lose their feminine graces: 'Elles auront le cœur engarçonné' (II, 727). Can 'Vive la différence!' be a pro-woman slogan?

The body, at its most gripping in women, also has its constantly laughable dimension: clumsiness, sexual fiasco, physical idiosyncrasy. It lends itself to caricature. Caricature seizes on one feature and aggrandises it, so that it dominates the supporting cast. It is a form of objectification or freezing, though many caricatures have preserved, in a second sense, those who might otherwise be forgotten. *Charge*, wider in French than English, embraces: burden, military onslaught, indictment, exaggeration, and caricature. Vallès okayed Gill's dog-caricature of him with one word: 'Chargez': charge!; pile it on thick (Gille, pp. v-vi). Some imagine that pictures speak louder than words, that they have a more immediate and telling impact over the whole sensibility of the receiver. In nineteenth-century France, this belief led to prior censorship, not, as with texts, *post facto*. In an age of only partial literacy, images could affect a wider slice of the population than prose. Verbal caricature seeks to straddle the two domains.

A great fan of Daumier and Gill, Vallès's many portraits of people are often caricatural, in that they isolate for emphasis a salient detail (sometimes a string of them). The intention is not always cruel. Jacques Vingtras's much-abused bum, the highly articulate hands of his dumb aunt: here the part for the whole partakes of a humanising process which calls for sympathy. It rarely seems like a dismembering. Like physiognomists, and most of us, Vallès believed there was a direct correspondence between inner being and outward manifestation. His frequently stated conviction of his own ugliness is, for Bellet, partly a borrowing of the idea of dangerous unattractiveness in Romantic or revolutionary heroes—so different from the flawless *sang-froid* of ancient statuary—and partly a resuscitation of the topos of the grotesque, *le monstre* (I, 1600). Yet contemporary accounts belie this self-dramatising myth; and Courbet's portrait captures a handsome man. In *Le Bachelier*, the pathetic tale of Edgard, the hydrocephalous child, chimes in with this taste for grotesquerie. As in cartoons, an inflated head on a foreshortened trunk. The story might well be in callous taste, but infant draughtspeople also bloat the head / face to the detriment of the totality. It is also a black pun about marketable *misérabilisme*, for Jacques writes the commissioned story in the hope of becoming 'une grosse tête' of the magazine (*Bach.*, pp. 636-8).

Caricature obviously falls within the area of press freedom. Vallès held, whistling in the dark, that it was an honour to be an Aunt Sally. The trouble with this argument is that it could lessen the impact of derision. On the whole, he preferred social to political caricature (at least in the 1860s): 'Je m'amuse plus devant le ventre de Robert Macaire que devant la poire de Louis-Philippe' (I, 586). Yet caricature should be unreservedly iconoclastic in spirit, and democratically comprehensive in its targets (*ibid.*). All is fair, even the unjust, and better out in the open than festering inside.

Death, of course, is no joke, or only blackly. One of the blackest ironies (or *quiproquos*) in the life of Vallès, who eulogised irony, was that other people were shot in his place, mistaken for him, in the Bloody Week that terminated the Commune. This is especially ironic in that earlier his life had been bought by the system of paid substitutes for military service. Apart from native rhetorical flourish, a lifelong reason why Vallès declaimed his readiness to die for his beliefs is that another route to premature death—potentially giving your life for your country—was denied him. As Vallès loathed proxy living, he may have felt some shame at proxy dying. Is focussing on death an obsession, or a sign of health? Pascal, whom Vallès read with interest, enjoins us to think much of death. The difference is that Pascal sees this practice as an essential training for the life to come, whereas Vallès sees death as the chief enemy of this unique life. 'J'aime ce qui est vivant, au point que je ne sais pas comprendre ce qui semble mort' (I, 1561).

Duels dramatically juxtapose the two. They are, in theory, the perfect form of combat for the individualist, who can choose (with his opponent) the time, the place, the weapon and (off his own bat) the adversary. Vallès fought at least two duels and was wounded in one of them, probably in the late 1850s. It was an often sought-after occupational hazard for journalists at that time, tacitly supported by the regime on the principle of divide and rule. 'C'est au nom de la responsabilité personnelle des journalistes, et contre toute idée de responsabilité collective du périodique, qu'on les obligeait, sous le Second Empire, à signer tous leurs articles. Cette personnalisation, favorisant les polémiques et les duels convenait parfaitement au pouvoir impérial' (I, 1388), as Bellet points out. Yet Vallès switched to criticising the duel, in the 1860s, as a barbarous and stupid non-solution to differences, while keeping his hand in for the sake of self-reliance (p. 755). Just as, in that period, he turned against Blanquist theories of political violence, so he saw this private variant as brutality (p. 866). Yet he never makes a clean break, seeing as he does the duel as a sign of revolt, the protest of caged men (p. 872).

Boxing, generally if not inevitably less lethal, met with his less ambiguous enthusiasm. His whole existential style was to keep coming back for more, less like Oliver Twist than like a boxer refusing to throw in the towel. If Flaubert is a heavyweight and Jules Renard a featherweight, Vallès is a welterweight in French literature. His love of 'la vie d'échange' involves copping it as well as dishing it out. 'Tit for tat' can be hostile (retaliation) or sociable (return of favour). What Vallès valued in boxing—especially the French variant, *la savate*, using also the feet—is a controlled violence, self-expenditure, and that *retenue* he rarely displays elsewhere. It combines physicality and grace (in this respect like ballet), and prowess at it gave Vallès the confidence that often eluded him in other ventures. The British form of barefist pugilism appalled, and magnetised, him (*RL*, II, 1296). Even there, however, the sudden swerves, feints and so on appealed to a man forever quick on his feet. Boxing is a serious sport, and surely Bellet is right to comment: 'Vallès rêve d'une harmonie entre ce qu'il faut appeler (le rapport qui jure est juste) la savate et la littérature' (*JVJR*, p. 236). Jarring connexions are central to Vallès.

Though Vallès does not mention rugby, he envisions life as a scrum: 'Ce fut une mêlée, et je m'y jetai à corps perdu' (*Enf.*, p. 339). The playground taught him more valuable lessons than the school-room. Even the gym, too regulated, had to be resisted. 'Virer sur une barre, c'était comme faire des versions grecques ou des vers latins; tourner pour la gloire, suer pour la galerie, travailler *dans l'espace*. Il me fallait toucher ou essayer de toucher le danger, avoir une cible à atteindre et des coups à redouter' (*SEP*, p. 95). This refusal of being a star turn, of showing off in 'exercices à mine romaine'; the sense that this form of pedagogy, too, loses contact with the common ground; this preference for the risk of two-sided conflict, reminds that a favourite cliché of the defenders of classical studies was the mental gymnastics that they supposedly promoted. What was perverted in reality (physical education) was championed in theory (Latin is a test of the mind's muscles). An American visiting teacher reported that 'gymnastic apparatus was almost unknown; practically all the swimming exercises referred to in the official syllabuses were performed on dry land; the boxing was a series of formal movements against imaginary opponents'.[6] This may be why shadow-boxing is such an insistent feature of French intellectual life, together with 'going through the motions': fulfilling formal requirements, the letter rather than the spirit.

What of the body politic? Vallès's plea for sport is part of a wider campaign. Even the myopic, overweight Zola pleaded for a greater stress on the body's fitness in schools. Barrès, of course, wanted to divert this to military training, saying that Napoleon's campaigns were 'de prodigieuses parties de footing'. Maupassant blamed the cerebral *baccalauréat* for mass-producing spindly youths. [7] In *La Rue à Londres,* Vallès explicitly attributes a good share of Great Britain's (then) predominance to its sporting traditions, which the French should emulate. More specifically, he suggests that international bouts are a continuation of war by other means, and preferable ones: a country 'defeats' another in the person of its representative pugilist. The film *All Quiet on the Western Front* restates this intriguing variant of pacifism.

The Setting

The body at play or at work cannot exist without a context, a physical milieu. We must start where Vallès originated, in the provinces, but stressing, as he did, more the countryside than the small town. In all his writings, he exploits the countryside as a buffer state both against the prison-like home and against the big city. Metaphorically speaking, as Vallès habitually does, we could say that he was cyclically tempted to beat his militant sword into a pacific ploughshare. As Gille said, Vallès was disarmed by nature. [8] If there was any element of seeking Romantic consolation there, Vallès was of course responding like millions of townees. Permanent in Vallès is the need for a truce, an oasis, a warrior's rest. His whole use of the happier memories from provincial childhood is this switching off, letting up. It is another unusual aspect of his militancy, like his humour. For once like Rousseau, at such time he enjoys just existing, *le doux far-niente,* the sweet sensation of being alive with no distractions or ambitions. The activist off duty (*flânerie* in Paris fulfils the same need). Here Vallès edges near the ancient myth of the Original Oneness, the melting of all those barriers and hierarchies which the Mother tried to beat into him.

A further myth embraces 'Auvergne' (a loose-fitting term in Vallès's word-hoard). His approximateness, his hit-or-miss approach, extends to geography. His native Velay at times embraces, somewhat drunkenly, the Auvergne and even the Cévennes. It is the image, the passionate stereotype, that matters more to him than topographic accuracy. The Cévennes adds a more revolutionary bite to the Auvergne.

> Pays curieux que ce Velay, où les torrents ont fait les chemins et où les volcans grondent sous la neige! Race étrange, dont les fils portent tous au cœur un besoin terrible de liberté, et même l'instinct de la révolte, si bien que leur vie est toujours troublée, et qu'ils meurent, un à un dans l'ombre, écrasés par leur propre force, victimes de leur fierté farouche (I, 392).

This sounds sombrely grandiloquent, yet a historian like Eugen Weber speaks of 'the especially strong individualism of Auvergne and Velay'.[9] A partial reason for this annexation of the Auvergne was that, in Paris, current mythology bloated the numbers of *Auverpins*. Often a kind of stand-in Jew, and the focus of resentment, intra-French racism. In addition, Vallès clearly wanted to equip himself with suitable forebears, to fit himself into a rebellious tradition located in a harsh, dramatic landscape.

On the area's peasants themselves, Vallès fluctuates. As well as exalting their resistance to authority, he can also see their wilful self-blinding. 'Ces pays-là, désolés et montagneux, deviennent des nids de fanatiques: fanatiques de n'importe quel Dieu, catholique ou jacobin' (I, 977). At other times, he echoes the standard view of peasants as cautious, conservative, self-centred, but recognises (as in *Les Blouses*) their willingness to erupt in *jacqueries* if pushed too far (II, pp. 1374-6). Even so, Vallès's peasants are not seen from the fearful distance of urbanites like Zola, Huysmans or Maupassant, mythologists like George Sand, or provincial bourgeois like Flaubert. If Vallès does mythify the peasantry, at least he spared it the traditional stereotype of bestial ignorance (the peasant as original sin, in the eyes of one charitable country priest), an inferior race hardly human at all. He largely omits superstition, sorcery, the cult of local saints, faith-healers—all still common during his century even in increasingly dechristianised regions.

In the city, Vallès retained his great love of flowers, a luxury he could ill forgo. 'J'adorais surtout les fleurs brillantes, le reflet rouge des pivoines, la bigarrure des tulipes, l'orgueil des lys. Je me repaissais de la joie des yeux: il me fallait les hautes tiges, les grands panaches, et je préférais une rose vermeille sans odeur à une rose pâle qui embaumait' (I, 668). He never lost this love of strong primary colours. As for wider nature, his moods vary. In one, he can write: 'C'est moins, je crois, que le spectacle est beau que parce qu'il est vaste qu'on aime l'Océan, la plaine: cadres sans bornes que l'horizon arrête, où la pensée étend à son aise les ailes' (p. 678). This has its more melancholy aspects: 'On n'est pas impunément, que voulez-vous? le fils d'un pays triste et grand, si triste et si grand que l'homme y disparaît. [...] Il n'est plus maître du paysage; c'est le paysage qui le domine: la nature l'écrase' (p. 977). More often, despite his fondness for occasional stasis, he records a lay Pascalian horror of immensity, of manless space and sterile contemplation: 'Le détail se noie dans l'infini' (*ibid.*). This holds true for the sea as well as the land. At Jersey, he writes: 'La mer m'a toujours attristé, d'une tristesse sans grandeur. C'est vide, vide! et ça roucoule comme une colombe bête. [...] Pour me plaire, la mer devrait hurler contre un navire en détresse, elle devrait au moins être couverte de bateaux de travail, être une rue menant à Terre-Neuve ou plus loin, une rue vivante' (II, pp. 1981-2). The term 'rue' is significant. Once he had known Paris, Vallès could hardly avoid being comparative, and using it as a yardstick.

In many cultures, the opposition metropole/provinces is felt as chic versus hick. With Vallès, it is more a shuttle. He evokes the country most lyrically from the city, and vice versa. The provinces represented principally his past, his childhood and youth. Like many temperamental (non-ideological) anarchists, he was loath to see any of what he cherished vanishing in the dubious name of progress. This oscillating temperament, while it thrived on periodic refurbishment in the country, could not live fully without the stimulus of city activity. As well as broad vistas and clean air, he needed the promiscuous contact with his fellow creatures in the cramped quarters of Paris. But neither pole can be divorced from the other; he sometimes felt that the ideal would be six months in the capital and a half-year in the country (I, pp. 702-703). While he loved stillness in nature, he detested it in museums or on city streets. When he went back home to Le Puy shortly before his death, he hated it. Even London, for *un Parisien parisiennant* such as he had become, would be better than a small provincial town (II, 1394). He learned to be deeply grateful for Paris. 'J'aime ce Paris, de toute la reconnaissance de mes douleurs. J'y ai tant combattu et tant souffert, sur ce pavé! J'ai de la peau de moi collée aux cloisons de garnis et aux pierres des rues' (*TP*, p. 34). He can wax as lyrical about it as a nature-poet about nature. 'L'air de Paris, lui, grise et ne saoule pas. Cela s'aspire, comme se siffle un verre de vin qui vous pique la langue et vous chatouille la cervelle, avec des douceurs de languette de soie' (II, 1334). In Paris, even the poor can live it up, in dream; enjoy ocular possession of the good things of life. While knowing that lavish shop-displays are a come-on sales-gimmick, he wonders: why not extract some profit from this profiteering and feast on the spectacle? (p. 1335).

Un-Parisian (it would be unfair to say un-French) enough to refuse to be a creature of fashion (intellectual, if not vestimentary), Vallès's 'articles de Paris' in the 1880s were not *articles de Paris* in the other sense: luxury items. Surroundings go deep.

'La rue' is the crucial term. 'Celle qui mène au boulevard et celle qui aboutit au faubourg: la rue que tous traversent, pour aller à l'hospice ou au bal, au bureau ou à l'atelier, à la Bourse, à la Halle, à la Roquette, au cimetière! [...] Pleine d'odeurs, de bruits, pavée de hasards, où tous se rencontrent ou se retrouvent' (I, 936). *La rue,* democratic space, merits its time-honoured metaphor, is truly an artery, the life-blood of the city. *La rue* is smaller-scale than *le boulevard,* and does not carry the connotation of smart frivolity stuck to that word. It houses work and pleasure, life and death; it is the open air, not the cloistral indoors. Bellet quite rightly stresses that, in his journalist role, Vallès often used a leg-man to prospect for him, and that much of his material came from readings. Thus, *la rue* was already literarised before Vallès's version (*JVJR*, pp. 110-11). He had a good reporter's sense for relevant detail, the gist, but this of course leaves much out. Vallès's Paris is as lacunary as his Commune or even his autobiographical fiction. What he never leaves out is women, respectable or marginalised, parading cynosurely on *la rue.*

However profound a Parisian he later became, in the Commune, as an ally of the federalists, Vallès favoured decentralisation: responsibility for government given back to local communities. After its long history of dominating, ruling and bleeding France, Paris tried to offer itself in 1871 as an exemplar of self-emancipation. Even though the Commune was not, as its enemies diagnosed, a disease, it did aim to be contagious. It failed in this, as in most of its other experiments. As a result, after the Commune, and exile, Vallès became a full Parisian, partly because of the near-total anti-Commune stance of the *ruraux,* which upturned Paris into the underdog and thus endeared it to Vallès.

And yet he remained to the end, to convert Renard's *bon mot,* 'un parisien du Danube', [10] a plain-speaking yokel. Léon Daudet exaggerates his discomfort when he calls him 'un transplanté social douloureux', [11] though the term 'transplanté' is more accurate than 'déraciné' (with its Barrésian overtones) or 'déclassé'. As Vallès once said: 'Nous sommes une nation de déclassés' (I, 922). If all are, nobody is. Zeldin reminds that, in the nineteenth century, 'social mobility was still called *déclassement'.* [12]

After the uplift of the Commune, Vallès could write more confidently of man and *physis:* 'La nature prend le ton et le pli que les hommes lui donnent, si forte qu'elle paraisse et quoiqu'elle semble nous tenir captifs dans ses bras' (*TP,* pp. 328-9). The same confidence gave birth to the Trilogy.

Chapter Six

L'Enfant

In *Foucault's Pendulum*, Umberto Eco writes: 'The literature of memory: he knew himself that it was the last refuge of scoundrels'. Sometimes, no doubt, but for Vallès the past was the true homeland. The only convincing fiction he could write (and he applied the same criterion to other writers) was born when he could master his facts. If home is 'the place where, when you have to go there, / They have to take you in', [1] it is also starting blocks. By the standards of ordinary success, Vallès, who never called his three novels a trilogy, was a late developer.

His fiction is heavily autobiographical, but not umbilicist. Just as simplicity cannot be swotted up, nor a sophisticate easily go native, so a grown man cannot rebecome his earlier self. He has, ineluctably, hindsight, and can hardly spurn the benefits of experience. All he can sanely aim for is to locate what is left of the child in the adult and use this to enrich his vision. Pedantic forms of keeping faith with an earlier self are self-denying and counter-productive. His old friend, Arthur Ranc, said in 1905: 'Il n'y a pas, à ma connaissance, de faussetés dans les volumes *Vingtras,* tout au plus quelques exagérations sans importance'. [2] The fact remains that Vallès took considerable liberties with the chronology of his life and omitted some significant experiences. Autobiographical fiction is a kind of double vision, which notoriously blurs, distorts, overlays. Vallès had to tackle the problem of getting X from A to B and onwards. Is it a smooth trajectory, or a zigzag (two steps forward, one step back)? If one of his profoundest desires was to avoid repeating his parents, being a chip off the old blockheads, then his retelling of his experience must refuse to imprison his hero. A kind of freedom, if not that indeterminacy so seductive to recent theorists, must be engineered.

Throughout the trilogy, life is lived and seen as a series of only partly resolved contradictions. Jacques Vingtras is frequently on the brink of throwing in the sponge, but then finding the will to come back for more. In each volume, life is a combat zone, with truces, parleys, assaults, cave-ins, harangues, wounds and deaths. It is an *exchange.* As he was permanently in opposition, Vallès thinks oppositionally. In the trilogy, he gets his own back: avenges himself, and reclaims his past.

A good deal of its material had been already aired, indirectly or proudly, in journalistic pieces, well before its actual composition. The trilogy reselects and reorders all this scattered material, and more. The two major first runs are *Lettre de Junius* (1861) and *Le Testament d'un blagueur*. In the first draft, the trio is an aunt, uncle and child—an obvious displacement, and a masking. Yet the aunt prepares for the mother, with her vetoes on coddling, the awful clothes and endless rules of etiquette she imposes on the child. The uncle is a cold fish. In an early version of the 'Victimes du livre' theme, he is spoilt by his 'Roman' idea of parental duty: 'Le pater familias antique, l'oncle familias moderne' (I, 133). We should note, however, that Vallès is more conventionally respectful here than in *L'Enfant*. Even so, in an anticipation of Nizan's outcry—'J'avais vingt ans. Je ne laisserai personne dire que c'est le plus bel âge de la vie'[3]—Vallès claims also to counter a received idea: 'Attaquer [...] une vieille phrase qui court le monde, à savoir: que l'enfance est le plus bel âge de la vie' (p. 129). *Lettre de Junius* is more cut-and-dried in its presentation of family conflict, and lacks the complexity. and the brio of *L'Enfant*.

   Le Testament d'un blagueur edges nearer to *L'Enfant*, though as a whole it is unsatisfactory, since the mystery of the hero's suicide is never elucidated. Nor is there much evidence of his supposed countervailing capacity for *la blague*. In this version, the parents are unremittingly cruel, and the mother is far more religious, breeding fear of hell-fire in the child. Although Vallès occasionally strikes the exact sardonic note ('On m'a envoyé à Paris en qualité de *bête à concours*. J'aurais pu venir par le train des bestiaux'—I, 1121), the derisive disgust more often sails unproductively over the top. On his education, he says:

> Je vais mâcher et remâcher, broyer, digérer, sécréter l'hexamètre, toute la saison. On ramassera mon fumier, et l'on recueillera mes rejets comme ceux d'un empoisonné: je les ravalerai par un trou de ma mémoire et le jour du grand concours, un matin de juillet, je recracherai le tout sur le papier, comme un nègre *rend*, derrière un buisson, le diamant qu'il a volé! (p. 1122).

This last simile forms part of a very contorted set of images of ingurgitation and regurgitation, already classic, of course, in student mythology. This testament contains a good many people, places and events that will reappear in *L'Enfant* (Mlle. Balandreau, la Polonie, clothes as imprisonment, the desire to be an artisan, and the complaints against classical education). But they seem more like beefing than indictment. Perhaps Vallès needed to get away from the scene of the crimes against the person before he could organise his fiction. Bellet remarks that this text was recited, at dinners, before it was written down, or rather dictated to a secretary (p. 1737). An over-genial, captive audience was the last thing he needed to test his authenticity.

   One of the commoner uses of the novel since its inception has been the educational: educating the hero or heroine and, in the process, enlightening the reader —the novel of growing up, being schooled (by family, school and society). This option involves not only the largely linear narrative that most storytelling requires but also an instantly recognisable experience. We have all been children; few of us have hunted whales or built a cathedral spire. Was it English understatement that made Vallès write to his faithful friend, Malot, from England: 'Des mémoires de moi seraient presque intéressants' (*Corr. M.,* p. 60)? He was actually talking of his larger-scale project, but the attitude—voiding himself into his work—is constant: 'Je mettrai sans doute là-dedans tout ce que j'ai, j'y logerai ce qui est *moi*, je me dépenserai jusqu'au bout, et quand ce sera fini, il se peut bien que je n'aie plus rien dans le ventre' (p. 146). More specifically on *L'Enfant* itself, he declares: 'La politique ne sera qu'incidente et viendra tard. Ce que je veux faire c'est un bouquin intime, d'émotion naïve, de passion jeune—que tout le monde pourra lire' (p. 98). He admits predecessors, for instance Alphonse Daudet's *Jack,* but feels sure he will create something fresh: 'Mon roman [...] est très vert, très ironique, original en diable il me semble' (p. 101). Its alternative, sardonic, title could be: *Les Plus Belles Années de la vie*. He had a clear sight of what he was creating: 'J'ai voulu faire un livre de sensations, presque de pensées, primesautier, coupé—avec une leçon terrible au bout malgré les ironies voulues, les grossièretés de parti pris' (p. 110). Although all the quotations above might strike a reader as typical of that song and dance, that *boniment*, that so fascinated Vallès when practised by *saltimbanques* , I believe Vallès had to talk through his project with his friend Malot, since, otherwise, he would have been talking largely to himself. He needed, here as elsewhere, 'la vie d'échange'.

The material and psychological conditions of the gestation of *L'Enfant* were harsh and dramatic: exile, censorship in France, considerable debts, self-doubts, and oscillations of ambition. Would he attempt a vast sociohistorical fresco, or stick to autobiographical fiction? He was not made for the invention of a purely imaginary world, and English society remained largely alien to him. Writing *L'Enfant*, Vallès could hear a crying, suffering child in the next apartment. He sent the contraband manuscript, disguised as padding for a doll, in a sardine-box resembling a small coffin, soon after the death of his love-child born of a liaison with a teacher. This sequence is over-determined; anyone can make a meal of it, though the loaded package was in fact a practical solution to escape the eyes of authority. Thus Philippe Bonnefis can comment: 'La finition est un problème d'obstétrique et non de simple rhétorique'. [4] For himself, Vallès explained: 'Je crois que je ne devrais pas dicter la colère. [...] C'est le lecteur qui, je l'espère, criera ce que je n'ai pas crié' (*Corr. A.,* p. 250). He appeals, then, to a free reader, but is not averse from jogging each of us in the ribs.

As well as the displacement effected in *Lettre de Junius* (and still, on occasion, in *L'Enfant*), there is that of pseudonyms. Despite his intense egopetality ('egocentricity' does not fit), Vallès often used pseudonyms out of a kind of *pudeur*, a desire to give aesthetic distance to real-life models, and, of course, at several crises in his life, a desire to survive by disguise. He felt an aversion not only from Baudelaire but from 'le coeur mis à nu' (see *Corr. M.*, p. 60). The disguises are often transparent. He wants to be caught, like the child playing hide-and-seek. In *Lettre de Junius*, repeating the tactic of *L'Argent*, he confesses: 'Je suis un inconnu qui a voulu forcer l'attention, me faire un nom en cachant le mien' (I, 129). It resembles the *roman à clef*, where readers' guesses at true identities are encouraged. Several of the pseudonyms he used while writing the trilogy in exile are connected either with his family history (Pascal—mother's maiden name) or provincial roots (La Chaussade, Colomb). They are giveaway, like *armes parlantes* in heraldry, to those who have minds to twig. Instinctively, he wants to stand up and be counted, to come clean. Vingtras itself may have been the name of a French doctor in London, or coincidentally that of a French occultist condemned by the Pope in 1843, and certainly an assonantal partner to Vallès.

L'Enfant

> They fuck you up, your mum and dad.
> They may not mean to, but they do.
> They fill you with the faults they had
> And add some extra, just for you.
>
> (PHILIP LARKIN: 'This Be the Verse')

> Vous ne réussirez pas à me dénaturer
>
> (DIDEROT: *Supplément au Voyage de Bougainville*)

As Sartre, and common experience, tell us, society is first mediated, transfused, to us via our families. It was inevitable that Vallès should begin at the beginning, where we are all made, unmade, or make ourselves. Just as Nizan wanted to smash the iconic view of youth as the best years of our lives, so Vallès worked to dispel the foggy myth of idyllic childhood. *L'Enfant* tells of child-abuse. It cuts very close to the bone, and is a crucial first stage to Vallès's wider indictment of all forms of victimisation. It is no joke, and very funny. Its hero, Jacques, gags (jokes/retches) against parental gags (vetoes).

The basic opposition within *L'Enfant* is between home as prison, punitive and restrictive, and various efforts to escape. In a typical instance of pointed hyperbole, Jacques finds the local jail gayer in atmosphere than home or school. In addition, of course, he is attracted to *irréguliers* (especially one inmate who had killed a gendarme). It is clearly a kind of inverted snobbery, of reversed values, but it serves to underline how anti-natural the parental home is, totally lacking in laughter, light, common-or-garden flowers. The novel begins in ordinariness, semi-anonymity: 'Voilà le petit Chose qu'on fouette' (p. 141): thingamabob, which, like *chose,* embraces indiscriminately objects and people. Though not an exhibitionist mooner like Rousseau, Jacques offers us his belaboured rump as an image of a brutalised, not loveless but misloved, childhood. From the start, his parents, especially his mother, seek to impose a severe system of demands and sanctions, and their son in response seeks ways of circumventing it. A kindly neighbour, Mlle. Balandreau, offers to stand in as beater, but merely slaps her hands to simulate the punishment, and dresses his previous wounds. The system seeks also to inflict guilt, as when the father cuts his hand while carving a rough toy for the child. While knowing he is an innocent culprit, Jacques admits his guilt in a childish mixture of injured innocence and assumed culpability. 'Ma mère a bien fait de me battre' (p. 143). He makes prodigious efforts to justify her irrational logic:

> Elle se sacrifiait, elle étouffait ses faiblesses, elle tordait le cou au premier mouvement pour se livrer au second. Au lieu de m'embrasser, elle me pinçait;—vous croyez que cela ne lui coûtait pas!—Il lui arriva même de se casser les ongles. Elle me battait pour mon bien, voyez-vous. Sa main hésita plus d'une fois; elle dut prendre son pied. (p. 202)

This is Romantic irony: the second part of the last sentence militates against the spirit of the first half. As such, it is a mock defence. Vallès records her beatings as virtuoso performances; she is a one-woman-band with her son as the instruments. It sounds like Ravel's *Bolero,* a mechanised set of variations on a process: 'Elle m'a travaillé dans tous les sens, pincé, balafré, tamponné, bourré, souffleté, frotté, cardé et tanné' (p. 258). In fact, when she leaves off beating him at one period, he feels lost: 'Ce chômage m'inquiète' (p. 259). In such ways does the abnormal become the norm. He worries that his hide will go soft. He even stretches his understanding of her behaviour to include the pleasure she takes: 'Ma mère est contente quand elle me donne une gifle—cela l'émoustille, c'est le pétillement du hoche-queue, le plongeon du canard' (p. 197). This sounds almost approving. What is going on?

First of all: why should a child be any less illogical than grown-ups? Jacques is governed by a perverse but dogged logic: the effort to find good, or a less gratuitous evil, in parents to all appearances monstrous. This is a clear sign of a split consciousness. The child, wanting to be loved or at least to be allowed to live more naturally, assumes the logic of his opponents, whilst retaining an instinctive sense that this is not the way for people to live together. To understand is not to forgive all, but it is to mitigate resentment and to fellow-feel. Vallès here goes against the grain, though more down-to-earthly than Huysmans's Des Esseintes. In literary terms, the reminder that there is generally more to most people than meets the cursory or jaundiced eye is surely one of the prime functions of a good novel: a learning, or relearning, experience for the reader as for the protagonist. So, Vallès makes the boy apparently internalise his mother's force-feeding. The product is a strange kind of irony (not unlike free indirect speech, which can be similarly ambivalent), since surely the child cannot be so totally on his tormentor's side. Vallès allows for the well-attested fact that battered children very often do blame themselves for their suffering, and protect their parents by all kinds of subterfuges. Jacques joins in the conspiracy that puts him in the wrong. His semi-conscious wish is to find a rationale for irrationality. Besides, he even enjoys his mother's tyranny to the extent that it recognises him as a rebel, which flatters his ego. Even so, she brainwashes him so unrelentingly that it takes all his instinctual resources not to believe with her that 'il ne faut pas gâter les enfants'. Gâter = ruin / treat. He withstands the former, and holds out for the latter as a right. In all this, he works hard to understand the enemy: an invaluable lesson that he will go on adding to in adult life. Miming the enemy, taking her/him off, is a prime way of resisting and indeed of striking back.

The mother is energised by the fairly universal doctrine that 'Mother knows best'. As she has no outside work, she can focus on her only child the burning rays of her Spartan solicitude. Vallès presents Jacques's childhood as a rigorous training scheme in stoical endurance. Children, in the mother's view, must not be spoilt, pandered to, nor allowed to exercise freewill. Only Jacques's mother-wit saves him from his genitrix. And yet, unwittingly, she teaches her son craftiness, the art of survival: per absurdum ad astra! Everything she stridently disapproves of, he values. She steels him to rebel. One of the many ironic contradictions of her programme of upbringing is that, destining him for conformity, she thinks she is doing the opposite. When she stops him licking some windfall sweets, she adds sententiously: 'On commence par lécher le ventre des bonbons, on finit par lécher...' (p. 182). She drifts off into euphemism, as befits her pseudo-petit-bourgeois 'gentility'. She wants not only to chastise her son's flesh, but chasten language. Her vetoes include rationing rare pleasures. The child wants freedom, not parole. Of sweets he says: 'Je les aime quand j'en ai trop' (p. 183). With perfect naturalness he loathes seeing pleasures corrupted by ethics. She never sees that kindness (and she does have sporadic onsets of humanity, when she drops her guard and lapses into simplicity) would have disciplined him far more effectively than severity ever has.

All she retains of whatever religious velleities once animated her are the twin tenets of crime and punishment. The forgiving God is terribly absent from her scheme of beliefs. She has a near-total lack of commiseration, not only for Jacques but for any unfortunates. It is not that she has no feelings, for she puts real passion, misapplied, into her regime. She often talks of her son in the third person, distancing and impersonalising him. Obsessed with him, she discounts and belittles him. At least, however, the child knows where he is with such a rigid person: she is consistent, not random. Yet it can only be sadism, a refinement of the lust to damage, that makes her, at one point, decide against a beating, for her son is largely inured to that, and opt for the worst sanction a sociable child can suffer: being deprived of his friends. (It is also part of her scheme to detach him from plebeian contacts). This act Jacques cannot justify: it is true, wicked cruelty. This swivelling between presenting the mother as comprehensible or as alien adds complexity to a figure who could have become an automaton and nothing else.

A conditioning programme, Pavlovian in its rigour, forces Jacques over five years to eat what he most loathes: onion hash. [5] The very day that he can stomach it without looking queasy, his mother takes it off the menu, for it was self-denial that she has been drumming into him. The progression goes from (those terrible French infinitives of legislation) 'ne pas s'écouter' to 'se forcer'. It is a regime in every sense. Life is not about pleasure. The mother labours constantly towards edification. 'Tu as pour mère une Romaine, Jacques!' (p. 280), as the hero ruefully notes. She works by aversion therapy. What he does like to eat, e.g. *gigot*, she gives him an over-bellyful of, so much, he relates, that he nearly ended up baaing (p. 219). The father, for once, teaches a far gentler and more durable lesson about respect for bread (p. 162). On the other hand, the mother's would-be genteel strictures about table-manners cause Jacques, when visiting, to respond hypocritically to offers of tasty food. Such conditioning goes some way towards setting up a divided nature, training versus impulse, with falsity as the end-product. When he lets her down, it is usually because she has hoisted him to a false and unsuitable height.

The mother adds etiquette (outward behaviour) to self-denial (inward constraint). She embarks Jacques on deportment lessons, in her overall plan to make 'un Monsieur' out of him, but, after months of practice, by a kind of saving gracelessness, Jacques reaches only the level of a theatrical bumpkin. Trying hard to slide his feet in the approved manner, he disembowels the headmaster's carpet with a nail protruding from his shoe. Scenes such as these are knockabout farce, silent comedies. Father and son, bending at the same moment to pick up an umbrella, bang their heads together. Even rare family kisses are mistimed, misplaced. The presentation of flowers to his father on his name-day involves a lengthy period of rehearsal and anticipatory dread, before the inevitable fiasco. A kind of unconscious pun places his laboriously hand-written card in the *table de nuit*: the accompaniment to the *pot de géranium* next to the jerry. Jacques has to clamber up to the high parental bed to present his gift, helped by the father hoisting him by the seat of his pants. The whole charm and ceremonial nature of the occasion is turned literally arseways round. Jacques spills the pot, soils the bed, and is booted out of the bedroom (pp. 185-7). With the most deadly serious intentions, the family trio, when changing abode, create traffic jams with their piled-up belongings, their always excess baggage. It is an unwilled number, a vaudeville routine, and there are repeat performances. Vallès milks such joke situations for all, at times even more, than they are worth. In his own life, reports present Vallès as an expert at clanging gaffes. So often, after a reasonably successful run in a job, he was fired for putting his foot in it. Yet this kind of failure is the most endearing part of Vallès, for it often rescues him from compromise.

Sartorial fiasco forced on the boy expands the attack on the parents, but also subjects the young hero to much mockery. This deflates him while inflating the description of grotesque clothes, ludicrous to behold, and constricting or abrasive to wear. Though his mother frequently accuses him of being a monster of ingratitude, the hideous clothes she foists on him turn him into *un monstre,* a freak. The habit makes the monkey. Once, the boy is dressed so weirdly that a traveller takes him for *une curiosité du pays,* and gallops up to inspect him. His mother's clothes reify him: 'J'ai l'air d'un poêle' (p. 166). They make him the odd one out. In exile, Vallès writes: 'Et il m'est donné, au sein même de ma ville natale, à douze ans, de connaître, isolé dans ce pantalon, les douleurs sourdes de l'exil' (*ibid.*),. They distance, imprison; they are killjoys. They remove him so far from normality that on occasions his own mother, the perpetrator, can hardly recognise him, were it not for the stigmata on his bottom. The irony is that she wants to show him off, but is foolish enough to imagine that such hotchpotch accoutrement, such patchwork quilts, will do anything but make a spectacle of him. Vallès often mentions breeches splitting, and the dangers of unmeant exhibitionism, but, given looser bags, Jacques resembles 'un canard dont le derrière pousse' (p. 295). As clothes, for Vallès, are always political badges, Jacques is concerned that some of his make him look like a Legitimist. Vallès connects clothes and ideas, education. In both cases, Jacques is made to inherit the rags and tatters of the past, reach-me-downs, just as he eats the left-overs of school meals. His makeshift apparel is forever a hindrance to unaffected existence.

Economy rules his destiny. 'Jusqu'ici je n'ai rien eu qui fût à moi, pas même ma peau' (p. 222). Although the mother trails bribes to egg him on to win prizes at school, she renegues. Via her control of family finances, she is the power behind the throne, or rather the rickety *chaire*, but she is unaware of the low esteem in which teachers like her husband are universally held. As Carassus says: 'Jacques ne peut rien dépenser, ne peut même pas se dépenser; il lui faut tout économiser: les habits, le gigot, les forces aussi. [...] Il lui faut mener une vie de caisse d'épargne. Seules gifles et fessées sont distribuées à profusion'. [6] The *tirelire*, savings to 'buy a man' to avoid military service, symbolises the future that never coincides with the present. Saving postpones; Jacques wants to enjoy life now.

As well as ubiquitous brainwashing, there are ritual ablutions. Historians of hygiene tell us that washing, at any social level, was at that time in France a rare event, seen as unhealthy if overdone. Jacques's mother seems ahead of her time in her ruthless persecution of dirt. She scrubs him with floor-soap weekly. Vallès's allusion to the Galatea legend (his allusions of this type are often hit-or-miss) is more of a joke than an invitation to depth (or even epidermis) psychology:

> Ma mère me jetait des seaux d'eau, en me poursuivant comme Galatée, et je devais comme Galatée—fuir pour être attrapé, mon beau Jacques! Je me vois encore dans le miroir de l'armoire, pudique dans mon impudeur, courant sur le carreau qu'on lavait du même coup, nu comme un amour, cul-de-lampe léger, ange du décrotté! Il me manquait un citron entre les dents, et du persil dans les narines, comme aux têtes de veau. J'avais leur reflet bleuâtre, fade et mollasse mais j'étais propre, par exemple. (pp. 219-20)

The classical reference is flanked, and its implications altered, by the culinary reminder: the boy is a hunk of meat. While there is undoubtedly a narcissistic element of self-delight, there seems no valid reason to import Oedipal overtones into this fresh scene of coarse refurbishment. As well as assaulting his nasal passages to 'clarify' them, the mother also brainwashes him with her pedantic saws; and seeks to launder his language via euphemisms: whitewash, or eyewash. When it comes to involving Jacques in housework, as usual she overdoes her instructions. In response, he piles it on thick (or takes off too much surface); 'il force la dose'. In this as in so many other ways, he and his mother form a kind of Jewish double act, exaggerating reciprocally, upping the ante.

Blatantly, Jacques is the *souffre-douleur*, emotional drudge, whipping boy, scapegoat, and safety valve. He is, therefore, useful. He is also a source of entertainment—the stooge, sidekick, or fall guy of the family show, 'comme l'ahuri des pantomimes, comme *l'innocent des escamoteurs*' (p. 198). In whatever role, he is the cynosure, *le point de mire.* [7] He acts as a buffer state 'entre le discours de [sa] mère et l'effroi de [son] père' (*ibid.*). He is either the apex of a triangle whose base angles gang up on him, or the white ribbon in a tug-of-war. Never does he enjoy the pair of them as parents. He functions as a crumbly mortar just holding together this grouplet threatened by collapse.

We have, then, to consider the trio, the unholy, holey trinity. Though irregularly capable of kindness, the father falls into the old teacher-parent's trap of avoiding favouritism by favouring victimisation. Here as elsewhere, the child is father to the man, for Jacques is glad to help out his father in their double bind. Vallès always looks for the desperate bonus of every situation, and here the son's acceptance of scapegoat status stops him being regarded by classmates as guilty by association. In the midst of humiliation, Jacques takes pride in being a tough, uncomplaining loser. As with the mother, he tries to adopt the logic of his father's motives: 'C'est moi qui ai tort. Je le déshonore avec mes goûts vulgaires, mes instincts d'apprenti, mes manies d'ouvrier' (p. 246).

The traffic of suffering is not all one-way. Jacques witnesses the progress of his father's affair with the frankly sensual Mme. Brignolin. He is not jealous or ashamed; he simply feels a gooseberry. The father's infidelity is an attempt for once to assert some individuality, to yield to pleasing temptations. Mme. Brignolin loves dancing, even draws the normally anti-hedonistic Mme. Vingtras into it, who looks a sight next to the vivacious other woman. Jacques feels pity for his mother, the pitiless one, when her husband betrays her. When the drama breaks, 'il parle à ma mère d'une voix blanche, qui soupire ou siffle; on sent qu'il cherche à paraître bon et qu'il souffre; il lui montre une politesse qui fait mal et une tendresse fausse qui fait pitié. Il a le coeur ulcéré, je le vois' (p. 267). Even a young child is capable of registering such strains. It is a fishy, hurtful situation, caught exactly and poignantly by Vallès. 'Il a passé un courant de vieillesse sur ma vie, il a neigé sur moi. Je sens qu'il est tombé du malheur sur nos têtes' (p. 265). Jacques has been schooled by his parents to eschew spontaneity, and so he has to bottle up his torn feelings. The father now becomes savage in his beatings, though Jacques still tries to read his reasons: 'Il voyait tout à travers le dégoût ou la fureur!' (p. 268). He lies to Jacques, which hurts more than any leathering, by making out that his son has got him into trouble with the inspector, when it was his own adultery that had earned an official rebuke. Like his son, M. Vingtras has had unwilling choices made for him as a child, and all his adult life he has had to submit to the humiliating imposition of lowly work and status. As with the mother, an element of posturing enters into the relationship with his son: 'Il s'épuise à la fin, à force de vouloir paraître amer' (ibid.). Despite the grating non-coincidence between two sensibilities, father and son do enjoy a rare truce (e.g. on the boat to Nantes), a windfall of camaraderie.[8] The sleeping mother cannot abort their drinking together. Indeed, whenever the father shows signs of relenting, Jacques feels a soft spot for him. All in all, he is more of an accomplice, conniving at his wife's ill-treatment of their son, a collaborationist poltroon. He is not an ogre, but a moral pigmy, which makes it that much harder for his son to rise up in rebellion against him. All he can teach his son is essentially negative: what he must not do or be. And what he positively wants his son to do—to follow in his footsteps—the son rejects violently.

In spite of her longings to conform to a petit-bourgeois model, the mother remains something of an irregular. She puts on genteel airs when all around her is plebeian or peasant, but in middle-class circles she betrays her peasant origins. Like Jacques, she is ill-adapted; she does not fit in anywhere. This is displayed marvellously, excruciatingly, on a school social occasion when she charmlessly tries to re-seduce her straying mate. On the dance floor, she achieves clodhopping, strident gaiety—brave, provocative, blundering—when she executes her peasant stomp and erupts into raucous folk ditties. It is a grotesque performance. Despite having worked so long to overcome them, she has regressed to her origins. Though mortally embarrassed—less, however, than the onlookers—her son cannot help admiring her self-destructive courage. For once in her dowdy life, she lets her hair down and loosens the strait corsets of her pinched existence. Her son might well agree with her that the *bourrée* is as good as a fandango, for he too values peasant exoticism over the more foreign variety. Unlike him, however, she has little or no sense of the ridiculous, whereas he has it in the highest degree.

The father is ashamed of her public disgrace. He forbids her to use words from Auvergnat dialect, thus hoisting her by her own petard, for she tried to raise her son above his station, and now her husband attempts to jack her up. (A national programme promoting French to the detriment of local languages operated through the nineteenth century). In response, she puts their child in an impossible position by obliging him to spy on his father's goings. The marriage is palpably coming apart at the seams. Her own probably impoverished sex-life makes her enviously caustic towards more candidly erotic women.

Throughout *L'Enfant,* in contrast or counterpoint, are happier families, significantly supported by manual work (artisans or peasants). What young Jacques values on his stolen visits is their enjoyment of work and their noisy, disputational fun, so different from the grey grimness of his own home: 'C'est cordial, bavard, bon enfant: tout ça travaille, mais en jacassant; tout ça se dispute, mais en s'aimant' (p. 200). When the mother's away, the unmouselike Jacques can play. In these families, children are allowed to be kids. When Jacques escapes domestic pedantry to play with the cobbler's children, he notes that these phonetically slaphappy kids 'parlaient avec des velours et des cuirs; —c'est le métier qui veut ça' (pp. 201-202)—a perfectly pointed pun. As Jacques himself is unfailingly drawn towards improper liaisons, his remark is more matey than snobbishly censorious. Dimly aware of the tradition of anarchist shoemakers, Jacques would like to be a cobbler 'pour chanter et taper tout le jour' (p. 202). He is 'presque de la famille' (p. 200). One of the major reasons why *L'Enfant* is so vivacious a book is that its child-centre is a fully-fledged, if at times almost skinned-alive, member of a family unit (however ill-cemented), as he is of a larger family and local community. Hence the gossipy tone, the sense of shared experience, of mutual aid or malevolence. Street battles furnish Jacques's first encounter with barricades, tactics, defence and attack. No longer an only child, he learns the ethos of gangs and peer groups.

Annual holidays with relatives on the land clear his lungs and open his eyes, indeed all his senses. 'C'est le temps des vacances qui est le temps fécond pour l'enfant. Il a des heures à lui pour voir avec ses yeux et non avec les bésicles du maître' (II, 747). Tramping through fields, rolling in the hay, he immerses himself 'dans la vie familière, grasse, plantureuse et saine' (p. 190). His love of country life embraces hard work in the fields, for even in his utopia he includes industriousness: 'Les pays où l'on souffre, où l'on travaille, mais où l'on est libre' (p. 214). Always he compares with home. His father, who scorns peasants as clodhoppers, has to bow and scrape to superiors far more than they; he is worse off, in terms of self-respect, than a hired hand. Vallès undoubtedly, in *L'Enfant*, theatricalises and mythologises peasants, while keeping them solidly attached to the soil. Jacques loves the pell-mell meals linking family and farm workers. In contrast with the laughterless home, 'ils rient comme de gros bébés', and, untroubled by etiquette, wipe their noses with their fingers (p. 176). They carry nature with them, on them, in them. Their coarse, weather-beaten skins have areas of tender whiteness, 'comme un dos de brebis tondue ou de cochon jeune' (p. 117). Amongst them, the townee Jacques is 'un animal de luxe' (*ibid.*). The child loves sinking himself in furrows or grass, uttering bird-calls or rolling about like animal young. His killjoy mother tells him to take his Latin grammar with him, for she mistrusts vacancy. For his part, Jacques needs these oases in his generally bleak young life: these moments of stillness, pure existence, usually out of doors. He needs moments of peace, as well as brusque outbursts of violent exertion, solitude as well as crowds. In this whole area of truces, Vallès reveals his faith in alternation, his general sense of life as swings and roundabouts. This attitude injects hope into despair, but reminds hope that it is menaced.

As well as a cobbler, Jacques would want to be a farmhand. This does not represent thraldom but liberation: the possibility to unbutton himself, sprawl, expand. (Vallès omits the constraints and multiple hardships of peasant life, but Jacques sees it only on holiday, and the idealisation is passionate, not milksop). More widely, he is impressed by peasant hostility to the forces of law and order trying to enforce senseless regulations. Peasant fêtes (such as *le reinage*) are also mythologised, as the folk-names given to participants hint, but what matters is the celebration of explosive pleasure—buttons popping, wine flowing. Even an intervillage punch-up is accepted as natural, an overspill of energy. Work, *fête*, fighting (or in Western film terms the range, the hoe-down and the bar-room brawl). In contrast, when the family moves to Nantes, Jacques dislikes the local peasants: 'Ils ne sentent pas l'herbe, mais la vase. [...] Je leur trouve l'air dévot, dur et faux, à ces fils de la Vendée, à ces hommes de Bretagne' (p. 294). Political preference here biasses him against counter-revolutionary peasants.

Jacques finds welcome otherness not only away from the family, but also within it, when he visits relatives. His deaf and dumb aunt Mélie engrosses him with her frenetic body-language, yet begets an interchange: 'Ses yeux, son front, ses lèvres, ses mains, ses pieds, ses nerfs, ses muscles, sa chair, sa peau, tout chez elle remue, jase, interroge, répond; elle vous harcèle de questions, elle demande des répliques. [...] Il faut se donner tout entier' (p. 148). Vallès energises, ventriloquises all he touches. Even the lacemaker's frames of his pious aunt Agnès are talkative. Though her looks repel him, he gazes steadfastly: 'Sa tête rappelle, par le haut, [...] une pomme de terre brûlée et, par le bas, une pomme de terre germée' (p. 149). Although he finds her affection suffocating, he extracts a consolation from her bed curtains which amuse him, especially if he looks at them with head between knees. Then he perceives fanciful creatures; he is literally seeing things. His artisan uncle Joseph has a lively body, so unlike the rigid corpse of the teaching profession. Another uncle, a *curé*, keeps no surveillance on Jacques. The mountain air clears the boy's head, and he enjoys the icy pleasures of fishing in streams. He meets other priests, whom he mistrusts when they betray anti-Protestant prejudice belied by his sighting of one in the flesh, who strikes him as an ordinary mortal. Jacques learns to unlearn on these escapes from school. His time with this uncle is a sequence of magic days followed by dreamless sleep, 'étourdi de parfums, écrasé de bonheur' (p. 242).

But he has to go back to school. This novel swings between the quick and the dead. Throughout *L'Enfant*, its *indécrottable* hero resists, with only partial success, the enforced psittacism of upbringing and schooling. He is by turns, or concurrently, *fort en thème, bête à pensums* and *bête à concours*. His education is principally a training in imitation: 'Mettez-vous à la place de Thémistocle' (p. 319). How can I, wonders Jacques, impersonate Mucius Scævola without the benefit of a charred wrist? Writing Latin verses as an exercise (mental callisthenics), Jacques parrots a pastiche of a poem about parrots: psittacism squared. Such reliance on the readymade leads inevitably to plagiarism. He first practises by forging indulgence-notes for a fellow pupil who owns books coveted by Jacques. Books lead him into crime: a

nice twist on 'victimes du livre'. Yet he is a counterfeiter of some
scruples, as he will not fake his father's signature in order to obtain
some frogs. Vallès parodies confessional literature *à la* Jean-Jacques: 'Il
m'est pénible de faire cette confession, mais je le dois à l'honneur de ma
famille, au respect de la vérité, à la Banque de France, à moi-même' (p.
214). Of course, this self-indictment is ironic, since anything getting a
child off school punishment is fair game to Vallès. By a twist of fate,
Jacques, chastised for non-crimes, gets off scot-free for real ones,
however venial. As when he refused earlier to see convicts as villains,
'je n'ai jamais eu le teint si frais, l'air si ouvert, que pendant cette
période de faussariat' (p. 215—this is also a prophetic skit on
Lombrosian deterministic theories of criminal physiognomy).

More gravely, Jacques plagiarises his schoolwork; he will press any
material into service. In a splendid pun, as he cobbles up spondees and
dactyls, he declares: 'La *qualité* n'est rien, c'est la *quantité* qui est tout'
(p. 320). Hating Robespierre, Vallès could never create a sea-green,
incorruptible hero. When Jacques confesses to a teacher that his
successful *copie* has been a medley, he hears this frank justification of
the system: 'Relevez-vous, mon enfant! Avoir ramassé ces épluchures et
fait vos compositions avec? Vous n'êtes au collège que pour cela, pour
mâcher et remâcher ce qui a été mâché par d'autres' (p. 321).
Forgetting this lesson, later in Paris, 'je mets *du mien* dans mes devoirs.
"Il ne faut pas mattre du vôtre, je vous dis: il faut imiter les Anciens"'
(p. 336). The nearest Jacques ever gets to his cherished craft of
shoemaking is 'le retapage et le ressemelage' of pre-existent materials
(and, preparing his *agrégation,* his father is also a mosaicist,
reassembling bits and pieces). All the time, however, Jacques keeps his
eye and other senses on true values; reality, the present, win hands
down: 'Je me moque de la Grèce et de l'Italie, du Tibre et de l'Eurotas.
J'aime mieux le ruisseau de Farreyrolles, la bouse des vaches, le crottin
des chevaux, et ramasser des pissenlits pour faire de la salade' (p. 321).
His choice of contrasting things is wilfully elemental; he does not want
to inhale the fumes of what he thinks of as academic shit.

Nowhere more sharply does Jacques see the deficiencies of his
education than in mathematics. As we saw in the previous chapter
concerning gymnastics, it was the abstract nature of the teaching that
appalled him. In *Souvenirs d'un étudiant pauvre*, the hero complains:
'Les cuistres, eux, obligeaient mon esprit à suivre des explications *dans
l'espace;* les gens du Grand Conseil de l'Université ne voulant pas
matérialiser la science', and later: 'Au lycée, on en est encore à ce que
j'appellerai bondieusarderie de la mathématique, à l'étude sans base
visible et sans arêtes tranchées' (*SEP*, p. 67). Elsewhere he confesses to
that literary disdain for numeracy which enrages scientists (I, 479). A
variant of *Le Bachelier* widens the complaint to theoretical study itself:
'La théorie, qu'est-ce que c'est que ça! [...] Je n'ai que quatorze ans! Je

voudrais savoir comment on fait, voilà tout! Je n'ai pas besoin de savoir
pourquoi c'est comme ça?'(II, 1674). I should stress that Vallès's
hostility to education as practised in his time is not that of *un cancre* but
of a generally quite-achieving *bête à concours*. He changes his tune
when he receives some far more valuable tuition from an Italian
exile—a real Roman, not a textbook figment. This ex-mason uses
fragments of plaster as visual and tactile aids in geometry lessons that at
last mean something to the boy: *leçons de choses* in the proper sense.

A *leçon de choses* (*per absurdum*) is provided by the philosophy
teacher, Beliben, who proves the existence of God by arranging beans
on a table. Jacques counters this pedant with a kind of peasant dumb
insolence. Of an academician who had devised two ethical systems
instead of one, Vallès comments drily: 'Abondance de bien ne nuit pas'
(p. 343): store is no sore. Vallès was fond of linking scurrilously
philosophy and constipation,[9] though it is more than a joke, for
Bergougnard's 'constipation' turns him into a puellicidal father. It is
surely the adult Vallès who jibs and gibes so pointedly against finalism:
'Au lieu de pousser tant de haricots dans les coins, pourquoi M. Beliben
ne dirait-il pas: "Voyez si Dieu est fin et s'il est bon! que lui a-t-il fallu
pour raccommoder l'époux et l'épouse qui se fâchaient? Il a pris le
derrière d'un enfant, du petit Vingtras, et en a fait le siège du
raccommodement"' (p. 199). Eschatology and scatology linked: the final
issue of things.

Not surprisingly, Vallès describes a prizegiving ceremony in circus
terms: the platform of notables as a line-up of performers, the
uniformed officials like equestrians. The description switches rapidly
from camels to elephants to seals. A man in an elephant-coloured suit
gives Jacques his prize: 'Je croyais qu'il allait dire "Papa" et replonger
dans son baquet' (p. 170). Little Jacques himself is a learned freak, a
bachelier nain. If humour, belittlement are forms of retaliation and
escape, books (hated when prescribed) are another. In detention late at
night, Jacques finds a copy of *Robinson Crusoe*—the archetypal tale of
self-reliant survival in your own preserve—and is totally absorbed in it
till darkness blots out the words. 'Je peuple l'espace vide de mes
pensées' (p. 211). It is a lifebuoy of a book, and a consoling comrade.
Jacques is not its victim, but its devotee. It encourages him to plan a real
escape from his prison-home: he will run away to sea. Having
previously wished to be a peasant or an artisan, he now would settle for
being a Negro, as he imagines Negro mothers love their children. The
escape proves abortive, and Jacques has an early experience of being let
down by fellow rebels. When he welcomes his father's thrashings
because they harden his skin for the tough maritime life, it is not clear
how much this is loaded irony, how much a defensive tactic of making
virtue out of necessity, or how much exuberant hyperbole. When the
family moves to Nantes, Jacques entertains great expectations of high

seas and long-haul ships which are rapidly disappointed. Even in escapism, he is conscious of plagiarism, the takeover of ideas and phrases from books. When he dreams of stowing away, he is indeed a stowaway on the flights of others' imaginations, though he injects also his own drive.

In Paris, he finds his fellow pupils even more obsessed with competitive examinations and prizes than in the provinces. He sticks out like a sore thumb. He finds again that clichés rule; he must imitate the *tours heureux* of great writers, the rhetoric of trite images (Boileau: 'Boire un verre de vin qui rit dans la fougère'), and of periphrases—the rifle as 'une arme qui vomit la mort' (p. 344). On his way to a *concours*, Jacques notices a wretch washing his handkerchief in the river with a book beside him: undoubtedly an impoverished *bachelier*. It is a traumatising insight into his own likely fate, a dire warning to all swots. Jacques fails the *concours*, and, back in Nantes, his *baccalauréat*, which, to him, is solely a matter of contacts, string-pulling, toeing the line and parroting (but he had listened to the wrong bird—p. 375).

This dashing of his father's high hopes and the severe strain on the family caused by the father's liaison poison the home atmosphere. The father grows more 'Roman' than ever, and he quotes to his son the Roman law concerning a father's right, if dishonoured, to kill his son. (This may well be a stand-in for the real-life event of having his son locked up in an asylum, which is a kind of execution). Even within the *Code Napoléon*, the father has the right to threaten him with the police. As for the mother, when she visits Jacques in Paris, she is seemingly more mellowed, though naturally he remains on a war-footing.When she remarks that he is the image of her, he instantly counters, in his own mind, with a refusal to acknowledge. Swivelling back to her old ways, she accuses him: 'Ah! tu n'es pas le fils de ta mère' (p. 351). Jacques wonders briefly: 'Suis-je un enfant du hasard?' (*ibid.*). Now, rather than executing a crypto-Freudian song and dance about the several references, in *L'Enfant*, to the mother's not recognising her son in various contexts and get-ups, I take these incidents as black metajokes about the topos of the foundling, the aristocratic bye-blow, so common in literature. Jacques would certainly prefer other and better parents, and indeed seeks out substitute ones, but he can never kid himself that his real genitors do not exist. When it comes to the crunch, mother and son do not fail to identify each other. She has, after all, marked him for life. It is possible to have a tight and fraught relationship with a mother without incest or sado-masochism explaining anything of value.

In Paris, Jacques accuses her, in his head; the mother-wit which has supported him all his childhood is largely *esprit de l'escalier*. Most of the time the mother has been unanswerable; eventually the years of pent-up grievances explode, and he shocks her into a partial admission of her wrongs against him. She has been both magnet and Moloch, in either case a strong polarisation. She is a martyrant, a blend that is unpronounceable, and almost unspeakable. Like many a mother, she makes a great show of self-sacrifice, twisting or inventing facts to fit the myth of herself as the self-abnegatory pelican. Is she a monster? She surely has robotic tendencies, but machines can surprise us. She oscillates, belittling Jacques while wanting him to walk tall. Her variability is that of life itself, socking you when you least expect it. This is a valuable, if dolorous, lesson for the apprentice Jacques. In a beautifully ambivalent phrase, Jacques admits that he can do nothing 'sans exaspérer son amour' (p. 259). Yet she is rarely maternally protective, just spoilsport. (A friend said, picturesquely, of Vallès's mother: 'Elle n'a pas plus d'instinct maternel qu'une tortue n'a de moustaches'[10]). At least she does not seem to have culled her system from books, but from a mish-mash of folk, *petit-bourgeois* wisdom, proverbs, bromidioms, a kind of collective unconscious—though it is she who assembles and cooks the ingredients. 'Behind the laughter is the nagging suspicion that Jacques might have had a somewhat brighter childhood had he been placed, at an early age, in the capable hands of a well-meaning female gorilla'.[11] Vallès bites the breast that (might have) fed him (Jacques is in fact unsure whether he was farmed out to a wet nurse. He was certainly brought up *by hand!*). Very French, very un-English is the 'religion de la famille' invoked by the Goncourts.[12] No doubt it derives from a confusion of mother and motherland, so that it comes to seem unpatriotic to attack your mother. Though psycho-analytical readings would have Vallès hankering to return to the womb, and though he is keenly aware of how much he missed out on as a child, Jacques, on the contrary, strives mightily to slice the umbilical cord choking him. The last chapter of *L'Enfant* is entitled 'Délivrance'.

The family seems damned and doomed. In a fight, where the father rains nearly murderous blows on his son, Jacques at last resists, having formed the clear question in his head: why should parents have such unjust rights over their children? (In the 1880s, Vallès was to propose a league for the protection of children's rights). And yet, after this confrontation, Jacques physically defends his father against the irate parents of a pupil he slapped in class by fighting a duel against the oldest son of the family. This testimony of loyalty at last drags honesty out of M. Vingtras. Gradually, he moves from the impersonal *on* to the first person. 'Ce professorat a fait de moi une vieille bête qui a besoin d'avoir l'air méchant, et qui le devient, à force de faire le croquemitaine et les yeux creux... Ça vous tanne le cœur... On est cruel... J'ai été cruel' (p. 387). Jacques overhears his parents' shamefaced mutual confession, which the father fears making face to face, lest it harm his authority. He is as pedantic domestically as at school: 'Je lui parlerai toujours comme à un écolier' (p. 387). He asks his wife to act as go-between, and to tell the boy that his father is, against most of the weight of evidence, fond of him. He is a pathetic case of professional deformation, a distortion imposed on him but abetted by a deeply flawed, diminished but very recognisable humanity. Brupbacher expresses this astutely: 'Au prix de mille avanies, il s'est, si l'on ose dire, haussé à plat ventre de sa condition de fils de paysans pauvres au rang de pseudo-professeur'. [13] Jacques also discovers that, at the time of the duel, the father was on the verge of having his son locked up, as allowed by the law of the land. In a letter to his friend Arnould while writing *L'Enfant*, Vallès declares: 'Je hais l'État avant tout. C'est même l'État qui fait les pères féroces en sanctifiant l'autorité, en mettant au-dessus de la tête d'enfants comme des têtes d'insurgés un droit providentiel, une religion indiscutée, le respect de père en fils du respect de la loi' (*Corr. A.*, p. 143). Inculcated respect prevents real respect.

Does the child stand in, here, for the citizen? Vallès suggests that we citizens are in the position of children: spoken for, talked down to, kept in our place, which is to be seen and not heard. For Vallès, rebelliousness, like charity, begins at home. He was indelibly scarred, and vigorously spurred, by his childhood experience. When Jacques nerves himself to confront and resist at last his tyrannical parents, he is well on the way to political militancy. He starts reading about the French Revolution, though the images he evokes are those of peasant uprisings and artisan revolts, not crowds of city workers. These readings vault Jacques from dead languages to a living world. 'Être libre? je ne sais pas ce que c'est, mais je sais ce que c'est d'être victime, je le sais, tout jeune que je suis' (p. 364). He gets his first sight and smell of journalism, linking the ink of printing with the blood of revolution in that primary, passionate imagery so characteristic of Vallès. He sees his first political cafés and clubs: 'La blouse et la redingote s'asseyaient à la même table et l'on trinquait' (p. 366). Overall, though, Vallès saves his hero's proper political baptism for *Le Bachelier*. In *L'Enfant*, he is on the way. Vallès gives *L'Enfant* a deliberately bathetic ending: the mother more interested in the trousers lacerated in the duel than in the fight to defend family honour. For his part, Jacques will cherish his duelling scar, as he curiously values the marks of his mother's whippings. They identify him, what he is and where he comes from. His parents' attempts to denature, or re-nature, him make him prize the natural above all. Truly, if perversely, they have made him what he is. Throughout, Jacques's true education, acquired against scholastic or familial indoctrination, takes the form of a contest between common-sense and fakery or unnatural absurdity, in which pretensions are cut down to size. Likewise, his psychological growing up entails the transfer from superstitious fears of the unknown to authentic fears of the known: the world of oppression. It involves a loss of innocence, but even more a loss of naivety.

L'Enfant makes as much space for the parents' woes as for their son's. They are in a false position: *déplacés, déclassés, dépaysés, dépaysannés:* rootless, stranded between different traditions into none of which can they integrate themselves. They are 'ces paysans mal parvenus'. [14] Like their son, they are in-betweens; hence his occasional indulgence and fellow-feeling. *L'Enfant* describes the difficult-to-express but commonly-felt phenomenon of love despite, love against the grain, so that criticisms of Vallès as parenticidal are misplaced. The family trio is, severally and collectively, accident-prone. No project ever properly works out for them. Not, then, a facile matter of Me versus Them, but, more resonantly, of the three of us in a collective soup. This, at least, is the rough-and-ready balance sheet by the end of the novel, though, in details, on the way there, the scales bang up and down violently. To deny them out-of-hand, as many children would be tempted to do, would seem to their son like denying himself. It is over-nice rhetorical balancing when Léon Daudet speaks of 'Jacques Vingtras, qui ne blasphéma la famille que par besoin ardent de tendresse familiale'. [15] Feelings do not come as neatly on tap as that. Jacques's revolt is not, as Brombert claims, conservative. If he were an emotional tory, he would want the past reborn as it was, or as he invented it in rose-tinted retrospect. He wanted it better than it was. His nostalgia is prospective. He does not blame 'Society' entirely for the parents' delinquency. Not an anti-Rousseauist for nothing, he knows how romantically futile it is to blame the 'System'. Their individual, and dual, responsibility is made very clear. The mother is mean-hearted, the father a coward. Like all of us when pushed, Vallès is an essentialist. In terms of fictional fact, Jacques is not starved, battered systematically, kept locked in for long periods. He is treated harshly, cruelly, but, all told, it is doubtful whether, even today, his parents would be found guilty, in law, of criminal ill-treatment.

Is his family the exception or the rule? If it is exceptional, that implies idiosyncrasy, and he must cherish it, like all eccentricities. While he enjoys oases of joy with other families, he also witnesses there more murderous sadism than in his own. When Bergougnard, an old schoolmate of the father and ex-philosophy teacher, meets him again, he tells him that he, M. Vingtras, embodies 'l'Imagination folle', whereas Bergougnard is 'la Raison froide'. Pompously put, this has a grain of truth, for the father's other side visibly struggles to emerge in his extra-marital affair. As Vallès comments in a pointed wordplay, 'il dit cela presque en grinçant des dents, comme s'il écrasait un dilemme et en mâchait les cornes' (p. 313). Indeed his coming brutality is a kind of aphrodisiac, like rhinoceros horn. The lead-in to his awful attack on his little daughter is comic, though with grating, sinister undertones. He has been brought in to tutor Jacques. He lectures on child chastisement from Greco-Roman classics—the authority; he beats to prove who is boss.

The story gets blacker as we home in on this household where Bergougnard's philosophising is put into practice. 'La maison du sage. Tout d'un coup ses fils apparaissent à la fenêtre en se tordant comme des singes et en rugissant comme des chacals' (p. 315). Some of his children are sadistic, too, trapped in a production-line of brutality. Jacques hates young Bonaventure for his cruelty to animals, and envisages with equanimity crushing the tormentor to death. His violence thickens the emotional stew, as Bergougnard systematically beats Louisette, 'qui demandait pardon, en joignant ses menottes, en tombant à genoux, se roulant de terreur devant son père qui la frappait encore... toujours. "Mal, mal! Papa, papa!" ' (p. 316). Terror and madness coexist. The narrator remembers the screams of an octogenarian madwoman he once heard, hallucinating that she was being murdered. Thus 'la Raison froide' beats sense out of a young head. Jacques again feels vengeful: guillotine the man, or bury him alive. Oscar Wilde could not have been so facilely cynical about this almost unreadable scene of horror and pathos. You start off racking your brains, and you end up braining your child.

We can of course select out the sentimentally loaded words: *mignonne, ange, menotte,* but they do not soften the power of this scene. Sentimentality, besides, is one of those terms that resemble a peasant's bedsock: into it may be accommodated gold currency, or just smelly feet. In Vallès's case, it can be a matter of over-persuasiveness, bludgeoning the reader, rather than of that under-conviction which produces spurious writing. Coincidences, for example, are generally in *L'Enfant* exploited as a joke, one of life's capers, as when Jacques ends up unwittingly eating the rabbit which he earlier won at a fair, carried painfully inside his shirt like the legendary Spartan fox, and eventually let escape. One scene, however, veers close to the naked sentimentality for which Dickens is notorious: the death and disposal of a cherished dog, 'un être qui m'avait aimé, qui me léchait les mains quand elles étaient bleues et gonflées, et regardait, d'un œil où je croyais voir des larmes, son jeune maître qui essuyait les siennes' (p. 275). The parents' callousness in ordering the corpse to be thrown on the midden was sufficiently eloquent without the author rubbing our noses in the wet mess like tyro puppies. One further instance of sentimentality, involving untruthfulness to facts, comes when, reading about the poor people who participated in the French Revolution, Jacques says: 'Et je n'aimais que ces gens-là, parce que, seuls, les pauvres avaient été bons pour moi, quand j'étais petit' (p. 363). Like the slack tolerance of Camus's *La Peste* towards the end, this is sentimental because patently untrue to the previous facts of the text, in which several better-off people treated him kindly and some poor people refused him help. Even so, a couple of sentimental episodes do not scupper a book so vigorous overall as *L'Enfant*. Besides, Jacques's occasional sentimentality is varied by his pleasure in watching force-fed turkeys turn blue. A child can house both extremes. Vallès does not merit the strictures placed on Dickens by Carey: 'Such plastic children bring tears to grown-up eyes, because they represent an innocence which the grown-up wrongly imagines he once possessed himself'. [16] However much he grieved for himself, Vallès never forgot to embrace other children's sufferings, like those of Ricard, a bed-wetter, shamed by having his dank sheets put on public display each day. Mme. Vingtras is mean; the novel that she dominates is generous.

*****

Whatever his sufferings, much of *L'Enfant* celebrates a highly sensuous and sensual child's sensations, for the most part intensely (if often unorthodoxly) pleasurable. Forbidden to play riskily on swings or trapezium with other kids, Jacques wonders roguishly whether he is more fragile. Has he been restuck together like a broken salad bowl? Perhaps his bum is heavier than his head, but he cannot weigh it separately to find out the answer. In a pertinent image, he jumps around the equipment 'comme un petit chien après un morceau de sucre placé trop haut' (p. 164). As with his aunt's curtains, he wants, like any child, to be upside down, to see the *mundus inversus,* which is precisely what Vallès himself is doing in this novel: adopting the posture of the child, giving us the child's slant. Jacques feels animal urges: to graze, to gambol; but he longs not only for such natural expansiveness, but also for man-about-town suavity, such as tipping a bootblack.

L'Enfant runs the whole gamut of the five senses. Taste (often imagined, given his Spartan diet). As regards religion, Jacques cannot help not taking prayers seriously, and the family attend midnight mass mainly because it is free entertainment, which the boy's imagination transforms into a pagan orgy. Passing pork butchers' shops laden with Christmas fare, Jacques experiences hallucinations of pork meat, obsessively, through the ritual:

> Le cordon de cire au bout de la perche de l'allumeur, le ruban rose, qui sert à faire des signets dans les livres, et jusqu'à la mèche d'un vicaire, qui tirebouchonne [...], la flamme même des cierges, la fumée qui monte en se tortillant des trous des encensoirs sont autant de petites queues de cochon que j'ai envie de tirer, de pincer ou de dénouer; que je visse par la pensée à un derrière de petit porc gras, rose et grognon, et qui me fait oublier la résurrection du Christ, le bon Dieu, Père, Fils, Vierge et Cie (p. 188).

Even sharp, irritating sensations of touch are welcome, as in 'le foin, où l'on s'enfouissait, jusqu'aux yeux, d'où l'on sortait hérissé et suant, avec des brins qui vous étaient restés dans le cou, le dos, les jambes, et vous piquaient comme des épingles' (p. 147). Jacques can find delight in the

unlikeliest places, for instance a stray, impish sunbeam shining on a
mountain of chamber-pots in a dormitory, 'pour y faire des siennes, s'y
mirer, coqueter, danser, le mutin, et il s'en donnait à coeur joie' (p.
170). French has the evocative term *lèche-vitrines* for window-
shopping, and Jacques gazes at objects behind glass so hungrily (boots,
for example) that they appear to come alive (p. 172). Some descriptions
are exquisitely precise, as in this of peasant knife-handles: 'Des manches
de corne, avec de petits clous à cercle jaune, on dirait les yeux d'or des
grenouilles' (p. 176). Is this the eye of a child or an adult poet? Cocteau
said: 'Tous les enfants de neuf ans ont du génie, sauf Minou Drouet'.[17]

Jacques, like Juvenal with money, accepts all smells, whatever their
provenance. Of a tannery, he notes 'cette odeur montante, moutardeuse,
verte—si l'on peut dire verte,—comme les cuirs qui faisandent dans
l'humidité ou qui font sécher leur sueur au soleil' (p. 173). He speaks of
'mon nez reconnaissant' (*ibid.*): recognising / grateful. Vallès
orchestrates sounds, as in this concert for three hungry stomachs:
'J'entends les boyaux de mon père qui grognent comme un tonnerre
sous une voûte: les miens hurlent;—c'est un échange de borborygmes;
ma mère ne peut empêcher, elle aussi, des glouglous et des bâillements'
(p. 279). Jacques opens up all his senses ('j'ouvre des yeux énormes;
j'écarte les narines et je dresse les oreilles' (p. 286)), and what he takes
in 'double mes sens' (p. 237). At times, the descriptions blend all the
senses into synaesthesia, as in this evocation of New Year presents, the
bright spot of his grey year: 'Ces tons crus et ces goûts fins, [...] ces
gloutonneries de l'œil, ces gourmandises de la langue, [...] ce libertinage
du nez et cette audace du tympan, ce brin de folie, ce petit coup de
fièvre' (p. 183).

Vallès is as perceptively evocative, as lyrical, about urban scenes as
about nature. For instance, a market, crammed with uproar, movement
and pungent smells, an open-air Noah's Ark running amok: 'Il y a des
engueulades qui rougissent les yeux, bleuissent les joues, crispent les
poings, cassent les oeufs, renversent les éventaires, dépoitraillent les
matrones, et me remplissent d'une joie pure' (pp. 190-91). Some
descriptions become apoplectic, as in this contrast of country fields and
town allotments, where he notices that 'quelques feuilles jaunâtres,
desséchées pendaient avec des teintes d'oreilles de poitrinaires. [...] Des
melons qui ont l'air de boulets chauffés à blanc; des choux rouges,
violets—on dirait des apoplexies' (p. 173). Even when pejorative in
intent, Vallès's descriptions are excited, dynamic. Reading itself can
transfer the living world into Jacques's sensibility. A fictional fishing-
expedition: 'Un grand filet luit au soleil, les gouttes d'eau roulent
comme des perles, les poissons frétillent dans les mailles, deux pêcheurs
sont dans l'eau jusqu'à la ceinture, c'est le frisson de la rivière' (p. 160).
A hyperreal text. Not to be outdone, here is nature herself: 'La rivière
en bas—qui s'étire comme un serpent sous les arbres, bornée d'une

bande de sable jeune, plus fin que de la crème, et piqué de cailloux qui flambent comme des diamants' (p. 156). Few French writers (so many take French leave of their senses when they write) achieve this physical density, this uncerebral joy in sensations. I think of Giono, and again when I turn to sexuality.

From an early age Jacques is jealous of men getting the older women he fancies. Above all, he loves, and desires half-consciously, his superb country cousin Apollonie, and her 'blocs de beurre fermes et blancs comme les moules de chair qu'elle a sur sa poitrine. On s'arrache le beurre de la Polonie' (p. 154)—a double entendre: people would give anything for her butter / breasts. She teases him, caressing and tickling him; she smells of raspberries. From the rear she reminds of a pony which he does not quite know that he wants to mount. He makes do, very satisfyingly, by riding behind her, gripping hard as she rides bare-arsed. The whole scene is bathed in frank sensuality:

> Je sens la tiédeur de sa peau, je presse le doux de sa chair. Il me semble que cette chair se raffermit sous mes doigts qui s'appuient, et tout à l'heure, quand elle m'a regardé en tournant la tête, les lèvres ouvertes et le cou rengorgé, le sang m'est monté au crâne, a grillé mes cheveux. (p. 156)

Women and horses are linked again in the delectable shape of the circus equestrienne, Paola: 'Elle tord ses reins, elle cambre sa hanche, fait des poses; sa poitrine saute dans son corsage, et mon cœur bat la mesure sous mon gilet' (p. 192). He is a would-be peeping Jacques, and the passion becomes farcical when he is so absorbed in stalking her that he trips over a serving maid and grabs whatever is to hand, 'à pleine chair, je ne sais où; elle a cru que c'était le singe ou la trompe égarée de l'éléphant' (p. 193). In an impoverished childhood, copious flesh is cherished. In the Gnostic tradition, the 'pneumatic' are the elect. Jacques is grateful for big mercies, as in a scene on a coach: 'La grosse femme a une poitrine comme un ballon, avec une échancrure dans la robe qui laisse voir un V de chair blanche, douce à l'œil et qui semble croquante comme une cuisse de noix' (p. 194).

Mme. Devinol plays the classical French role of the older woman who breaks in the pubescent. When she takes his arm, he pumps up his biceps to near bursting point. Vallès does not omit the less glorious aspects of courtship—Jacques shaving prematurely: 'Je racle et je racle, et je fais sortir de ma peau une espèce de jus verdâtre, comme si on battait un vieux bas' (p. 331). Mme. Devinol grows more pressingly forward, and offers truffles (a reputed erotic stimulant hardly necessary when his own tuber is swelling). Stripping off in an inn after getting wet in the rain, their budding coitus is interrupted by intruders: Jacques can never conceal his identity; his telltale hat has been identified. As Vallès plays between youth and adult, in these sexual matters, the text grows equivocal, if seldom coy.

Puns are *équivoques*, supremely. They can be unmeant, as when Jacques's trouser leg rides up and his mother shouts out 'Jacques, baisse ta culotte' at the prize ceremony (p. 169). Or simple, as when Jacques lets the camel ('qui a bon dos') be blamed for his indiscretions at the circus (p. 194). They can be excruciating, and deeply serious, as in a heavily charged scene of family dispute. Jacques breaks a picture frame: 'Je suis bien content tout de même d'avoir dérangé ce silence, *cassé la glace*, et ma famille en arrache les morceaux' (p. 198). The sentence swivels between literal, metaphorical and back to literal again. It is a serious pun because it leads into an extended section suggesting that the son's pain helps to heal the parents' rift. Other puns can be laboured. Jacques approaches the much-beaten Ricard about running away: 'Je tâte Ricard; quand je dis je tâte, je parle au figuré: il me défend de le tâter (il a trop mal aux côtés)' (p. 250). This is pedantic, clumsy. Others are snappier. The cuckolded chemist, M. Brignolin, 'est toujours dans les *cornues*' (p. 258). Vallès even puns, in a variant, in his mock family escutcheon: 'Nous sommes une noblesse d'écurie. Du côté de mon père, on élevait les cochons, dans ma lignée maternelle on gardait les vaches. Nous portons pied de cochon sur queue de vache, avec tête de veau dans le fond de l'écusson' (II, 1711). (In slang, *tête de veau* = dumb cluck, *queue-de-vache* = mousy-coloured, *pied de cochon* = dirty trick. As 'un cochon' is a *remplaçant* for military service, his father did 'élever des cochons' after a fashion).

Puns often twist meanings in new directions. After the rhetorical question 'Qui remplace une mère?', Jacques answers: 'Mon Dieu! une trique remplacerait assez bien la mienne!' (p. 212). 'Triste comme un bonnet de nuit', Mme. Brignolin says sadly to M. Vingtras. This usually occurs as 'une histoire triste comme un bonnet de nuit', a dull-as-ditchwater story. Here the sense is melancholy: the father is a sorry specimen (p. 254). A common form of twisting is exaggeration, comic hyperbole. A hat brushed against the pile makes Jacques look as if his hair were standing on end. 'Il a vu le diable, murmuraient les béates en se signant' (p. 168). A rare bout of affection from the mother has this result: 'Elle me donna un baiser à ressort qui me rejeta contre le mur où mon crâne enfonça un clou' (p. 273). This is probably a twist on the stock idea of knocking the nails of ideas into blockheads. The family threesome all exaggerate. The mother *charrie* in her upbringing (and downcasting) of Jacques; the father *renchérit* on the need to kowtow to superiors, *il force la note;* Jacques matches, mimes them; and Vallès often goes over the top in narrating all of this. We should ponder, nonetheless, the Jewish saying: 'Crooked parents can produce straight children'.[18]

All in all, Vallès handles so confidently the resources of rhetoric that we could talk of the mother, for instance, as a composite rhetorical figure: a living paradox, an oxymoron, a mixed metaphor, a chiasmus, a pun—all of these figures suggesting tugs and tensions, layered meanings. In the hated school, Vallès learned his lessons well, even though French pedagogy was back-to-front, *adverso pectore,* as Jacques notes (p. 320).

As for the structure of *L'Enfant,* the narration often suggests that something has only recently happened: 'Je m'étais piqué à une rose l'autre soir' (p. 144). Reflecting on his forgeries, Jacques wonders whether he might end up in prison: 'Et qui dit que je n'irai pas?' (p. 216). Vallès is here looking forward from a refound past to a future presented as still unfinished. The time-scheme of this novel is evidently slippery. An associative mind links, or more often juxtaposes, fragments; a patchwork quilt is being assembled. Let us consider a section, 'La Petite Ville' of Chapter Four.

The Porte de Pannesac is in the lower town of Le Puy. Jacques rejects his father's reverence for Roman monuments, but is fascinated by the grain trade centred on this area, which also houses the local baking trade and, as a sideline, hunting equipment, including fishing-rods. The text evokes the vivid sensations of fishing, and calls to his mind his reading of Captain Cook's travels among Pacific island fishermen. There follows a section on smells, good and bad (e.g. fish-glue), and a grocer's shop, packed with strong odours, including salt-cod. Back on the street, Jacques's life is endangered by grain waggons driven by flour-covered men who remind him of Italian mascarades.

In contrast, in the upper town lies the teacher-training college, which keeps the figure of M. Vingtras in mind. Jacques, playing circumspectly to order with the director's son, wonders why other parents appear so unconcerned about their children's safety in playgrounds. The chapter ends on a note mingling quietude (after the uproar) and frustration. Jacques sitting on a bench like a little old man, both enjoying the stillness and dying to leap around like a young animal. The whole section comes no full circle, and follows no linear progress, but the associations of idea, sentiment or sensation give it a vital interconnectiveness, with swift shifts of mood that have their own inner logic. Even when, elsewhere, a situation seems about to develop in an orderly way, the narration often sidesteps or backtracks. Such shifts reflect Vallès's sense of the randomness of daily life. The journalistic experience explains much: the often feverish pace, the arresting headlines, followed by often jerky explication. The use of the graphic present promotes the illusion that much is just now happening; it aids immediacy.

Jacques acts as eye- and ear-witness, not always understanding what he sees or hears, though the hindsighted Vallès intimates that the boy has adequate inklings. Generally, the hindsight is disguised, as though by dark glasses. Jacques receives fragmentary hints (oranges, sign of gay living; he hears his parents arguing over 'elles', and only later understands his father's infidelity). Vallès knows how to spin out suspense, and to mimic the patchy business of twigging. Though narrated in the first person, the speaker frequently records an objectification of his self which derives from the gaze or attitudes of others: parents, teachers, bystanders. The impersonal idiom 'comme il faut' is at the core of his mother's programme: this third person who does not exist, this god at the apex of a triangle whose base-angles are Me and Other People. This source of authority is located no place, hovering, like the 'petit bonhomme' struck to the classroom ceiling in mockery of God. The choice of the first person, in contrast, is self-affirming.

Vallès narrates through the vigilant eyes (and skin) of a brutalised child, to which is superimposed on occasion the grown man's more lucid indignation. Lejeune assumes he is doing Vallès a favour by enlisting him, on account of the superimposition of different voices which produces 'un texte vacillant', in the ranks of 'modern' autobiography. [19] For me, the often switchback narration is more agelessly a matter of an adult reliving a childhood and putting himself imaginatively into the adult shoes of the mother and father. There are alternances with the text—the parents taking it in turn to be inhuman/human. However disconnected L'Enfant often seems, the process of learning (and unlearning, de-indoctrination) that is at its heart is mainly a matter of making the right connexions. The child who enjoys seeing turkeys asphyxiating at the start is resolutely against all forms of enforced suffering by the end.

*****

After bracketing L'Enfant with Darien's Bas les cœurs! and Céline's Mort à crédit as three great 'livres d'enfance', Campagnoli and Hersant make it clear that such books use the child as an operator: 'L'enfant n'est pas l'objet d'un discours paternaliste, mais sujet d'un discours subversif'. The usual tradition, they argue, which passes from Fénelon through Hugo to Jules Renard, begets 'un jeune adulte, un *juvenis senex*'. Even if the child is in practical terms impotent, his powerlessness increases clear-sightedness, and in contrast we see the childishness of many adults. [20] In a wider view, Coveney states:

> If the central problem of the [nineteenth-century] artist was in fact one of adjustment, one can see the possibilities for identification between the artist and the consciousness of the child whose difficulty and chief source of pain often lie in adjustment and accommodation to environment. In childhood lay the perfect image of insecurity and isolation, of fear and bewilderment, of vulnerability and potential violation. [21]

This thoughtful comment leaves out the toughness, the powers of the child to resist onslaught, which are plentifully embodied in *L'Enfant*. Though some lines of Wordsworth might be transferable to Vallès's way of looking ('Shades of the prison-house begin to close / Upon the growing Boy', or 'As if his whole vocation / Were endless imitation'), no heaven lies around Jacques's infancy, and the child as visionary is hardly Vallès's *tasse de tilleul*.[22]

The *Bildungsroman* records a process of growing up, apprenticeship, acculturation and initiation. In *L'Enfant,* however, Vallès offers little clear sense of what his hero is heading towards, though a strong idea of what he is kicking against. In this respect, *L'Enfant* is open-ended. In ways very different from Sartre's Hugo in *Les Mains sales,* Jacques is 'non récupérable', incorrigible, *indécrottable*. He lives by trial and error; he is sorely tried and he errs frequently. At times, no doubt, the emotion in this novel, like the boy's backside, is raw, but if convincing recall depends on preserving into maturity the emotions and sensations of the child, then we have to take the raw with the cooked. Despite his above-average suffering, Jacques comes across as a normal child.

Zola, who had a lengthy if guarded relationship with Vallès, judged *L'Enfant* 'un livre vrai, un livre fait des documents humains les plus exacts, et les plus poignants. Voici dix ans qu'une œuvre ne m'avait remué à ce point'. Less keen on its exclamatory interventionism and the 'bouffonnerie inutile' of some pages, and writing after the Commune, for which he felt little sympathy, Zola ends with: 'Comment un homme du talent de M. Jules Vallès a-t-il pu gâter sa vie en se fourvoyant dans la politique. Jamais je ne lui pardonnerai'.[23] Politics is fit only for failures. Alphonse Daudet said of Vallès: 'Il avait l'embouchure, le vocable, le cri: rien à mettre dedans'.[24] Sounding brass, where Daudet was a tinkling cymbal. Given his fey facetiousness, his anaemic, weak-willed characters, his inability to capture the child's voice, his biologically snobbish Petit Chose and his unconvincing Jack, Daudet was in no position to pass judgment.

Jules Renard is altogether more interesting. His *Poil de carotte* has often been thought of as plagiarising *L'Enfant* (Léon Daudet and Barrès used to call Renard 'Poil de Vallès').[25] Renard's copy of *L'Enfant* was heavily scored with blue-pencil marks, though this could imply censorship as much as casing the joint. In his diary, Renard admitted: 'Pour être original, il suffit d'imiter les auteurs qui ne sont plus à la mode'.[26] Even more revealingly, he states: 'J'ai été élevé par une bibliothèque'.[27] Not something Vallès could have accused himself or his parents of, for, though strongly affected by childhood reading—both models to reject or to endorse (Plutarch / Defoe), he is less bookified than many French writers, *livré aux livres* (even these words seem akin). Any touches of sadism in *L'Enfant* are wholly different in kind from those on show in *Poil de carotte,* where the whole family stands alien to the reader, and where the young hero stonily tortures and massacres little animals at great length. The mother's *méchanceté* is given, unexplained: an essence. Guichard contrasts the two writers in this way:

> Constamment, Vallès se laisse emporter par sa verve, et donne le coup de pouce à la vérité, avec sa jovialité brutale, alors que Renard pince les lèvres, parce qu'il serre les dents. Vallès s'épanche alors que Renard se retient, se contrôle. L'un délaie quand l'autre décante. L'un ajoute quand l'autre biffe. L'un 'en remet' quand l'autre en enlève. Vallès est un 'débondé' quand Renard est un 'constipé'. [28]

Where does the balance fall in this Gallic symmetry? Speaking in his own name on this issue, Renard says:

> J'ai lu très jeune *L'Enfant* de Jules Vallès. On m'a souvent dit plus tard que *Poil de carotte* était une imitation de *L'Enfant.* C'est inexact de fait; mais vous pensez bien que ce reproche m'honorait, car je considère *L'Enfant* comme un livre de premier ordre, un de ceux que tout écrivain français doit lire le plus tôt possible, un livre de direction. [...] C'est d'ailleurs surtout l'humour de Vallès qui m'a frappé. Je restais, étant sans doute trop jeune, plus insensible à l'amertume, aux plaintes sociales, un peu trop développées à mon goût, de Jules Vallès. [29]

This indeed rather tight-lipped, constipated hommage is as near as Renard ever gets to generosity towards another writer. 'Chaque fois que le mot "Jules" n'est pas suivi du mot "Renard", j'ai du chagrin'. [30] Truly, he was like 'une araignée au centre de mon moi'. [31]

Vallès is generous. The epigraph to *L'Enfant* is 'à tous ceux qui crèverent d'ennui au collège ou qu'on fit pleurer dans la famille, qui, pendant leur enfance, furent tyrannisés par leurs maîtres ou rossés par leurs parents' (p. 139). *Le Bachelier* shows Jacques Vingtras widening out further from the initial base of *L'Enfant*.

Chapter Seven

Almost My Story: *Le Bachelier*

J'ai couru au-devant du ridicule.

(II, 595)

Vallès told Malot that the book he was working on could be 'mon histoire, mon Dieu—ou presque mon histoire' (*Corr. M.*, p. 98). What would be eventually entitled *Le Bachelier* is indeed a story of approximation, near-misses, and, as such a cautionary tale for would-be rebels (*Corr. A.*, p. 91). '*Te voilà bachelier...* mot dit par [M.] Vingtras à son garçon quand il revient avec son diplôme. Ça lui faisait une belle jambe! Enfin! Ce sera justement l'histoire de cette belle jambe' (*Corr. M.*, p. 277). Though Jacques will be complimented on his shapely supports by a bootmaker, his paper qualifications will indeed do him a fat lot of good. 'J'ai essayé de mettre en relief une idée dans ces *Mémoires d'un Révolté*, celle-ci. C'est farce et sottise, on n'est qu'un blagueur et un fou, d'espérer VIVRE SUR SON ÉDUCATION' (p. 348). This proposition met, and meets, with much sympathy and widespread condemnation. Vallès chances his arm more with *Le Bachelier* than *L'Enfant*. When it first appeared as a serial in a newspaper, its administrator, Callet, remarked: 'Votre roman a un grand succès dans un certain public, étudiants, écrivains, etc., ouvriers lettrés, mais il n'est pas populaire' (quoted II, 1631).

Vallès was obliged to hack his text about considerably in order to pacify editors and subscribers. If he cut himself, did he not bleed? 'Quelle douleur, ces saignées!' (*Corr. M.*, p. 325). He had to leech his text to make it paler and less alarming to consumers. The time-scale is roughly between mid-1848 to around 1860, but Vallès takes liberties with the chronology of his life within this block.[1] A pursuit of freedom cannot kowtow to mere calendars.

Significantly, the dedication of *Le Bachelier* is composed of a play on words about Greek and Latin *roots*, and the impossibility of living off paper qualifications in them. Two levels are juxtaposed here and for the duration of the text: learning and feeding, mental and physical force-feeding or malnutrition. Jacques's belly will often be empty, but his brain remains stuffed. *Le Bachelier* releases (on parole) the pent Jacques into a hand-to-mouth existence in Paris.

The text itself starts with a pointed pun on *carrière*, eminently apt as it concerns a penniless *fort en thème* driven to suicide by careering from a stone quarry. The novel is thus placed under the sign of excruciation, the coexistence of competing strains. Setting out for Paris on the stagecoach, Jacques switches rapidly from hoping he will be free at last from parents and teachers to wondering whether other policemen lie in ambush. Spotting a gendarme next to the driver, he swiftly minimises his own alarm by ridiculing in his head the official's uniform, with its leather straps 'couleur d'omelette, des épaulettes en fromage' (p. 448). Keyed up by his own daring, he then recalls in an escalating paroxysm an incident from *L'Enfant*, where a whole village resisted an attack by the *gendarmerie*. Jacques swears that it is honourable to be executed for such acts, whereas it is deemed ignominious to counter a father's aggressivity by knocking him aside. The circle closes, from father back to father, with resistance to authority at its core. The telescoped emotions of this sequence derive from a heavy load of past fears, and apprehension of what the future holds in store. Playing and quaking, Jacques tastes the mixed blessings of independence.

He is free:

> Je puis secouer mes jambes et mes bras, pleurer, rire, bâiller, crier comme l'idée m'en viendra! Je suis maître de mes gestes, maître de ma parole et de mon silence. Je sors enfin du berceau où mes braves gens de parents m'ont tenu emmaillotté dix-sept ans, tout en me relevant pour me fouetter de temps en temps. (p. 448)

After possession (of a diploma), self-possession. Jacques leaves infancy (that is, speechlessness). In *L'Enfant*, Jacques's every move had been surveilled, in intention if not in practice, by his parents, though he managed all kinds of mini-escapes by a kind of internal emigration. Now he is free, awesomely so, but also exhilaratingly: 'Une moutarde d'orgueil me monte au nez' (p. 449). He is indeed being reborn, his heart beating like a baby's in the womb. The swinging moods of the novel are there from the start, however, as his excitement yields to melancholy, and open spaces change from betokening liberty to suggesting the void. He is unsure what to do with his new-found freedom, and more certain of what he is fleeing than what he is heading towards.

His mother had inscribed his name and provenance in the shape of a cross on his trunk, as if she were burying his new life, or possibly as a way of warding off the evil eye. For someone so long deprived of anything to call his own (even his skin!), his hole-in-the-corner lodgings inspire animal joy: his own space, a refuge and fortress. He needs this retreat, to be himself and to hear himself think. He is an educated Noble Savage:

> Vingt-quatre sous, dix-sept ans, des épaules de lutteur, une voix de cuivre,
> des dents de chien, la peau olivâtre, les mains comme du citron, et les
> cheveux comme du bitume. Avec cette tournure de sauvage, une timidité
> terrible, qui me rend malheureux et gauche. (p. 450)

Like his old helpmeet Robinson Crusoe, he starts off with a life to
construct, but with very sparse equipment. Vallès is very astute on the
posturings enforced by need and embarrassment. From early on, he
suggests not only the youth's fear of being caught out and humiliated,
but the whole intrusive atmosphere of watchfulness and suspicion in a
budding police-state. 'Mon attitude était louche, ma rôderie monotone,
inquiétante' (p. 455). A suspect before he has done anything (as he was
at home). He could be taken for a criminal or a nark, as he prowls the
streets of Paris.

What has he come to? In the middle of the nineteenth century, Paris
was not yet an important industrial city. Rather it was a centre of
administration, shopping, craftsmen and service-agencies. Under Louis-
Philippe, the population had rapidly increased, largely because of the
rural exodus, yet there was insufficient employment to provide for these
extra stomachs. In the 1850s, large numbers of 'students' crowded into
Paris, a good many of them hoping to publish their writings. Economic
crises hung over from the 1840s, but charity was inadequate and
government assistance negligible. The new cry, which Jacques echoes on
reaching Paris, was 'le droit au travail!' Jacques will cling to the idea of
remunerated work during the day, followed by study and writing at
night. Apart from the practical necessity of such an order of priorities,
this dream also shows how he felt that he had to earn the right to read
and compose, and that experience must precede reflexion.

At the other end of the social scale, a wave of economic expansion,
largely fuelled by speculation, followed the establishment of the Second
Empire, and bred a small race of *nouveaux riches,* often lacking in
taste. It was an age of pleasure for the well-off, but also an age of
material envy and growing interclass hatred and fear. The stock image
of the Second Empire is that of *la vie parisienne,* typified by the well-
oiled forces of Labiche and the exuberant music of Offenbach (admired
by Vallès for his ironical use of motifs from classical antiquity). Yet it
was equally a time when *l'ordre moral,* a rough French counterpart to
Victorian values, put Flaubert's and Baudelaire's masterpieces on trial
for immorality. In *Le Bachelier,* Vallès offers a corrective to such stock-
images, a kind of below-stairs view of daily living, which makes no
mention of the Crimean War or of the Paris World Exhibition of 1855.
Vallès is fully alive to the politico-social issues fermenting behind the
opulent façade of that society, in which Jacques moves from subjection
at home to bohemian self-help.

By the middle of the century, the *baccalauréat* had become such a
desirable (if not inevitably marketable) qualification that a whole

industry of cramming establishments grew up. In 1850, there were only 4,000 new *bacheliers*. As such they might have been a privileged caste, and that would help to explain, if not justify, why Jacques so often assumes that a piece of paper should guarantee the holder a secure job and financial reward. Instead, he finds that it is a handicap of a privilege. In addition, he harps on entitlement because he is more generally keen on asserting rights (such as free speech). How to get on without thereby becoming a *parvenu* or an *arriviste,* and without reneguing on your origins and becoming *déclassé par le haut* ? In truth, Jacques's great expectations aim lower than the heroes of Balzac, Stendhal or Flaubert. Far from cosseting himself with the delusion that the world owes him a living, Jacques would settle for enough to eat, decent accommodation and unpatched clothes. His view of Paris is never panoramic à la Balzac or à la Hugo; it is scrappy, never an overview but a mêlée—more like Fabrice's encounter with war in *La Chartreuse de Parme*. Jacques's peripatetic description dwells on *hôtels* (scruffy boarding-houses) and cafés, as these represent the twin poles of his material life: *la pâtée et la niche*. Like Nature, he abhors a vacuum; empty Sunday streets frustrate him. When he is of a mind to praise it, he links Paris, especially those areas scarred by past uprisings, with revolutionary values. The one space for escape, the sky, is a screen on to which he can project his changing moods, fears and aspirations. [2]

'J'ai de l'éducation' (p. 447): a possession that generally proves to be a white elephant. Indeed, much later, after several failures to hold down a job, he cries in mock-despair: 'Comment devient-on bête? Comment oublie-t-on ce qu'on a appris?' (p. 680). His head is a ragbag of examination quotes, of miscellaneous and largely inapplicable 'culture'. Though he sports with his classical impedimenta, making it serve the purposes of comedy, retaliation, and occasionally even of winning him a short-term livelihood, he finds straightaway that he is over-educated and untrained. In interviews, his reply to the question 'What can you do?' is the bald statement: 'Je suis bachelier', as if he were by formation an essence. Attracted by the idea of becoming an apprentice-printer, he is warned that he would only be *un saute-ruisseau,* a gofer, and besides, *déclassés* are unpopular in the trade. A veteran worker comments that Jacques still smacks too much of *le collège:* 'Vous auriez des airs de monsieur' (p. 471): what his mother always wanted. When Jacques mentions politics—with which he links printing in his mind—the worker advises: 'Prenez votre parti de la redingote pauvre. [...] Si vous résistez, vous resterez debout au milieu des redingotes comme un défenseur de la blouse. Jeune homme, il y a là une place à prendre!' (pp. 471-2). This prophecy has a profound effect on the young man, for its promises him an activist's role, however reduced, while denying him integration in the working-class. Because he has no *état,* however, he is suspected by a landlord of being a pimp (p. 568).

As he is *un enfant de la balle universitaire,* and because of that
growth of crammers mentioned earlier, teaching beckons. Finding
himself in a seedy *pension* which is at bay to creditors, Jacques is ready
to swallow his pride. As well as teaching basics (the alphabet), he is also
in effect lumbered with menial extras which involve an apparent sex-
change: *bonne d'enfants* (p. 578). Like a dog-pound handler with strays,
he collects his small charges by blowing a whistle; he wipes their snotty
faces, and replaces dangling shirt-tails. He takes absurd pride in such
minuscule skills: 'J'ai le geste pour ça, presque coquet, il paraît, *un
tour de main* [...]. *A moi le pompon!'* (pp. 580-81). For Jacques, it takes
more guts to plead for work than to fight on the streets, where the
enemy is known and visible, whereas poverty is a spectral presence.
Jacques has condemned himself by his aversion from swearing the oath
of allegiance to the State to accept shoddy employment in the private
sector. Not lazy by temperament, he shows willing in his various jobs,
but he never fits in. Though he at times lands windfall jobs (e.g. with
some *saltimbanques,* where his facility in the classics briefly comes in
useful for the pompous spiels of sideshows), much of *Le Bachelier* deals
neither with regular work nor with true leisure. I am reminded of the
Liverpool concept of the fret-worker: work one day and fret for four.
Yet Jacques envies installed workers, even if he does not fall for the
boss-class stereotype of the non-troublemaking *bon ouvrier.* He lives
much of the time like a vagabond, errant and aberrant, hence his
frequent frenzy and frustration: no fixed abode, living from hand to
mouth.

His journalistic experience is equally at the lower end. As a *teneur
de copie,* he reads texts aloud to a *correcteur:* only a channel, with no
personal input except his loud voice. He scrabbles in a petty press hardly
distinguishable from commercial prospectuses, and in fact is paid in
kind (coat, shoes) for his efforts. On *La Nymphe* (in real life *La
Naïade*), a free sheet on waterproof paper, he acts as a beater, a one-
man claque, demanding the paper vociferously in bathing-
establishments. In a parodic version of Vallès's own tendency to
misérabilisme, he writes for a tear-jerk woman's journal, but he relates
there a true story about real poverty which proves too much for the
editor. Jacques is out of step again, and even when showing willing he is
provocative. Similarly, an article on the youth of the Latin Quarter
proves too hot to print, in the climate of fear after 1848. He is in a
Catch-22 situation: if he imitates the mode, he produces stupid copy; if
he writes from the heart, he is unpublishable. When he tries to trim he
feels ashamed of his articles: 'Je les cache comme des excréments' (p.
640). His father reappears as an additional censor. When he hears that
Jacques is about to attack *les universitaires* in print, afraid for his job he
puts his foot down. Not for the first time, his son caves in to parental
blackmail.

He tries piecework (on anthologies and dictionaries). He is on a permanent restart programme. As he is grateful even for such miserable hack work, he often feels he is a lucky Jacques. In the chain-gangs of lexical groupuscules, Jacques, as at school, learns fraud: inventing quotations (he excels at pseudo-Bossuet). In a splendid scene he overhears pedants squabbling over his cooked-up citations. In a real sense, he must 'possess his classics', as one of them acknowledges, or he would not counterfeit so plausibly. Again exploiting his schooling, as a paid satirist (a kind of verbal hit-man), he mugs up classical models. Though this remunerated bitchiness pays off briefly, he runs out of vituperative steam; he rarely works well on command.

Office work sees Jacques again as a square peg, a misfit. His humanities education had scorned not only mathematics but also fine handwriting as fit only for lesser lights, and so he cannot keep down a job as a script-copier. When clerking in a factory, he finds that Latin structures and phrases come first to mind when he has to frame business-letters: 'Je *pense* bien mieux en latin. Je traduirai après' (p. 678). His whole education had indeed been a matter of translation and mediation, not of concentration on essentials.

Bouche-trou, cache-misère: making do embraces work, clothes and food. Poverty breeds invention. Jacques undergoes more than once 'le vertige de la faim' (p. 457). Much of his existence in Paris could be summarised by the idiom: 'bouffer de la vache enragée'. The restaurant name 'Au hasard de la fourchette' symbolises his spasmodic eating: pot luck (on rare occasions potlatch, beano). Faithful to his roots, Jacques would prefer hearty peasant food and its accompaniment of conviviality (*cum pane:* company). What he gets more often is scrag-ends, or even virtually imaginary fare. His artifice of self-preservation, his dietary whistling in the dark, rely on dodges like waving his tasteless crust in the odour of frying fish percolating from a neighbour's flat (p. 570). The old idioms come to mind: 'manger son pain à la fumée du rôt', 'tromper sa faim', 'dîner par cœur'. Jacques has 'quelque chose dans le ventre' in one sense, but frequently not in the other.

Just as he never totally starves, he is never actually nude, but he has endless problems with clothes. Clothes, in Vallès, are characters. When Jacques props up his huge overcoat, it frightens strangers like a scarecrow. It is a present encumbrance, but also a cherished relic. Behind much of Vallès's obsession with clothes lies the myth of the tunic of Nessus, a fatal, poisoned gift to Hercules, a source of intense irritation and an inescapable gaol. (Cf. Pip's clothes in *Great Expectations*, 'like a kind of Reformatory' which prevents 'the free use of my limbs').[3] Whereas he would like to be a moderate dandy, with the merest 'pointe d'orgueil' but no intention of humiliating others, in fact he attracts far more attention when he is monstrously attired than on the rare occasions when he can dress smartly: 'Pantalon qui a deux yeux par derrière, redingote à reflets de tôle, [...] souliers à gueule de poisson mort' (p. 600). He is a sideshow on the streets of Paris: 'un dandysme à l'envers'. [4] Off to a crucial interview, and jumping stiffly downstairs feet together, in agonising discomfort because so many pins hold his begged and borrowed, jerry-built suit together, he can still summon a joke about 'la raideur anglaise', which he attributes elsewhere to the English having swallowed whole the flagpole of the Union Jack (pp. 601-603; 1161). Vallès knew very exactly how much material things affect confidence, behaviour, or success. No wonder that, as with hunger, Jacques has hallucinations about clothes.

For him, they are badges of political affiliation, an 'advertisement for myself', and he borrows in some anguish gear from merely moderate republicans. It is strange that one so individualistic should stress so much the uniform of ideas. The reason may be that he links growing up and away with picking your own apparel, as many youths today believe: 'Je voyais dans le triomphe des idées nouvelles le moyen de n'être plus vêtu avec la défroque des générations anciennes' (I, 131). Sartorial farce dogs all his efforts, just as his stylistic incubus is the classical rhetoric dinned into him at school: 'Ma tête avec ce qu'il y a dedans: thèmes, versions, discours, empilés comme du linge sale dans un panier!' (II, 598). He needs to burst out, for 'j'ai toujours étouffé dans des habits trop étroits et faits pour d'autres, ou dans des traditions qui me révoltaient ou m'accablaient' (p. 695). In clothes, as in all else (cf. his 'bridging meal', half-lunch, half-dinner), he remains in-between, as with his 'costume de demi-saison'. Ever since Eden, many of us have been unduly concerned with clothes, the big cover-up. For Vallès, the cover dis-covers; it is a signifier, team colours.

A born dropper of clangers, Jacques both tries to watch his tongue (a difficult contortionist feat), for the secret police and their grasses pullulate, and manages to blow the gaff, as when, having discovered that it is easier to get fish-heads on tick than a whole fish, he is called 'l'homme qui demande des têtes' in front of a possible informer (p. 571). Wilfully or accidentally, Jacques is forever speaking out of turn. While this is serio-comic in the above instance, his other existential gaffes cost him jobs. He oscillates between being turfed out or dropped in it: 'flanqué dehors' or 'mis dedans'. He is often a self-saboteur. Vallès's humour often relies on slapstick, but is no less to the point for that, and silent comedy is, after all, all that soundless books can offer. Comic scenes in his work are often breathless, for physical comedy notoriously hangs on timing and velocity.

As we have seen with wardrobe farce, the body and its paraphernalia have a political dimension. As well as a temperamental, Jacques is a corporeal anarchist; his limbs lead resistance movements. *Gauche* is left-wing as well as clumsy; rebels are sore thumbs or all thumbs. In more ethical terms, Jacques possesses (and I need to coin) *maladroiture*, a redeeming gracelessness. His accident-proneness is meant to strike readers as a solvent for basic honesty. Language, like clothes, is revelatory: 'Ces cris allaient m'échapper comme une culotte trop courte que j'ai failli laisser tomber [...], ayant oublié dans le feu de la conversation de la retenir en l'empoignant par le derrière' (p. 607). In several senses, Jacques hangs on.

His feet, which lend this book its title, are crucial. If you are forever *à cheval,* astride, your footing is essential. 'Réfractaire, quiconque n'a pas pied dans la vie' (I, 138). Like the Tower of Pisa, to live aslant needs a solid base. Séverine describes Vallès's gait in terms of a rolling, effortful strut: 'Dans la marche pesante et cadencée, le roulis du gabier [= topman] et le dandinement du porteur d'eau'.[5] Vallès, even on *terra firma,* had sea-legs. An unlikely source, Jacques Lacan puts the seat of reflection at the opposite nether extremity: 'Nous croyons penser avec notre cerveau. Moi, je pense avec mes pieds, c'est là seulement que je rencontre quelque chose de dur; parfois je pense avec les peauciers du front, quand je me cogne. J'ai vu assez d'électro-encéphalogrammes pour savoir qu'il n'y a pas ombre d'une pensée'.[6] This puts the emphasis on physical, whole-body thinking and the usefulness of physical collision with reality. Feet likewise keep Jacques on the ground.

The body calls up not only banana-skins, bulls in china shops, the *lapsus corporis* to accompany *linguae, mentis, calami* and *auris,* but also prowess and grace. In *L'Enfant,* Jacques amazes his country cousins by jumping feet together over a gate, whereas his mother specialises in unsure-footed social alpinism. He talks elsewhere of his 'besoin de sauter à pieds joints dans la lutte' (*SEP,* p. 39). In *Le Bachelier,* his tongue trips over in a splended mixed metaphor when he tries to speechify: 'Ainsi finissent souvent ceux qui brûlent leurs vaisseaux devant le foyer paternel pour se lancer sur l'océan de la vie d'orages! Que j'en ai vu trébucher, parce qu'ils avaient voulu sauter à pieds joints par-dessus leur cœur' (p. 628). In other kinds of standing jumps, *savate* for example, he achieves real physical dexterity: 'Je dois à mes pieds de gagner ces cinq francs deux fois par semaine' (p. 597). He knows that his head is not a patch on his feet, and he takes real pride in his skill. *Savatier* or *savetier*: either would be a real craft, and better than his abstract *bachot,* that millstone. He prefers *savate* to wrestling, because, even when defeated in it, you don't signal that you submit.

Whether we call it Sod's Law, Resistentialism (Paul Jennings) or *contre-finalité* (Sartre), back-firing ironies assail the ironist Jacques; SNAFU threatens him non-stop. But cussedness can be a property not only of material reality, but also of human will, or whim. Jacques is pugnacious, and oppugnable (i.e. subject to doubt). Nowhere is this more palpable than in his conflictual relationship with the groupuscules of his coevals. There his foot-in-mouth disease (the Duke of Edinburgh, who has raised it to a fine art, coined 'dontapedalogy') frequently puts him in quarantine or Coventry. The quick-footed Jacques, his friends find, can often be *casse-pieds,* and shoot himself in the foot.

They form a marginal sub-class of down-at-heel 'students', who today might be called dropouts, though Vallès's versions are more inclined to drop in. In his time, they were numerous, and many a young man talked of going to Paris to 'faire sa bohème', as other and graver youths crowded there to 'faire leur droit'.[7] Vallès's account of this bohemian stage is much more panicky and concerned with the crucial facts of life, and for that reason more compelling, than Murger's saccharine tales. Vallès's belief in the educative effects of poverty are altogether different from his predecessor's.

Vallès's account starts, prophetically, with the pointed description of male embraces between Jacques and his re-found schoolmate, Matoussaint—a kind of loving competition: 'Je n'ose pas lâcher le premier, de peur de paraître trop peu ému. [...] Il y a longtemps que je crois avoir été assez ému, et Matoussaint me tient encore très serré' (p. 462). This sets the tone for the close out-of-stepness of Jacques's relations with his peer group. Jacques, throughout, will be seldom in tune with the customs, thinking, dress or verbal mannerisms of his co-rebels. Much of the time, he is also the odd man out as a bachelor, as the rest have steady women. Yet he has no leadership-potential, for he appoints Matoussaint, even while having his doubts, chieftain of the clan.

He differs, firstly, on references back to the glorious revolutionary forerunners. 'J'ai un jour appelé Robespierre un pion et Jean-Jacques un "pisse-froid" ' (i.e. a shifty, cold fish—p. 481). Though, to keep the peace, he retracts these insults to the glorious dead, he persists in thinking (like many of Rousseau's readers, no doubt): 'Il ne rit jamais, ce Rousseau, il est pincé, pleurard; il fait des phrases qui n'ont pas l'air de venir de son cœur; il s'adresse aux Romains, comme au collège nous nous adressions à eux dans nos devoirs' (p. 482). As for Voltaire, it is the writer of the *contes philosophiques* that he values: 'C'est le Voltaire qui donne des chiquenaudes à Dieu, fait des risettes au diable, et s'en va blaguant tout' (*ibid.*). He refuses automatic veneration (for Béranger, for example). Matoussaint, as a result, accuses him of contradiction-mania: 'Il ne sera jamais de l'avis de tout le monde, ce Vingtras!' (variant, p. 1647). Jacques, of course, immediately counters, and thereby underlines, this stereotyping, by claiming that, on the contrary, he feels at times that he is 'un religieux à rebours, [...] un moinillon de la révolte, un petit esclave *perinde ac cadaver* de la Révolution' (p. 483). This joke, with its reference to Loyola's demand on his Jesuits, points up Jacques's less pedantic concept of political militancy. He accepts the gang ethos when there is a need to muster forces for a demonstration or a street fight against political opponents, but rejects it when ideological argument erupts. However muddled and subjective he knows his convictions to be, he clings to them; his companions borrow most of theirs. Though never entirely independent from the group's view of social reality, he distinguishes himself from them by bloody-mindedness. He knows the fate of mutual-congratulation societies.

An especial bone of contention is the verbal style, the congealed rhetoric, of revolutionary clichés: ' '93, CE POINT CULMINANT DE L'HISTOIRE; LA CONVENTION, CETTE ILIADE; NOS PÈRES, CES GÉANTS' (p. 481). Jacques senses he is back to school, being flunked if he does not parrot the politically correct, homogenised formula. The Revolution has its sacrosanct classics, too. Jacques wonders whether he has simply left 'une cuistrerie pour une autre, et si après les classiques de l'Université il n'y a pas les classiques de la Révolution—avec des proviseurs rouges, et un bachot jacobin' (p. 515). His instinct is to mock such café politics, such armchair rebels and their vast Romantic imaginings (in which he includes himself, for he is an insider-outsider): 'Nous avons dix-huit ans [...]; nous voulons sauver le monde, mourir pour la patrie' (p. 513). He ridicules in particular Matoussaint, with his outdated passion for secret societies, the Blanquist tradition. Cloak-and-daggery haunts their get-togethers: 'Nous nous assemblons [...] en séance extraordinaire presque toujours' (p. 521). And yet Jacques recognises the boosting effect of peer-group pressure: 'Mon courage me viendra beaucoup de ce que j'ai juré d'être brave dans ces séances à la chandelle' (p. 522). Something of value emerges from farce and fiasco: being put on your honour teaches you not to flinch. His group sneers at another ('une crémerie d'opinions pâles') that plays cautious by signing a protest in a circular list of names, to avoid any standing out as ringleader (p. 490).

Though hostile (as Vallès was in the Commune) to lynching, Jacques is in favour of punch-ups, where you take your chance, just as he advocates exemplary, even if unsuccessful, demonstrations. Their japes often have near-lethal consequences (Championnet is very badly beaten up in one). Jacques himself is not to be trifled with: 'J'ai à faire sortir les coups que j'ai reçus. Ne me touchez pas! Prenez garde!' (p. 476). Yet there are moments of stillness, quiet sadness, amid all the rumbustiousness; it is far from a carefree existence. Being what he is, however, Jacques cannot breathe without humour. 'Je n'aime pas qu'on m'ennuie; si pour être révolutionnaire il faut s'embêter d'abord, je donne ma démission' (p. 482). Horseplay as well as fights, student larks and verbal jousts are all part of the fabric of their political lives. 'On n'imite pas Danton tout le temps [...], on est un peu *farce* aussi; et après le tocsin de 93, c'est le carillon de nos dix-huit ans que nous sonnons à toute volée. C'est le grésil du rire après les tempêtes d'éloquence' (p. 506). Even here, however, Matoussaint seeks to politiciser their games: blind man's buff, he asserts, trains you to spot spies (p. 512).

One living figure focusses their energies: Michelet. At his lectures in the Collège de France, which chills Jacques because it is an old man's *collège* (and what real advance is that?), Jacques feels uncomfortable in the role of part of a *claque*, responding on tap. He is, after all, a permanent member, often the only one, of the awkward squad. [8] He finds Michelet insufficiently clear on what he proposes, and would want him (like Hugo) to be more 'terre-à-terre' (p. 486). The *claques* erupt on cue. Out of step again, and as clumsy as in his childhood deportment lessons, Jacques mistimes his laughs and other responses. His grievance against Michelet is that he is only sporadically on a par with his written self; his books had been lucid, inspiring, heart-warming. When he orates, however, though the flame is still there, the lecture seems artificially stoked up and leaves an ashy taste in the mouth. Though Vallès describes Michelet mainly in terms of direct, physical impact, and hardly mentions any specific topics of his lectures (the man was a highly metaphorical writer himself), he does offer a nuanced critique, with changes of gear and mood as the occasion progresses. Michelet remains a noble figure, though a variant stresses much more the *comédien* aspects (p. 1650). While admitting that revolutionary rhetoric perhaps needs such props, Jacques still hungers for a less histrionic and more truly moving performance. Jacques dislikes his niggling response to critics, yet as soon as Michelet is under threat (his lectures banned), he drops all his reservations and organises petitions. The actual demonstration is, expectably, a farce. It is badly equipped—no banners ready—and as it is teeming with rain, it takes place unheroically under a screen of umbrellas (p. 491).

When, with seeming inevitability, Jacques and his friends plan a newspaper, it transpires they are strapped not only for cash but also for ideas. Not having outgrown yet the sepulchral Blanquist tradition, Jacques offers to do 'les tombes révolutionnaires' (p. 510), though he is more tempted by vengeful necrologies: 'Je serais accusé sûrement de *baver* sur les tombeaux; car il y a des morts que je jugerais à l'Égyptienne et dont je souffletterais le crâne' (*ibid.*). He knows in his bones that he cannot make obeisances to Plutarch or revolutionary greats. His independence is an awesome limitation, but it is all he has: 'Je le sens bien, je n'ai rien dans la tête, rien que MES idées!' (p. 512).

Louis-Napoléon's takeover on 2 December 1851 arouses his violent indignation. He is amazed that other people show so little stomach to resist; ordinary folk go on playing cards. This disillusionment could well have proved traumatic, but Jacques is too busy to lose heart. Instead of obeying the watchword 'Fatiguer la troupe', he manages only to 'exaspérer mes amis' (p. 527). Does he know himself what he really wants? A gesture, exemplary; a possible spark set to the mute anger of the workers? Anarchistic as so often, he laughs at his comrades' insistence on discipline and hierarchy. He receives yet another squelch from a veteran workman: 'Jeune bourgeois! Est-ce votre père ou votre

oncle qui nous a fusillés et déportés en juin?' (i.e., 1848—p. 529). Moral
shame and political impotence overcome Jacques's grouplet. It is a cock-
down theory of politics; demonstrations have become engorged, but
then detumesce. In an earlier text, 'Un Chapitre inédit de l'histoire du
Deux Décembre', Vallès relates this period, and the plot to kidnap
Louis-Napoléon, in a melodramatic, presumptuous fashion which tries
to make out his friends and he could have changed the course of history:
'Le coup de maillet du 2 décembre! [...] beaucoup en sont devenus fous.
[...] Nous sortions en 1850 du lycée; en 51, nous étions déjà des vaincus!
[...] Mais ils ont été la génération la plus maltraitée de l'histoire' (I, pp.
1076-7). This is an absurd claim. In the novel, the abortive event fails to
take place, appropriately, at the Opéra-Comique.

Vallès is clearly a combative writer, but who or what is the enemy?
Sometimes it seems to be the hero's worst foe, himself—with his
clumsiness, his impetuosity, his only spasmodic self-control. Is it, then,
his upbringing and conditioning he rebels against? For Marx or Engels,
Vallès's brand of anti-dogmatic revolutionary fervour is admirably
suited to moments of mass uprising (such as the Commune), but
nefarious in the much more lasting periods of protracted struggle, grey
endurance, for it lacks self-discipline and is, of course, for them hardly
theorised at all. He can only be in their eyes a petit bourgeois. He is
certainly not a proletarian, either by tastes (the good life) or in
experience (of the serious working world), though, as Jean Prévost
maintains, he is of *le peuple* 'par ses grosses colères, ses airs farauds,
son goût de la prouesse physique, ses fusées de bonne et de mauvaise
humeur'.[9] He is separated, though, as if by a pane of glass from the
workers, for whom he would want to act as a loudspeaker and a
standard-bearer, but who understandably mistrust his motivation. He
needs (but so did de Gaulle) 'un bain de foule' from time to time:
'J'éprouve de la joie à reposer mes yeux sur la foule des plébéiens; il y a
chez eux de la simplicité, de l'abandon, des gestes ronds, des éclats de
gaieté franche' (p. 650). Travelling through Lyon at one point, Jacques
pays shame-faced homage to the whole-hearted rebels of the textile
industry there, *les canuts*. Nonetheless, he remains immersed.
Throughout, his political idealism and the brute facts of life are not only
counterpointed; they overlap and contaminate each other.

Just as he progresses from counter-productive thoughts of regicide to
a realisation of the wider target: 'le mal social', so *Le Bachelier*
struggles to escape the prison-world of *L'Enfant*. As well as student
groupuscules, Jacques still has to contend with the (disintegrating)
family trio: the mother 'promène sa douleur muette entre nos deux
colères' (p. 532). Vallès displaces the whole affair of the internment in a
lunatic asylum on to a colleague of his father, who has now deserted his
wife. It seems an exaggeration when Jacques says: 'Il avait une nature
d'irrégulier, et le hasard l'a mis dans un métier de forçat' (p. 655).

Vallès even provides strong reasons why the father is so ready to have his son locked away: Jacques's reiterated desire to become an apprentice manual worker, his neglect of his studies, and his dangerous involvement in capital politics. On a trip home, Jacques rediscovers his own countryside: 'Tout parle à ma mémoire' (p. 656), and grows lyrical: 'Ah! je sens que je suis bien un morceau de toi, un éclat des tes roches, pays pauvre qui embaume les fleurs et la poudre, terre de vignes et de volcans' (p. 658). Passing peasants 'sont mes frères en veste de laine [...] ils sont pétris de la même argile, ils ont dans le sang le même fer!' (*ibid.*). A chill grips his heart on reaching home, furnished with keepsakes, piously kept by his mother: 'les miettes du passé' (p. 655). This 'reliquaillerie' gets in the way of full sympathy for her state of abandonment. We should remember that, for much of the period covered in *Le Bachelier*, Jacques is still in hock and in thrall to his parents; he has a meagre allowance, which he budgets strictly, as he had been brought up to do. He uses his mother's maiden name as a pseudonym for his first piece of journalism.

One of the reasons for Jacques's trip home is his mother's desire to find him a good wife. Already in Paris he has had a liaison with Alexandrine, whose affections he wins by relinquishing his pose as radical bohemian and speaking with frank simplicity of his embarrassment. He shacks up with her at her father's house, where he pays for his keep. It is a stable, happy period, where he lives for once like a fighting-cock. He has occasional doubts, in the best French boy-scout tradition (à la Saint-Exupéry or Malraux), about such comforts distracting from militancy, though he is moving away from the idea of women as warriors' rests to that of female co-fighter. When Alexandrine later leaves him for another, he is unvengeful and grateful for what they have had. All the time in Paris, he enjoys the sexy spectacle of women on the streets, in the Tuileries: 'Oh! ces remous de jupe, ces ondulations de hanches, ces mains gantées de long, ces éclairs de chair blanche, que laisse voir le corsage échancré!' (p. 556). Hunger is sexual, too: 'Un bifteck avec des pommes soufflées autour, comme des boucles de cheveux autour d'une tête brune [...] Des femmes ont de la poudre de riz sur les joues, comme il y a du sucre sur les fraises' (p. 557). Women are good enough to eat, in every sense. Food and sex also cohabit in the comic episode where Jacques gets off the absurd charge of attempted rape on the unappetising wife of his employer, Entêtard, on the grounds that he has been so poorly fed that he would have not possessed the strength (p. 585). It is frequently older women (cf. Mme. Devinol in *L'Enfant*) who fancy him. The mother of one of his pupils presses her nipples against his unprotesting shoulder; and Vallès leaves us something to contribute imaginatively: 'On entrouvre un grand peignoir à raies bleues, bordé de dentelles fines, et qui moule un corps de statue' (p. 613). [10] The girl lined up by the mother blows her chance

when, walking through an impoverished district, she makes plain her
distaste for the poor. Typically, Jacques questions his own scruples when
he rejects her for this: 'Je regrette mon acte de courage' (p. 665).

Several instances suggest that Vallès was far from averse from
sharing something of the opposite sex. At the *pension,* Jacques gladly
performs an inter-sex role. A woman writing to thank him for his sad
tale 'La Tête d'Edgard' says: 'Vous cachez sous un nom d'homme la
grâce d'une femme' (p. 638). Although he prefers clear distinctions of
dress (as badge of gender or of political affiliation), in terms of
personality he welcomes some overlap. Before the duel with his friend
Legrand, a second comments that the problem with their warring duo
was that there was no female element in it; a touch of the female would
have averted a senseless duel. Just before it takes place, however, an
admiring girl offers her luscious body to Jacques if he wins (p. 689).

The nadir of Jacques's experiences occurs when he rejoins his family
in Nantes. Villat nicely suggests that Vallès had it in for Nantes by a
misplaced anger, because it wasn't Saint-Nazaire (a true ocean port).[11]
Barges lie mainly motionless on oily waters: 'C'est le sommeil de l'eau.
C'est le sommeil de tout' (p. 534). It is a wretched locale, from which
he is tempted to emigrate. He feels like barking in misery, not only for
himself but also for all who live there (p. 536). Awful memories of his
schooldays there add up to this sensation: 'Mon passé se colle à moi
comme l'emplâtre d'une plaie' (*ibid.*). The woman, who, on his
mother's behalf, spied on him as a boy, still persists: 'Il me semble
qu'elle me vieillit en arrêtant sa prunelle ronde sur moi' (p. 537). He
sees duffers who have succeeded, and belittles his own scholastic
triumphs as those of an animal performing before a circus band: his
mother (p. 538). Even peasants, in this urban setting, repel him; the
common people are not authentic *peuple;* and the middle-classes are
reactionary. Finding that he is undercutting his father's rates for private
tuition, he is obliged to give up his little earner. With his friend
Legrand, whom he remeets and will meet again in Paris, he mixes in
some despair with the fast set, 'les têtes brûlées' of Nantes. Jacques
admires their expenditure—of money, energy and self—while
remaining aware that it has self-destructive seeds. 'Ces viveurs
méprisent la pauvreté, point les pauvres' (p. 547), an aristocratic
attitude that awakes a spark in him. Legrand and he witness a duel, a
prefiguration of their coming encounter.

Back in Paris from Nantes, Jacques recalls Rastignac and Lucien de
Rubempré, and, in a different mode, *Jérôme Paturot à la recherche
d'une position sociale* (Louis Reybaud), but such bookish, grandiose
ambitions, shaking a fist at Paris, are beyond him. Still, a little better
off as a result of Mlle. Balandreau's legacy, over which he haggled with
his parents, he enjoys the pleasures of eating out, for once, in some
style. 'L'égoïsme m'empoigne!' (p. 555). Though his night shadow

walks tall, 'il s'agit de me faire une place aussi large au soleil' (p. 558). Meanwhile, if he minimally prospers, the society around him has changed for the still worse. The former rebels have been subdued by a police-regime of spies and informers. Jacques always copes better with pitched battles than with wars of attrition. As so often, he finds a comic image for his pain and frustration: 'Ceux qui ont des voix de stentor doivent se mettre une pratique [= squeaker] de polichinelle dans la bouche' (p. 562). He also sums up expertly his mixture of obduracy and defeatism: 'Contre quoi se cogner la tête?' (p. 566). He and his erstwhile co-rebels are simply making a shindig in a vacuum.

At school in Nantes, Legrand had deployed an effective tactic of dozing to counter brain-fag and mind-stuffing; a studied role of invincible ignorance had been his version of dumb insolence, and an artifice of self-preservation, which Jacques envies without being able to emulate. When they are reunited in Paris and living together in penniless promiscuity, the territorial imperative comes into operation. The constant gooseberry in their *ménage* is poverty. Vallès deliberately fosters a sexual interpretation by talking of 'ce long accouplement forcé' (p. 700). As in those *collages* which engrossed Huysmans, the two young men rub each other up the wrong way, squabbles over trivialities breed insults, and friction yields to anger. The face-to-face of the brewing duel is prepared for by the polarisation they both choose; the Catholic Legrand declares: 'Je crois à *Celui d'en haut,* tu crois à ceux d'en bas' (p. 687). They live 'en chien de fusil' (p. 572): curled up small in their garret, and like a cocked gun-hammer. They will progressively talk themselves into a duel, which both acknowledge to be symbolic. Each of them is wittingly a stand-in for the real adversary: *la misère* (Cf. the founding unholy trinity of father/mother/son, which also had to break down. Like another great antithesiser, Balzac, Vallès might well have though that 'il n'y a que Dieu de triangulaire').[12] The actual pretext for the slap precipitating the duel is brushed aside as irrelevant. The event is remote-controlled, built into their situation.

Both desire an explosive settlement of their differences—in truth, a recognition of difference. Serio-comically, they have to pawn belongings to buy the weapons. A mediocre marksman, Jacques cares little whether he kills or is killed, but is buoyed up to feel that they will at least be spared decrepitude. After the hemmed-in garret, they will enjoy the open space of countryside and sky, and commandeer it instead of being its prisoners. An apt black pun crops up, on *sapin:* both a cab and a coffin (p. 693). Jacques is eager to see how he will measure up to the test (cf. Stendhal's notion of 'la scène probante'). At Robinson, they are in Céline country, and a shooting-gallery foreshadows their coming gunplay. A resurgence of sexuality before imminent death excites Jacques with memories of full-breasted peasant girls at *reinages*: 'Ma chair qui s'éveillait parlait tout bas; aujourd'hui qu'elle attend la blessure, elle parle aussi' (p. 693). There is something 'over-determined', and certainly grotesque and crazy, about the long lead-up to the duel. Céline noted perceptively: 'L'une des rares scènes de délire que l'on trouve dans la littérature française [...]. La littérature française ne délire presque jamais—elle lyrise avec regret'.[13]

Scattered close or distant sounds lend the outing an air of threatening expectancy, as in the seduction of Emma Bovary. With more justification than Julien Sorel, Jacques claims that his action of shooting is on behalf of other *irréguliers* also (p. 695). His moods swivel rapidly. He whistles joyfully, then recognises in a Cornelian phrase, undercut by the whistling: 'Je diminue la belle cruauté de notre duel' (p. 697). The duel starts with near-misses. So near to death, Jacques greedily sucks in the world about: 'Je bois avec les narines et les yeux tout ce qu'il y a dans cette nature. J'en remplis mon être! Il me semble que j'en frotte ma peau' (*ibid.*). In a cinematic double-take, Jacques realises Legrand's smile is a grimace of pain; he has been hit (p. 698). When a friend goes to cut open his boots, Legrand stops him; they are his only pair. He has no grievances against Jacques, for whom the bitterest irony of so many in this novel is that he ends up not leading a charge on his class enemies, but nearly killing a good friend. The lugubrious procession—the bleeding Legrand in a wheelbarrow—is not taken seriously by partying bystanders, who think that he is drunk (p. 699). All involved now discard their earlier grandiloquence, the dross, the poses, and become simplified: 'Ma sensibilité ne joue plus la comédie' (p. 700). Even in such circumstances, Jacques locates a bonus: 'Il viendra peut-être un peu d'air frais par ce trou-là!' (p. 701). Yet he knows in his bones that day-by-day courage and resistance to oppression are worth more than such exotic one-off affairs. A chill notation lays a final shadow on the day: an ice-pack dripping on to Legrand's serious wound: 'Cette larme de glace m'est tombée sur le cœur' (p. 702). The whole episode has been a shifting sand of bravado, bravery and bravura.

The last phase of the novel—and this ending may be why some commentators underestimate its vitality—dwells on largely blank years in Paris. Jacques works in libraries, but his fellow-readers are no rebels, 'gamins de soixante ans, qui puaient encore l'école à deux pas de la tombe' (p. 704). He plods on the spot in the narrow circuit of the Latin Quarter streets. When his father dies, Jacques resurrects his old lament that neither of them should have deserted the land—a fond myth of their foundations. His father's corpse is a baleful warning of the dangers of submitting to the wrong choice of life. Jacques's one moment of proud self-assertion in this period comes when he remeets his old bully of a teacher, Turfin, and takes revenge, not only for himself but for other unfortunates in his classes, though typically Jacques saves the old wretch from an even worse drubbing (pp. 684-5). A brief spell as a removal man—the only time he could have worn the *blouse*—is followed by a builder's refusal to take him on as a hod-carrier; he cannot even put his physical strength to gainful employ. With his mother leaning increasingly on him, he decides to give in to the obvious, and become a (junior) teacher, *un pion*, while mouthing wild oaths to get his own back in time (p. 714). At the end, Vallès distances him from us. His old cronies around the Odéon gather to pass round the news that Vingtras has capitulated: 'Sacré lâche!' (*ibid.*). He had been tempted to suicide when he realised what he must do. Becoming a *pion* will, in his eyes, be a moral *auto-da-fe*. Readers, however, retain their previous knowledge that Jacques usually makes the best of a bad job, and bad jobs seem to be his lot in life.

'Toujours sur le qui-vive! Je monte la garde depuis le berceau devant mon amour-propre en danger' (p. 610). Jacques is a better man when protecting his aboriginal pride than when he indulges in trivial vanity. At such times, he is aware that he treats himself like a stock-market commodity: 'Le *Vingtras* est en hausse' (p. 612). Striving continuously to combat his past conditioning and to cope with his present dilemmas, he has frequently dumped himself in ridiculous and demeaning situations, out of which he has to posture his way. He is hyperconscious of his image in other people's eyes. Tugged between past and present, he is forever scrabbling to keep semi-upright on 'la pente de la lâcheté'. His ambitions never preserve him from stupidity, for much of the time he keeps up grudges unfruitfully, gets involved in rumpus rather than revolt, and batters his head against closed doors, instead of patiently working to pick the lock or going round the back way. Not a cynic, he often expresses regret at having scruples.

He is not a finality, but a tension. As a developing teenager, he cannot stall into a resumable character. An in-between, permanently suspended between adolescence and manhood, stretching to link students and manual workers, rooted in the provinces but caught up by the streets of Paris, between two stools (cowardice and courage). Small wonder, then, that, *à cheval* (as the pun straddles two meanings with one sound), Jacques experiences life as if it were an excruciating pun, a criss-cross he has to bear, if possible with a grin. While fully believable, he is anything but dully average. He has all the vigour of his creator. His existence is day-to-day and hand-to-mouth. Such a fluctuating life (cf. the motto of Paris: *Fluctuat nec mergitur*) begets passing moods, of cowardice, bravado, vim or listlessness. Changeable, then, but there are constants, held together by the oxymoronic notion: 'J'ai eu le courage d'être lâche' (p. 668—cf. William Empson: 'Courage means running'). He has the restiveness, the deflating humour, the fear of being suckered but also the willingness to give instant support, the scepticism towards his elders (and coevals), that typify the best kind of adolescent. He is keenly aware that higher things are governed by lower ones, the head by the feet, and that courage is diminished by shoes that pinch.

Bachelier, like bachelor, means also a tyro who followed the banner of an established knight. While Jacques is undeniably a greenhorn, he is not beholden to any chivalrous tradition of apprenticeship. He is thoroughly modern, and, despite his conditioning, he teaches himself as he goes along. He is a picaresque hero, but far from unscathed and frequently questionable, constantly exposed, by insecurity of tenure, to repeated humiliations.

*****

A moody, often a broody writer, Vallès often proceeds by phrases such as 'qui me botte' or 'qui ne me va pas'. This stress on being suited comes from a preference for instincts and a dislike of intermediaries. *Le Bachelier* is a destabilised, if not deconstructable, text, composed of ups and downs, every success menaced by fiasco, windfalls compensating for deprivation; apogees and nadirs of despair and elation. It is a jumpy text. The narrative leaps ahead to the resolution of the duel before Jacques and Legrand agree on one (p. 687), just as visualising the Emperor's spilt blood puts Jacques off thoughts of regicide. Journeys, to Nantes or Le Puy, introduce change of scene, variety. The graphic present, as in *L'Enfant,* brings immediacy, the full present flavour of events. Vallès refers dialogue to reported speech, because of his belief in letting people speak for themselves. There are fewer portraits than in *L'Enfant* (which is more static, running—or squirming—on the spot), or *L'Insurgé* (with its historic actors needing to be caught). The young, growing cast of *Le Bachelier* define themselves by their assertions, their actions or failures to act. More rarely than in the other two volumes does the narrator sum them up definitively. Emphases are often idiosyncratic, as when he lingers on petty details and neglects major ones.

All in all, Vallès declares war also on classical construction. The overriding rhythm is staccato, highly appropriate for a picaresque novel where the hero is buffeted from pillar to post. Even though little is allowed entry unless it affects Jacques directly, the resulting impression is less of a self-centred blindness to external reality, a narcissism, than of a physical plunge into a very definite context. Many times, Jacques addresses himself. This is a rhetorical device, but also a sign of self-division—not schizophrenic, but life-supporting, for the one part contradicts, questions, urges on or checks the other, as in the Stendhalian heroic self-harangues. Also, since in *L'Enfant* his mother often referred to him in the third person, he makes up now by using the first, or the second. Either way, it is a form of self-affirmation, even when it introduces scepticism or criticism. The repertoire is not restricted to comedy. As a writer of moods, Vallès can capture torpor (the Nantes section) as well as frenzy, or the slow grinding of time (and teeth) as in the post-duel period, as well as the uproar of student brawls. He can move between comic deflation and grave lyricism. He remains attuned to atmospherics, inner and outer weather.

I have described Jacques as an existential pun. *Le Bachelier* features much wordplay, and at one point Jacques earns a modicum plagiarising puns from other collections for a new one (p. 652). Pointed, political punning: 'Les buissons d'écrevisses—emblème du recul—fleurissent où hurlaient des hommes d'avant-garde! Cette maison, où l'on cassait la coquille aux préjugés, a pris pour emblème: *A la renommée des escargots*' (p. 484). Crayfish go backwards, and snails cower under cover. This chop-house become restaurant has renegued on its former clientèle of revolutionary paupers; its novelty is a retrograde step. A protest-march under pouring rain: 'Etes-vous trempés?' (ready for battle / soaked to the skin) (p. 492). Self-lacerating: on 2 December, 'je n'ai pas reçu une blessure, je ne saigne pas; je râle' (p. 529). The unmarked youth emits the death-rattle / bellyaches. Moving from literal to figurative: 'Ce printemps dans les arbres, ce printemps dans nos têtes! [...] Les oiseaux qui battent la vitre, nos cœurs qui battent la campagne!' (p. 507). Even when no actual punning is involved, Vallès's urge to pull together disparate things promotes a kind of excruciation. In a shabby waiting-room stand wooden chairs blackened by the ink of worn and touched-up trousers, shiny like the same breeches from over-use, and with wobbly legs like those of the impoverished sitters (p. 586).

As always, the crucial question is one of control. At times, Jacques stupidly allows himself to get bogged down in pettifogging details, e.g. a couple of pages on the fiddly business of coping with a decrepit hat, whose unreliable movements on his head keep wrecking his concentration. Jacques, and Vallès, can be sidetracked in this way (pp. 681-3). At the other extreme, Vallès's readiness to go the whole hog with his wordplay, to risk outgrowths, to avoid apologising for them, can pay off with excellent results. For example, when Matoussaint lands a job of writing the biography of a philanthropist who used to distribute soup to the poor:

> Sa famille veut élever une statue, elle a pensé qu'un livre, où seraient les *anas* de sa bonté, aiderait à consolider la gloire du défunt, que sa renommée tiendrait là-dedans comme une cuiller dans une soupe d'Auvergnat, et c'est Matoussaint qui a été chargé de tremper le bol. Il s'en acquitte consciencieusement, écumant les *bonnes actions*, les *traits de charité* qui surnagent dans la vie du défunt, comme des yeux sur un bouillon. (pp. 484-5)

'Écumer la marmite' also means to sponge, which is precisely what Matoussaint is doing. He is paid in kind and grows portly: 'Il est entré dans le pot du bonhomme', a punning twist on 'la peau du bonhomme', a theatrical term for getting into a part, as he does in fact. The climax of the episode is Matoussaint's ungrateful and unspecified pollution of the family tureen (could it be pea soup?), an ending which further deflates the already mock-heroic pretensions of the prolonged wordplay, which embraces parasitism, skimming off profits and impersonation. Just as there are 'métaphores filées', we could here talk of 'calembours enfilés'. Vallès does not make a mess, but a satisfying meal, of this pottage. Puns are never incidental in Vallès. It is on the occasion of Matoussaint's release from his prison-tomb and the pun 'Au Lazare de la fourchette', that Jacques asserts roundly: 'Le calembour n'empêche pas les convictions' (p. 503).

*****

Quite fairly, Pillu notes that *Le Bachelier* opens with a reference to death (suicide in *une carrière*), and ends with the father's death and his son's moral suicide, after a near-fatal duel: the shadow of death looms over the whole novel. [14] Other critics see this novel as a transitional work, a trough in the waves, a marking-time, and its general mood as more sombre and defeatist than that of *L'Enfant* or *L'Insurgé*. Much hangs on how we take the point of the humour in *Le Bachelier*. Is it desperate? Is it a branch of revolt in itself? Is it fatalistic? For me, it is not a side issue, certainly not a luxury: it is a vital necessity. While hardly an optimistic book, it is basically tonic, though often like a bitter-tasting medicine. Vallès's honest sense of humour moves him to expose his hero at his worst as well as his best, and at his median: that blankness, that absence of anything special, which make up a great part of most normal lives. Overall judgments depend on what value we give to the tone of statements like these: 'Mourir, allons donc! J'ai encore à faire avant de mourir' (p. 547), or 'Il faudra qu'on me tue pour que je meure' (p. 661). Jacques undergoes ups and downs, but, on a switchback, the downs are as stomach-lurching, as exhilarating, as the ups. The humour, existential, teams up with the tactic of making virtue of necessity: Jacques's tiny garret concentrates his mind wonderfully (p. 570). The grating quality of the humour chimes (or clanks) with the often excruciating circumstances of his experience. Compare these two declarations: Vallès: 'Je l'ai pourtant montré sans pitié, pourtant avec le rire aux lèvres. N'ai-je pas arrosé de gaieté la leçon dure au fond et sèche dans la forme?' (*Corr. M.*, p. 348); and Dickens, on his picture of the notorious Yorkshire schools: 'I have kept down the strong truth and thrown as much comicality over it as I could, rather than disgust and weary the reader with its fouler aspects'. [15] Laughter as leavener, against laughter as integral part of the complex equation.

Reactionary writers (such as the younger Anatole France in his *Les Désirs de Jean Servien*, 1882) exploited the same theme as *Le Bachelier*, as did Barrès in *Les Déracinés*, but from a radically different angle. They extracted the moral: do not leave home; do not entertain ideas above your station. Bourget joins the chorus: 'L'ascension purement individuelle [est] un principe de malheur personnel et de danger social'.[16] Upward mobility (*brûler les étapes*) must be discouraged. Bourget's *L'Étape,* anti-egalitarian, pro-status quo, is the opposite of Vallès's trilogy. The older Bourget got, the more dangerous Vallès appeared to him. Jean Richepin is more nuanced in his criticism. Vallès, for him, pleads a special case and should not have generalised. 'Ce livre, pris au mot, serait tout simplement l'apologie de l'impuissance envieuse. [...] Qui diable vous a dit qu'une fois ce parchemin en poche, vous n'aviez plus qu'à vous laisser vivre en attendant que les alouettes tombent toutes rôties?' Besides, if Vallès did survive and eventually come through, the much-cursed *bachot* must have been a helpmeet. He was lucky. What about the hordes of non-qualified poor? Instead of urging the abolition of the *baccalauréat,* we should demand its accessibility to all. Then, Richepin concludes slightly deliriously, when everyone has the same qualification, let the race begin. [17] After egalitarian education, Social Darwinism. Like many a *gueux* grown Tory with age, Richepin orders, in effect: stop whingeing. Zola's review celebrated the unique resonance of Vallès's trumpet voice, but, as with *L'Enfant,* the question is put: why, when he hates regimentation, does he get involved in politics? Seeing politics in largely parliamentary terms (e.g. opportunism), he calls Vallès a 'révolutionnaire d'instinct qui n'entend rien à la politique et qui est seulement bon pour la bataille'.[18] Zola's generation, putting its faith in the triumph of scientific progress, not politics, is superior to Vallès's conspiratorial youths. Even though mainly belittling, Zola came to regret this article as too favourable, and was later reported as saying: 'Dans ce livre tout est blague, mensonge, qu'il n'y a aucune étude d'humanité, et il répète deux ou trois fois avec une espèce de colère comique: "Pour moi, Vallès, ce n'est qu'un grain de chènevis"'.[19] What is wrong with hemp-seed is a mystery to me.

At the other extreme of political interpretation, in an otherwise thoughtful study of the question, Caryl Lloyd makes this questionable claim: 'The identification with the collective good and simultaneously the rejection of an individual ironic perspective make *Le Bachelier* a significantly revolutionary work'. An overlapper, Vallès does not polarise the matter in such terms. 'Irony, the distance between what ought to be and can be said, is the exact reflection of Jacques's economic situation'. This puts the stress, in neo-Marxian fashion, on the imposed recourse to irony, and underplays the wilfulness of the choice. Overall, Lloyd attempts, laudably, to switch the emphasis from the private and psychological to the public and the sociopolitical, but does not admit the possibility that Vallès seeks always to remain his own man while redirecting his militancy. [20] I started this chapter by claiming that *Le Bachelier* is the story of a near-miss. *L'Insurgé* will give this theme its most dramatic embodiment.

Chapter Eight

The Commune and *L'Insurgé*

C'est beaucoup plus simple et plus dangereux que cela.
(Letter to HECTOR MALOT)

The above was Vallès's counter to the broadcast view of the Commune as a bout of communal insanity (*Corr. M.*, p. 89). The Paris Commune of 1871 is a shibboleth. How you pronounce on it helps to define you. It became instantly and has remained a myth, not only in France but across the world and through history. In fact, it lasted only fifty-three days and so had little time to attempt or achieve anything durable. ' "The Commune" was always more of a slogan than an institution. It can better be approached by the hopes that it aroused than by its behaviour'. [1] It made bad mistakes (the ungrateful and cruel treatment of Cluseret and Rossel), and all participating, including the National Guard, were unsure of their roles or their powers. In line with Vallès's own anti-theoretical theory of the cock-up nature of public events, 'accident and circumstance did much to shape the course of the Commune once it was elected'. [2] Its hour-by-hour decision-making by non-oligarchic delegates (which must have recalled to him journalistic deadlines) suited Vallès's antiprogrammatic mentality and temperament; living in the present instant, at a high pitch, but preserving a sense of *fête* and of humour gave him an environment at last to his taste. Vallès was fond of symbolic gestures, exemplary show, if not the frozen attitudinising of Antiquity or its present-day neophytes, and the Commune was above all a symbolic event, a proof in action that actively-willed change is possible, or at least conceivable.

Audacity cohabited with timidity. The fighters felt most at home behind a barricade, and showed little keenness to go through open countryside, to carry the fight to Versailles. They fought best when inspired by 'chauvinisme de quartier', protecting their *patria chica*. The Bank of France was never expropriated, and the Commune seems not to have though of it as a powerful bargaining counter with Versailles. There was no obvious leader, and indeed the Commune puritanically voted to pay its members only fifteen francs a day, though Vallès undercut this by suggesting ten, on a par with foremen in certain industries. With Ranc and Lefrançais, Vallès wanted the Commune to be 'a simple executive organ directly expressing popular sovereignty through handing over responsibility to the workers' associations and arrondissement organisations'. [3] The whole process was close to anarchic, as the Communards attempted the difficult feat of organised spontaneity. As one of them commented: 'Les hommes de la révolution communale furent au-dessous de leur tâche—on est toujours au-dessous d'un peuple soulevé'. [4] Eastern Europe is currently relearning this lesson. The Commune legitimised *enfants naturels*. It was itself something of a bastard, and certainly hybrid in social composition. As befits the French addiction to verbalisation, the slogan 'la Commune' preceded any attempt to turn it into a working idea; a slogan without a programme, a brandished fist. Much reference was made back not only to the *commune* in the French Revolution, in order to grant the successors a paternity, a greater legitimacy and of course glamour, but also to those medieval cities that declared themselves independent of feudal lords. The spirit, then, was one of separation, although the Paris Communards appealed to and hoped for comparable uprisings in the provinces; they wanted their local attempt at decentralisation to be generalised. The provincial forces, however, apart from short-lived *communes* in a few regional centres, were in fact the most recent and dangerous enemies of Paris in the Assembly elected after the armistice with Prussia. The supporters of the Commune had excellent reasons for wanting to overturn the official regime: Paris enjoyed less real autonomy than any town in France.

Though the Commune lacked basic funds to carry out most of its more progressive measures, education was one area of achievement. Real efforts were made by the special commission, on which Vallès served, to make education free, obligatory, lay (in effect anticlerical and indeed atheistic), and much more fully rounded in its goals. In schools, the 'experimental method' should oust the old consecrated abstractions. This was much to Vallès's tastes. Despite his own warm sympathy, Dommanget is obliged to conclude, after quoting yet another grandiloquent declaration: 'On a peur que ces clichés n'aient tenu lieu de réalisations positives'. [5] Even so, many of their ideas were taken up by more moderate republicans in the 1880s; the Commune was ahead of its time in so many ways. In a related area, art, Courbet, accompanied on one occasion by Vallès, saved many treasures. As with education, the ideal goal was to open up art to all, and to strip it of its mercantile aspects. Courbet was not in a position to order the demolition of the Vendôme column, as he was later indicted, though undoubtedly he approved of the act of dephallusisation of this rampant symbol, built to glorify the exploits of Napoleon's Grande Armée and thus an emblem of cocksure Caesarism.

People make of the Commune what they will. For Ross:

> The failure of the Communards in the 'mature' realm of military and

politico-economic efficacy is balanced by their accomplishments in the Imaginary or preconscious space that lies outside specific and directly representable class functions—the space that could be said to constitute the realm of political desire rather than need. [6]

This is the Situationist angle (American branch). The Communards visibly loved *fête*, but they also had and represented concrete needs. And what is so marvellous about unconsummated desire? Of comtemporary writers, Villiers de l'Isle-Adam was, with Vallès, virtually alone in celebrating the Commune. He was genuinely exhilarated by the popular uprising: 'Quand un homme de bonne foi passe auprès d'eux aujourd'hui, il comprend qu'un nouveau siècle vient d'éclore, et le plus sceptique reste rêveur'. The joyful atmosphere delighted him: 'Quoi! Paris se bat et chante! Paris est à la veille d'être assailli par une armée implacable et furieuse, et il rit!' [7] Paris had to bear not only military assault, but a large campaign of propaganda and disinformation conducted by men of letters, the government, the press and military commanders. [8]

Few of the literary gentlefolk who waxed homicidal against the Commune witnessed it at first hand. Théophile Gautier was more tearful about the fate of zoo animals than that of Parisians. Even if anti-bourgeois (while living *bourgeoisement*), many writers saw no reason to root for the great unwashed. Some had been traumatised by 1848, and retreated to various kinds of ivory fallout shelters. Others felt threatened in their pockets: property, or investments; and a good number had simply sold out during the Second Empire, by accepting pensions, invitations to imperial dinners, or decorations. The literary circus was very largely tamed. Established writers felt as much aversion from bohemians and *réfractaires,* such as Vallès, as from the workers. Flaubert, Taine, Renan, the Goncourts, Barbey d'Aurevilly, Leconte de Lisle, Théophile Gautier all imagined themselves an intellectual mandarinate, anti-egalitarian. Maxime Du Camp, a twelve-carat *arriviste* himself, summed up his two-thousand-page account of the Commune (which earned him a throne among *les Immortels,* the living dead of the Académie) in these terms: the Communards were 'de petits bourgeois déclassés, des ouvriers désespérés de n'être point patrons, des patrons exaspérés de n'avoir point fait fortune; ce sont des journalistes sans journaux, des médecins sans clientèle, des maîtres d'école sans éléves'. [9] Their motives were envy born of frustration or greed. An equally common diagnosis was the pathological one (much favoured in our time by the CIA, KGB, MI5 and so on). If an individual can become deranged, then so can a whole society. The medical yields to the theological: a 'tache originelle' is at the root of such destructive, anti-social behaviour. In such views, existing society is a well-oiled machine being wrecked by loony mechanics. Guilt by association *roolz,* and decrees that bird-brains of a feather flock together. [10]

All the common people desired was booze and orgies. Especial venom was reserved for the women of the Commune, because many already misogynistic writers could not stomach feminism, and shuddered at the very idea of women's greater sexual voraciousness. It is amusingly amazing how often they protest, overmuch, to be disgusted at the sight of female thighs under skirts hoisted for work or breasts plopping out of torn bodices. Very little notice was taken of specific actions by the Commune. It self-evidently possessed an evil essence, beyond analysis as well as beneath contempt. The whole myth of the Commune is a perfect example of the lethal power of clichés in action, of escalation by stereotype. Vallès betrayed none of the essentially racist fear of the common man, and woman, which disfigures the writings of the great men listed above. He could never have mustered this thought of Renan: 'Le grand nombre doit penser et jouir par procuration. [...] Quelques-uns vivent pour tous'. [11]

Zola could not summon the moral, political or imaginative energy to view the Commune very differently from most of his colleagues. His *La Débâcle* hovers somewhere between horror and gleefuly morose delectation, as he charts a sickness, a madness which, in its apocalyptic finale, yet had, in his myopic eyes, the effect of cleansing France. Decay, Chaos, Renewal (coming from honest peasant values): Zola is more taken with his pattern-making than with the complex reality of the Commune. A more measured view comes from Tombs, a historian unsympathetic to its cause:

> The Commune was indeed opposed to the liberalism dear to moderate republicans and Orleanists; it was, in spite of its patriotic rhetoric, damaging to the nation and its interests as most men saw them; it did become noticeably less popular with Parisians and irksome to the middle classes at least; its leaders did include foreigners and men of dubious character. [12]

Myths, of course, are often thus partly true.

How did Vallès himself fare in this general onslaught against all involved in the Commune? One contemporary critic, Caro, after overestimating the number of writers who were Communards, exaggerates the political influence of books like Vallès's *Les Réfractaires,* in his urge to demonstrate that a major cause of the Commune was 'une barbarie lettrée'. [13] Caro reads the later event back into an earlier book: not so much logical deduction as cuckoo-projection. Even more cuckoo is Paul de Saint-Victor's labelling of Vallès as 'un bâtard de Marat, dans le *Cri du peuple*. [...] Bohème de lettres, aigri par une jeunesse misérable, affolé d'orgueil, ulcéré d'envie, sa poche à fiel crevée s'était répandue dans son style. Son talent réel, mais lugubre, faisait des grimaces et des contorsions de damné. [...] L'incendiaire couvait sous l'énergumène. Après avoir craché sur l'*Iliade*, il est tout simple qu'on veuille brûler le Louvre et faire sauter

Notre-Dame'. [14] Apart from 'talent réel', every word in this is wrong. It is true that an 1857 throwaway gag of Vallès had welcomed the burning down of Paris monuments (see I, 78), but when challenged with being a firebug, Vallès replied: 'Je n'ai aucune disposition pour ce métier-là. Voilà une heure que j'essaie d'allumer mon feu et je ne peux pas y arriver'. [15]

In a characteristically stab-and-pat piece, Edmond de Goncourt offered this inflationary gloss on Vallès's presence on the Education Committee:

> Risum teneatis [= *keep your face straight*]. Jules Vallès est ministre (!) de l'Instruction Publique. La bohème des brasseries occupe le fauteuil de Villemain. Et, il faut le dire cependant, dans la bande d'Assi, c'est l'homme qui a le plus de talent et le moins de méchanceté. Mais la France est classique, de sorte que les théories littéraires de cet homme de lettres font déjà plus de mal au nouveau gouvernement que les théories sociales de ses confrères. Un gouvernement dont un membre a osé d'écrire qu' Homère était à mettre au rancart [...] apparaît au bourgeois plus émouvant, plus subversif, plus antisocial que si ce même gouvernement décrétait le même jour l'abolition de l'hérédité et le remplacement du mariage par l'union libre.[16]

As with Caro, this is a marvellous, self-cancelling syllogism. It is impossible to mix politics and serious literature, but, when you do, you produce only destructive effects on society. Vallès, and his ilk, are simultaneously comic, negligible, and dangerous.

Engels at least belittled Vallès from a firm political standpoint:

> Vallès is a dilettante or, even worse, a miserable phrasemaker and a worthless fellow who, due to his lack of talent, has gone to extremes with tendentious junk to show his convictions, but it is really in order to gain an audience. In the Commune he only talked big, and if he had any effect at all, it was detrimental. [...] This *drôle de fanfaron*, this foolish loudmouth. [17]

And from the opposite wing, B. de Fallois, while admiring him ('Tout est encore vivant chez Vallès') and seeing exemplary qualities in his failure, chooses to present Vallès and the Commune in schoolroom terms. 'La Commune tout entière ne fut finalement pour lui qu'un immense chahut. [...] Pour quelques heures, le drapeau noir flotte sur les murs du collège. Tout cela est vain, tout cela va rentrer dans l'ordre'. [18]

As most often, Bellet offers the most balanced and accurate assessment: 'La Commune de Paris fut la négation triomphale de toutes les négations de Vallès. [...] Elle fut la surprise et l'étonnement révolutionnaires' (*JVJR*, p. 397). On the first page, I mentioned a debaptised school. On the centenary of the Commune in 1971, the pupils and teachers of the Lycée Thiers refused to see any longer their school named after the Versailles leader, and petitioned the *proviseur* to rebaptise it after Jules Vallès. At the time of the Commune, even *The Times*'s soul was sickened at the mass executions following the collapse, though Thomas Cook tours were up and running by June the same year to view the blood-soaked ruins of Paris. We are back where we started: the multiple meanings and uses of the Commune. After it and its predecessor the Franco-Prussian War came moral rearmament and the start of the *revanchard* impetus, directed not only against the Huns but also against the 'internal enemies' of the true France. Rather surprisingly, Marx offers one of the soberest judgments on the Commune: 'The Paris Commune [...] was merely the rising of a city under exceptional circumstances. [...] With a modicum of common-sense, however, it could have reached a compromise with Versailles useful to the whole people—the only thing that could be attained at the time'. [19] One of the many attractions of *L'Insurgé* is that it proves in action how the powerful appeal of common-sense goes under amid a welter of even more powerful counter-appeals.

L'Insurgé

Je ne tiens pas à être immortel après ma mort:
je tiendrais seulement à vivre de mon vivant.
(II, 891)

Around 1870, Vallès's image was substantially that of a bolshy humourist, a champion of marginals, a failed parliamentary candidate,—all of this summed up in the Goncourts' verdict (which betrays their customary fixation on accessories, and their malady of adjectivitis):

> Vallès, un homme de talent; il a l'épithète de l'écrivain; il a fait deux ou trois chefs d'œuvres d'articles. Et puis rien, il en reste toujours au *boniment* de ce qu'il menace de faire. Un tonnerre qui accouche d'un pet! [20]

In fact, Vallès's dudgeon was low in the couple of years before the Commune. His second paper, *La Rue,* had failed in 1870, lacking any real focus. The failure to make militant capital out of the murder of the young journalist Victor Noir by Napoléon III's cousin, Pierre Bonaparte, deepened Vallès's mood of near-despair, in which he talked of emigrating, and addressed his old friend Arnould thus: 'Le Vallès passionné et violent que tu as connu, ce Vallès-là se fait ermite' (I, 1148): an unlikely tale. He piles on the agony: 'Moi, je suis libre. Libre de mesurer ma prison—libre, dans ma misère, de ne parler ni de la cherté des loyers ni du prix du pain, [...] libre sous une loi qui pend au-dessus de ma tête comme un couteau' (pp. 1147-8). Writing *L'Insurgé*, which would embrace this low ebb before the explosive Commune, moved Vallès from the particular to the general, while always retaining the subjective. As George Barker wrote: 'By being miserable for myself I began, / And now am miserable for the mass of man'.[21]

Ready always to redistribute his chronology, Vallès reshuffles events so as to make a bridge between *Le Bachelier* and *L'Insurgé*, and to refer back to *L'Enfant*, for the third volume starts off with Jacques Vingtras back in school, this time as a *pion* at Caen. To this extent, Vallès allows his hindsight to affect his fictional re-creation. The first two volumes present a kind of apprenticeship for the third. It is an ironised one, in that it shows how unfitted Vallès was to play a leading role in the Commune, if fully equipped to be a participant, or agonist.

L'Insurgé begins, then, with Jacques at peace, and well-fed for once: 'Et Vingtras le farouche n'a plus la rage au cœur, mais le nez dans son assiette' (p. 879). For once he compares his father favourably with himself; the old man was never such a contented pig at the trough in his schools. Jacques, of course, is over-compensating for long periods of going hungry, and the whole lead-in adroitly blends self-indictment and self-justification. Like Julien Sorel at the seminary, however, Jacques cannot help blowing the gaff on his true self. When he says to another inmate: 'Je me fais petit, je suis décidé à être lâche', the reply comes: 'Peut-être, mais on voit que vous ne l'êtes pas, et les pleutres devinent votre mépris' (p. 883). Acting as *agents provocateurs*, the head and the chaplain set a trap, by sparking off a dormitory shindig. Jacques is caught *in flagrante delicto*, banging a candlestick against a chamber-pot, inciting the boys to riot against the *pion* (i.e. himself). As he has blown the job, he decides on a Parthian shot. Standing in for the *rhétorique* teacher, he makes an impassioned speech against the educational system: all learning will cease, dominoes will take over, and the youngest can shove paper-darts up the anuses of flies (p. 884) — *enculer des mouches:* to nitpick, the main goal of schooling, in his eyes.

Back in Paris, in his next post at the registry of births, he undergoes his usual fiascoes, but becomes also quote adept at the minimal task of verifying the sex of babies. For once, regular work gives him the chance of writing in the evenings. Vallès recalls here his early attack on the 'fausse Bohème' of Murger, and his first major article on *réfractaires*. He prides himself on the social utility of his cautionary tale; he has saved battalions of youth from falling for a mirage (p. 895). Writing against fake bohemianism, Jacques experiences a Spartan variant: he has to robe himself like a monk to keep warm; it is a hard-working garret the anti-Murger lives in.

Vallès introduces the first of his historical actors, Villemessant and Girardin. The latter looks like a zombie, but he is 'un des soubresautiers du siècle'. In telegraph-style, he calls Jacques 'Irrégulier! dissonant' (p.

903). Jacques learns that Girardin fears that the aspirant's cacophonous trumpet will drown the more piping clarinettists in the magnate's band (p. 903). Jacques cannot manage the house style. Taken up by Villemessant on *Le Figaro*, Jacques succeeds, in Trojan Horse fashion, in slipping some political fervour into his articles on *saltimbanques*. What is recorded here is the gradual emergence of a previously buried man: 'Cette fois, il me semble bien que je suis arrivé. J'ai plus que le visage hors de terre, je suis délivré jusqu'à la ceinture, jusqu'au ventre' (p. 906).

In contrast with the displaced effect of printed texts is the direct impact of the spoken word: the notorious public lecture on Balzac. Jacques presents himself as the joker on the evening's programme, *le singe* — not a plagiarist, but an entertainer capable of savage nips (as Villemessant had acknowledged when he said Jacques's articles had bite, and 'du chien'). Jacques implies that the lecture is extempore. Beyond Balzac, with whose wilful, ambitious heroes he expresses sympathy, he attacks wider targets: not only Napoléon III but the society he has moulded. Vallès keeps up the military motif in an extended image of the freebooter: Jacques is a one-man charge of the light brigade. He blatantly enjoys his moments of demagoguery: 'Je tiens ces gens-là dans la paume de ma main, et je les brutalise au hasard de l'inspiration' (p. 898). He knows, all the same, that his triumph is a one-day-wonder, but it has served, like a duel, as a purgation.

On gaining some response from his readers, too, Jacques starts to swell up, but, always on the alert, deflates himself:

> Heureusement je me suis vu dans la glace: j'avais pris une attitude de tribun et rigidifiais mes traits, comme un médaillon de David d'Angers. Pas de ça, mon gars: Halte-là! Tu n'as à copier ni les gestes des Montagnards, ni le froncement de sourcils des Jacobins, mais à faire de la besogne simple de combat et de misère. (p. 907)

He admits all the same his pathetic desire to be loved by his substitute family of readers (p. 908). His second period on *Le Figaro* gives him the confidence to refuse the role of 'amuseur du boulevard' (p. 910). He is in demand at last. Recalled by Girardin, he is given free rein to bark, as he has 'du chien'. Jacques attacks in print the colonial general Yusuf, which again makes him unemployable. The more Jacques remeets and rethinks Villemessant and Girardin, the more he sees beyond their misleading personae. Vallès here reenacts the process of learning to distinguish the essential from the accessory. It is time for the first *La Rue*, for Vallès's resounding article 'Cochons vendus', and for his imprisonment in Sainte-Pélagie. There, despite some spats with socialist ideologues, followers of Pierre Leroux, Jacques can state: 'Cette captivité n'est point pour moi la servitude: c'est la liberté. En cette atmosphère de calme et d'isolement, je m'appartiens tout entier' (p.

929). Indeed, the regime for political prisoners there was very relaxed.

The 1869 legislative elections immerse Jacques in orthodox politics for the first time. As always, he admits his lack of experience and training, stresses the impromptu nature of his speeches on the stump, and undergoes moments of self-doubt and desire to flee. A further cause of anxiety is the accusation that he has tapped slush funds in his campaign. (The evidence seems to point to a set-up—see Bellet's account, II, pp. 1869-70). A strong reason for Jacques's sense of being a fish out of water in this domain is that, when he goes with others to politely beard republican leaders about their position on a planned demonstration, they all (Ferry, Simon, Picard, Pelletan, Favre and Gambetta) wriggle out of committing themselves, with varying degrees of frankness or deviousness.

After these villains of the piece,we move to a gallery of portraits of leading socialist orators, (Briosne, Lefrançais, Ducasse), the militants after the *députés*. Ducasse is a substandard body secreting passion and strength of commitment. He enacts the executioner's part ('faire *couic* à un aristocrate' [p. 954]: a lethal onomatopoeia). In Vallès's treatment, such militants are partly comical. Either Vallès spreads out to kindred spirits his own medley of humour and conviction, or he looks for such a mixture before he can truly warm to the person.

The first real test for men of the left is the murder of Victor Noir. Some militants virtually welcome this death as providentially good for the cause, a martyrdom. Vallès sees clearly the farce present at such moments of tugging over a corpse. [22] He records the big talk, and the loss of nerve: can a small group take on itself such momentous decisions involving possibly hundreds of thousands? Rochefort almost faints (p. 964). For his part, Jacques is, as ever, unsure of the extent, if any, of his popular appeal: 'Journalistes [var. formalistes] que nous avons été!' (p. 958). All this time, Vallès stresses the inner divisions, the heterogeneity of the left, though he commandeers proudly the frightened cliché of the *bien-pensants* ('l'hydre de l'anarchie qui sort ses mille têtes, liées au tronc d'une même idée' (p. 961). Jacques feels more in tune with the general angry sentiments of the marching crowd than with any particular ideological camp. He thinks of leaders as foci, 'écriteaux vivants': 'Personne ne commande, détrompez-vous! [...] Je suis pour ce que le peuple voudra' (pp. 962-3). He is very alert to changes of temperature, of fervour. Victor Noir's brother 's'est refroidi en même temps que le cadavre' (p. 963). Crowds are a law unto themselves and pretty unreadable: 'Elles portent en elles leur volonté sourde, et toutes les harangues du monde n'y font rien!' (p. 964). As in the duel-section of *Le Bachelier,* Vallès excels in registering the switches of mood, anticlimaxes and exhilarations. In what is probably the result of hindsight, Vallès has Jacques decide that the moment is not ripe for public upheaval.

As Vallès did not serve in the Army, he works a vanishing trick on the Franco-Prussian War, which, for different reasons, is as conspicuous by its absence in *L'Insurgé* as in Huysmans's splendid story 'Sac au dos'. Jacques sees this war as a pretext for stemming the upsurge of revolutionary socialism. He is totally against war, and risks being lynched for publicly declaring this opinion. Even a good many left-wingers rediscover chauvinism. For once, the people, with their bellicism, have let down his expectations. Variants show that, despite Vallès's own proud touchiness, the whole business of diplomatic insult (a nice oxymoron) that precipitated the war leaves him cold (p. 1885). Jacques suffers a nose-bleed, his sole contribution to patriotic blood-sacrifice. The bellicose crowd are offended, for it will frighten the babies, incidentally all strapped up in *zouave* outfits (p. 970).[23] 'Mon pif en tomate les gêne!' (*ibid.*). He is moderately derisive of journalists who volunteer for ambulance-service, one 'un brave garçon, belliqueux comme un paon' (*ibid.*). In prison briefly for defeatism, Jacques meets a poltroon called Francia, who makes patriotic sculptures (p. 974). The whole war footing is presented as farcical. So much energy being directed to futile ends abroad that could have been channelled to urgent needs at home.

Jacques experiences another near-miss when he becomes partly involved in the failed Blanquist *coup* at La Villette. While ready to collaborate with such doctrinaires for the good of the cause, he spots their inner splits, and remains largely true to his instinctive preference for the collective uprising over the conspiratorial. Even so, he still criticises Gambetta: 'Les gens de cœur l'inquiètent; c'est une menace pour l'avenir' (p. 980). The one-eyed demagogue has always an eye to the long-term strategy, which alienates him from the mainly spontaneist Jacques. Yet even his antiparliamentarianism is not overly sanguinary. He would be glad to 'faire passer toute cette députasserie par les croisées—sans défendre pourtant d'étendre des matelas dessous, pour qu'ils ne se fissent pas trop bobo!' (p. 984). He notes the scrabbling for posts in the new republican government, in which some journalists jump on the bandwaggon and look at him 'de chien repu à chien pelé' (p. 987).

The International Workers' Association meets with more approval: 'C'est le Travail en manches de chemises, simple et fort, avec des bras de forgeron' (p. 991). Their simpler style of militant rhetoric, as opposed to the hieratic Jacobins and the secret societies' conspiracies, gives Vallès hopes of real advance towards desired goals. Jacques himself never forgets the practicalities, the need for food and drink as a fuel for fervour. He approves also of the *Comité des Vingt Arrondissements,* for this federation goes against standard French centralisation. As he explained later to Malot, 'ce n'est pas la politique politiquante, entendez-vous, mon cher Malot, qui amène ces explosions'

(*Corr. M.*, p. 275). Jacques is more at home in the push-and-pull, the lobster quadrilles, of crowds.

When he accepts the post of battalion commander in the National Guard, in order to give more credence to his activities as a 'tribune', he lasts only fifteen days. Totally lacking in military experience, tripping over his sword, he is—the story of his life—vexed by sartorial problems; his men vote him a pair of boots (p. 995). In an attempt to take over a *mairie,* he wrestles with the mayor for his sash, has him locked in a cupboard, and gets into hot water for illegal requisitioning of food for his men (p. 1007).

He finds a more suitable niche in the small team working on the text of 'l'Affiche rouge': ghost-writers for the masses. The twin pitfalls of public discourse, platitude and declamatoriness, awe them (p. 1017). They are wording the imminent Commune. Jacques, in fact, is on the run even before it begins, because of the charge of taking part in the affair of La Villette; his paper *Le Cri du peuple* is briefly suspended, but reappears in time to salute the proclamation of the Commune:

> La voilà donc, la minute espérée et attendue depuis la première cruauté du père, depuis la première gifle du cuistre, depuis le premier jour passé sans pain, depuis la première nuit passée sans logis—voilà la revanche du collège, de la misère, et de Décembre! (p. 1023)

That is the purely personal gut reaction. A few days later, Vallès celebrates the Commune in a lyrical passage where all the senses are brought into play to evoke the high hopes of those involved:

> Ce soleil tiède et clair qui dore la gueule des canons, cette odeur de bouquets, le frisson des drapeaux! le murmure de cette Révolution qui passe tranquille et belle comme une rivière bleue, ces tressaillements, ces lueurs, ces fanfares de cuivre, ces reflets de bronze, ces flambées d'espoirs, ce parfum d'honneur, il y a là de quoi griser d'orgueil et de joie l'armée victorieuse des républicains. [...] Fils des désespérés, tu seras un homme libre! (p. 1031)

Jacques overhears a reader's reaction: ' "Il a tout de même le fil, ce sacré Vingtras!" [...] Je ressens une ivresse profonde' (pp. 1031-2). Prose has to take over from poetry. Vallès's *Cri du peuple* went on to urge legality, moderation, cooperation, return to work, the freedom of the press. Hardly a lack of positive proposals, if all of them were commonsensical. *Le Cri du peuple* acted as a forum and did not embark on knocking jobs on papers of different persuasions:

> Quand nous entendons passer un cri de passion, alors que ce cri-là déchirerait nos oreilles et irriterait notre conviction, disons-nous que c'est un autre convaincu qui parle, et en ces jours de trouble et de misère, soyons larges, ayons plus d'indulgence que de colère et plus de douleur que d'orgueil. (II, 16).

The blackest irony is that *Le Figaro*, which Vallès fought not to have banned, said, when the government troops finished off the last insurgents, that clemency would be lunacy.

Once on the Central Committee, Jacques again is deeply conscious of his shortage of qualifications, his lack of acquaintance with most of the other members, and the precariousness of the whole situation, struggling as it was against a rival mayors' organisation. In sessions, Vallès protested against the regime of solitary confinement, arbitrary arrests and preventive imprisonment. Though he intended to include in *L'Insurgé* lengthy accounts of sessions (see II, 1818), in fact Vallès omits from his novel most of the legislative work of the Commune and most of the military manoeuvres of April and May 1871 (no mention, for example, of Rossel). 'Allez donc peser les théories sociales quand il tombe de ces grêlons de fer dans le plateau de la balance!' (p. 1033). It is possible to see such omissions either as artistic selectivity, or as self-censoring deletions, though I find it hard to see what the point of these would be, a decade after the events. He focusses mainly on the uprising, the collapse and the savage repression. Equally surprising is the lack of coverage of the food question during the Siege of Paris, for Vallès could surely have made comic capital out of this black material. (A man fattened up a huge cat which he planned to serve up surrounded with mice, like sausages; and lamb offered to a British correspondent 'ironically turned out to be a wolf').[24]

Instead, Vallès delights in recording the iconoclasm of a minor figure, Grêlier: 'Il signe des ordres pavés de barbarismes, mais pavés aussi d'intentions révolutionnaires, et il a organisé, depuis qu'il est là, une insurrection terrible contre la grammaire' (p. 1033). All of this is a joke about the metaphorisation of political discourse, the idea that words can be concretely subversive or kill: 'Cet homme [...] fusille ainsi l'orthographe' (p. 1034). He was always as fascinated by misshapen speech as by deformed bodies, as if freakishness were a more natural state than normalcy. Another oddball, Rouiller, on the education committee (where Vallès served, but he does not mention his contributions) declares: 'Je chausse les gens et je déchausse les pavés!' (p. 1035). But Jacques sees that Rouiller, for all his boozy, Rabelaisian personality, has a more intelligent understanding of what needs to be done than supposed experts.[25] Vallès is here inverting his snobbery, for the chairman, Vaillant, was a serious and well-informed educationalist.

In the full sessions of the Commune, Jacques, like a good many other Communards, presages defeat from the outset, but the moral imperative to see it through to the bitter end outweighs the political considerations. Like Malon, Vallès sees only too clearly the enormity of the obstacles to success: 'Les nécessités de la défense et de la guerre intestine ont mangé jour par jour, heure par heure, l'étoffe que chacun pouvait avoir en soi. [...] Personne n'a donné sa mesure' (variant, p. 1936). He is clearly less concerned about the small mark he himself left on the proceedings than about the failure of the total effort, all the more so as he joins the minority faction. Similarly, he does not waste time registering his opposition to the Committee of Public Safety, headed by the fanatical Blanquist and lethal atheist, Rigault. 'This was a strange anachronistic mixing of contradictory elements from the first Revolution, for it had been the Committee of Public Safety under Robespierre that on behalf of the National Convention had crushed the Commune of Paris'. [26] After studying the workings of the official political police under the previous government, Rigault had set up a ruthless system of counter-espionage.

The only description of barricades is of incomplete ones: Oh! what a holey war. Jacques sympathises with those *fédérés* tugged away by domestic loyalties, and understands the local roots which transform the battle against the Versailles troops into district-by-district encounters. Even in the blood and smoke of battle, Jacques asks himself the perennial poser: 'Est-ce que ça sait quelque chose, un éduqué?' (p. 1055). He answers honestly, when accused by a citizen of wanting, in his moderation, to keep his hands clean for posterity (or for tribunals): 'Oui, l'on veut paraître propre dans l'histoire, et n'avoir pas de fumier d'abattoir attaché à son nom' (p. 1058). When people turn to him as a representative of the Commune he has nothing, no strategy nor tactic, to offer. All he can do is to try, vainly, to prevent summary injustice. When asked to authorise incendiarism, he makes a distinction between the necessary and the indiscriminate. The Panthéon, used as an arsenal, is saved by the ridiculous speech of an aged bystander who opines that, if the Communards blow it up, they should, for honour's sake, go with it. This daft proposal amuses the crowd, who desist from their plan (pp. 1066-7). It is a good example of the comic sense being a sense of proportion. Its value is again shown when Jacques and others decide on a non-liturgical last supper: 'On taille un jambonneau, et une bavette. [...] Puisqu'on est sûr de la défaite, on peut bien boire le coup de l'étrier, avant de recevoir le coup du lapin': truly pointed zeugma and punning (p. 1067). Besides, as Jacques had said earlier, it is a final gesture against deprivation: 'Corrompu que je suis! Je voudrais dîner royalement avant de partir, [...] finir comme un viveur, après avoir vécu comme un meurt-de-faim' (p. 1049): a perfect chiasmus.

This is a truce amid chaos: lynchings, the massacre of the rue Haxo, the murder of the Archbishop of Paris, (probably provoked by Thiers). Vallès lets facts speak for themselves: 'Un feu de peloton, quelques coups isolés d'abord, puis une décharge longue, longue... qui n'en finit plus...' (p. 1076). As Jacques says, he has had more fights with *fédérés* than with Versaillais, but he feels proud not to have taken part in any butchery, and to have tried his best to stop atrocities. One of the several legends concerning Vallès is that he escaped eventually dressed as a priest. [27] This would have been foolhardy, as priests were favourite targets for revenge matches. In fact, Jacques, like Vallès, escapes disguised as a medico, and suffers several near-misses of recognition, particularly by Maxime Du Camp (p. 1085). Picking up corpses in his van, he reflects how death is helping him to survive (p. 1083). Expecting to be caught, streamlined by fear, he still has a moment to think of poses: 'la toilette à rafistoler, la phrase à léguer, l'attitude à prendre!' (p. 1086). Simplicity is a difficult art. As he goes into hiding, he experiences a sense of peace: 'Mes rancunes sont mortes—j'ai eu mon jour. [...] Bien d'autres enfants ont été battus comme moi, bien d'autres bacheliers ont eu faim, qui sont arrivés au cimetière sans avoir leur jeunesse vengée. [...] De quoi te plains-tu?' (p. 1087). Heading for Belgium and exile, he looks back to the sky above Paris: 'On dirait une grande blouse inondée de sang' (*ibid.*). His *Cri du peuple* had earlier pleaded with Parisians not to snipe at Prussians parading through the city: 'Les héros ne sont pas ceux qui disparaissent, mais ceux qui restent' (II, 20). Or those who flee to fight another day.

*****

We saw earlier that antiCommunard orators were less royal purple than puce; the rhetoricians of the Commune were, comparably, not so much red as crimson. [28] Words went on a spree: *démagoguette*. Jacques is constantly aware of the congealed mindlessness of much revolutionary discourse, including on occasion his own: 'J'ai honte de la métaphore sans carcasse' (p. 942). It is full of potholes over which he himself often trips. He is particularly conscious of the facility of automatism. 'Il n'y avait, devant ce public, qu'à faire ronfler la toupie des grandes phrases' (p. 941). Asked to improvise a funeral oration, he forgets the name of the deceased. Thinking quickly on his feet, but still offending the family, he transfers his aim to the theme of unknown soldiers (p. 994). Material conditions are crucial. The sloping amphitheatre where Commune *séances* are held is not suitable for tribune oratory: 'La déclamation a du plomb dans l'aile' (p. 1040). He is not averse from rhetoric as such, but only from its misuse at the hands of a Gambetta. He takes care to distinguish between sincere histrionics and Gambetta's ham acting, for he knows any public performer needs an element of show, *parade*. In the consumptive Briosne, Vallès relishes the living paradox of a weak-lunged eloquence, a riddled giant. In Lefrançais, Vallès responds even to a totally different style from his own: 'C'est le plus redoutable des tribuns, parce qu'il est sobre, raisonneur... et bilieux ' (p. 952). The insistent theme of deceptive appearances cohabits with an unspoken wish that people looked like what they are; that their essence surfaced in their existence. To this end, he gives each of the revolutionary orators that he singles out a dominant image, a leitmotif (Ducasse, 'un écarquillé', a permanently wide-eyed verbal executioner).

Neo-Freudian critics refer more rarely to *L'Insurgé* than to *L'Enfant* or *Le Bachelier*, for in it the Vallès up to his ears in public events is uppermost, and there is smaller room for 'family romances' to drool over. The relationships Jacques has with others succeed each other at a rapid pace. '*L'Insurgé*, says Bellet, 'est un grand texte à ruptures; il est fait de morceaux cousus, décousus et recousus. C'est un texte à sauts et à soubresauts, à vitesses variées' (II, 1812). In this novel, Vallès captures, mimes, keeps faith with chaos. This is Vallès's realist reply to the old aesthetic conundrum: does the artist have the right to depict chaos chaotically? A telling image of the disintegration of crowd unanimity could be applied to the novel as a whole: 'Toujours est-il que la foule se morcelle et s'émiette. Le serpent se tord dans la nuit. La fatigue le hache en tronçons qui frémissent encore. Deux ou trois saignent' (p. 983). He had plans for many more portraits of historical figures than the text now presents. In many ways, Vallès is more interested in the self, the essence, of those he evokes than in what they did. Though the portraits, typically, are dynamic ones, they do stall the narrative, or give it the appearance of a passing parade. In some ways, *L'Insurgé* is a multiple obituary or memory-book. Several times, Vallès blinkers his hindsight, his 'aft-boding' (Ogden Nash), in order to keep faith with the less-informed man he was at the time of the events. What is obvious is that the frantic life of the Commune is irreducible to any classical kind of artistic representation. A student of the manuscripts, Silvia Disegni, finds that the many *blancs* in the text are deliberate and often result from wilful deletion of bridging material, so as to produce a disconnected effect that would try to match the rapidity of change in 1870-1871 itself. [29] Bellet is equally convinced that Séverine's editing of the manuscript involved ordering, not insertions or deletions (II, 1815). We have, in substance, the text willed by Vallès (*ibid.*, p. 1818).

'Le narrateur de cinquante ans est celui-là même qui, à la fois, s'engage passionnément dans son récit et le tient à distance critique' (Bellet, II, 1810). Though distanced by a frequently comic perspective — telling puns, Daumier-like grotesquerie of characterisation, and ebullient irony — events and moods in *L'Insurgé* come across with shocking immediacy. The humour infuses, and does not merely leaven, the prose. While it is true that, as *L'Insurgé* builds up steam, the jottings of events grow too hectic to allow for punning on the scale of the more leisurely, often time-marking *Le Bachelier*, Jacques refers to himself as 'un écolier aux moustaches grisonnantes' (p. 1056). If life is a game, the rules keep changing at a frenzied rate, and the insurgents find themselves enmeshed in a more deadly variety, the *Kriegsspiel* conducted by Bismarck and the Versailles authorities. [30] For all that, Jacques does not decide that the game is not worth the candle, for even in defeat he remains immensely grateful for the experience he has lived through. Even in its gravest moments, *L'Insurgé* seldom misses a chance, as we have seen many times, for a generally pointed piece of wordplay. Vallès cultivated glaring oppositions (as in the nose-bleed episode), because he believed that they would appeal to the common reader. 'Le peuple aime la grimace burlesque et hardie' (p. 954). Just as the Commune embezzled or recycled churches for use for political meetings, so verbal *détournement* 'is no mere Surrealist or arbitrary juxtaposition of conflicting codes; its aim, at once serious and ludic, is to strip false meaning or value from the original'. [31] Vallès achieves this by diverting clichés and slogans. When Jacques hears a demagogue spouting commonplaces about ancestors in 1793 ('Nos pères, ces géants'), he reacts by pointing out that his grandfather was nicknamed 'Short-arse' in his village (p. 927). Another *détournement* is the reinvesting of Christic images (Golgotha, Barabbas, Calvary, Judas) in a revolutionary text and context (see Bellet, II, 1811).

Even allowing for the unfailing self-mockery of any serious Vallès text, *L'Insurgé* displays, understandably, more pride than *L'Enfant* or *Le Bachelier*. His life effort, comments Duvignaud, was guerrilla warfare: 'Mais la guérilla est chose rurale. [...] Vallès la prolonge à Paris, en écrivant la "Grande Jacquerie" '.[32] For Bellet, *L'Insurgé* scoops Malraux: 'sans "philosophisme", sans lyrisme épique; dans de simples dialogues de personnages, dans des séquences juxtaposées: dans une filmographie révolutionnaire'. [33] In a less triumphal vein, Vallès is quoted by Séverine as saying in his last years: 'Qui sait s'il ne vaut pas mieux qu'elle [la Commune] ait été vaincue? Nous aurions été, peut-être, bien embarrassés de la victoire'. [34] Against this we should place Bellet's view that, even after the defeat, Vallès would never again have the sense of being 'un vaincu' (II, p. x). I myself feel that, given the place of fiascoes in Vallès's total experience, he half-consciously read the Commune as another one: ill-prepared, mismanaged, fundamentally hopeless—and magnificent. Not a few commentators, even sympathetic to its goals, have judged the Commune as setting back the cause of the downtrodden by a decade or more. Then again, but for the almighty fright it dealt the establishment, would anything have changed in France for even longer than that? Whatever the political effect of the Commune, I agree with Bellet (p. 1809) that Vallès found in it his true (enlarged) family—the one you choose, not the one dealt out to you by biological fate. He presided over the last session of the Commune.

*****

Even though Vallès failed in the common nineteenth-century ambition of writers to become a successful dramatist, in his fiction he sees, and renders, dramatically. There is an insistent theme of role-playing, indeed of role-imprisonment, both in the family home, in student bohemian Paris, or on the political stage (Gambetta can hardly stop striking poses). One of Vallès's most devoted readers, Louis Guilloux, puts beautifully this weariness of having always to repeat the same lines: 'Ce qu'il y avait d'intolérable, c'est que c'était toujours l'épicier qui était l'épicier, l'avocat, l'avocat, que M. Poincaré parlait toujours comme M. Poincaré, jamais, par exemple, comme Apollinaire et réciproquement'. [35] Vallès sets his play *La Commune de Paris* (1871) in a longer historical framework and tradition (back to 1848): the past as millstone, trampoline, shaper. It is an apologetics, written very soon after the historical events, and so is affected by self-censoring; its characters are fictitious, though Vallès is transparently present. Though this epic drama interested the Berliner Ensemble, and was first performed in 1983 in Peking, shorn of many tirades and speeded up in narrative, under the title *Le Temps des cerises* (after the popular song by Jean-Baptiste Clément), it is hard to disagree with the verdict of Carassus: 'Brecht et Adamov, moins métaphoriques, moins imagés, seront en fin de compte moins abstraits. [...] Cette illustration défensive et glorificative rejoint souvent l'image d'Épinal'. [36] Vallès forgets in his theatre what he practises in his fiction: interaction, interplay: in *La Commune de Paris*, the figures declaim at each other. He went on caressing theatrical ambitions to the end of his days; as Alexis reports:

> L'idée de [...] *La Baraque* (ou *la Dompteuse*), pièce à grand spectacle, avec parades, cage de dompteuse, bêtes féroces—peignant le monde des saltimbanques, que Vallès avait étudié—la vie des irréguliers. [...] Je l'ai entendu, plein d'enthousiasme, m'expliquer ce désir 'de donner un coup de corne' dans les conventions scéniques actuelles, et nourrir l'espoir que les préoccupations tout autres apportées par son nom et sa qualité de militant lui permettraient d'oser davantage et de faire accepter plus facilement ses audaces dramatiques.[37]

Circus, irregulars, the shuttle between literature and politics, going over the top, desiring wide appeal: much of the essential Vallès rests in this spectacular and unavailing ambition.

Within the Trilogy itself, *L'Insurgé* is obviously the most epic volume. Vallès practised increasing discontinuity and widening social and political coverage as it progressed. Because of the magnetic mother, *L'Enfant* has a fixed pole. *Le Bachelier* moves off into the picaresque (even if Jacques's travels often involve juddering on the spot). *L'Insurgé* reflects and brings chaos; the picaresque hero runs up against the ultimate sanctions: imprisonment and death. After struggling to escape parents and poverty, Jacques has to escape for his life, into unwanted exile. The Trilogy, for all these threads and patterns, is not perfect. The very idea would have appalled and convulsed Vallès, who had a deep distrust of the finished object (e.g. statues). If imperfect, however, the variants of the Trilogy reveal a Vallès no less spontaneous and outgoing, but much more self-critical than is often imagined.

Chapter Nine

Exile and Return: *La Rue à Londres*

Exile

Long before he was forced into it, Vallès hankered for a chosen
exile, an expatriation (or 'exmatriation'). [1] Eight years before his first
trip to England in 1865, he observed some Englishmen in Paris:
'L'Anglais garde, dans son faux col trop raide et son coatchman [*sic*]
trop large, un air étrange et distingué. Il est muet, il a caché sa langue
au fond de sa valise; s'il ose parfois s'en servir, s'il parle, on ne
comprend point son langage' (I, 63). An unpromising introduction:
stiffness, reserve, incomprehensibility, otherness, and yet an imposing
idiosyncrasy. When he actually set off for England, the unwitting
dramatic irony as regards the future is intense: 'Je n'ai point le
douloureux honneur de partir proscrit, rien ne m'oblige au rôle d'exilé'
(p. 771). And again at the end: 'Après trois semaines de séjour à
Londres, je m'aperçus que pour pouvoir parler de l'Angleterre, il fallait
y passer dix ans. —Je regardais et je ne voyais pas; j'écoutais et
n'entendais pas: je n'aime à parler que de ce que j'ai entendu et vu. Je
me moquai de moi-même et repassai la mer' (p. 793). This honest
admission of his limitations is typical. On the more positive side, he was
already grateful for the haven offered here to (post-1851) *proscrits;* and
impressed by policemen sorting out a brawl: 'Au lieu d'être violents
parce qu'ils représentent l'État, ils étaient indulgents parce qu'ils étaient
la loi' (p. 1559). He salutes the beneficial effects of self-control: 'Dans la
rue comme au parlement, le *self governement* [*sic*] s'exerce et
l'individualisme est en campagne' (p. 1566). When the trip became an
exile, from late 1871, or early 1872 onwards to 1880, these mixed
reactions to things and people English had ample time to develop in
complexity.

He was sentenced to death *in absentia;* the ultimate sanction for
taking French leave. Although he experienced England in many ways as
a prison, a far from magnificent hulk, and was kept under surveillence
like other political refugees, in fact his freedom of movement was
constrained only by his financial state. This was adequate at the outset,
by reason of receipts from *Le Cri du peuple* and a windfall inheritance,
of which, despite legal tangles, he managed to get part; but for the bulk
of his time in London he was severely strapped for cash. As he knew
and partly gloried, his style was too blatantly telltale for his journalism
to appear under pseudonyms in Paris papers. When this subsequently

became more feasible, he badgered his friend Malot unmercifully (as he had already in the early 1860s) about loans, contracts, approaches to editors and publishers. Frequently using images of safety valves in his correspondence, Vallès occasionally apologised: ' Pardonnez ce qu'il y a d'égoïste dans ces exhalaisons à outrance' (*Corr. M.*, p. 187). When another friend, Arnould, rebuked him for his one-sided view of friendship, Vallès, cut to the quick, responded speciously (*Corr. A.*, p. 285). His main defence was that he underwent, in effect, an eight-year fit of *le spleen*, the exile's blues. Even his affair with a Belgian schoolteacher, who bore him a daughter whom he loved deeply, ended tragically when the baby died after nine months on the fateful date of 2 December.

He enjoyed little comradeship or agreement with the other Communards in exile, finding, as always, the Marxists too aridly theoretical, and the Blanquists obsessed with armed insurrection. Indeed, Vallès seemed to be veering towards venture capitalism. He nursed various fruitless projects: a wine business, porcelain painting, a non-political weekly aimed at a comfortably-off English readership and bringing news of cultural life in Paris. This might in turn spin off a luxury art shop. Together with other exiles, he founded the short-lived French Athenaeum, a meeting place for lectures and language tuition. The even briefer-lived *The Coming P* (the title, suggesting a damp squib, shows Vallès's shaky grasp of English. The full 'People' would hardly have been incriminating, anyway) displays Vallès's energetic efforts to get into print (he tried as far afield as Russia, via Zola). [2] From about 1876, his correspondence talks repeatedly of a novel, a kind of *Vingtras IV*, for which he mooted various titles: *Les Réfractaires de Londres, Les Mystères de Londres, Les Misères de Londres, Londres infâme*. Much of the material for this project was used instead for *La Rue à Londres*. He started work on *L'Enfant* in 1876. He mentions reading few books in these years (though he kept up to date with the Paris press). Swotting up some books on banking and commerce, he commented: 'C'est lourd comme le plomb, ces livres sur l'or' (*Corr. M.*, p. 262). His trips away from London were to Belgium and Switzerland and, within Britain, to Brighton, Kent and Jersey; he did not venture to the industrial Midlands, North, Scotland or Wales.

As for psychological exile, Wittlin, on the basis of the Spanish *destierro* (deprivation of homeland) coined *destiempo:* 'The exile lives in two different times simultaneously, in the present and in the past. This life in the past is sometimes more intense [...] and tyrannises his entire psychology. [...] An exile, as it were professionally, moves backwards'. [3] Home thoughts from foreign parts are normal, and the Irish Bull tells us that the exile is not at home when he is abroad. In some ways, Vallès in London thinking of Paris resembles Vallès in Paris recalling his provincial childhood. 'L'exil', he recognised, 'est une province. On n'y voit pas plus loin que le bout de sa manie!' In this perspective, even Paris becomes parochial: 'Sans autre parisiennerie que celle de la Commune racontée, re-racontée, jugée, re-jugée— parisiennerie effroyablement provinciale!' (*Corr. M.*, pp. 81; 223). Exile reinstated the climate of childhood (and thus helped the writing of *L'Enfant*): Vallès complains frequently of being left out in the cold, starved of warmth, contact and news. He is like a lover, or a desperate child, waiting for the postman in high anxiety and deeply frustrated when there is nothing for him. He refuses to understand why he does not get responses by return of post to his pleas, questions and demands. He sums up his state in these terms in a letter to a Paris editor: 'Vous avez la goutte, moi j'ai l'exil. Je ne veux pas vous arracher des larmes, je ne pose pas au martyr, je ne me drape pas, je m'embête. C'est embêtant, le manque de patrie!' (quoted II, p. xxxiv). Yet he learned to know in his bones that his exile changed his writing for the far better, that, in this area, it paid off handsomely. 'Il est à constater que le brouillard de Londres n'a jamais endolori le talent ni voilé la flamme dans les têtes françaises. Au contraire, il a trempé des styles, comme l'eau boueuse du Furens trempe les armes' (*TP*, p. 259).

La Rue à Londres

Vallès's documentary groundwork for *La Rue à Londres*, finally published in 1884 after a dozen or so years of fits and starts, was essentially the reading of French visitors to these shores: Flora Tristan, Ledru-Rollin, Louis Blanc, Alphonse Esquiros, Taine and Louis Enault (with wood engravings by Gustave Doré) (see II, 1983). *La Rue à Londres*, similarly, had drawings and etchings, by Auguste Lançon, an ex-*fédéré*. Possibly needing to boost his own morale, Vallès boasted to Malot in 1876: 'Ce serait le premier livre impartial sur l'Angleterre. Tous ont menti jusqu'ici depuis Esquiros jusqu'à Taine. Mettons qu'ils se sont trompés' (*Corr. M.*, p. 129). *La Rue à Londres* is not impartial; it is passionately wrong-headed, with moments of insight. In its admission of defeat (the English are beyond summary, if not beyond judgment), its rueful acknowledgment of the complexity of the subject, it is closer to interesting fiction than to a sociological survey feigning accuracy.

Much of the text is mnemonic. Afraid of losing Paris for good in fact or in memory, Vallès recites its characteristics, in opposition to those of London. Just as mother and son bounced off each other originally, Vallès always needs to play off polarities in this way, favouring now one, now the other, in a cross-Channel shuttle. He starts with *la rue*, his favourite space, in both cities. The streets of Paris win hands down: light, gay, not overcrowded and gloomy like their London

counterparts. Here, there is little conversation, that 'vie d'échange' that
Vallès needs like oxygen. He cannot tell the English apart, for they are
like interchangeable mechanisms: 'Ils vont, ils viennent comme des
pistons de machines, ils passent comme des courroies se mêlent, comme
des trains se croisent' (II, 1135). Thus running together the Industrial
Revolution and individual Londoners, Vallès gives fair notice of what
will be his regular tactic of overstatement, of demonological (and, much
more rarely, angelical) procedure. London 'n'a pas pour deux liards de
fantaisie' (p. 1137). Exiled, he rosifies Paris, polarising even public
drunkenness in both cities: 'C'est la soulaison noire, point l'ivresse rose'
(p. 1139). He was especially disgusted by female drunks, vomiting on
the cobblestones (*ibid.*). He wilfully underestimates French alcoholism,
accusing Zola of slandering *le peuple* in *L'Assommoir* (p. 1309).
Shuttling, however, he notes that London streets are less military than
Parisian ones: fewer soldiers, and they stroll unarmed (p. 1139).

Disoriented, he misses landmarks. 'Rien ne s'accuse en traits nets et
logiques' (p. 1140). He sounds here like the quintessential neo-Cartesian
Frenchman he never was. Though he accuses England of
compartmentalisation, this is in fact what he misses: in London the poor
and the rich live cheek by jowl (p. 1148). He offers a stereotyped
French notion of English antisystematic thinking: 'L'esprit anglais ne
sait pas classer ni déduire, voilà pourquoi mes voisins de la bibliothèque
anglaise, tout en bûchant plus qu'on ne bûche chez nous, ne feront pas
sortir du sol des idées nettes et claires. Leurs pensées flottent dans le
brouillard, comme leur soleil s'y noie' (p. 1303). Amid all such
diametrically opposed patterns, however, his eyes are open to a
phenomenon still observable today: 'Une cité où les sergents de ville ont
l'air poli et où les gentlemen ont l'air féroce' (p. 1140).

We have to wonder how many English homes Vallès penetrated, and
in those he did how often he was slighted by long waits in the halls. (We
must also wonder how many middle or upper-class homes Vallès was
familiar with in Paris). Against the common British sense of French
homes as impregnable bastions, Vallès presents English homes shut up
against the world outside: 'Pays hostile, race murée!' (p. 1142). Vallès
kicks against the cliché of 'le confortable anglais' (though I for one find
little physical ease in French furniture): 'L'Angleterre est le pays du
mal-vivre, du mal-loger, du mal-manger, du mal-s'asseoir, et du mal-
dormir' (p. 1206). In these areas, Vallès misses concierges, a *table de
nuit* for the jerry, and sauces on food (pp. 1207; 1211; 1213). Churches
are no more welcoming than homes. Protestant temples are lugubrious,
have less garish colour and smell than French Catholic ones; reformed
religion offers an 'implacable tristesse' (p. 1144), and infiltrates
everywhere. Like Stendhal before him, Vallès was appalled at the
British veto on breaking the Sabbath. The English Sunday lasts all week:
'La platitude du jour sacré' (p. 1194). Vallès almost renegues on his

godlessness: 'La simplicité crue du protestantisme m'effraie plus que la grâce enivrante et enflammée du catholicisme', but luckily he pulls himself up short: 'L'encens et les bouquets font presque oublier Dieu dans les chapelles embaumées de France' (p. 1196). A few pages after the largely black-and-white opening, Vallès admits the complexity of the subject, and his own perplexity: 'Quelle ville!... toute pleine de contradictions énormes, amas de confusions!' (p. 1146).

The biggest contradiction is the coexisting grandeur and misery of London. Whereas the poor in Paris 'ont la pudeur de leur misère', the English paupers flaunt theirs, using the doorstep as a sofa (pp. 1146; 1148). 'On ne connaît point la blouse à Londres' (p. 1140). As ever, Vallès looks for badges of membership, identity tags, forgetting that the *blouse* concealed a host of different political persuasions. English workers prefer 'avoir l'air d'un commis, d'un clerc, d'un monsieur', as they buy reach-me-downs cast off by their social betters (p. 1283). Clothing unmaketh the man. In Petticoat Lane, he gives this sartorial ideology a rest, and reverts to his lifelong anxiety about arse-out breeks: 'N'es-tu pas las aussi de montrer ton derrière, pincé par le vent, et qui a la chair de poule? [...] Pour un shilling seulement, si tu ne tiens qu'à être pudique, tu auras une culotte à pont' (= full-fall trousers—p. 1279). He prefers, however, French skill in making-do and mending, wifely husbanding of resources (p. 1149).

While profoundly anxious about the fate of children in the gin-soaked slums, Vallès recognises that children are freer, allowed to be children more than in France (pp. 1150; 1215). Their parents, remaining standing to drink in pubs, are thus prevented from the real get-together for the exchange of ideas that large French café tables offer (p. 1170). It has been pointed out by Tholoniat that, in concentrating on the squalid public bars, Vallès neglected the back-room meeting-places of dissident groups. [4] He sees the *isoloir*, and not the snug. Perhaps his visceral need for drinking in company, compotation, was hindered by the level of his English and his disrelish for draught beer. All the time, and naturally, he holds it against England, his unnatural second home, for not being France. He remains, however, open to new experiences. Lacking small-group discussions, he enjoys open-air mass meetings (e.g. Hyde Park Corner). Even if there are no political slogans or graffiti on the walls, no revolutionary historical markers, even if the English 'n'ont point senti le tremblement social' (pp. 1140-41), Vallès is moved by large numbers freely speaking their minds in public, just as he admires elements of British justice such as *habeas corpus* (p. 1146).

He spends a lot of time on leisure activities, presumably believing that you can tell a great deal about a people by examining its pleasures. Theatre, dances and music halls are all dismissed as inferior in London. Vallès dislikes the auctioneer-style hammer of the master of ceremonies, which affords an attack on automated pleasures, piston-like movements of artistes: 'l'éternelle marche *à la soldat!*' (p. 1165). All the same, while finding English stage-movements gross, he still admires 'ces friands de l'énergie, ces gourmands de vigueur' (p. 1167). The cross-dressing, the drag routines, so central to the English tradition obviously troubled him. One area that delighted him was music-hall satire, mocking Crown and Government. He voices a bitter complaint against all the spying on and censoring of free-tongued pleasure in France: 'Gabelous de la morale, gardes-chiourmes du goût' (p. 1162).

Vallès admitted to Séverine (and the phrases are delectably double-layered): 'La *Femme anglaise* ne m'a jamais enthousiasmé', and 'J'ai attaqué la femme anglaise, que j'ai coupée en deux' (*Corr. S.*, pp. 151; 73). While admitting eventually that pleasure with women is obtainable in London and its up-market tarts less blasé than French *horizontales*, Vallès misses *demi-mondaines* (in-betweens like himself) (p. 1271). He misses flirtatiousness, the come-on, the clear confidence that the girl or woman is the cynosure of male gazes. In England, women go off rapidly: 'On avait une gazelle hier, on a une girafe demain' (p. 1136). In contrast, 'la femme de trente ans, comme nous l'aimons, grasse et blanche, ou souple et dorée, appétissante comme un fruit mûr, irritante comme une odeur sauvage, on ne la frôle point, on ne la sent pas sur le pavé de Londres' (*ibid.*). English girls can be delectable (if boyish) up to a certain age, but then their blatant pursuit of marriage partners withers them. Perversely, he states that the very availability of English girls, the absence of social obstacles as in France, kills passion (p. 1261). On a more practical level, though finding breach of promise cases rather ludicrous, and though paternity payments derive from a mercantile logic, he finds them more humane than French practice. Reverting to male chauvinist wolfishness, he misses the ocular whistles of Latin men: 'C'est le seul pays d'Europe où j'aie vu circuler les gens sans regarder les passantes' (p. 1263). He obviously enjoys the chat decorating such lust, for he says of Englishmen: 'S'ils s'y mettaient, ils les examineraient comme des chevaux, tandis que le boulevardier sait fleurir de politesse et ouater de discrétion son audace de suiveur, son grappin d'abordage' (*ibid.*). The aggressive last metaphor gives away the violence beneath the violets. In all his discussion of women on both sides of the Channel, Vallès keeps sliding betwen classes, so that he blurs the whole issue. Parisiennes are more hard-headed and more romantic; Englishwomen go in for *far-niente* (which class?) (p. 1265); they are also do-gooding campaigners, which transmutes them into a third sex, neither female nor male (p. 1272).

As for sport, (within 'le dur sport de la vie' (p. 1285)), while having some reservations, Vallès is full of praise. Derby Day is a *mundus inversus:* 'L'Angleterre s'y montre la tête en bas, les pieds en l'air' (p. 1284). In this land of compartments, this is a free-for-all, promiscuity: 'Cette inondation de la foule, cette éruption de volcan, dans ce pays de cellules sociales et de mutisme pénitentiaire' (p. 1285). By this stage of his account, Vallès has wearied of being a registering eye: 'On veut être à la fois acteur et observateur dans la pièce' (*ibid.*). He revels in the jovial matiness of the omnibus ride ('une kermesse entre quatre planches' — p. 1286)). Then, by a cinematic double-take, he realises he has conned himself. The joviality has blinded him to the have-nots, the beggars. Vallès feels anger at the insulting charity thrown to them: cruel scenes of mendicants made to beg like dogs or to jig about (p. 1290). As in theatres, however, vigour plays off against coarseness. 'Nulle part', he writes of the mass return home, 'jamais, il n'y eut ce pêle-mêle, cet encombrement, cette verve sauvage, cette fureur de casse-cou' (p. 1292). In this way, throughout *La Rue à Londres,* the rush to moralise has to take on board the extra-moral.

Fascinatedly appalled at bareknuckle boxing, he still believes that sporting prowess (strange how England was once reputed for it) helps to explain British world dominance: 'C'est à ces mœurs du *ring* et du *turf* que l'Angleterre doit d'être le champion de la résistance dans le champ clos du monde' (p. 1299). Picking up his previous attacks on the under-emphasis on physical education in France, he praises English schools (public schools, designed to produce élites — but Vallès focusses on the formation of self-reliance): 'Au lieu d'être élevés comme des métaphysiciens ou des poètes, les adolescents sont dressés comme des fils d'hercules ou de maîtres de natation' (p. 1294). In contrast, in Soho, he notes the degenerate scum of French expatriate society (p. 1196). Critical of many English forms of pleasure, he unreservedly lauds (after Dickens) the English Christmas: the presents, the fun, the good cheer and drink (for once), and the reading of popular romances and ghost-stories (pp. 1215-16). He appears to mistranslate Boxing Day as an occasion for drunken punch-ups in the streets (p. 1220). He enjoys pantomime, despite the cross-dressing, for there the (earthly) 'gods' rule the roost (p. 1221).

For all the emphasis on garish colours and ubiquitous advertising, Vallès never loses sight of the reverse picture. The sections on workhouses record his visits to these organised, measured infernos, with their highly programmed dispensing of charity. He is too streetwise not to realise the ambivalence of the whole workhouse phenomenon: it can abuse regulars, and be abused in turn by spongers and shirkers. Here again religion interferes. Some women there catch 'la névrose de la religion, ce qui est l'avortement des âmes' (p. 1246). In the world of actual work, at London docks, the visitor marvels in horror at the huge scale of operations generated to service the maritime colossus of the nineteenth century, the runaway growth of mechanisation. He notes the indigo warehouses where the workers salivate blue, the massive stores — a carceral cornucopia (pp. 1227-8). He tries unavailingly to anthropomorphise forbidding buildings: 'On voudrait leur voir un front, des yeux, des lèvres, [...] des fentes larges par où rirait un peu de lumière—des rides ou des cicatrices, au besoin! Non! c'est comme une colossale bedaine de pierre, ronde, unie, à la peau brune et tendre' (p. 1232). He remains open to the call of the open sea, ships off to the ends of the earth: 'Cela écorche et éblouit les yeux, cela aussi recule le paysage et ouvre à l'affamé un horizon profond' (p. 1233). But the stevedores who have to stay, performing repetitive, uncreative tasks of loading and unloading, lack all rebelliousness; they are 'ces fakirs du chômage' (p. 1232). Human labour comes cheap: 'A quel prix est payée la balistique humaine?' (p. 1233). In keeping with their context, 'leur vie fait eau de toutes parts' (p. 1231). He watches the recruiting sergeants, and notes, by a bitter twist on 'cochons vendus', poor wretches paying to get into the army. As for the underclass of hooligans with their violent horseplay, Vallès feels a mixture of fear and distaste:

> C'est une race terrible, allez, et je ne voudrais pas que ma patrie devînt leur ennemie—ni leur amie. [...] Musulmans sans soleil, ces fils de la Grande Bretagne! Ils ont la résignation muette des Orientaux, sous leur ciel de fer. Ils sont fiers d'être Anglais, c'est assez—et ils se consolent de n'avoir pas de chemise en regardant flotter un lambeau de drapeau. (pp. 1276-7)

Have things changed so much today?

'Qu'on le sache bien, l'Anglais a la haine instinctive, aveugle, de ce qui est français' (p. 1205). This is probably truer than we want to think. Periodically, Vallès reverts to the initial polarisation, and can then slump into cliché: 'Ainsi nous sont-ils hostiles de toute la force de leur tristesse et de leur patriotisme religieux et glacial. C'est le brouillard furieux qui en veut au soleil; c'est le rire blême qui en veut au rire clair; c'est le duel de la bière et du vin!' (p. 1205). He makes the standard charges: we are non-enthusiasts, whereas the French need to 'penser tout haut' (p. 1260). And yet he recognises a futile quality in his own country's humour, in comparison with English phlegm: 'Nous paraissons des gamins souvent, à crier ainsi contre le vent, et à envoyer des chiquenaudes au nez des avalanches' (ibid.). The Englishman practises not only 'le rire jaune', but also 'vit jaune' (Corr. A., p. 201).

At one point, Vallès spends two whole paragraphs, inflating the problems of getting back into the crowd at a procession to a symbol of the impenetrability of English society. So doing he points to the crux of the exile's dilemma: 'On ne pénètre pas dans un milieu où l'on n'a pas racine' (p. 1275). Like the crowd in the Commune, England remains unreadable. Like the Thames: 'Cette eau ne reflète rien, elle est comme le visage des Anglais' (p. 1153). An abyss of twenty miles lies between Calais and Dover (p. 1325). For all that, Vallès remembers to express his authentic gratitude for lessons in freedoms, and especially for the transnational haven of the British Museum Library, far better stocked on French history than the Bibliothèque Nationale: 'J'ai pu vivre en pleine terre nationale pendant neuf ans d'exil' (p. 1306).

Hyperbole is the commonest mode of *La Rue à Londres*. 'Par esprit de patriotisme, parce qu'ils ont le Derby et la mer, ils ont tous des têtes de cheval ou de poisson' (p. 1135). The reader, even non-English, is tempted to respond: 'What! All of them? Why do rabid individualists so often generalise manically?' Lugubrious conceits occur frequently, as in this Thames-side scene: 'On voit se balancer dans l'air des sacs mous qui oscillent au bout des poulies avec des pesanteurs et des gigotements de pendus. On pend ici; c'est laid et sourd, cela plaît bien' (p. 1155). Perhaps he prefers the sharp clunk of the guillotine.

It is a patchwork text, 'cousu de pièces découpées, rapportées, accolées' (Bellet, II, 1982). Vallès was fully conscious of this himself, as he makes clear in his instructions to his secretary, Séverine: 'Cela aura *l'enlevé* d'un croquis, le je-ne-sais-quoi saisissant des observations collées chaudes mais sans suite sur le papier. A vous d'étayer et de dresser cela comme on pare un plat fait de morceaux' (*Corr. S.*, p. 90). Tholoniat detects a dominance of the colour yellow in these fragmented descriptions:

> L'Anglais vit jaune, il rit jaune dans sa barbe de même couleur; le brouillard est couleur merde d'oie; la Tamise, les murs, les écriteaux ont des reflets jaunâtres. L'énergie du couple rouge-noir atteint son entropie avec les couleurs seulement définies par le terne, le pâle et le blafard. [5]

In a generally overheated article, trying to enlist Vallès into German Expressionism, Blanc accurately observes: 'Vallès gauchit les perspectives, tourmente les lignes, noircit le tableau. La *vision* remplace la vue'. [6]

As Bellet puts it pungently, but for once with inadequate nuance, apart from political freedom, Vallès relished virtually nothing about England, for whose life he felt an aversion as visceral as that which, as a child, he had felt for onions (II, p. xii). Any English person hailing from outside London would exclaim how unfair it is to judge all England via the capital, which many natives find every bit as alien and hateful as do many foreigners. Critics underplay the shuttle or seesaw tactic of *La Rue à Londres*, which at different points seems to have been written (as indeed it was) from opposite sides of the Channel, so that Vallès refers at times to England as 'là-bas'. Two principal critical approaches predominate. The documentary (Tholoniat): Vallès's account is lacunary, inaccurate and biassed; and the aesthetic (Blanc): never mind the lesser contact with observable reality, what internally coherent picture does Vallès create? On the issue of his non-visits to provincial cities, where, Vallès recognised, working-class militancy would have been more obvious, Tholoniat suggests that the experience of the Commune—the provinces refusing to emulate Paris—might have blinkered him. Vallès, besides, was reluctant to admit that other forms of worker organisation—trade unions, provident societies—offered more gradualist forms of activism than he was yet ready to value. [7] To his credit, he did not exaggerate the scale of poverty in London, but, like Taine, did little to analyse its causes, only its consequences. Cardboard cities are not recent inventions. Tholoniat points out that the number of skilled and well-paid workers was much higher than that of exploited semi-skilled or unskilled workers: 'Ce manque d'homogénéité de la classe ouvrière—et non la résignation—peut expliquer son apparent manque de combativité'.[8] My own estimation is that the facts Vallès incorporates are generally accurate, but that he omitted—more through ignorance than perverseness—crucial areas. What is unforgettable about *La Rue à Londres* is the sense of a man mortally afraid of but fighting back against *étouffement:* asphyxiation, silencing, anonymity: a forgotten man lost in the crowd.

'Unlike the London residents of other origin, the French Londoner [...] remains above all a Frenchman, and retains all the feelings, characteristics, and customs of his race'. [9] Of course, Vallès did not realise how French he was until he had to live in England. Yet, while undoubtedly as quintessentially French as Montaigne or Diderot, he seems 'Anglo-Saxon' in many ways, and even before he set foot here. His love of sport and of country fresh air; his fondness for eccentrics, all those who march to different drummers; his empirical bent which made him suspect all systems, Marxist, Jacobin or Proudhonist; his awareness of overlap and contamination between all would-be clear divisions of thought and behaviour; his passion for exploiting, by wordplay and coinage, the often underused potential of his native tongue; his support of and identification with the underdog, the plucky loser ('Il faut toujours applaudir aux révoltés, surtout quand ils sont vaincus'—I, 343). Though he spent a long time in England, he did not get far with assimilating the language, but in attitudes he comes part-way to meet the anti-extremist. Playing the shuttle too, I would repeat that Vallès is very un-French in his near-immunity to intellectual incest, yet very French in his belief that cultural devaluation might seriously shake society, and very un-French again in his unworldly-wise capacity for surprise. 'Suis-je devenu Anglais en détestant John Bull? Ai-je perdu le flair et le tact français? Je ne crois pas. J'ai gagné comme tous les camarades, au contraire, le dédain des ficelles, et le désir de netteté en affaires. "Oui: non". Ah! l'on gagne cela en Angleterre!' (*Corr. M.*, p. 264).

At a low ebb when trying to get another *La Rue* off the ground in 1879, he writes to Parisian correspondents:

> J'en suis à me réjouir d'être resté dans un exil rigoureux, dans une Angleterre où les placards éclatent comme des pétards, où il y a des manifestations de 100,000 hommes. Vous m'ôtez le courage. Nous

sommes plus gais et plus Parisiens à Londres que la moitié des Parisiens
que j'ai revus. [...] Vous parlez de mon normandisme d'aujourd'hui. Eh
bien, mon cher, appelez ça anglaisisme et vous aurez trouvé le mot. Je ne
ferai rien, rien, rien avec quelqu'un sans traité à l'anglaise, sûr, indéniable,
débattu, défini, et convenant à tous les deux. [10]

The blatant hypocrisy, the up-front reserve of the English ('perfidious
Albion') have given way in Vallès's mind to this reliability. Vallès
clearly plays one side off against the other, depending on circumstances.
He was too French for the English and too English for the French. *A
cheval*, again: in mid-Channel.

Return and *Le Cri du peuple*

His problems with this *La Rue*, which lasted only one month,
demonstrate how little Vallès was cut out for working by proxies, or
doing anything from a distance. He came alive only in the scrum—the
least Olympian, the least *point de vue de Sirius* (Beuve-Méry) of French
journalists. He could not, as he hoped, address the sons of his political
enemies without joining them in the fray back in Paris, which had been
largely quiescent during his exile, after the Commune. Would his return
reveal him as an anachronism?

Edmond de Goncourt aimed to freeze Vallès in a stereotype: 'L'amer
que Vallès a en lui, il le soigne, il le caresse, il le dorlote, il le travaille,
il le porte en ville, pour le tenir toujours en haleine, comprenant fort
bien que s'il venait à le perdre, il serait un ténor dépossédé de son *ut* '. [11]
It is true, and understandable, that on his return Vallès made frequent
references backward, trying to reknot broken threads. As usual, he
came clean. Turning down in 1881 offers of two Paris candidacies, he
stresses that he fights lost battles: 'J'aime mieux être le porte-parole du
passé [...] C'est un rôle qui vaut bien l'autre—je serai le député des
vaincus. [...] Je veux être l'historien de la grande foule anonyme qui se
révolta et fut écrasée en 1871' (II, pp. 717-18). Although he accepted
that workers value their dearly-won suffrage, he seemed to feel a near-
anarchist disdain about using his own vote. His mistrust of professional
politicians remained intact. 'Nous ne sommes pas des politiciens, nous
sommes les soldats et les peintres de l'idée sociale', manning 'notre
barricade sans fusils' (pp. 395; 397). The Palais-Bourbon, in his eyes,
was fundamentally unserious, a theatre or even trestles, 'l'asile des
phrasassiers' (*Cri du peuple*, 30 mai 1884).

It is not surprising that he steered clear as much as possible of any
adherence to constituted parties or doctrines: anarchism or collectivism.
'Je ne vais pas m'enfermer dans un bivouac, quand j'ai devant moi tout
le champ de bataille révolutionnaire'. Don't fence me in. As before, he

stresses that it is the will, the intentions, that matter in political action, and not class provenance. Here the habit does not designate the monk. In a twist on the idiom 'montrer patte blanche', he says no one needs to 'montrer main noire'; it did not matter in the Commune (II, pp. 440; 444). As Bellet comments, 'la vieille terreur vallésienne du clos, du circonscrit, du fermé, du muré, de la grille et de la chapelle, trouve sa correspondance idéologique et politique dans le refus de choisir une "école" socialiste au lieu d'une autre' (*JVJR*, p. 450).

As for Marxism, Vallès makes no mention of the First International until around 1870, and generally betrays little sense of class in the normal sense. In the 1870s surfaced a tendency, for French left-wingers, especially those in exile in London, to amalgamate Marx and Bismarck (perhaps a phonic coincidence, the second being almost the first twice over) on the grounds of pan-Germanist ambitions. In his letters to Arnould, Vallès asked him to boil down *Das Kapital*, 'si difficile à lire!' He heads straight for Marx's powerful metaphors: 'Sais-tu que c'est beau, cette définition du Capital: travail mort qui comme un vampire suce et dévore le travail vivant! [...] Et que cette idée de la marchandise, travail cristallisé, solidification de la peine, mérite qu'on y pense' (*Corr. A.*, p. 219). While he had little grasp of the more abstract concepts of economics, he did retain a fascination with the Stock Market and the world of banking (*JVJR*, p. 451). As we saw in Chapter Two, Vallès coincides, all the same, with Marx in his hostility to historical plagiarism.

> The social revolution of the nineteenth century can only create its poetry from the future, not from the past. It cannot begin its own work until it has sloughed off all its superstitious regard for the past. [...] In order to arrive at its own content, the revolution of the nineteenth century must let the dead bury the dead. [12]

In harking back to the Commune, Vallès was hardly even dreaming of seeing it replicated. It was the spirit, and the justice of the Communards' cause, that must be kept alive, and pursued by other means. Though he defended Kropotkin, Vallès wrote against terrorism: 'L'assassinat politique isolé ne porte pas' (II, 1425). As in the previous two decades, he placed more trust and hope in the free exchange of ideas, 'le terrain de rendez-vous' (the word used less in the amatory sense than in that of a duelling-space) represented by his second *Cri du peuple*. He wanted to coalesce, or help to make coexist, the mutually exclusive and reciprocally destructive forces of the left. Such an effort at neutrality was very necessary for the times and the situation in France.

Readers' letters were invited, thus hoping to convert the French press from its traditional tribune stance into more of a dialogue, 'une tribune ouverte'. Generous space was given to popular *feuilletons* in

order to increase circulation by making the paper more reader-friendly.
Similarly, small emblems were placed at the head of each column to flag
its contents at a glance: a bell (for parliamentary affairs), a trowel (for
workers' meetings), or an eye (for police news). As an editor and
journalist, Vallès always worked for the eye-catching, but not cony-
catching. *Le Cri du peuple* campaigned against colonial expeditions to
Tonkin ('La vivisection humaine va commencer' — II, 1093), for
teachers, for reforms in the judicial system (especially the abolition of
the death penalty). In Vallès's ideal republic, every citizen would do a
stint as a constable (*Cri du peuple*, 5 avril 1884). He always stressed the
'social question' over politics (i.e. ideology, which he left largely to
Guesde in the pages of the paper), though he never resolved the question
of how you could separate the two.

    In a campaign for children's rights, Vallès stresses that he wants
prevention of cruelty, not revenge against brutal parents (II, 1369). One
of his last articles protests the brainwashing of children by didactic
plays disguised as fantasies. Children's dreams are essential, but not at
the cost of abolishing reality. This is presumably why *Robinson
Crusoe,* which combines exoticism and hard work, is so central to
Vallès's canon. Why not awaken children to the exciting new world of
science and industry, as in Jules Verne's work? (pp. 1422-4). On the
question of progress, he can seem backward-turned, as when he
criticises capitalist enterprises for taking over rubbish-collection in
Paris, thus depriving hundreds of *chiffonniers* of a livelihood. He
neglects the improvement in sanitation. Yet even here he has a point.
Such *biffins* supplied other service industries (including restaurants)
with recyclable materials. Greens might find these practices easier to
stomach than others. Vallès is as well-informed on the daily budgets of
biffins as he was earlier of those of *saltimbanques* (pp. 1105-1107).

    Again and again, he returned to the primordial things: work, roof,
bread, blood, tears, sweat. To his old category of society's *forçats,* he
added the large numbers trapped and alienated in soulless factory-work.
He came to see strikes as the only effective weapon available to workers.
One of his last public appearances was at a solidarity meeting for the
miners of Anzin in 1884, when desperately ill with the diabetes which
would kill him in a few months. That the government was nervous
about the popular appeal and influence of *Le Cri du peuple* is indicated
by the Ballerich affair, when two policemen broke in and started
shooting at the editorial staff. When one of the two was killed by self-
defending fire, Vallès's apartment and even his sick-bed were violently
searched. Perrot sums up the political standpoint of *Le Cri du peuple* in
these terms: 'Un socialisme sans doctrine, protestataire et humanitaire,
nostalgique et messianique, généreux et confus, perpétuellement
résurgent dans la tradition française: un socialisme style flamboyant'.[13]

    Vallès's helpmeet after his return to France was Séverine. She used

her husband's money to launch *Le Cri du peuple* in 1883. Their deep
relationship, intimate but seemingly non-carnal, is encapsulated in her
cry on Vallès's death: 'C'était mon père... C'était mon enfant!' Her
frankly warm-hearted encomium makes a nicely sexist division of his
influence on her: 'Il me donna un cœur de citoyenne et un cerveau de
citoyen'. [14] When she eventually left *Le Cri du peuple* in 1888, after
disagreements with Vallès's successors over its increasingly sectarian
slant, she frequented, in a very Vallésian phrase, 'l'école buissonnière de
la Révolution'. [15] She and Vallès enjoyed an exceptional osmosis; she
assimilated his ways of thinking and expressing himself, and he trusted
her judgment implicitly. His utter reliance on her puts a more benign
slant on his perennial anxiety over plagiarism. As a cleric commented,
she was a splended mixture of a *pétroleuse* (in words, not deeds) and a
sœur de charité. [16] Fittingly, in the same way that Vallès escaped 'la
Semaine sanglante' in an ambulance, so the director of that service, Dr.
Sémerie, introduced Vallès to Séverine and her doctor husband in
Brussels. She would nurse his remaining years, when his lifelong taste
for heavy peasant food did little to help his diabetes. She brought him
comfort and stability, after a life of much insecurity and frequent
deprivation. She played a major part in running the paper and in
preparing *L'Insurgé* and *La Rue à Londres* for publication. She
protected Vallès when alive and after his death. In *La Rue à Londres*, he
makes a moving dedication to Séverine: 'Vous avez fait à ma vie cadeau
d'un peu de votre grâce et de votre jeunesse, vous avez fait à mon
œuvre l'offrande du meilleur de votre esprit et de votre cœur' (II,
1133).

Committed Literature

The idea of committed literature pulls together Vallès's two lifelong
concerns: politics and literature. There, above all, he is in his
characteristic position: *à cheval*. This straddle is archetypically that of
the committed writer (of the left), reneguing on his generally middle-
class or *petit-bourgeois* origins, yet rarely, if ever, integrated into and
adopted by the working-classes. He is thus often stranded in no man's
land, caught in the crossfire. This situation can be alternately or
simultaneously exhilarating and anguishing. Of course, all of us live less
dramatically in a murky middle ground between metaphor and concrete
reality, the spirit and the letter. Tension reputedly energises. Vallès was
not *un écrivain de chapelle,* and so was largely unforgivable to any side
in the French literary church.
  Mi-figue, mi-raisin, in his first book, *L'Argent,* Vallès was
proclaiming the need to live with your times. At no point did he adopt

the posture of the intellectual fakir. Indeed, so convinced was he always of the necessity to have convictions, that he was ready to salute those of his political opponents, for instance Barbey d'Aurevilly: 'Je hais la politique autoritaire et dévote de M. Barbey d'Aurevilly. [...] Mais il est resté *lui,* avec toutes les vertus de ses vices' (I, pp. 349; 348). There is a strong element of the willy-nilly in all this ('en dehors de toute volonté de l'écrivain' (II, 1340)); the writer has to respond to historical reality, which is much bigger than any individual. 'Tout se tient. La littérature change de tour quand la politique change de face'(I, 400). Vallès always persisted, however, in distinguishing the social from the political: 'J'aime mieux, après tout, la littérature qui refait les moeurs que la politique qui fait les lois' (p. 435). These terms suggest that he places far more weight on how society regulates itself (with some guidance from the likes of Vallès) than on abstract theories of how it ought to be organised. As Bellet comments: 'Il a le sentiment, aigu et profond, de la rencontre inéluctable des mouvements artistiques et sociaux, quelles que soient les différences de leurs rythmes propres et même si, souvent, le rythme des mouvements artistiques et littéraires, plus rapide, devance tous les autres' (p. 1418). That is, the writer is not only in step; he may be prancing ahead. Whatever he does, he must never fear, as Nietzsche urged, 'to trespass upon actuality'. [17]

Not all agree. Tocqueville spoke of the crisscross contamination of politics and literature, each aping the other, so that politicians often talk like books, and authors think they can set their countries to rights. [18] The grass-roots American novelist James Farrell puts his spoke in: 'Literary men have the habit of rushing into the periphery of politics, and they contribute to political struggle—not knowledge, not practical experience, not theoretical analyses, but rhetoric. Rhetoric is the one commodity in politics of which there has never been a scarcity'. It is possible that, when Socrates spoke of 'the unexamined life', he had in mind much political discourse, and much literature that marches in too tight a step with it. We are all so hardened to jargon, cliché and double talk (in electioneering, party manifestoes and press conferences) that we sometimes fail to appreciate the much richer and denser ambiguities of good literature. Many, besides, want fiction to be more obviously up-front than it can or should be; they want it akin to pamphleteering, political correctness. Against such persuasions, a committed writer like Vallès demonstrates how resistance to ideology (mind-bending), even that of your ostensible allies, is every bit as important as endorsement of it. 'Commitment', besides, is not a good translation of the Sartrian *engagement.* It has legal, forensic overtones, and misses the input of *gage* (promise, wager). Commitment sounds like that which is imposed on you; *engagement* what you will yourself to choose (as in 'engaged to be married').

Most Naturalists were essentially 'down there on a visit': slumming.

They were exploiting a seam, less like miners than like investors. They rarely sided with the oppressed creatures they described. Even though Vallès, in the 1860s, termed the Goncourts' style 'tourmenté, prétentieux, *scudérique'*, and described their stance as 'le coin d'un cénacle, mais ce n'est pas la vie', he was generous enough to conclude: 'Ce n'est pas senti, mais comme c'est observé!' (I, pp. 350-53). He did not practise 'l'onanisme rétinien' of which they boasted. [19] Zola did not relish Vallès's calling him 'un rouge en littérature, un communard de la plume' (II, 120). It is fairly comical to watch each bank of the divide tugging the communal blanket to one side in these ways, Vallès claiming that Daudet, the Goncourts and Zola were revolutionary despite themselves, a prophetic twist on the Soviet notion of 'objective guilt'; and the Naturalists trying to water down Vallès's firebrand writings. Gradually, however, Vallès's rough logic made him openly hostile. Naturalists were 'maniaques de la constatation, mouleurs de michés, point mouleurs de vrais mâles!' (a pun on *michés* and *godemichés:* brothel clients and dildoes). They waste their talents on lubricious tales, instead of speaking up for real suffering (pp. 1100-1101). Despite seeming to be censorious about subject matter here, it was the pretence of political neutrality that Vallès really could not stomach.

Many of these matters came to a head when Vallès engaged in a polemic with a spokesman for the Zola school of Naturalists, Paul Alexis, who hoped for the advent of a press 'où [...] la politique, n'occupant plus que la place qu'elle occupera alors dans la vie des peuples, sera reléguée entre le Sport et les Annonces, piteusement'. [20] He was reacting no doubt to earlier charges addressed to him by Vallès: 'L'homme qui dit n'avoir pas d'opinions politiques en a une. Il est le collaborateur et le complice de tous ceux qui ont mis la main sur le pouvoir' (II, 812). Vallès scoops Sartre here. The only alternative to *engagement* is parasitism: 'Ou insurgé ou courtisan: il n'y a pas à sortir de là'. Vallès goes on to compare would-be abstentionists with the 'platonic' (i.e. non-participatory) clients in brothels (*ibid.*).

Already in the 1860s, Vallès had mocked one such illustrious abdicator, Baudelaire, whom he presumably could not forgive for reneguing on his young man's fling with revolution in 1848 (*'Le 2 DÉCEMBRE m'a physiquement dépolitiqué'*). [21] Like Sartre, Vallès homes in on the posturing man and neglects the writer. He is totally wrong, as a result, in judging that Baudelaire's fame will be short-lived. For Vallès, Baudelaire is the perfect mugwump, on the fence, or on both sides of it at once. He hedged his bets on the religious issue. No doubt, too, Vallès's harsh attack on Baudelaire, whom he knew from bohemian cafés, is part of his general attack on the unquestioning cult of genius, the *monstre sacré*. The crucial criticism is that of bad faith: 'Il n'avait pas la santé d'un débauché et avait dans son enfer une petite porte masquée par où l'on pouvait remonter au ciel' (I, 973). In other

words, in all his pacts with Satan, Baudelaire always inserted an escape
clause. 'Il y avait en lui du prêtre, de la vieille femme et du cabotin.
C'était surtout un cabotin' (p. 971). It is ironical that he accuses
Baudelaire of being a ham actor, when this was the regular complaint
about Vallès's public persona. He misses the point of the dandiacal,
wilful mystification.

Another *preuve par l'absurde* of the value of *engagement* is the sad
André Gill. Vallès felt strong sympathy for this excellent caricaturist
when he went insane and was locked up. While he could forgive, he
never could forget, and Gill's earlier contribution to the cause of
contestation had not been followed through; indeed in the Commune
Gill had been a turncoat. For Vallès, true commitment preserves sanity,
a view which runs absolutely counter to the common twentieth-century
dismissal of all political passion as neurotic (II, 721). Before he lost his
reason, however, Gill struck home with these remarks about Vallès's
stance: 'On a eu dans sa vie une heure pendant laquelle on s'est trouvé
particulièrement beau, on s'est *gobé;* dans la glace on s'est trouvé des
airs de héros ou de martyr. [...] Héros et martyrs! Vous en riiez
autrefois. [...] Ne soyez pas une vieille barbe, l'Homère entêté d'une
épopée ratée'. [22] Vallès's problem was a common one: even when you are
right, it is hard to avoid appearing self-righteous. Vallès recognised that
courage is not on tap to everyone, but inciters must possess some,
otherwise they have double standards: calling for blood, then running
away (see II, 116). Surely Vallès makes the lily-livered reader at least
temporarily ashamed, when he talks of 'ces gens qui se sont fait de leur
impuissance un piédestal, et parlent du haut de leur impuissance comme
Démosthène du haut de la tribune' (I, 954). Vallès's work is a reminder,
writing against the self-induced amnesia both readers and writers so
facilely fall into. 'Forgetfulness, especially of classes and class conflict,
is a common theme of bourgeois culture, a theme which can be related
to the concept of art as a transcendent form of activity'. [23] While never
approaching the later notion of 'socialist realism', Vallès's views are
certainly close to what has been called 'critical realism', already present
in Vallès's lecture on Balzac and later acknowledged as a significant
category by Engels: 'Est-ce que les socialistes socialisants ont écrit
contre la famille, la vertu et l'or des pages plus cruelles que Dumas fils,
Flaubert, de Goncourt, Zola?' (II, 1340). Vallès detects the ideological
dimension, the would-be manipulation, even of children's literature:
'Tous [...] montraient le doigt de Dieu, partout où il y avait un trou où
le fourrer' (p. 744). The Jesuits always knew that you have to catch
them young.

Even when denied for ideological reasons, the urge to political
partisanship is ubiquitous in a cultural tradition like the French given to
embattled polemic. You have to take sides, make your bed and lie on it.
None of this entails crude propaganda. As Engels said of *Tendenz-*

Literatur: 'I believe that there is no compulsion for the writer to put
into the reader's hands the future historical resolution of the social
conflicts which he is depicting'. [24] The just society can be talked about, if
at all, only in the optative mood. *L'Insurgé* in its practice concurs with
this theory. Does this view concede that written attacks can only ever be
paper tigers, that political novels can never pack any political clout?
Significantly, it is a writer most removed from the fray, Mallarmé, who
makes the wildest claim: 'La vraie bombe c'est le livre'. [25] This
statement is pathetic in the truest sense, but a Symbolist poet supporting
anarchist explosions would tend to take metaphors for actualities, and
experimental writing for a revolutionary deed (a pathos still to be found
in some deconstructionist criticism). Vallès knew full well that the pen
is never mightier than the sword, but he believed that it may on
occasion give added impetus to the sword-arm. Above all, Vallès never
suspects or seeks impunity: a price has always be to paid for any
decisions acted upon.

I have mentioned Sartre (a self-confessed 'victime du livre' if ever
there was one) before in connexion with Vallès. *Les Mots* unmercifully
probes the posture of writer-as-saviour. It is regrettable that, by a
strabismic oversight, Sartre missed a powerful trick when he all but
omitted Vallès as a vigorous forebear (with real claws) of *littérature
engagée*. In *Qu'est-ce que la littérature?* he mentions only, in contrast
with seventeenth-century social satire, 'la grande satire de
Beaumarchais, de P.-L. Courier, de J. Vallès, de Céline'. [26] At least he
puts Vallès in suitable company. He and Vallès share a similar revulsion
for Baudelaire's *cabotinage*. Both see the writer as a free consciousness
addressing a free reader linked by a relationship of trust (a leap in the
dark). When Vallès turned down the offer of a seat in the Académie
Goncourt, and indeed denounced the whole project, he recalls, all due
allowances made, Sartre's refusal of the Nobel Prize. Neither of these
committed writers wanted to be rewarded with a *prix de sagesse* for
being literary good boys.

Shortly before Vallès's death, Edmond de Goncourt recorded an
anecdote that I would prefer not to be apocryphal: 'Robert Caze, parlant
de la maladie de la pose chez Vallès, raconte qu'il l'a vu manger une
choucroute dans une brasserie du Quartier Latin, avec un tablier de
franc-maçon, dont il s'essuyait les lèvres'. [27] If true, it would
demonstrate his durably iconoclastic attitude to congealed rituals. I
wonder what he would have made of his own funeral in 1885: a suitably
mixed event, a rehearsal for Hugo's even more massive funeral three
months later: very large crowds, scuffles and punch-ups, some German
socialists provoking cries of 'Down with Germany'—ironical in that
Vallès was never keen on Marx or Germany.

The next and last chapter will examine how, in terms of rhetoric,
style and structure, Vallès himself mixes it.

Chapter Ten

Rhetoric, Style and Structure

Rhetoric

Vallès's opponents often carved up his form and his subject matter (a great stylist; a public enemy), so why a second refrain? It is of course impossible to chop up a living corpus in this way, and cross-references will rule. Even so, the language question is of the essence. As Rosenberg noted: 'The French language is heavy with old literature. The Frenchman has so much tradition that he can easily say anything except what he wants to say. To be conscious of his own feelings, to see with his own eyes, he must restore freshness to his language'. [1] Without being a Grandma Moses, for he constantly refers to and re-employs his egregious scholastic training, Vallès both mocks and exploits the stock in trade of his mother tongue. For him, language is a trap to be mistrusted, and a springboard to take off from.

So alert to overlap in all walks of life, and thus never fully convinced of class war, in rhetoric also Vallès sensed the interaction of many of its categories (metaphor and wordplay for one). He was sane enough to know that rhetoric is not the preserve of the great washed; whatever the linguistic divide between the owning and the lacking classes, each has its own rhetoric, and nobody talks absolutely plain. As the neo-classical rhetorician Du Marsais pointed out: 'Il se fait dans un jour de marché plus de figures qu'en plusieurs jours d'assemblées académiques'. [2] With his deep respect for artisans, Vallès naturally was fully awake to 'les idiotismes du métier', both in its sense of idiolect (the technical language of cobblers, journeymen or *saltimbanques*) and in Diderot's reworked sense (in *Le Neveu de Rameau*) of an incorrigible man's convenient and idiosyncratic exploitation of conventions attaching to his profession. Rhetoric suits us down to the ground.

Rhetoric, that public address system, is, equally, a posh name for the failure to distinguish between words and action, the temptation to think that to verbalise is to solve, a common vice of politicians and literary critics. Vallès's consistent complaints about ideological rhetoric amount to an attack on jargon, that is: words used so as to bind insiders and to blind outsiders—the exclusive club of bafflegab, and, as such, anti-democratic. As the name promises, parliaments are talk shops. We saw earlier how Vallès frequently mocked the demagogic rhetoric which habitually referred back to the giants of the French Revolution. These in

their turn were often recapitulating what they had been taught at school:
'C'était surtout avec une rhétorique de collèges, de Jésuites,
d'Oratoriens et de Parlements que les révolutionnaires avaient accédé à
la tribune des assemblées'. [3] A dizzying, infinite shuttle between school
rostrum and political platform. Vallès's account of Robespierre's
oratory is no doubt partial, but blinkered eyes can still see straight.
Schama locates something self-defeating in the premium placed on
rhetoric in the Revolutionary period: 'The dilemma for successive
generations of those politicans who graduated from oratory to
administration was that they owed their own power to precisely the kind
of rhetoric that made their subsequent governance impossible'. [4] For all
this, and even when attacking empty demagoguery (in Gambetta, for
instance), Vallès is always French enough to associate militancy with
eloquence. Even a 'spontaneous' uprising, in his view, needs a verbal
fillip. For Barrès, Vallès talked himself into insurgency: 'Vallès fut hissé
sur les barricades par des métaphores et par toute la truculence de son
vocabulaire'. [5]

Vallès is such a vital animator that he gives life to what he is
describing as dead: e.g. Sorbonne rhetoric: 'Il n'en tombe rien, rien que
des paroles, des périodes connues, des exordes dont la tête est chauve,
des péroraisons dont la queue est pelée' (II, 741). He humanises, or
animalises, discourse in this way, because he dwells far more on the
delivery, the physical impact, the crowd reactions, than on the contents
of speeches. He *reads* performances, like a novelist analysing character
or conduct. Often he finds the physical elevation of the dais alienating,
and warms for preference to 'l'instinctive éloquence' (p. 1103). Orating
in public, you have to be yourself, be convinced and speak in your own
name, not merely parroting imported scripts.

More than once caricatured as a dog, Vallès certainly had much of
the barker in his ideas and his practice of public communication. A
terrier, noisily worrying away at bones of contention, but never
anyone's lap-dog. *Bonimenteur, aboyeur, puffiste*—he always stressed
the importance of presentation, of *parade*. Often, of course, like any
barker, he promised without delivering, contravening all kinds of trades
description acts; beating the drum, blowing the trumpet. We talk of
political speechmakers as hucksters, setting out their stalls. Vallès never
expected to grab any audience's entire attention, though obviously he
enjoyed the rare occasions when he got it. As he said of *saltimbanques*
and their patter: 'Il faut attirer l'attention du public, le maîtriser, et
étouffer sous ses plaisanteries ou son tapage la concurrence. Il suffit
d'un incident, d'un rien, pour détourner la foule' (I, 710). This is the
area of 'la contrecarre': rivalry, diamond-cut-diamond; the sharper
edge of 'la vie d'échange': cut and thrust. He trusted public argument,
whether on the fairground, in the press, or in parliament, to regulate
itself; in a free-for-all (that lovely, hopeful term), without recourse to

guillotines of any variety. *Parade* means also 'parry': such a view of rhetoric is defensive as well as aggressive.

Not only a dialogue with competitors is involved, but also one with the receivers. Vallès relied on interaction, on picking up clues, responding to them, creating a collective momentum. On district meetings, probably his favourite kind of political gathering, he said he wanted an active public: 'Rédacteur en chef, la foule' (p. 1152). Naturally he could not wriggle clear of the double-bind corseting all orators. While the honest orator is loath to bend minds, what would be the point of the art of persuasion that is rhetoric if it did not attempt this? It is related to the question of leadership, about which Vallès always felt uncomfortable. Those who claim to speak for others tend to speak down to them. There are victims, suckers, of speech as there are of books.

Vallès's putative public, whether readers or listeners, and however idealised, seemed to him real. He allowed little sense of talking to himself in a void, or to a few acolytes, as a whole phalanx of writers from Flaubert to Mallarmé alternatively complained or boasted they were doing. Memories of the *cours magistral* in school, and family lectures about his behaviour, fidelity to his aversion from statues on pedestals frozen in mid-gesture, these helped to keep him aware of the drawbacks of speechifying, either for deliverer or receiver. Whatever the dangers, all the same, for Vallès talk was a necessity. Even when he worked for forums of ideas he could never be a pacifier, a dummy (and remember his dummy aunt, speechlessly eloquent). This outspokenness does not rule out craftiness. In his account of his Balzac lecture, he says: "J'ai grandsièclisé ma parole—ces imbéciles me laissent insulter leurs religions et leurs doctrines parce que je le fais dans un langage qui respecte leur rhétorique, et que prônent les maîtres du barreau et les professeurs d'humanité' (*Ins.*, p. 898): a splended instance of commandeering the enemy's weapons. Sometimes—plagiarism is so rampant in human affairs—he filches less consciously: 'Je le dis comme je le pense! Ce n'est point seulement pour faire une phrase sonore,—quoique je m'y laisse aller malgré moi, tant il m'est resté des souvenirs de 48 et 51, tant j'ai le regret des grandes harangues, tant j'ai la nostalgie du tumulte et de l'éloquence plébéienne!' (*CP*, p. 327). At times, it seems, as when he praises the top barrister Lachaud, that the ideal would be to be so original (though with fake motives, in this case) that everyone copies you: 'Il avait un tempérament et, comme on dit, il *faisait dans sa nature*. On n'est quelqu'un qu'à ce prix-là' (II, 850). This is to move beyond low-grade *cabotinage* into high drama. But Lachaud at the bar is not checked by audience reaction, as is an orator at a public popular meeting, where 'toute harangue gonflée et creuse est interrompue par l'auditoire. [...] Ce n'est pas en flattant les basses passions et en faisant des moulinets d'éloquence qu'on gagne l'oreille du grand tribunal en cotte et en bourgeron' (pp. 113-14).

As in the structure of his prose, Vallès has a high regard for interruption, as in this delightful anecdote about a meeting:

> — Qui interrompt? a demandé le président.
> — C'est moi, a répondu un homme sur les gradins.
> — Vous voulez parler?
> — Non... je voulais faire une interruption. (I, 618)

Vallès likes to interrupt, others or himself, in order to make the inertial flow of words more discontinuous, staccato and thoughtful. This often happens by accident, for the fiasco-prone speaker's gift of the gab often turns into the white elephant of the gabble. Vallès makes a good deal of sport with the pitfalls of enunciation, which makes him tolerant of other people's phonetic solecisms. Besides, whereas the *lycée* taught *abondance,* the impoverished Jacques's whole life exemplifies Diderot's aside in *Jacques le fataliste* that the only riches the poor can enjoy is the gift of the gab. Dumb insolence can also speak volumes. Vallès's stress on rhetoric and verbalisation is tempered by his recognition of those situations where words are either excessive or not enough (e.g. in the brooding silences of family crises). When words fail, gestures may step in. Addressing, with poor command of English, a London crowd, Vallès got his message across by gesticulation and enacted passion (p. 576).

Slogans and Clichés

Keats said: 'We hate poetry that has a palpable design on us'.[6] Vallès always has palpable designs on us. I myself prefer the palpable to the impalpable, just as I prefer the voluptuous to the scrawny. I like to know where I stand, or what I stand to for. Vallès's rhetoric runs the gamut from the aside (irony, wordplay) to the tirade (inky indignation). It concentrates itself in the form of slogans.

Vallès shares the French fondness for maxim-guns: 'Je crois qu'une proposition formulée en langue claire, dans quinze lignes, sert l'humanité autant et plus que les livres obscurs de tous les métaphysiciens' (I, 822). This boiling down clears the ground for formulae, placards, what Vallès called 'phrases brûlots', like one of his favourites, Proudhon's 'La propriété, c'est le vol'. Slogans are magic, or counter-magic, a hex on mystification. (Like Lamennais's 'Silence au pauvre', which sets the saying 'money talks' in a new light: to run a popular newspaper, you need money to be able to talk).[7] Vallès, however, fights his own sucker-instinct for lapidary phrases. On Proudhon's, he adds that no proprietor has been hanged and that God owns a lot of property in Paris (p. 1590). Despite his hostility to *syntagmes figés*—clichés, watchwords from the past reiterated in the present and intended to dictate the future—Vallès is at his most political, and journalistic, in his prolific skill at coining resounding formulae. No wonder he was enlisted for the 'Affiche rouge'. Slogans, of course, tell us what to achieve, but not how to achieve it. They can be paper tigers, roaring harmlessly. Equally they can be lethal if acted upon ruthlessly. People can and do kill each other for telescoped fixed ideas. These laconic stereotypes can freeze the brain, imagination and sympathy. They are knock-down arguments, a fact made clearer by the older spelling 'slug-horn': rallying calls, war cries. They save time and space, and economise on mental effort. Indeed, and this is where they overlap with clichés, they want us to *think automatically.*

In turn, clichés link up with Vallès's lifelong fixation on clothes. The standard metaphors for clichés are predominantly vestimentary: threadbare, down-at-heel, off-the-peg, reach-me-down. As Vallès tends to jib against automatisms, set occasions, performing on cue, and to prefer improvisation, he naturally resists clichés, which claim to be the last word on a subject and so inhibit thinking for oneself. They are not unthinking, as they have designs on us, but they are un-self-critical. They are ubiquitous, on lip or pen, for after all the common place is where we all live, the stamping-ground, pounded and infertile. This includes hallowed places: churches, schools, political platforms or court-rooms, in all of which we so often pay lip service in language afflicted by verbal or semantic fatigue: convenience language. Then again, clichés give us a break. However vacuous, they fill a void, a lull in conversation (just as pictures do furnish a room). Many of our apparently most spontaneous utterances are clichés; we often have reflexes instead of reflexions. This is language as social cement or lubrification. Clichés are labour-saving devices, and risk-avoidance. Listening to counsels of prudence after Sedan, Jacques comments: ' "Pas encore!... Laissez *pisser* le mouton. [...] Petit à petit l'oiseau fait son nid!" [...] Je laisse *pisser* le mouton! mais il me semble que depuis que je suis au monde il ne fait que pisser devant moi, ce mouton, et je suis toujours condamné à attendre qu'il ait fini' (*Ins.*, pp. 983-4).

We have to ask how adept Vallès was at revising or countering his own stereotypes and lazy options, at thinking against himself; how arthritic were the joints of his mind. He has that kind of associative mind which, when it hears the word 'clarinet', thinks immediately not of the instrument, but of a blind busker. He needs clichés for his own purposes, as well as for counter-attacking those of others. Take his habit of personalising issues, so that Homer = the classics, and Robespierre = revolutionary rhetoric; or his tic of Latin tags. These are often deployed ironically, but they still suggest a kind of dependence, *un revenez-y.* It all depends, naturally, where clichés come from and what fresh energy can be invested in them. For example, the commonplaces of adventure stories are used blithely and excitedly by the young, and the older, Jacques, whereas most of those stemming from school classical traditions are used derisively. The son's struggle against his mother is one waged against her existential clichés, her attempt at an imposed voice of authority, a *doxa*. Resisting them by not conforming, he learns the precious lesson that change, familial or social, comes about via resistance to cliché; by asking 'Is it so? What does that mean?' Any reader of Vallès has to sort out the sheep from the goats (*le peuple, les blouses, le sang*), the herd-like from the capricious and the sprightly. One thing stands clear: he cannot help energising even cliché-mongers: 'Les légendes qui courent le monde, qui dansent sur les lèvres des banalistes' (II, 1206).

Neologism

One source of energetic counter, the quick against the dead, is neologism: the coining of words to replace or add to time-honoured phrases. As at a sabbath, of course, it is hard to say which are the quick and the dead in language. Many coinages abort; many clichés flourish. Still, neologising is training in self-assertiveness (as well as show-off, verbal stunts). Not inventive in terms of plot or character, Vallès is prolific in word-creation, linguistic do-it-yourself. *Réfléchissoir* ennobles Jacques's minuscule garret which serves to focus his thinking (*Bach.*, p. 571). Eating a boiled egg becomes different when you call it *coquicide* (*Enf.*, pp. 150-51). Many of Vallès's coinages are derogatory; his foes excite his innovatory verve. Waldeck-Rousseau is 'le ministriculet de l'Intérieur', which buries *cul* inside the word (*Cri P*, 11 février 1884). *Romantasserie* or *diablotinisme* (attached to petty neo-Romantics), or 'bas-bleus, sabots bleus!' (referring to precious, pseudo-bucolic writers). [8] *Députasserie, politiquaillerie* speak for themselves (*Corr. A.*, pp. 103, 147). Vallès uses a nice neologism to denounce literary plagiarism: 'le Daudetlinage d'une tête taillée pour vivre elle-même'. [9] 'Il n'y a même pas le chien derrière le convoi: on l'a mangé un jour qu'il faisait faim' (II, 12), which encapsulates the wintriness of hunger, in the besieged Paris of February 1871. His coinages are tightly based on existing words or phrases, to which he gives extension or twist. Undoubtedly in so doing he fills gaps in the French lexis. As he said of his neologism 'Actualistes': 'S'il n'a pas d'avenir, au moins il n'a pas de passé' (I, 891). He makes up words to strike back against indoctrination: 'Il y a peu d'hommes qui aient été aussi énéidés que j'ai été' (II, 742). Hostility to word-making is the mark of linguistic purism, which is not unrelated to purges or doctrines of racial purity. Any conservative power seeking to put a curb on the tongue or the mind angered Vallès. He joyously forged words to stretch (and to stick out) his tongue. In *L'Insurgé* he could justifiably claim: 'Je n'ai eu ni le respect des tropes, ni la peur des néologismes' (p. 895). They add to his already capacious vocabulary of the concrete, for which the alert reader hardly needs the dubious benefit of computers.

Metaphor

A further area of inventiveness is metaphor: finding links between previously disparate entities. Vallès's sane mania for comparing Then and Now (youth and adulthood), Here and There, Town and Country, Them and Us, springs from his instinctual thinking analogically rather than linearly, from his admitted soft spot for nostalgia, and from his egalitarian impulse to contrast the lot in life of different social groups. Bringing two planes together is not always pacificatory, ecumenical (finding common ground). It is also a way of keeping separate and competing units in a relationship of tension and confrontation. 'C'est par la comparaison qu'on contrôle les sensations et les idées' (*TP*, p. 398). Metaphors are his form of analysis. By them he lassos a topic, and constant strings of them help to pull together a life and a work always threatened by dispersal. The insistent circus images of the earlier journalism and fiction evolve in *L'Insurgé* to an image of the Commune as a multicoloured merry-go-round, which gradually spins out of control, and finally begets a *danse macabre*.

In his journalism of the 1860s, when censorship made it dangerous to write nakedly, metaphors, more dolled up, often carried clandestine protest values. Indirect discourse is the very stuff of literature, and of its half-breed brother, the press. Vallès's urge to contrast and compare both helped his rebelliousness ('Why this rather than that?'), and preserved a tolerant, embracing quality ('There must be links between this and that': a first stage to understanding). His revolt did not spring from a rhetoric, but is clearly consubstantial with one. The analogical, associative mind can thus back up the cooperative urge. At the same time, even Vallès's more pacifist writings resort often to warlike imagery (blood, weapons, flags, wounds). His images retain militancy; they give as good as they get.

Their most marked feature is their concreteness, which is sometimes rendered by onomatopoeia, in keeping with the general mimetic line of Vallès's rhetoric: 'Le *fla-fla* des phrases, que signifie-t-il à côté du *clic-clac des sabres?*' (*Bach.*, p. 523). 'J'ai honte [...] de la métaphore sans carcasse', says Jacques of his 1869 electioneering in *L'Insurgé* (p. 942). Blood features so often that when 'le candidat des pauvres' projects emigrating to America to become a revolutionary adventurer, he instinctively refers to 'le trop-plein de mes veines' (*CP*, p. 383): he has a surplus of it; he envisages its being let, or spilling that of others. Blood and ink, another favourite, are interchangeable. *L'Enfant* places 'une encre qui est à peine séchée' right after 'du sang de révolté' (p. 364). In the same text, Jacques states: 'J'ai touché la vie de mes doigts pleins d'encre' (p. 271). Writing is bleeding oneself. Blood and wine have traditional links, on which Vallès overlays ink: 'J'irai l'an prochain aux vendanges, et pour faire mousser ma chronique, je mettrai du vin dans mon écritoire' (I, 87): which is presumably better than 'baptising' wine. Ink has other uses—for disguising worn or discoloured clothes, for instance (*Bach.*, p. 601). Its primary function is to bind, like metaphors in general, different realms, e.g. a republican print shop and a stable (*Enf.*, p. 365). This is the rich, inebriating stink of ink, not the mortifying stench of classrooms. Even in these, ink can be appropriated. Vallès talks often of eating paper and drinking ink at his boyhood desk (see *ibid.*, p. 247). This perhaps is meant to indicate that he had writing in his blood. Or perhaps a kind of back-formation has operated, from the vehicle to the tenor. It could be that the idiom 'buveur d'encre' (a penpusher) has been translated back into a literal consumption. Vallès, in fact, is so widely metaphorical that literal and figurative frequently seem osmotic. What might seem stylistic ornamentation becomes the norm, organic and indispensable.

Just as 'comme si' often introduces a telescoped fairy story, an exaggeration, not to be taken too literally, so metaphors can be excessive, over-pushed, e.g. 'La clarinette mordit jusqu'au sang le nez de son instrument' (I, 269). Discussing a landscape poet, Vallès has it both ways, mocking and indulging preciosity: 'Il ne fait pas leur toilette aux buissons et ne repasse par les collerettes blanches des marguerites, filles des prairies' (p. 421). Going over the top is imminent in *métaphores filées*. On the communard Rouiller, unlettered but clear-eyed, able to distinguish treacherous swine from pigskin, Vallès strings along a series of shoemaking puns and metaphors:

> il en sait plus long en histoire et en économie sociale, ce savetier, que n'en savent tous les diplômés réunis qui ont, avant lui, pris le portefeuille dont il a, avant-hier, tâté le ventre, avec une moue d'homme qui se connaît plus en peau de vache qu'en maroquin. [...] Et, à la tribune, il sait faire reluire et cambrer sa phrase comme l'empeigne d'un soulier, affilant sa blague en museau de bottine, ou enfonçant ses arguments, comme des clous à travers des talons de renfort! (II, 1036)

Intricate, and undoubtedly doing its job of ennobling a plebeian, this almost takes off into a separate domain of self-celebration. Another passage of *L'Insurgé* hovers between extended and mixed metaphor; at first it talks of patchwork, but then modulates gratingly into butchery:

> J'ai pris des morceaux de ma vie, et je les ai cousus aux morceaux de la vie des
> autres, riant quand l'envie m'en venait, grinçant des dents quand des souvenirs
> d'humiliation me grattaient la chair sur les os—comme la viande sur un manche
> de côtelette, tandis que le sang pisse sous le couteau. (p. 895)

At its best, a *métaphore filée* like this can ensnare the reader's attention.
At its worst, it is a kind of vamping, a way of sidestepping thought.

Mixed metaphors, Irish Bulls, follow on naturally. 'Renoul n'aurait
pas été bercé *sur les genoux de cette tête vénérée*' (*Bach.*, p. 504,
Vallès's italics). Or the Mother speaking, with her inimitable logic: 'Je
voudrais que tu fusses bien malade une bonne fois, ça te guérirait peut-
être' (*Enf.*, p. 213). The out-of-place, or above-her-station imperfect
subjunctive shows she is trying to talk fancy but making a pig's ear of it.
Vallès himself was the most metaphorical of men,—hardly a sentence
without a comparison of some kind—yet his aim was plain speaking (not
that direct appeals rule out figurative speech, Christ knows). Despite his
championing of *vise-droit* writing ('Moi, je veux une langue pour les
truands, claire, transparente, avec des mots en cristal de roche, au
travers desquels on voit l'idée! C'est pour cela que j'ai fait des
barricades' [10]), the Stendhalian varnish style would have ill suited him,
in fact negated him. There is no real paradox here. While never
revealing all (who ever does or can?), he offers himself with few
ambages or other verbal fig-leaves. He addresses his readers directly,
vocatively, and in truth could very well do without us scholiasts. Like
God in the Portuguese proverb dear to Claudel, he writes straight in
crooked lines. [11] Metaphor is his daily bread.

The fan of *savate* adores catching words off guard, on the wrong
foot. He boxes (and coxes) with them. It may be because Vallès is so
metaphorical a writer that he pauses so often to literalise metaphors, as
though to remind us and himself of the ground beneath the airy talk.
Metaphor (like irony) pleads: 'Do not take me literally; read between
my lines'. Literal-mindedness resists this soft soap. In *L'Enfant*, when a
fatuously reverential teacher eulogises Racine: 'Il ne reste plus qu'à
fermer les autres livres', the practical Jacques mutters: 'Je ne demande
pas mieux'. When the teacher plugs away: 'Et à s'avouer impuissant',
Jacques disassociates himself: 'C'est son affaire' (p. 343). This is a
variety of punning that detects other meanings beyond the intended one.
Another variant is the extended idiom ('brosser le ventre': to go without
food): 'J'ai tant de fois brossé mon ventre sans faire reluire l'espoir
d'un dîner' (*Ins.*, p. 877). A further one is self-deflating Romantic
irony: 'Je suis resté huit jours à m'arracher les cheveux; heureusement
j'en ai beaucoup' (*Bach.*, p. 615). Literalisation brings back to earth
what seeks to remain other-worldly; it takes at face value instead of as
gospel. Even when translating at school, Jacques aims for literalism: 'Je
suis le second en version. J'ai *fait* encore trop près du texte' (*Enf.*, p.
373). Didier detects scatological wordplay in 'fait'. Though I, a

puntheist, see puns everywhere, I cannot in this case. [12] On the other hand, when Jacques rides behind Polonie, I take this as a literalisation, a delectable embodiment, of his existential metaphorical position, *à califourchon.*

Twists and Zeugma

No metaphor is ever truly dead; it is merely lying doggo, and by a kind of voodoo can be reanimated. Sayings long inert can be reactivated and, like trampolines, give bounce to ideas and words. It is principally highly conventionalised utterances, proverbs, idioms, slogans or clichés, that lend themselves to and invite distortion. This process of twisting clearly partakes of a desacralising urge, or sabotage. By the start of his journalistic career, in 1861, Vallès was already making clear his tactic.

> Je vous ai promis d'écorcher quelques préjugés, de bouleverser les clichés sur lesquels se tire la Bible de la sagesse contemporaine! Je vais faire d'une pierre deux coups: vous donner ma biographie et attaquer, par le miroir, une vieille phrase qui court le monde, à savoir: que l'enfance est le plus bel âge de la vie! (I, 129)

'Par le miroir', reversing the image; twists do 'kill two birds with one stone'. 'Clichés' retains here its original connexion with printing, but the following lines show the meaning slipping over into 'hackneyed ideas'. In a similar spirit, truisms can be reutilised as home truths: 'La jeunesse est un âge, et non pas un talent, pas plus qu'une vertu' (p. 472). As we saw earlier, his resounding article 'Cochons vendus' redirects an already metaphorical phrase to new, pointed and wider uses: venality in large areas of public life. Social change can be helped to come about by such challenging of received ideas: innovation by reaction. The ludic instinct is the heckler at the back of our mental meeting-halls.

As elsewhere, Vallès's revising mockery moves inwards as well as outwards. 'Moi, louveteau de Panurge' (p. 686) boosts himself: he could never be *un mouton* (an informer, or a follower-on), while reducing himself to a cub, not a pack leader. Ever on guard against turncoats, he rarely misses a chance for the comic turnaround. Reporting a scam whereby crooks sold water as an elixir, then drank all the profits: 'Ils avaient mis beaucoup de vin dans leur eau' (p. 763), he twists on the twisters. After a duel in which Jacques is amazed to find himself emotionless, despite a wound in the thigh, he says: 'Ça ne me faisait pas plus qu'un cautère sur une jambe de bois' (*Enf.*, p. 386). This phrase means usually something of no earthly use, but here it is transferred to: making no impression. It is a picturesque way of dramatising a non-occurrence. A further twist on this idiom: 'C'était comme un cautère sur une tête de bois, cette latinasserie qu'on m'appliquait sur le crâne' (*Bach.*, p. 538), conjoins wasted effort and boneheaded obstinacy. Jacques twists and turns in order to survive: 'Ah! tant pas, je prendrai la vache enragée par les cornes!' (*ibid.*, p. 653). Vallès records the poor people of London protesting about economies in the Lord Mayor's Show: 'Ils voudraient en avoir pour leur débine' (II, 1274). Some of Vallès's twists are passably pointless ('Caleçonner des pipes' for 'culotter' — to break in a pipe — *Ins.*, p. 880), but most give a new edge to the teeth of old saws. The surviving brother of the murdered Victor Noir is his spitting image: 'Ils se ressemblaient comme deux gouttes de sang' (*ibid.*, p. 958). Our contemporary coinage 'rejasing' (reusing junk as something else) suits Vallès's linguistic ecology.

A related rhetorical figure, the zeugma, similarly enables a bifurcation, a kind of mental splits:

> On a rétabli les foires dans les communes et les faubourgs, à la grande joie des pauvres, qui, tous les soirs, peuvent faire voir trente-six chandelles à leur spleen ou à leurs gosses: les aigrettes du gaz et les mèches des lampions crèvent, non seulement l'ombre de la nuit, mais aussi le noir des idées. (*TP*, p. 83)

In a self-portrait at the age of seventeen, Vallès describes himself as: 'Petit émeutier précoce, il parlait haut d'ordinaire, cassait les verres, les vitres, froissait les jupes et les gens. Il jouait à l'homme' (I, 312). The zeugma miscegenates the posh and the demotic, as in this account of kids' street fights where 'on éteignait mutuellement son enthousiasme et ses lampions' (p. 670). As well as being one of the jokers in the rhetorical pack, the zeugma brings down to earth, reminds that few things in life escape their prosaic accompaniments: 'Je prends mon courage à deux mains et ma malle par l'anse' (*Bach.*, p. 452). It lends itself to the pell-mell, with a twist in the tail: 'On découvre une lacune dans son roman, une invraisemblance dans sa pièce, des trous à son pantalon' (I, 247). After a passage relating Jacques's games with the children of a cobbler and a grocer, Vallès says they called him in 'à propos de bottes ou de marmelade; il y avait toujours quelque tonneau, quelque baquet, quelque querelle ou quelque pot à vider' (*Enf.*, p. 203). This is a delightful mixed bag of menial task, squabbling and convivial tippling, playing on the literal and figurative senses of *vider*, and a good example of Vallès's sliding technique.

Puns

In the separate chapters on the three novels, I have already shown puns *in situ* and in action, and want here to recapitulate and generalise rather than to list many more examples. Literalisation, twists and zeugmas are all blood brothers of punning, the rhetorical weapon most often in Vallès's hands. [13] Puns, the stock in trade of the lowest comedians and the most refined wits, have been partly rehabilitated nowadays, but scarcely possess as yet *lettres de noblesse*. They are thus tailor-made, as his clothes so rarely were, for the rogue Vallès. They remain in a limbo, practised everywhere by nearly everybody, but sheepishly, whereas all puns should be intended, spoken with pride and not apologetically. If we have to add anything to a pun, we should say, not 'so to speak', but 'and no mistake'. One reason why children in particular love them so is that they bring about mock marriages, illicit mixtures, of the high and the low ('Un calembour, qui est une espèce d'adultère', said Valéry). [14] For Vallès, it is not too much to say that life itself is a pun: excruciating, pointed or pointless, full of coexisting but not necessarily compatible demands. It can make us laugh, openly, or on the other side of our face. This existential punner, this ludic activist, punned for his dear life. Organic punning lies at the heart of his experiencing and his exploration of reality.

Punning is part of eloquence itself: 'Il lançait des *postillons* d'éloquence sur tous les chemins' (II, 409. Vallès's italics). It makes words do double duty, and offers a bargain: two meanings for the price of one word or phrase. It is thus a device of economy, but also an excuse for expenditure; and the budget-conscious Vallès always checks both sides of any balance sheets. 'J'ai réglé ma vie—le livre de comptes est là, près du livre de souvenirs—mon budget est inexorable' (*Ins.*, p. 890). As well as one-liners, Vallès's wordplay can be intricate, as in this equation of traditional republicans with food. I have managed, he says, to 'rayer de mon doigt la poussière sur ces *pots* de tradition confite, et gratter au couteau les *tartines* de ces pseudo-révolutionnaires' (I, 773; my italics), which calls to mind complacent potbellies and rambling harangues.

Jacques Vingtras is often split-minded, and so the duplicitous, forking, ambivalent pun comes naturally to him. A pun is a Janus, 'un mot à deux têtes' (p. 760), and two heads are better than one, as Vautrin urges Rastignac. It is an ideal vehicle for mixed feelings, for 'cohabitation sémantique'. [15] Vallès, however, rarely uses it for innuendo. Even when a much cuckolded chemist in *L'Enfant* is described by his neighbours as being 'toujours dans les *cornues*' (p. 255), this betrays a community zest for gossip rather than prurient sneakiness.

Jacques fluctuates between the twin poles described by the verbs *crâner* and *caner* (and the two sounds come perilously close to each other): brazening it out, or caving in—the two options, also, of the arm-chancing punster. 'Il me fallait toucher ou essayer de toucher le danger, avoir une cible à atteindre et des coups à redouter' (*SEP*, p. 95). This tit for tat forms part of what Vallès means by 'la vie d'échange', though this term also embraces less aggressive, more companionable impulsions. The pun is both attack and defence, like *savate*, duelling or urban guerrilla warfare. Receivers often register puns as an aggression or outrage, while punsters often retaliate against oppressors. One meaning of 'to pun' is to batter. *Le Canard enchaîné*, which fittingly honours Vallès amongst its forerunners, is fond of 'le calembour-massue', and Vallès indeed frequently clobbers his readers with his wordplay. Most of his puns hit the bull ('la blague ayant toujours sa cible sérieuse'—*Ins.*, p. 918). In an exam hall crowded with scoffing students, Vallès enjoys 'le calembour français riant au nez de la poésie romaine'(I, 851). In these circumstances, playing with words is a muffled but still audible protest of growling underdogs. The availability of puns reminds us that, while we are all subject to the 'System' or to multiple subsystems, there remains play in the system, elbow room. After all, wordplay can suddenly unmask the latent resources of language, and those of the human spirit. Like irony, it can smuggle in forbidden ideas. It is a kind of aside, out of the corner of the mouth or the mind, a glancing blow. It is 'semantic kidnapping'.[16] Yet, hard to pin down for long, this slippery customer can be blatant, as well as clandestine. Vallès often highlights his by italicising them—the equivalent of the stand-up comedian's wink. An above-board writer in the main, he thumps his cards on the table, unkeen on 'cette guerre d'allusions voilées' (p. 772).

As Freud knew, none of us can control the polysemy of language. When Jacques says: 'J'avais insulté les fayots de collège', he may have had in mind only beans, but *fayots* also signifies swots, re-enlisted soldiers and teachers (*Ins.*, p. 887). He is clearly being wry, as so often, for example when an editor congratulates Vingtras on a hard-hitting article: 'Cristi! vous avez de l'estomac'. Jacques ponders: 'Beaucoup trop! Je m'en suis aperçu souvent: les jours de jeûne surtout' (*ibid.*, p. 894). This points up how the more estimable things in life are conditioned by the grosser. Such awareness rarely depresses, however, for wordplay acts generally as a morale boost. 'Cet habit à queue de morue dessalée par la misère' (I, 139): a swallowtail (in French, a codtail) coat is both soaked by poverty and made streetwise by it. The wearers of such coats pun in their very behaviour: 'Ils consentent à passer pour fous, à condition de paraître moins pauvres; ils laissent dire qu'ils *déménagent*, pour avoir l'air d'avoir des meubles' (*ibid.*, p. 140). This unrealistic pun mirrors their delusion; they move between crazy-houses. On their behalf, Vallès here uses the pun as a buffer zone, to keep at bay unfaceable reality. In his own name, it is most often a way of coping with problems, rather than evading them, as frequently occurs in the punning Victorian, Thomas Hood.

Apart from its properly serious uses, the pun is often an agent of sociability, an icebreaker: 'Fouille-au-pot jeta, comme un pont, un calembour salé, la glace se fondit et nous parlâmes' (p. 247). It is an equaliser: 'Chacun, gâcheur de plâtre ou gâcheur de vers' (p. 843). It can betoken simply fun, though even so remain pointed: 'C'était le bon temps du poil à gratter, et le négociant en démangeaisons faisait des affaires brillantes. On est aujourd'hui moins chatouilleux et l'on a la peau plus dure' (p. 724). The thick-skinned find it hard to laugh. Some of Vallès's puns are pure verbal high spirits ('Le calembour, cette rime dévergondée'[17]), shamelessly exploiting phonic coincidences. Verbal pantomime, larking about, acting the goat. Vallès everywhere derides *l'esprit de sérieux*—that great bogy also of Sartre. In his hostility to gravity (*gravitas, gravitatis...*), his words can take off on an antic life of their own, performing somersaults, and, inevitably at times, coming a cropper. Vallès can match Prévert's 'grand homme d'état trébuchant / sur une belle phrase creuse / tombe dedans'.[18]

Literary exiles are often given to punning: Joyce, Nabokov, Ionesco, Beckett, but not Conrad. Even before his enforced expatriation, Vallès was always something of a resident alien in his homeland (deported as a child into outrageous clothes). Puns lie around in languages, waiting to be picked up, released. The alien eye can spot these opportunities (Nabokov: 'What is this *jest* in majesty, this *ass* in passion?').[19] Puns make receivers backtrack, do a double take, have second thoughts, which explains their unpopularity with many. Others feel that their mental agility is being appealed to. Punning, like dirty, minds think alike. Even so, Vallès is able to think against his own preferences. Among the many *galériens* and *forçats* of *La Rue* is 'le forçat du bon mot'. There are pun machines; a century earlier the Marquis de Bièvre was one such. 'Je ne connais pas de métier plus fatigant [...] que celui de "causeur amusant", qui court après le calembour bizarre, [...] comme un nain à califourchon sur les dents d'une *scie'*: a truly excruciating pun, and posture. For all his clubbability, Vallès dislikes factitious gaiety, 'la fécondation artificielle, les travaux forcés de l'improvisation hâtive', when 'on attend, comme un œuf sous la poule, la plaisanterie fine ou salée' (I, 799-800).

Although at times it might appear as if Vallès were only a linguistic playboy, in fact both he and his hero are extremely sensitive to the weight and import of words. More than once Jacques claims that his father's verbal lashings hurt him much more than did his physical blows. On a wider social scale, in a strongly censored society such as that of Vallès, the responsible uses of literacy acquire even more urgent significance. The pun, as Empson says, is 'a crucial point',[20] as well as being saddled with the label 'excruciating'. Vallès put wordplay to work; he made play work—that is, function effectively. Wordplay enables him to detect not only incongruity, but previously unnoticed congruity. It is grossly inadequate to declare, like Bonnefis: 'Le

calembour, chez Vallès, n'est jamais laudatif. Il est toujours réducteur'.[21]
This omits all the festive, celebratory, hyperbolic, and indeed politically
committed puns. Remember: 'Le calembour n'empêche pas les
convictions' (II, 503): puns don't mean that you don't mean it. Of the
Trilogy, it is *Le Bachelier* that houses the most wordplay, perhaps
because adolescence involves sowing wild oats. The young child was too
severely hemmed in, and the grown man too caught up in frantic public
events for either to have quite as much time as the largely suspended
bachelier for verbal antics. Nevertheless, all three books have a high
incidence of punning. Vallès measures his wordplay out not with coffee
spoons but with soup ladles. However dire the circumstances, Vallès
commonly and unabashedly resorts often to punning comment. It is one
of his favoured modes of authorial intervention. It is his readiness to
play with words, to take risks by juxtaposing competing registers, that
gives his writing its self-igniting vitality, its bitty and variable
lifelikeness.

Exaggeration, Melodrama and Sentimentality

'J'écris à la diable et en toute franchise; la blague pourra paraître
parfois trop forte, elle ne sera que l'expression de la vérité, grossie par
le rire. Quand on rit, les joues gonflent' (*SEP,* p. 84). If revolution
begets exaggeration, why should not a revolutionary? In his defence of
the fittingness of hyperbole, Vallès has weighty supporters. Baudelaire
talked of 'la vérité emphatique du geste dans les grandes circonstances
de la vie', and Barthes glosses, apropos of the French Revolution: 'Ce
qui paraît aujourd'hui de l'enflure, n'était alors que la taille de la
réalité. Cette écriture, qui a tous les signes de l'inflation, fut une
écriture exacte: jamais langage ne fut plus invraisemblable et moins
imposteur'.[22] Exaggeration can come from violence; it can be, to use a
favourite image of Vallès, a release valve: a frustrated banging of the
head, or the tongue, against the wall. Political impotence gives rise to
verbal over-compensation, talking big, in order to minimise the enemy.
Vallès's comic amplification belittles the official *amplificatio* of
scholastic exercises. His imagination often runs riot, and this embryonic
insurgent is forever on the lookout for riots he might whip up.

In addition to ideological motives, exaggeration in Vallès is innate,
medullary, like Thoreau's 'extra-vagance'.[23] Lepelletier comments:
'C'était tous les jours mardi-gras dans ses œuvres'.[24] We have seen many
instances of his comic hyperbole about clothes: the awkward conjunction
of a proud self and demeaning apparel. Exaggeration underscores,
heavily. Jacques says of sweets doled out over a year: 'J'ai léché—par
ordre—des bonbons qui semblaient venir de Pompéi' (I, 696). The fish-

tails that Jacques eats in Paris taste like candlewax: 'Avec une mèche, un merlan m'éclairerait toute la nuit' (*Bach.*, p. 570). A marvellous section of sustained hyperbole in *Le Bachelier* concerns a garret so miniscule that even the fleas are crowded out and Jacques cannot afford to let his nails grow. As in a hospital, he has to sleep with his feet in the air, and his friend Legrand with his head sticking out of a skylight. This swelling of the minimal is far more than a passing joke. It has real point, for the maladroit individualist can never fit himself in anywhere comfortably (pp. 572-4). As the passage moves from the metaphorical to the literal and on to the hyperbolic, we see exaggeration moderated, but not short-circuited, by a sense of irony, for Jacques is also pricking his bladder of pretension. Conversely, just as litotes (*extreme moderation*) is frequently hyperbole in disguise (they are not miles apart), so Vallès's undercutting often inflates. The Bachelier géant states: 'J'avais la fièvre dans le cœur et le feu dans la tête; on dit pourtant qu'il fait frais sur les cimes!' (I, 270). Perhaps stagflation is a better term for this paradoxical mode. Exaggeration, besides, is contagious, as when anglers vie with tall stories. Undoubtedly a hyperbolist, he attracts exaggeration (Vallès the monster; Vallès the lay saint). The hardest, and most necessary, thing is to see him straight.

Exaggeration naturally leads Vallès at times into melodrama and sentimentality (though many sob stories are, of course, authentic). It can be argued that his common melodramatising urge wells from his very verve, his relish in his own effects. His reiterations and underlinings, his verbal eye-rolling, are more often than not wilful rather than careless, and are designed either to damage a hated idea by repeated exposure, or to enhance a cherished one by heroic expansion. The fact remains that some of his harangues are pickled. It sometimes seems as though so much energy goes into joking at miseries that only melodrama remains for greater sufferings. If Vallès had the sort of mind that reads, with hindsight, omens into everything, we must remember that he was also a man to whom ominous things (asylum, prison, civil war) happened.

Sentimentality calls on stock responses (but so do beauty, tragedy and comedy). The difference is to do with the degree of effort—imaginative, moral—involved. It can, at its lowest ebb, be mere knee-jerk tear-jerking, as when Vallès, out of character, writes fakely of Maurice and Eugénie de Guérin: 'nous préférions pour lui, à une notoriété banale, une gloire discrète dont le rayon tiède tombât, comme le jour pâle des églises, sur des âmes pieuses et préparées' (I, 832). Yet, like much stereotyped response, sentimentality can be strong, as in Vallès's demagogic oratory in 1869: 'Quatre ou cinq *effets,* criards comme des images d'Épinal' (*Ins.,* p. 939). Just as the stockpot is invaluable in the kitchen, many stock responses are made to stock situations. Sentimentality also entails excessive response. It cannot be faulted on intensity, but only on disproportion or misapplication.

Although Vallès's constitution jibbed at onions, he was fully capable of the automatic onion effect. We have to remind ourselves, nonetheless, of our twentieth-century taboo on expansiveness, the hard-boiled topos of our age. Vallès is not as callous as children nor as blasé as adults often are. As the tough egg Léon Daudet noted, Vallès's language is 'de temps en temps, sous le mâle, d'une beauté féminine palpitante et sobre'. [25] Though Vallès himself claimed that there should be 'des larmes dans les yeux clairs des pamphlétaires', by the end of the article he is stressing: '*La sentimentalité nous tue!*' (I, 134-5).

He is, for all that, a self-confessed sucker for pathos, in art or daily life. It can take the form of an upturned preciosity which attempts to ring the changes and turn the tables for different sentimental reasons on a stock association. After noting that doves are conventionally linked with both purity and voluptuousness, Jacques takes pride in describing a scruffy dove which visits a poverty-stricken streetwalker neighbour, pecking on her squalid windowpane for a few scraps of rancid bread, and crapping on his sill (*Ins.*, p. 890). A clear sentimental streak, a love of the painfully obvious collocation produces patterns like this: 'Je ne voyais pas éclore mon avenir, mais je voyais pourrir mes fleurs' (*Bach.*, p. 475). He relishes opposing primary colours: white/red, red/black. It is useless denying that, on a good many occasions, Vallès's sensitivity lacks taste, proportion, and control. Vallès, whose life curve was a string of near misses (either triumphal or disastrous), culminating in an impaired survival, is an approximate writer, a man of lunges, who often loses on the roundabouts what he gains on the swings, and who therefore frequently flails about in some confusion. His ideas are quite often commonplace, indeed corny, though, as Camus reminded: 'On appelle vérités premières celles qu'on découvre après toutes les autres'.[26] Snobbishly, we might call this the 'popular' side of Vallès. He is 'un homme du peuple', like all of us, in that too often he relies on gut-instincts which are under-informed and half-baked. He himself recognised that his style, like his head, was a ragbag: 'J'ai fait mon style de pièces et de morceaux que l'on dirait ramassés à coups de crochet, dans des coins malpropres et navrants' (*Ins.*, p. 910). Vallès the rhetorical *biffin*. Like that other nineteenth-century cliché, the whore with the heart of gold, one stereotype of Vallès is that of the softy loudmouth. It should be added that Vallès himself went along with this high-toned portrait, piling it on thick, for example in the umpteen Pagliaccian variations on the theme of irony as a mask for vulnerability.

Irony and Euphemism

If irony is a mask, does it hide, distort, or create a new persona? 'Je couvrirai éternellement mes émotions intimes du masque de l'insouciance et de la perruque de l'ironie' (*Bach.*, p. 449). This is irony as would-be aristocratic defence, warding off intruders. Obviously, too, he gives his game, and his privacy, away; he makes a public spectacle, to his readers, of his camouflage. Against this we should place Vallès's protest against the rewriting, the editorial mutilation of his articles: 'Mon style c'est moi. Si l'on m'ajoute des verrues, on me défigure. C'est mon masque, et non mon visage; il suffit d'un clou [boil] sur le nez d'un grec pour en faire un pif; on m'a fait un pif' (*L'Époque*, 30 août 1865). Like irony itself, aiming at veiled visibility, Vallès wanted it both ways, but out of necessity. Having to keep watch on his tongue and attitudes at school and at home for many years, Vallès built up 'un emmagasinement d'ironie' (*SEP*, p. 87). It was his form of pseudo-dumb insolence. Like all programmatic strategies, it could be fake, 'une douleur blagueuse, une ironie de crocodile' (*Bach.*, p. 567). As well as being a double agent, it can serve a double function for Vallès—as natural as sweat ('L'ironie me sortait par la peau'), or provocative and healing ('Malgré soi, son vinaigre, qui avait cautérisé mes plaies, assaisonnait ma blague'—*SEP*, p. 87).

The uses of irony (double talk) are self-evidently complex, and even self-contradictory. Irony does not blow the gaff (and yet the blatant, salient language of Vallès rejoices in it perhaps *because* it is an in-between mode); it tips the wink, needles, or nudges. Even as a child, however, Vallès disliked the at-a-remove mode of allegory. On La Fontaine he comments: 'On parvint à grand'peine à me faire comprendre que c'était de l'allégorie—une supposition. / Un mensonge, alors!/ Depuis, je me tins en garde vis-à-vis de l'apologue et je regardai tous les fabulistes comme des blagueurs' (*Enf.*, variant, p. 1535). Like euphemism, irony is a code to be deciphered by an accomplice. It does not insult the intelligence of anyone, except for censors. It is an anti-authority authority: 'The free mind must have one policeman. Irony!' [27] As 'get at' means to refer to, often indirectly, and to attack, often head-on, irony is devious aggression. Sarcasm ('to rip flesh', 'to bite the lips in rage', 'to sneer') is irony stepped up; it is usually unmistakable. Irony, for its part, says more by specifying less. Working on the slant, it aims to put things straight: a pair of glasses to correct defective eyesight. Though not saying what it means, it does, on the whole, mean what it (indirectly) says. It is a shortcut that takes a detour, often more interesting than the highroad. Misused, of course, it can be merely hypocrisy, un-plain dealing.

Vallès seems to visualise irony almost literally as a weapon: 'L'arme de l'ironie toujours, un poignard à manche joli, à reflet de lame bleue, avec une petite larme blanche au bout et des taches de sang dans le fil' (*Corr. M.*, p. 116): a curious development of the stock image of irony-as-weapon, in which the *signifié* virtually comes adrift of the *signifiant*,

possibly via a phonic off-glide into *arme blanche*. At other times, he
calls irony a whip, a bayonet, and, of course, a safety valve (I, pp. 520;
608; 1026). It is all-embracing: 'J'aime toutes les formes de l'ironie,
adoucies, violentes, polies, barbares. Elle ne fait peur qu'aux faibles et
elle est la leçon et l'honneur des forts' (p. 583).

Jacques Vingtras stays on guard not only when face to face with
tyrants, but also when on his own, in soliloquy, a sign that he has
internalised the dangers, and the tactic essential for resistance. Often he
gets in first, via self-irony. He refuses to take even himself as gospel.
When a tailor asks him 'Quelle forme ont vos jacquettes, d'ordinaire?',
Jacques immediately thinks ruefully, in escalating self-mockery: 'L'air
d'un sac généralement: d'un morceau de journal autour d'un os de gigot,
d'une guenille autour d'un paquet de cannes' (*Bach.*, p. 607). The hero
of *Le Candidat des pauvres* reflects on his 'réputation de gaieté et
d'entrain à quelques mètres à la ronde' (*CP*, p. 353). As Geoffrey
Strickland perceptively notes, such self-deflation 'is not merely funny or
merely a device to endear Vallès to the reader. He is not a nineteenth-
century Lucky Jim'. [28] Nor is it that terminal English disease, false
modesty.

Irony is as central to Vallès as exaggeration or punning or
metaphors, because he experienced life as deeply ironical, bloody-
minded in its placing of obstacles to fulfilment. If his irony strikes some
readers as too omnipresent, they might reflect how deathlessly un-ironic
are the asseverations of many politicians, parents, teachers, lovers,
friends and, when we nod, so often ourselves. Irony is not necessarily a
debilitating mode, as Flaubert emphasises: 'L'ironie n'enlève rien au
pathétique: elle l'outre, au contraire'. [29] Devious, oblique, but not
inevitably evasive. Vallès extends the term too widely for it to be tamed
by a single verdict. Bellet lists: 'Rire de Voltaire, ironie proudhonienne,
gaieté factice et humeur farcesque des grands seigneurs irréguliers ou
des aristocrates déclassés, caricature, rire des cafés chantants, gaieté des
opéras bouffes, rire réaliste, rire de saltimbanque, fête populaire'
(*JVJR*, p. 292). Irony, for Vallès, is almost synonymous with breath and
speech: 'L'ironie me pète du cerveau et du cœur' (*Ins.*, p. 917). The
verb *péter* captures the healthy outgoing nature of this underground
trope.

Another type of un-plain speech is euphemism, which ranges from
near-complete cloaking to virtual transparency. As might be expected,
Vallès is towards the latter end of this spread. Where dysphemism is full
frontal assault, euphemism is a way of uttering the unspeakable, a prim
sin. Like circumlocution (or Céline's 'circonlocutasserie' which mimes
as it mocks lengthiness), [30] it sets up a puzzle, encouraging solution.
Words, however, cannot keep things incognito. The verbal fig leaf tries
unavailingly to be the opposite of the blatant codpiece. Willy-nilly, most
euphemisms backfire. Jacques is paid commission to pen an insulting

note. Euphemistically, he puts 'c—r' for 'cracher', but then panics at
the thought that this might be read as 'chier'—a splendid instance of
how euphemism draws attention to the forbidden word (*Bach.*, p. 647).
While not coy, Vallès rarely flaunts bodily functions, and 'baver sur les
tombeaux' in *Le Bachelier* (p. 510) might be a cop-out for Horace's
franker: 'We mercifully preserve their bones, and piss not upon their
ashes'.[31] An example of loquacious euphemism, noisily trumpeting what
it feigns to cloak, is this mock-heroic description of an English po:

> Là-bas, énorme, pansue, voyez-vous resplendir au ras du sol la lune de
> faïence, Phoebé consolatrice qui, chez nous, ne déserte pas l'autel avant la
> nuit profonde et attend que tout se taise pour écouter Endymion, mais qui là-
> bas, commère impudique, dont la bedaine luit à toute heure et pour tout le
> monde, tend ses joues, non pas seulement aux familiers, mais au visiteur
> inconnu que le *pst!* déconcerte—et émeut. (*RL*, II, 1211)

It comes complete with telling onomatopoeia, and in addition, is surely
a parody of all the arch, fine-sounding classical reproductions Vallès
was obliged to concoct at school. Much more down to earth is the boy
Jacques describing himself as feeling 'tout chose' (all of a doodah) over
seeing the edible cousin Polonie getting dressed—a very different
matter from his mother's 'chose [i.e. cul] de bouteille' (*Enf.*, pp. 154;
301). It is significant that Vallès's euphemisms do not etherealise, but
come back to things. His bromides are seldom self-administered. For a
feet-first writer, Vallès displays, nevertheless, much more tact (if not
squeamishness) than might be forecast. In a heavily-policed society,
veiled allusions are all that citizens dare allow themselves, but, in this
area of indirection, Vallès goes for the double-meaning pun, or irony,
much more than for euphemism.

Repetition

Vallès's post at Caen lycée was 'surveillant répétiteur', which
suggests a spy running on the spot, a theatrical rehearsal and, of course,
betrays the repetition central to education. One of the commonest
critical complaints against Vallès is his repetitiveness. Though a man of
many surprises, he is also one of countless automatisms (e.g. Homer is
always blind). In a book on plagiarism, Schneider reminds us how very
little any of us has to say.[32] So how can we avoid repeating
ourselves—as if consuming an everlasting radish? We all pillage
ourselves. Even God, the founding non-original, made humanity in
his/her own image. For Bellet, Vallès's repetitiveness grows organically
from his fidelity to cycles (agrarian, church or school calendars, to
which we must add revolutionary dates). These act as constants (*JVJR*,
pp. 307; 326).

When Vallès repeats himself (sometimes, but not always, with variations), no doubt he is guilty of self-plagiarism, but, as its best, the act of reiteration reconfirms an allegiance. Aimed at others, such hammering is that of a rhetorical Vulcan (or cobbler), endlessly restating what many do not want to hear, knocking nails into wooden heads or hearts: 'Je vous l'ai demandé, recommandé, répété, re-répété...'. [33] Strangely, Vallès is both short-winded and prolix, the prolixity coming from milking a phrase or a situation. Anger, the will to negate, militancy, all rely on repetition, as in Cato the Elder's famous 'Delenda est Carthago', with which he ended every oration (quoted II, 818). Freud links the compulsive repetition kept up by young children with the hunger for mastery. He notes that 'as a child passes over from the passivity of the experience to the activity of the game, he hands on the disagreeable experience to one of his playmates and in this way revenges himself on a substitute'. In turn, Freud compares this operation with artistic play. [34] Wordplay in Vallès combines with a pedagogic urge to teach his readers a lesson, as a compensation perhaps for all the mind-stuffing he endured as a boy. So doing, however, he hopes to promote deliverance, not impose incarceration.

Sometimes, repetition comes from and with Vallès's taste for grotesquerie, as in this harping portrait of the exorbitant Ducasse in *L'Insurgé:* 'Il écarquille ses yeux tout ronds; il écarquille ses coudes pointus; il écarquille ses jambes qui tricotent; il écarquille sa bouche coupée en fente de tirelire' (II, 952). In a different context, in *L'Enfant,* a junior teacher's minor vice of brandy-tippling is described as 'son péché mignon, sa marotte humide, son dada jaune' (p. 212), where the effort of dwelling upon the target presupposes an interest and the beginnings of compassion. Less kindly is this list judging a senior teacher: 'Insinuant, fouilleur, chafouin, furet, belette, taupe' (*ibid.,* p. 292); here the last word subverts the preceding ones, as blindness cancels acuity. As for *Le Bachelier,* we might remember that rebellious youths tend to latch on to catchphrases, slogans and passwords, especially when they set up in secret societies. Jacques's own refrains (e.g. 'Alea jacta est') betoken not fatalism, but rather the need for *débrouillardise.* His recurrent rhetorical questions, similarly, are not the traditional sort, whose answer is self-evident, but calls to action, self-harangues.

Vallès makes sparing but telling use of alliteration and assonance, as in the opening to *L'Enfant,* with its contrasting t-values: 'du temps où j'étais petit; dorloté, tapoté, baisotté; j'ai été beaucoup fouetté' (p. 141). Jacques spits out his distaste for the alien humanities: 'Tout ce latin, ce grec, me paraît baroque et barbare, je l'avale comme de la boue' (*ibid.,* p. 269). Too much of this, as of any repetition, would seem like flogging a dead horse, an inability to leave off and call it a day. When Vallès jams, as he does, on certain sounds or expressions, as though afflicted by a stammer or hiccups, or like a needle stuck in a faulty groove, it is generally either because he is choking with barely suppressed anger or excitement, or, of course, simply because he is carried away by the exuberance of his own verbosity. Masson talks of logorrhea, but that is sometimes necessary to clear out the system. [35] Nevertheless, banging can make a reader punch-drunk. An habitué of state prisons, obsessed with his own motif of *galérien/forçat*, Vallès is a stylistic recidivist.

Narrative and Structure

Vallès's narrative discontinuities immediately strike any reader. Maybe he took to heart the advice of Pascal (another rebel against classical order): 'L'éloquence continue ennuie'. [36] His prose switches or slides constantly from one register, source of reference or area of lexis to another, often within the same sentence or in adjacent ones. He acts as a pointsman. The rhythms are staccato, syncopated. The jaggedness of the narrative is a sign of the will to avoid fixture, monumentalisation, statufiction. It is his way of paying homage to chaos, or at least to bittiness and mess: the very stuff of life. Even in our post-everything age, many people do not want to encounter fragmentation. *La Nausée* remains very perceptive on our insistent retrospective ordering of experience. An author like Vallès who reminds us in his practice of these messy facts of life is reopening our shut eyes and not necessarily failing in his artistic duty as a shape-maker. Besides, all such talk is too neatly oppositional (even though Vallès habitually pairs opposites within a sentence, as when he says of England that she 'promène ses richesses ou ensevelit ses suicidés dans les flots boueux de la Tamise'—*TP*, p. 257). His structure is less truly binary than overlapping, a tension: home is ever present in Paris, the past in the now, the future looms today. Written discontinuity is still a kind of shaping, involving deletions, highlighting, underplaying: choice. It is a new order, not an absence of order. Vallès, for instance, possibly because of the journalistic habit of headlining, often given us the gist, the main news, before the details, the build-up: he jumps the gun. If anything, this adds to rather than destroys suspense.

He rarely lets the reader rest up. As on a roller coaster ride, we have to follow his hero's ups and downs, changes of tones and mood. Vallès writes of, and in, swings and roundabouts. Holding in (irony, reserve, litotes) alternates with expansion (anger, exaggeration, lyricism). It is the rhythm of breathing, vital, existential. And yet his commonest narrative structure, the scene—comic or dramatic, or often both simultaneously—would seem to militate against the impression of strenuous energy. Excerpting such scenes, as I have done throughout, is less unkind to Vallès than to many writers. He is jumpy, moody, theatrical, (fairground, music hall, circus), and it is the accumulation, juxtaposition and intensity of such scenes that give his works whatever unity they have. The sketches pile up into whole pictures. Each mood/scene is not a self-contained block. It contains the seeds, or the aftertaste, of other scenes.

In *Qu'est-ce que la littérature?* Sartre argues that most French novels of the Third Republic give the impression of having been written by fifty-year-olds. He targets Maupassant in particular in this onslaught on the posture of 'l'homme d'expérience', ensconced in a stabilised society, who has 'seen it all', and ends up disabused. This loaded mode of narration, seeking to brainwash the reader into asking no questions, appals Sartre because it would, if it could, rule out any freedom on the part of either the fictional characters or the reader. Everything is predigested and catalogued. Life in its variousness, unpredictability and strangeness is tamed, and well-nigh killed off altogether. [37] This is the vantage point, or rather the fence, of squatting adult *sagesse,* man-of-the-worldiness; account-book writing. In full contrast, Vallès, knocking on fifty when writing the Trilogy, stays young, was never cured of his youth. There is no privileged viewpoint. He never sees wild oats as a means of fattening up a complacent adult. His prose is lean and hungry. As Strickland comments:

> This unapologetic self-portrayal provides what is disconcertingly absent in Maupassant and Zola, an identifiable standpoint within the drama itself from which the behaviour of other people is observed; what it is really like therefore to be caught up in events and unable to know whether a decision will ultimately turn out to have been wise. [38]

Vallès was rereading Montaigne when building up to writing the Trilogy in 1876 (Bellet, II, p. xxxiii). It no doubt seems perverse to compare the highly cultured and sophisticated Montaigne with Vallès. I feel sure, however, that both made themselves 'expert in home cosmography'. [39] Both concentrate on the fleeting, difficultly graspable self, while retaining a strong sense of overall unity. Montaigne, and Diderot, are marvellous pathfinders in this domain of fruitful mixtures, self-contradiction, and the impossibility, *pace* Descartes, of severing mind from body. 'Pas de réaction, de sentiment qui ne s'accompagne d'indication d'attitude, de geste: [Vallès] étouffe de joie, craque de bonheur. [...] Pas de psychologie sans physiologie'. [40] Vallès keeps a sharp eye for the salient, revelatory feature or gesture, the special silhouette each of us projects. People in his work are on parade, but Vallès is a tolerant sergeant-major. With such concrete, if not rock-solid, foundations, the question of inventiveness seems of lesser importance. 'Je ne puis voir que ce qui est autour de moi [...]. Pas deux sous d'imagination' (*CP*, p. 254). Vallès rarely, if ever, invents characters, or even events, from scratch. When he does twist or convert actual material, it is *pour les besoins de la cause,* and seldom gratuitously. He rearranges chronology the better to dramatise and give point; he stretches and bends real happenings to create comedy. Thus, though thoroughly dependent on his experiences, and lacking in fabulating skills, he rejases what he has known. In addition, his verve generates new or alternative realities from these stimuli.

He knows how to animate, to dynamise, his apparently limited stock of material. Strong active verbs are crucial to this effort: 'Nous courons dans tous les coins, nous grattons tous les enthousiasmes, nous mettons les convictions à vif, nous chatouillons la plante des pieds à toutes les passions' (*Bach.*, p. 493). Similarly, tenses play their part: 'Le livre va paraître, le livre a paru' (*Ins.*, p. 906): the future shunted in the past/present in one brief sentence. Not keen on the past historic, the tense that implies all is over and done with, as if history could be controlled and its flux neatly chopped up, Vallès prefers the graphic present, for its immediacy, shock value and possibilities of jumpy discontinuity. He largely avoids the imperfect tense, the tense of analysis of *états d'âme.* No analyst, he seldom resorts to indirect speech, that smuggling in of authorial contraband. Though he is addicted to the indirection of irony or wordplay, indirect speech is too roundabout, too clandestinely manipulative for his generally blurting approach. It is replaced by active narration and snappy dialogue. Though Vallès is said to have rehearsed parts of his fiction in convivial company, I am not fully convinced of the view that Vallès is primarily an oral storyteller; [41] his prose is surely too disjointed to be easy listening for a public.

Finally, in this section on structure, I want to look at Vallès's typography, which is always self-aware and explicit, and as such an important branch of his general rhetoric. After all he wanted to be a printer and, as a journalist, had direct contact with typesetting. Bellet points out that exclamation-marks, in Vallès's writings on the Commune, were as pointed as the gleaming tips of bayonets (*JVJR*, pp. 399-400). We could talk of an automatism, so prevalent in this sign (which Queneau extended to 'le point d'indignation' (!!!!)). I am also reminded of the printers' term, 'interrobang'—a punctuation-mark for use at the close of an exclamatory rhetorical question, and very suitable for the crash-bang Vallès. More subtle is his use of blanks. As he instructed the tyro editress Séverine: 'Gardez le respect du blanc, de la feuille vierge et libre, avec seulement cinq lignes, au besoin, au milieu du ventre. De l'espace, de l'espace, de l'air, de l'air—à tout prix! Vous savez, j'étouffe toujours' (*Corr. S.*, p. 77). Apart from the physico-psychological dread of being stifled, this care for aeration of any text suggests an interplay between the said and the unsaid, a consciousness of emphasis, framing and the need to ventilate what might otherwise be a congested text.

Bellet stresses also the ludic element, Vallès playing at being the 'saltimbanque de l'alinéa' (*JVJR*, p. 332). Cascades, parades and mascarades of words produce a carnivalised text (*ibid.*, p. 330). The aim is to 'conjurer la pure successivité de l'écriture pour se rapprocher de l'image: comme s'il fallait *voir*, et non plus seulement lire' (p. 329).

Humour

In an otherwise dim presentation, Michel Tournier spots Vallès's most distinctive feature: 'Cet humour de Vallès mériterait une longue analyse, car il est plus révélateur qu'aucun autre aspect de son œuvre'. [42] I treat it last because it comes first, governing and informing all else. Vallès is serio-comic, joco-serious. Jacques complains there was no laughter in his home, yet *L'Enfant* is full of comedy. The parents are often unintentionally funny, even if there was no 'joking relationship' in this small tribe. Humour is the child's first tottering step towards emancipation, though Lessing soberingly reminds us: 'Not all are free who mock their chains'. [43] The humour of Vallès is not a dress, to be donned or taken off, though he often applies images suggesting decking or disguise. It is the thing itself. We can no more separate Vallès's humour from his general outlook than we could flay him and keep him alive. It is a tunic of Nessus, which 'colle à la peau'. Like the material forced on the child, which 'crève la vue et chatouille douloureusement la peau' (*Enf.*, p. 167), Vallès's humour tickles painfully. A sense of humour is an aboriginal as a tragic sense of life. It is not a makeshift, though it undoubtedly helps to make life more bearable. The commonest form of lying is humour. Where else do we so consistently bend, indeed reinvent, the truth of a situation in order to give it a point? Jokes are fictions in miniature, condensed novellas.

Among the many and always unsatisfying grand theories of humour are: the superiority theory; release from tension; the Bergsonian stress on automatism and professional deformation (Cf. Vallès's many jokes about *raideur*); the Freudian stress on unconscious desires and regression to childlikeness; and those of all the lab-technician psychologists who have demonstrated that if you tickle a baby, but not a rabbit, you may produce movement in the zygomatic muscles. Surely one of the deepest meanings of most significant functions of humour is to remind us that anything is possible; we can rewrite scripts.

In the mid-nineteenth century, the new intellectual proletariat for which Vallès spoke was as distasteful to establishment writers as were the working-classes themselves. The Goncourts, who failed to see the relevance of desolemnising irreverence for social and personal hygiene, wrote often like shrill Bowdlers: 'La Blague du XIXe siècle, cette grande démolisseuse, [...] l'empoisonneuse de foi [an unconscious pun on *foie?*], la tueuse de respect; la Blague avec son souffle canaille et sa risée salissante jetée à tout ce qui est honneur, amour, famille, le drapeau'.[44] In turn, their famous *écriture artiste* was alien to Vallès. *Blague* means variously: a throwaway gag, belittling mockery, vulgar humour, nihilating laughter (as in the pseudo-metaphysical laughter of Musset's Fantasio). In Vallès's usage, it often has the sense of *galéjade,* blarney, braggadocio, and embraces even the musical japes of Offenbach. Demystification (or the more physical term, debunking), parody as exorcism: humour, for Vallès, always has a militant edge. It may not be possible to laugh away despotism, which gets more brazenly brass-necked every hour, but resistants can ill do without a sense of humour. It keeps the pecker up, anaesthetises some pain, and its sociability gathers in brother and sister souls. Vallès can justifiably speak of his 'vie de blagueur et de convaincu' (*Corr. M.,* p. 116). He was a militant with an unkillable sense of humour, the 'fireproof laughter'of the Homeric gods, brought suitably back to earth.

Vallès could take a joke, but not all. He had a brief spat with the devotees of the *Chat Noir* club in 1883. These had repeatedly mocked him for his militant stance and had virtually accused him of being a *poseur.* His response, witty, slangy, if a bit ponderous, turned the charge round: the *Chat Noir* crowd shirked social reality, and as such were complicitous with the forces of order. They remained impenitent and made no mention of Vallès's death two years later.[45] Vallès was counterattacking (Cf. 'la contrecarre'), and certainly not seeking to muzzle dissenters, especially as he noted bitterly that the last stronghold of state censorship was satirical cabarets, probably because of audience participation (see II, 1116).

Black, or sick, humour focusses the ambivalence of humour acutely, for what seems brave sport to some appears callous indifference to others. But surely black humour can underline, and not trivialise, the seriousness of suffering. Without levity there is no true gravity; besides, overcoming gravity has been a persistent dream of humankind. I do not mean mere 'comic relief', but more that constant in Jewish humour: making a joke out of pain. Vallès's comic sense is indeed a cousin (*à la mode de Bretagne*) to Jewish black humour (which antiSemites, unless they are Jews themselves, rarely possess). Vallès describes the man who fell for the legless 'Vénus au râble' thus: 'Monnet passait sa vie aux pieds de Césarine!' (p. 721). Benjamin Franklin's pointed joke at the American Declaration of Independence in 1776 ('We must all hang together, or certainly we shall all hang separately') would be entirely in tune with Vallès's attitude in the Commune: gallows humour, punch lines of last extremists. In an article about the murder of a pauper by his daughter and her consort, Vallès exclaims in an optimistic, lugubrious conceit: 'O misère, c'est toi la première coupable! Le jour où il y aura de la farine pour tous les vivants, il y aura peut-être besoin de moins de son pour les guillotinés' (*Le Peuple,* 16 février. 1869). Even here, Vallès is not deadpan; he makes no secret of his intentions. *With* Renard for once, if challenged on the question of taste, which always crops up in any discussion of black humour, Vallès could well have replied: 'Je ne réponds pas d'avoir du goût, mais j'ai le dégoût très sûr'. [46]

Humour, of course, can be simply genial. As Vallès says of the zany Poupelin: 'Comme le métier de noircisseur de verres pour les jours d'éclipses, celui du faiseur d'Empire a ses moments de relâche; il y a des mortes-saisons' (I, 182). This joke is at the expense of a fool, but even fools have to survive on a budget. It is difficult to be guilty, in turn, of *Vallès-majesté.* While he was a proud man, he knew how to laugh loudly at himself. If he valued personal sovereignty, he mocked delusions of majesty. Like Vallès, humour is an awkward customer, unpigeonholable. All I am certain of is that Vallès speaks many true words in jests.

The Point of Style

If Vallès habitually talks, in traditional terms, of style as a covering, clothes (uniform, wig, rags), he knew that it goes deeper than that. It is a second skin, a second nature; it is the man himself. While fully aware and spasmodically proud of his own hotchpotch style, he always tried to resist the frills and furbelows of the journalistic mode of his day. Just as irony helps to dress his wounds, so other forms of *cache-misère* aim at dignity in undignified circumstances. However carnivalesque, his writing is rarely unkempt. How much other writing goes about like mutton dressed as lamb?

As we have seen in his typography and in his taste for strong verbs, Vallès is a gesticulatory writer. Editors were forever urging him to plane down the angularities of his prose, to produce a smoother, blander texture. If indeed he had a castration complex, it would be in part because censors were always attempting to chasten, chastise or castrate his naturally ungelded style. Though cool towards Vallès's politics, Albalat salvages him for stylistic reasons: 'Il nous répugne par sa démagogie révolutionnaire, et il nous séduit par l'aristocratie de son style'. More perceptively, Albalat recognises that 'son style vous prend parce qu'il saute aux yeux'. It has 'une sincérité sensationnelle', by which he means that it renders faithfully what Vallès's nerve ends (and intuitive antennae) registered. He salutes 'cette énergie continue et cette pleine santé de phrases'. [47] In another book, Albalat proposes Vallès as a model for aspiring writers, for his 'matérialité visible'. [48] I have already likened Vallès to Montaigne. Montaigne's recipe for good prose fits Vallès to a T: 'Tel sur le papier qu'à la bouche, un parler succulent et nerveux [...], non tant délicat et peigné comme véhément et brusque'.[49]

Whether or not we accept the view that Vallès's stylistic discontinuities embody his longing for a plural society,[50] we must see that Vallès wants to deconstrict language as a contribution to the emancipation of workers or children. The regular embedding of colloquial expressions in his prose, even when italicised, does not quarantine them. It is a registering of how people talk, a form of remembrancing, linguistic egalitarianism. Slang has been called the poetry of the man in the street. Vallès knew instinctively that language has to be used for multiple purposes: seriously, playfully, lovingly, mistrustfully, humorously, insolently, hopefully. His narrative gets close to the patterns of spoken French, with its exclamations, interruptions, parentheses, though obviously it cannot hope to be a straight recording. Like Céline and Queneau this century, Vallès works to democratise literary French, by reaching for the affective, mocking tones of popular speech, *and* its occasional lift-offs into rhetoric and fancifulness. Realism and socialism, after all, have something in common (grotesquely parodied in socialist realism), for both aim to secure full rights of entry and esteem for low and repressed subjects.

Like a boxer, a fairground barker, or a stand-up comedian, (or, sometimes, an ancient mariner), Vallès's delivery, staccato, seeks to buttonhole, to pin down the listening bystander. His tactics of displacement, his disconcerting shifts of emphasis—lurching, sidestepping, stepping on toes—recall his love of *savate*. But there is as much brain and mother-wit as brawn. Claude Roy, no doubt contaminated by Vallès's punning mania, had in mind the prose of Renan and Sainte-Beuve when he compared the alacrity of his writing with the potbellied gait of his famous contemporaries: 'Le style Second Empire est prodigieusement rond: ronds d'huile, ronds de jambe, ronrons'.[51]

Vallès's style is a proof (*une preuve par l'absurde*) of what his education did for him: he inherited and put to good use the muscularity, the incisiveness, the ellipses of the best Latin prose writers. Just as a corset accentuates the figure, so that prison-house of language perversely encouraged libertarian speech. Montaigne and Burton prove that absorption of others does not preclude and indeed can engender a most distinctive style of your own. Not all are convinced. Brombert sniffs at 'too unremitting an effort to attain hearty, comic effects, too much metaphoric verve'.[52] Just as there is a pain threshold, perhaps there is in some a barrier to aggressive styles? Though he favoured forums, Vallès had an innate mistrust of consensus.

Postlude

Ils m'ont maudit vivant; mort, me comprendront-ils?
(I, 1006)

'Moi expansif, sanguin, causeur, remueur'. [1] Among the plurivalent
meanings of the word *nature* in idiomatic French is that of a strong
personality who is blunt, uninhibited, gullible and unadulterated. A full-
blooded man succumbed to diabetes, which produces excessive discharge
of sugary, cloudy urine, emaciation and great thirst. Vallès's stock
images included: 'pisser de la copie', 'pisser sur les tombes', and 'pisser
du sang'. He ended up straightforwardly pissing, copiously. Before he
died he settled some debts dating back twenty-five years. He was both
complex and lacking in disguise.

He loathed all models and templates and never hoped to be
exemplary. One of the many tonic virtues of his work lies in its stout
resistance to the preachy, from whatever quarter. Yet inevitably he
teaches a lesson: do not take anyone or anything as read. We cannot tie
him down, and he would persuade us not to do this to him or to anyone
else. He is a moving target, a monolithic Proteus. He is more
oxymoronic than paradoxical. Though he customarily writes binarily,
exile brought home to him, in that it was both escape and prison in an
alien land, the coexistence, more often warring than peaceful, of
opposites. Despite his autobiographical confinement, he was a
gregarious individualist, outward-turned, wanting to share (what he had
and what others had). Obsessed by the figure he cut in others' eyes, he
refuses to allow others, whether parents, teachers, governments or
political allies, to define and dictate his self. In an unlikely likening, I
would compare his resistance to killjoy vetoes with Blake's attack on
'mind-forged manacles', and his awkward question: 'How can the bird
that is born for joy / Sit in a cage and sing?' [2] Yet, as in the work of
Guilloux, Vallès's criticism of turncoats is tempered by his
understanding of what makes us all weaken and yield to accommodating
temptations, and how randomly determined are our choices. On
Gounod, whom he admired, his verdict was: 'Affaire d'éducation—
d'origine, de hasard' (II, 439). He swivels, as we all do, between
determinism and voluntarism, essentialism and existentialism: 'Chacun
est esclave de la vie vécue' (I, 844). But 'les individus, comme les
nations, portent le poids de leur faiblesse et souvent ont fondu leur
boulet eux-mêmes!' (p. 801). Like a good son of his century, Vallès
recognises the importance of heredity, environment, upbringing and
historical 'moment', but he believes equally firmly in human cussedness.

Few remain unaffected by reading Vallès. The response of his

enemies indicates that he gets under their skin equally. Brunetière stands
for many such. In an essay, published a couple of weeks after Vallès's
death, he turns his target's own phrase 'la mort n'est pas une excuse'
against him. [3] Vallès bears the classical symptoms of the century's
malady; he is a *déclassé*, deeply immoral, wicked and dangerous. (In
another text, Brunetière declared: 'L'hérétique est celui qui a une
opinion'; presumably the orthodox do not trouble their brainbox at all).[4]
Vallès 'n'a rien aimé dans sa vie, pas même la Révolution, quoi qu'il en
ait voulu dire, et encore moins "le peuple", dont les "sueurs"
offusquaient son odorat d'aristocrate. Mais il a beaucoup haï,
prodigieusement haï, d'une haine inexpiable'. [5] How wrong can you be?
Brunetière reveals the lethal logic of conformist thinking when he ends
up regretting that Vallès was not a true fanatic and did not spark off
fires or urge atrocities in the Commune, which would have made more
consistent sense in Brunetière's eyes (*loc. cit.*, pp. 314-5). Even so,
Vallès deserves a place in the national Museum of Horrors, between
Hébert and Marat (p. 315). Léon Bloy made the same analogy with
Marat. For Bloy, Vallès was a lackey, who dishonoured his parents, and
who, cowardly, fled from the barricades of the Commune. Bloy
practises *l'amalgame*, blending Vallès with Jules Ferry and Edmond
About. It is a delirious misreading, partly compensated by a later
admission: 'Un rude écrivain, tout de même'. [6] All the same Léon
Daudet spots a link: 'Vallès est avec Bloy—avec toute la différence du
terrestre obstiné au mystique en armes—le plus expressif de nos
écrivains d'humeur et tempérament, à la fin du XIXᵉ siècle'. [7] 'Écrivain
de tempérament': an idiosyncratic voice with lusty ideas. Vallès belongs
to the race of bellowers like Bloy or Flaubert, and not to that of the
whimperers and whisperers.

I must acknowledge Vallès's limitations. The stock complaint is that
he lacks scope, unity and variety. There is undeniably monochordal
monotony in this colourful monolith of a man. 'Un homme, si fort qu'il
soit, porte-t-il en lui plus d'un livre?' (I, 386). He is not a great one for
nuances. Largely direct, he detested that allusiveness which is the
Masonic signal of the intellectual playing his in-games. It is true that he
lacked real powers of invention, and that he was, not unlike Huysmans,
one of those 'romanciers de soi-même' who excel in fragmentation,
instantanéisme, inflation and deformation, rather than in aesthetic,
pseudo-architectural unity. [8] Vallès was conscious of his limitations.
Jacques exclaims: 'Rien que MES idées à MOI, c'est terrible! Des idées
comme en auraient un paysan, une bonne femme, un marchand de vin,
un garçon de café!' (*Bach.*, p. 512). If Vallès was limited, inevitably, by
his nature, upbringing and adult experience, at least he was limited to
his own and not to someone else's. 'Un être unique dont l'unique raison
d'être est la révolte'. [9] Yet I want to argue his ordinariness, or in coined

French, since there is no *mot juste* for it, his *quelconqueté*.

First of all, the counter-view: 'Vallès charge son trait pour surenchérir, travaillant sa dégaine et son style, s'évertuant à faire l'original'.[10] Many of Vallès's contemporaries were also taken in by this blustering pose. No writer wants to be unoriginal. Angry at being misrepresented by a critic of *L'Enfant*, Vallès exclaimed, however:

> Sacrebleu, il n'y a rien compris. Il dit que les Vingtras deviennent fatalement des cachotiers, des moroses, des hypocrites, des tristes! Si je ressemble à ça, je veux bien que l'on me fouette encore! Dites-lui donc que je suis fait comme tout le monde, que j'aime à rire, et même à boire, comme Fanchon, et que je mange comme un ogre, assis sur un derrière qui a pardonné et qui, il pourrait s'en assurer, n'a pas gardé de cicatrices. (Quoted in *JVJR*, p. 425)

Indeed, his whole upbringing had been a concerted programme in the prevention of normality: getting dirty, playing rough games, mixing socially with all and sundry. Many have tried to make Vallès into a man of unremitting resentment, whereas a careful reading of *L'Enfant* reveals how hard he works to motivate even his oppressors. Like Paris itself, Vallès 'n'a pas la rancune noire'(II, 1333).

He does not, like Rousseau, pursue difference: 'Je ne suis fait comme aucun de ceux que j'ai vus; j'ose croire n'être fait comme aucun de ceux qui existent. Si je ne vaux pas mieux, au moins je suis autre'.[11] As Sabin comments:

> Rousseau's obsession with his uniqueness in the *Confessions* seems oddly inconsistent with his other philosophic positions. Rousseau frankly assumes that the idiosyncrasies of others are more conventionally accountable than his own. [...] He differs from other people more than they differ from each other.[12]

Vallès is quite other, and closer to the egalitarian arrogance of Sartre's self-estimate: 'Tout un homme, fait de tous les hommes et qui les vaut tous et que vaut n'importe qui'.[13] I am struck by the unexceptional nature of Vallès's ambitions: regular work, enough money to enjoy life, a reasonable reputation. Sainte-Beuve coined the term 'ouvrier littéraire': Vallès wanted to be a manual writer, and journalism was his nearest approach to that desired state. I happily concur with Jean Paulhan:

> Soit pudeur, générosité, simplicité réelle, il a beau s'occuper de lui, il néglige ou biffe tout ce qui le rendrait différent. Il ne fait pas rare, ni distingué. Il voudrait être savetier, garçon d'écurie, matelot, épicier. L'exotisme, pour ce petit bourgeois, commence à l'étage au-dessous.[14]

I have earlier remarked on the averageness of his not very extensive reading, much of it in the area condescendingly labelled sub-literature.

As a child, and more than residually as an adult, his hope in reading fiction was to lose himself, to play away on recognisable territory, which is probably what the common, and even the uncommon, reader expects of a novel: literature not as a narcotic or sedative, but as a transporter. As for literary creation, Vallès manages a feat quite rare in French fiction: to write in the common idiom (which does not exclude classical references) about down-to-earth things, without condescension and generally without that inverted snobbery which donates automatic pedigrees to the underdogs. Queneau once remarked that many practitioners of the demotic (Richepin, Céline) have been in outlook 'de fieffés réactionnaires'. [15] Everyone, for Vallès, has a tale to tell: 'Chacun de nous, s'il veut écrire avec franchise et simplicité, porte en lui un chef d'œuvre' (I, 941). This is base flattery, but it is also an invitation to an open house, as well as a dismissal of the tenet that literary creation is special and reserved for a tiny élite. The *nous* here is more cooptive than editorial or royal. As so often, Sartre was overstating when he said that man was yet to be invented. Man (men, women, children) is yet to be discovered, taken heed of, for we are easily overlooked, or converted to suit some less than human purpose.

One of the many ironies inhabiting Vallès, or my version of Vallès, which I piously hope resembles Jules like a long-lost brother, is that he was supremely ordinary, and yet was fascinated by monstrosity, and sometimes felt himself to be a freak. But then his earliest texts humanise monsters. If Vallès and his hero are normal, then it might be thought that it is those around them who are abnormal. This is dangerous logic. Many lunatics are convinced they are the only ones sane. The claim to sanity can also be heroic, in that it involves sticking to your guns and defending what we do not always agree unites us all. Many of Vallès's amateur and professional readers have been struck by the strange fact (not a paradox, a fact) that a man so taken with marginality should in effect be so central to an understanding of his age, and so accessible. Despite his hyperbole and his limitations, including ignorance and periodic obtuseness, he is a more reliable witness than many more renowned but less involved writers of his time.

Normality, perhaps, is the ultimate strangeness, for so few recognise it even when they trip over it. By stressing his ordinariness, I do not want to belittle or decomplexify Vallès, but only to suggest its rarity value. Though expressing himself frequently in polarities, Vallès was even more deeply aware of overlap, vestiges, coexistence. Too many of his critics opt for one pole, and thus offer an unbalanced Vallès. His parents saw him as mentally disequilibrated. In *savate* as in life generally, he sought *la pose des pieds*. It might be rocky, like a sailor's, but his feet remained planted on this earth, even if his head was often in the clouds. Vallès was more ordinary, and so more extraordinary, than he is usually cracked up to be. As well as being an admirable sore thumb, Vallès must also have been, many a time, a pain in the neck.

He does not strive to wriggle out of pigeonholes. He simply would not fit in one. He fitted rarely into groups, either, or clothes, or spaces (the exiguous *pied-à-terre,* or rather *pied-en l'air*), or jobs. The only fits he enjoyed were those of anger or hilarity. *Indécrottable, irrécupérable, inclassable,* indelible: after all the negations willed by Vallès, it is curiously apt to sum him up with a series of them, as long as we remember that *indécrottable* covers: oafish as well as bloody-minded, past praying for as well as incorrigible. We have taken from French the word *aplomb.* Why not also its antonym, *de guinguois,* as it would fit this awkward customer like a glove? Where much language is pedestrian, his is jaywalker. If you try to make a long division of Vallès, there is always a considerable remainder.

There is no impenetrable disguise in his world of words. He was a sign-reader long before today's variety claimed the monopoly and the invention. Is this unduly optimistic? Are there no unplumbable mysteries and indecipherable individuals? Vallès is more interested in the effects of misreading of signs, how seeing things comes easier to us than seeing straight. In addition (and before Freud) Vallès understood how the human gift of the gaffe acts as a giveaway; our slips are always showing. As regards himself, and despite the 'wig of irony', Vallès, unusually for a writer, does not wear a mask. 'Larvatus prodeo' would be the last motto he would flaunt. As the Goncourts said: 'Il y a du couche-tout-nu dans ce littérateur'. [16] More recent critics, wanting to rescue Vallès from the sidelines if not from outer darkness, have deemed it necessary to invent depths, false psychic garb, of a kind to make him more 'interesting' for imagined modern tastes. This urge to read between the lines, especially of so metaphorical and wordplaying a writer, to claim to know better than he what he was and believed, gets in the way of clear sight. I write as a certified myopic. Some of those reading this book will putably be woolly liberals. I doubt whether I am even that well-defined; more of a man-made mixture.

Despite the comic exaggerations in *L'Enfant* about the mother strangifying her son, Vallès had no real need to worry over his identity. He was unmistakable. Though he sometimes bemoaned not being able to escape his own bounds (he would still never have lamented, like Flaubert, that he was too small for himself), he was, I believe, fundamentally happy to be who he was. Not exactly at ease in his skin, as the French idiom has it, for that can connote complacency, but glad to be him. And this gladness communicates itself to readers. Students often ask teachers: 'Why is so much literature so depressing?' There are plenty of good answers to this query, which is neither stupid nor naïve. Vallès offers a fully-working alternative: anti-depressant writing. In the 'raideur anglaise' section of *Le Bachelier,* it is Jacques's very unnatural uptightness that gets him the job. Tables turned: the fact that we control little of what happens to us begets bonuses as well as mishaps. Vallès has a very unwordly-wise capacity for surprise, (shock, amusement, exhilaration, consternation), which reveals an openness to experience and a non-shut mind, which in turn militates against emotional anaemia or anorexia. Louis Guilloux recounts how he discovered Vallès for himself, when also a poor *pion,* on a secondhand bookstall at a fairground—so appropriately: 'Nous étions livrés aux professeurs, c'est-à-dire à la mort sous toutes ses formes. [...] Vallès m'introduisait à un monde dont j'avais soif, un monde de santé, d'audace, de fierté, d'ironie, d'insolence, de liberté, vrai monde de la jeunesse'. [17] Youth is not a talent, nor even an age; it is a state of mind. I trust this testimonial. All of the detail of my book (Vallès's warts and all) adds up to a recommendation to read him. It is a long-winded urging. Vallès, who experienced past and present with like intensity and yet managed to hope forwards, is a cheering writer. This book aims to express the appeal of Vallès, in both senses: how he projects himself in addressing us, and how we might receive him. He rarely exempts himself from the vices and idiocies of his fellow-creatures. For him, we are all in the soup together. More optimistically, what he proposes is *un bain de vie* ('La vie nous serre de près!'—I, 884)). Like a tub, his work is for enjoying as well as for cleansing; a place for behaving naturally, for disconnected but fruitful musing. He conveys a sense of the fullness (and, when fitting, the emptiness) of each moment.

I realise that the 'plain approach' is a stance like any other, just as anti-rhetoric is another rhetoric. I hope to have counteracted some misleading excesses, by my own version of *la contrecarre,* but the battle between the barkers outside Vallès's sideshow will remain, no doubt, dubious. There can be no winners, only competing challengers. That is how Vallès saw life, and so, in this respect if no other, we are all, collectively, being faithful to him. I need hardly add that this conclusion is not piously ecumenical. I am not sure whether it will be a good thing if or when championing this embattled, hit-or-miss writer changes from special pleading to *l'évidence même.* He squares up to us all. He was an unforgetful man and, once you get to know him, an unforgettable one. Even Veuillot concedes as much:

> *Pachionnard* (d'Auvergne) a vraiment fait sensation [...], criant que tout est vieux, que tout est bête et usé, et je ne prétends pas qu'il eut toujours tort; demandant du neuf et de l'extraordinaire et jurant qu'il en apportait et qu'il avait de l'inouï plein ses poches. [...] Tout est dans sa manière de prononcer les *rr.* Il vibrre, c'est son génie; il vibrrera toujourrs. [18]

His funeral occasioned punch-ups. His soul may long since have mouldered in the grave, but his body (of work), his unholy real presence, hectic and trouble-making, goes marching on. Vallès is hilarious, taxing, infuriating and, despite a hibernation of more than a century, intensely alive. Whatever I, or my brother or sister critical ambushers have said or might yet say, Vallès surely has the inalienable right to the last word, as in *L'Insurgé* (p. 1087):'Ils ne m'auront pas!'

Notes

Place of publication is Paris or London, unless otherwise indicated.

Prolusion

1. *AJV*, 7 (1989), 83.
2. *Corr. A.*, p. 17.
3. Callet, A. (ed.), 'Lettres d'exil', *La Revue du Palais* (1 janvier 1898), p. 3.
4. Lançon, A. (ed.), *Les Animaux chez eux*, in *Œuvres complètes* (*LCD*) IV, 1551-67.
5. Dumesnil, R., *Le Réalisme* (J. de Gigord, 1936), p. 180.
6. Didier, B., preface to *L'Enfant* (Folio, 1973), pp. 21; 24.
7. *Œuvres complètes* (*LCD*) IV, 406.

Chapter One

1. Huysmans, J.-K., excerpt from his *Calepin vert*, *Le Figaro littéraire*, 2-8 juillet 1964.
2. Veuillot, L., *Les Odeurs de Paris.* (Crès, n.d.), p. 89.
3. Guilloux, L., 'A propos de Jules Vallès', *NRF*, 35 (1930), 440.
4. Gill, A., *Vingt Années de Paris* (Marpon et Flammarion, 1883), pp. 28-9.
5. 'Prodigies' was in fact the term proposed by the Bishop of Winchester, when a protest meeting of the maligned ones demanded a new name. Some three hundred were put forward, in what was possibly a stunt arranged by the Barnum and Bailey public-relations team. See Fiedler, L., *Freaks* (Penguin, 1981), p. 15.
6. Lloyd, C., ' "L'Amour du monstre": Jules Vallès and *Le Bachelier géant*', in *The Monstrous*, Durham French Colloquies, 1 (1987), 29.
7. Malraux, A., *La Condition humaine* (Gallimard, 1946 [1933]), p. 46.

8.   Cf. Georges Brassens's song: 'Je me suis fait tout petit devant une poupée'.

9.   Marotin, F., 'Valeur polémique et satirique du thème des saltimbanques dans la pensée vallésienne', in Baader, H. (ed.), *Onze Études sur l'esprit de la satire* (Tübingen: G. Narr, 1978), pp. 153-4.

10.   Pillu, P., preface to *La Rue (EFR)*, p. 16.

11.   See II, pp. 1345 ff.; pp. 414 ff.

12.   Don Marquis, *Archy's Life of Mehitabel* (Faber, 1991), p. 15.

13.   Queneau's *Battre la campagne* plays with similar reverberations.

14.   Pontmartin, A. de, *Le Radeau de la Méduse* (Lévy, 1871), p. 213.

15.   Pontmartin, *Nouveaux Samedis* (M. Lévy, 1867), p. 78.

16.   Barbey d'Aurevilly J., *Le 19ᵉ Siècle* (Mercure de France, 1964), pp. 67-9.

Chapter Two

1.   Bellet, R., 'La Rencontre de la révolte et de la révolution sous la plume de Jules Vallès', *AJV*, 7 (1989), 29.

2.   Tournier, M., *Le Vent Paraclet* (Gallimard, 1977), pp. 87-8.

3.   Hemmings, F.W.J. (ed.), *The Age of Realism* (Penguin, 1974), p. 17.

4.   Schama, S., *Citizens* (Penguin, 1989), pp. 528-9.

5.   *Ibid.*, p. 577.

6.   *Ibid.*, p. 828.

7.   Zeldin, T., *France, 1848-1945* (Oxford: Clarendon Press, 1973), I, 489.

8.   For all of this, see Marx, K., *The Eighteenth Brumaire of Louis Bonaparte,* in *Surveys from Exile* (Penguin, 1973), pp. 146-9.

9.   Yeats, W.B., 'The Second Coming'.

10.   Foot, M., review of Mitzman, A., *Michelet, Guardian*, 30 August 1990.

11.   Renard, J., *Journal* (Union générale d'éditions, 1984), II, 481.

12.   Gille, G., *Jules Vallès* (Flammarion, 1941), p. 50.

13.   Zeldin, I, 461.

14. Marx, *Works* (Lawrence and Wishart, 1985), XX, 32.

15. Much of my material on Blanqui comes from Hutton, P., *The Cult of the Revolutionary Tradition: The Blanquists in French Politics, 1864-1893,* Berkeley: University of California Press, 1981.

16. Hutton, p. 24.

17. Vallès, letter to Callet, A., 'Lettres d'exil', *La Nouvelle Revue,* 37 (1918), 48-9.

18. Hutton, p. 11.

19. *Ibid.,* p. xiii.

20. *Ibid.,* p. 162.

21. Petrey, S., 'All God's Children Got Emes: Demystification in Jules Vallès', *Colloquium in 19th Century French Studies* (Philadelphia, 20 October 1979), p. 10.

22. Brupbacher, F., *Socialisme et liberté* (Pensée et Action, 1964), p. 341.

23. Though, etymologically, 'victime' means holy, sacrificial, set apart, not 'defeated'.

24. Gille, p. 193.

25. See Zeldin, I, pp. 611 ff.

26. Hi Sook Hwang, 'La Vision du peuple chez Vallès', *Modern Language Studies,* 15, 4 (1985), pp. 316-17.

27. Lafargue, P., *Le Droit à la paresse* (Maspero, 1965), pp. 43; 54.

28. Gallo, M., *Jules Vallès*(Laffont, 1988), p. 289.

Chapter Three

1. Alain Cottereau, preface to Poulot, D., *Le Sublime* (Maspero, 'Actes et mémoires du peuple', 1980 [1870]), p. 16.

2. The text of the medical documents is to be found in Dr. R. Benon, 'Jules Vallès à l'asile d'aliénés de Saint-Jacques à Nantes', *La Nouvelle Revue* (15 décembre 1918), pp. 353-5.

3. Gagne, P., quoted in Blavier, A., *Les Fous littéraires* (H. Veyrier, 1982), p. 697.

4. See Mehlman, J., 'Blanchot at Combat: of Literature and Terror', *Modern Language Notes,* 95 (1980), 811.

5.   Weber, E., *Peasants into Frenchmen* (Chatto & Windus, 1976), p. 292.

6.   Goncourt, E. & J. de, *Journal* (Fasquelle; Flammarion, 1956), II, 359.

7.   Williams, R.E., *Henri Rochefort, Prince of the Gutter Press* (New York: Scribner's, 1966), p. ix.

8.   Bellet, R. (ed.), *La Lanterne* (Pauvert, 1966), pp. 18-19.

9.   See Zeldin, II, pp. 494 ff. for an account of Girardin.

10.   Much in this paragraph is indebted to the excellent article by S. Disegni, 'Journalisme et littérature au XIXe siècle. Deux frères ennemis? Le cas Vallès', *Micromégas*, XV, 3 (1988), 39-68.

11.   See Bellet, *JVJR, passim,* for details of Vallès's various papers, and the history of fines, seizures and imprisonments.

12.   Callet, A., 'Lettres inédites de Jules Vallès', *Revue indépendante* (avril 1885), pp. 473 ff.

Chapter Four

1.   Montaigne, *Essais* (Garnier Frères, 1958), I, 163.

2.   For the following, I pillage Gerbod, P., *La Vie quotidienne dans les lycées et collèges au XIXe siècle,* Hachette, 1968.

3.   Sarcey, F., quoted in Gerbod, p. 192.

4.   A. Binet, quoted in Zeldin, II, pp. 193-4.

5.   Weber, *Peasants into Frenchmen,* p. 70.

6.   Napoleon, cited in Guerrand, R.-H., *C'est la faute aux profs!* (La Découverte, 1989), p. 37.

7.   Sorel, C., *Histoire comique de Francion* (Hachette, 1926 [1622]), pp. 2-3. Their very notebooks bore the revelatory name of *raptaria.*

8.   Céline, L.-F., *Bagatelles pour un massacre* (Denoël, 1937), pp. 166-7.

9.   Guerrand's book (see n. 6) uses Vallès's writings as evidence for his argument that too little has changed in a hundred and fifty years.

10.   Flaubert, G., *Correspondance* (Conard, 1929), V, 200.

11. Camus, A., *La Chute* (Gallimard, 1956), p. 77.

12. Tallis, R., *In Defence of Realism* (Arnold, 1988), pp. 154-6.

13. Sartre, J.-P., *Situations I* (Gallimard, 1947), p. 71.

14. See Zeldin, II, pp. 880; 767.

15. Bory, J.-L., *Musique 2: tout feu, toute flamme* (Julliard, 1966), p. 127.

16. Daudet, L., 'Jules Vallès', *L'Action française*, 14 février 1935.

17. Vallès became a freemason, probably in a *loge* reputed for iconoclasm (*JVJR*, p. 277).

18. Quoted in Péridier, J., *La Commune et les artistes* (Nouvelles Editions latines, 1980), p. 57.

19. Huysmans, J.-K., quoted in Fabre, F., 'Jules Vallès et le Naturalisme', *Les Cahiers naturalistes*, 8-9 (1957), 385.

20. Mallarmé, S., *Correspondance* (Gallimard, 1959), I, 95.

21. Camus, A., *L'Homme révolté* (Gallimard, 1951), p. 314.

22. Callet, A., 'Lettres d'exil de Jules Vallès', *Nouvelle Revue*, 37 (1918), 46-7.

23. For this survey, I make extensive use of Bollème, G., *Les Almanachs populaires* (Mouton, 1969), and *La Bibliothèque bleue* (Gallimard; Julliard, 1971).

24. Péridier, p. 18.

25. Flaubert, *Correspondance* (Conard, 1927), II, 79.

26. Vallès, *Des mots* (Tusson: Du Lérot, 1986), pp. 10-30.

27. Hugo, V., *Choses vues* (Gallimard, 'Folio'), II, 172.

28. Bancquart, M.-C., preface to *L'Insurgé* (Gallimard, 'Folio', 1975), p. 10.

29. Serge, V., quoted in Howe, I., *Politics and the Novel* (New York: Horizon, 1955), p. 206.

30. Carey, J., *The Violent Effigy* (Faber, 1973), pp. 74; 56.

31. *Ibid.*, p. 74.

Chapter Five

1. Cf. J.-L.Bory, *op. cit.*, p. 201, on Sue's 'réalisme policier'.

2.   Bourget, P., 'Jules Vallès', *Portraits d'écrivains* (Plon, 1903), I, pp. 141; 145; 153.

3.   Corbin, A., *Le Miasme et la Jonquille: l'odorat et l'imaginaire social, XVIIIe-XIXe siècles* (Aubier Montaigne, 1982), p. 258.

4.   For which Vallès may have written an unfinished and lost *Tanguiade* in verse.

5.   Cottereau, A., preface to Poulot, *Le Sublime*, p. 37.

6.   Zeldin, II, 185.

7.   See Carassus, É., 'Vallès journaliste sportif', in Premuda-Perosa, M.-L. (ed.), *Jules Vallès giornalista* (Perugia, 1987), p. 97. Bellet (I, 1533) reports that a promoter of the day married music and *savate* under the billing 'assaut-concert'.

8.   Gille, p. 492.

9.   Weber, *Peasants into Frenchmen*, p. 47.

10.   Renard, *Journal*, III, 995.

11.   Daudet, L., 'A propos de Jules Vallès', *Action française*, 13 juin 1932.

12.   Zeldin, II, 297.

Chapter Six

1.   Frost, R., 'The Death of the Hired Man', *North of Boston* (1914).

2.   Gille, p. 607.

3.   Nizan, P. : *Aden Arabie* (Maspero, 1960 [1931]), p. 65.

4.   Bonnefis, P. : *Vallès: du bon usage de la lame et de l'aiguille* (Lausanne: L'Age d'homme, 1982), p. 30.

5.   Before a projected dinner, Paul Alexis reminded Zola: 'Vous savez: pour le communard "ni oignon, ni ail, ni ciboule, ni ciboulette"'. In Bakker (ed.), *Naturalisme pas mort* (Toronto U.P., 1971), p. 182.

6.   Carassus, preface to *L'Enfant* (Garnier-Flammarion, 1968), pp. 23-4.

7.   'Cynosure' : dog's tail. Cf. the famous cartoon of Vallès as a mutt, on the cover of this book.

8.   The father 'était chien' (= stingy, nasty); the son 'avait du chien' (= spunky, sexy).

9.   Cf. Pléiade II, pp. 1565-6 : 'M. Taine est un constipé [...], assis sur les "origines" de la France, n'accouchant de rien'.

10. Frantz Jourdain, quoted in Choury, M. (ed.), *Les Poètes de la Commune* (Seghers, 1970), p. 221.

11. Rollin, R.H., *The Comic Spirit in the Trilogy of Jules Vallès* (Ph.D., Bryn Mawr University, 1976), p. 265.

12. Goncourt, *Journal*, III, 28.

13. Brupbacher, *Socialisme et liberté*, p. 331.

14. *Ibid.*, p. 330.

15. Daudet, L., 'Jules Vallès', *Action française*, 14 février 1935.

16. Carey, *The Violent Effigy*, p. 136.

17. Cocteau, J., quoted in Barthes, R., *Mythologies* (Seuil, 1957), p. 154.

18. Rosten, L. (ed.), *Treasury of Jewish Quotations* (New York: Bantam, 1977), p. 131.

19. Lejeune, P., *Je est un autre* (Seuil, 1980), pp. 14-15; 28.

20. Campagnoli, R. and Hersant, Y., 'Discours historique et discours romanesque', in *Ricerche sulla Comune* (Milan: Centro Grafico S, 1974), pp. 83-4.

21. Coveney, P., *The Image of Childhood* (Baltimore: Penguin, 1967), pp. 31-2.

22. Wordsworth, W., 'Intimations of Immortality', *Poems* (Penguin, 1982), I, pp. 525; 527.

23. Zola, É., 'Jacques Vingtras', *Œuvres complètes* (Tchou, 'Cercle du livre précieux', 1969), XII, pp. 589-593 (p. 592).

24. Daudet, A., quoted in Daudet, L., *Flammes* (Grasset, 1930), p. 171.

25. Daudet, L., 'Jules Vallès', p. 1. *Poil* here suggests both work-shyness and the hair of the dog that bit you.

26. Renard, *Journal*, II, 510.

27. *Ibid.*, p. 457.

28. Guichard, L., *Jules Renard* (Gallimard, 1961), p. 88.

29. Renard, *Lettres inédites* (Gallimard, 1957), p. 237.

30. Renard, *Journal*, III, 816.

31. Renard, *Journal*, II, 541.

Chapter Seven

1. *Le Candidat des pauvres* (1879, serialised just after *Mémoires d'un révolté*) and *Souvenirs d'un étudiant pauvre* (1884) have even more fantasy chronology, do not find a consistent tone, and suffer from too much gab and whining, though both fill in some of the gaps left by the Trilogy. I have occasionally used them as sources not meriting detailed study in their own right.

2. See Pillu, P., 'Paris dans la *Trilogie* de Jules Vallès', *Europe*, 470-72 (1968), 66-77.

3. Dickens, C., *Great Expectations*, Chapter Four.

4. Carassus, É., 'Jules Vallès et les marginaux dans *Les Réfractaires*', *AJV*, 2 (1985), 25.

5. Séverine, *Le Cri du peuple*, 16 février 1884.

6. Lacan, J., quoted by Georgin, R., 'Le Linguiste du monde occidental', in 'Jakobson', *Cahiers Cistre*, 5 (1978), 129. For umpteen variations on the theme of feet in Vallès, see my 'Dérapage vallésien : pastiche marron', *AJV*, 3 (1986), 11-21.

7. See Allem, M., *La Vie quotidienne sous le Second Empire* (Hachette, 1948), p. 243.

8. Cf. Pléiade I, 517: 'Plus d'un Romain [i.e. *claqueur*] avait l'enthousiasme sceptique'.

9. Prévost, J., preface to *L'Insurgé* (Livre de poche, 1964), p. 11.

10. Though *L'Enfant* is overall the sexiest part of the Trilogy, this is perhaps because, as the variants show, Vallès attenuated the erotic element in *Le Bachelier*.

11. Villat, L., 'Jules Vallès à Nantes', *Mercure de France*, 236 (1932), 258.

12. Balzac, H. de, *Illusions perdues* (Garnier Frères, 1954), p. 422.

13. Céline, L.-F., *Cahiers de l'Herne* (1965), II, 80. Huizinga's analysis of the modern French duel as ritual blood-play—*Homo Ludens* (Paladin, 1970), p. 116—is much too schematised.

14. Pillu, P., postface to *Le Bachelier* (Livre de poche, 1985), p. 403.

15. Quoted in Carey, *The Violent Effigy*, p. 71.

16. Bourget, 'Jules Vallès', p. 144.

17. Richepin, J., *Le Gil Blas*, 1 juin 1881.

18.   Zola, É., 'Souveraineté des lettres', in *Une campagne, Œuvres complètes* (1970), XIV, pp. 615-20 (p. 617).

19.   Zola, cited in Goncourt, *Journal*, III, 118.

20.   Caryl Lloyd, 'The Politics of Irony and Alienation : A Study of Jules Vallès's *Le Bachelier*', *Romance Quarterly*, 34 (1987), 25-33.

Chapter Eight

1.   Roberts, J., 'The Myth of the Commune', *History Today*, VII, 5 (1957), 297.

2.   *Ibid.*, p. 299.

3.   Edwards, S., *The Paris Commune 1871* (Eyre & Spottiswoode, 1971), p. 217.

4.   Malon, B., *La Troisième Défaite du prolétariat français* (Neuchâtel: Guillaume, 1871), p. 177.

5.   Dommanget, M., *L'Enseignement, l'enfance et la culture sous la Commune* (Librarie de l'Étoile, 1964), p. 69.

6.   Ross, K., *The Emergence of Social Space: Rimbaud and the Paris Commune* (Macmillan, 1988), p. 39.

7.   Villiers de l'Isle-Adam, 'Sous la Commune. Tableau de Paris', *Mercure de France*, 1080 (1953), pp. 587; 593 (text of 1871).

8.   Such propaganda went to current photo-opportunistic lengths of restaging an event for the cameras. Paris theatre actors posed for the 'massacre' of the rue Haxo; see Bourgin, G., *La Guerre de 1870-1871 et la Commune* (Flammarion, 1971), p. 373.

9.   Maxime Du Camp, *Les Convulsions de Paris* (Hachette, 1889), IV, 330, quoted in Lidsky, P., *Les Écrivains contre la Commune* (Maspero, 1970) — an excellent study of this whole question.

10. All these remarks are based on Dr. J.V. Laborde, *Fragments médico-psychologiques: les hommes et les actes de l'insurrection de Paris devant la psychologie morbide*, Germer Baillière, 1872.

11. Renan, E., *Œuvres complètes* (Calmann-Lévy, 1961), I, 623.

12. Tombs, R., *The War against Paris* (Cambridge: U.P., 1981), p. 122.

13. Caro, E.M., 'La Fin de la bohème', *La Revue des Deux Mondes*, XLI, 94 (1871), 241.

14. Saint-Victor, P. de, *Barbares et bandits* (Lévy, 1872), p. 246.

15. Quoted in *Le Cri du peuple*, 17 février 1885.

16. Goncourt, *Journal*, II, 754.

17. Engels, F., in *Marx and Engels on Literature and Art* (St. Louis : Telos, 1973), p. 123.

18. Fallois, B. de, 'La Malchance de Vallès', *La Revue de Paris* (janvier 1955), pp. 115-16.

19. Marx, in Marx-Engels, *Selected Correspondence* (Moscow: Foreign Languages Publishing House, n.d.), p. 410.

20. Goncourt, *Journal*, II, pp. 459-60.

21. Barker, G., quoted in Allott, K. (ed.), *Penguin Book of Contemporary Verse* (1954), p. 217.

22. I am reminded here of the political exploitation of the corpse of a murdered worker in Steinbeck's *In Dubious Battle*.

23. See Horne, A., *The Fall of Paris* (Macmillan, 1989), p. 38: 'The Zouaves paraded a parrot that had been taught to screech "A Berlin!"'.

24. *Ibid.*, pp. 178; 181.

25. Bellet (II, 1929) plausibly suspects that Vallès is ventrilocuting here

26. Edwards, *The Paris Commune*, p. 227.

27. Richepin, *Les Étapes d'un réfractaire*, p. 218.

28. This latter jibe is reported in Guillemin, H., *L'Avènement de M. Thiers* (Gallimard, 1971), p. 219.

29. Disegni, S, 'Journalisme et littérature', p. 53.

30. *Le Cri du peuple*, 19 mars 1884, recalls kids playing marbles behind the barricades. The same urchins also imitated, brutally, the adult street battles. See Dommanget, *L'Enseignement*, p. 79.

31. Ross, *The Emergence of Social Space*, p. 42.

32. Duvignaud, J., 'Une lutte de partisans', *NRF*, 282 (1976), 109.

33. Bellet, 'La Rencontre de la révolte', p. 37.

34. Séverine, *Choix de papiers* (Tierce, 1982), p. 28.

35. Guilloux, L., *Le Sang noir* (Gallimard, 1935), p. 191.

36. Carassus, É., 'Variations de Vallès sur la Commune', in *Ricerche sulla Comune*, pp. 61-2.

37.   Trublot (P. Alexis), 'Vallès auteur dramatique', *Le Cri du peuple*, 19 février 1885.

Chapter Nine

1.   Rogozinski, D., 'Franchise autobiographique', *AJV*, 1 (1984), 66.

2.   One of his few comments on this was: 'Je sais un peu l'anglais' (*Corr. A.*, p. 79). He mentions very few English acquaintances, and these usually spoke French.

3.   Dr. J. Wittlin, cited in Tabori, P., *The Anatomy of Exile* (Harrap, 1972), p. 32.

4.   Tholoniat, R., 'Vallès et Flora Tristan face à l'Angleterre victorienne', *L'Information historique*, XLV, 1 (1983), 35.

5.   Tholoniat, 'Jules Vallès imagier londonien', *AJV*, 7 (1989), 61.

6.   Blanc, J.-N., 'Une ville écrite: l'expressionisme dans *La Rue à Londres*', *AJV*, 10 (1990), 53.

7.   Tholoniat, 'Gavroche et Joë. L'Enfant et l'Insurgé. Deux mythes personnels de Jules Vallès face à la réalité anglaise', *AJV*, 1 (1984), 87-8.

8.   Tholoniat, 'La Pauvreté à Londres à travers *Notes sur l'Angleterre* de Taine et *La Rue à Londres* de Vallès', *Confluents*, 1 (1976), 92.

9.   Villars, P., 'French London', in Sims, G.R. (ed.), *Living London* (Cassell, 1901), II, 134.

10.   Callet, A., 'Lettres d'exil', *La Revue du Palais* (février 1918), pp. 397-8.

11.   Goncourt, *Journal*, III, 104.

12.   Marx, *The Eighteenth Brumaire of Louis Bonaparte*, p. 149.

13.   Perrot, M., foreword to Feller, H., 'Physionomie d'un quotidien: *Le Cri du peuple* (1883-9)', *Le Mouvement social*, 53 (1965), 68.

14.   Séverine, *Choix de papiers*, pp. 22-3.

15.   Quoted in Le Garrec, E., *Séverine* (Seuil, 1982), p. 306.

16.   Quoted in Gille, G., *Jules Vallès*, p. 520.

17.   Nietzsche, F., *The Genealogy of Morals* (New York: Doubleday, 1956), p. 235.

18.   Tocqueville, A. de, *L'Ancien Régime et la Révolution* (Gallimard, 1967), pp. 240-41.

19.   See Bellet's excellent article: 'Les Goncourt et Jules Vallès: une rencontre', *Francofonia*, 19 (1990), 130.

20.   Alexis, P., *Le Matin*, 17 août 1884. Alexis, however, wrote regularly for *Le Cri du peuple*, often under the pseudonym of Trublot. See also his curious story, 'Jean Vingtrin' (*AJV*, 2 [1985], pp. 49 ff.), where a writer switches off from the cacophonous gunfire of the Commune to concentrate, unperturbed, on his civilisation-saving life work.

21.   Baudelaire, *Correspondance générale* (Conard, 1947), I, 152.

22.   Delfau, p. 104.

23.   Rifkin, A., 'Cultural Movement and the Paris Commune', *Art History*, II, 2 (1979), 207.

24.   Engels, F., *Über Kunst und Literatur* (Berlin, 1949), p. 143.

25.   Mallarmé, quoted in Mauclair, C., *Servitude et grandeur littéraires* (Ollendorff, 1922), p. 116.

26.   Sartre, *Situations II* (Gallimard, 1948), p. 140.

27.   Goncourt, *Journal*, III, 446.

Chapter Ten

1.   Rosenberg, H., *The Tradition of the New* (Thames & Hudson, 1962), p. 87.

2.   Du Marsais, quoted in Reboul, O., *Le Slogan* (Bruxelles; Paris: Complexe, 1975), p. 77.

3.   Blanchard, M.E., *Saint-Just et Cie: La Révolution et les mots* (Nizet, 1980), p. 109.

4.   Schama, *Citizens*, p. 532.

5.   Barrès, M., 'La Leçon d'un Insurgé', *Le Voltaire*, 11 juin 1886.

6.   Keats, letter to Reynolds, 3 February 1818.

7.   A phrase from Lamennais's *Le Peuple constituant*, 11 juillet 1848.

8.   Quoted in Callet, 'Lettres d'exil', *La Revue du Palais* (1 janvier 1898), pp. 2-3.

9.   Delfau, p. 203.

10. Quoted by Bergerat, É., *Le Rire de Caliban* (Charpentier, 1890), p. 105.

11. Claudel, P., epigraph to *Le Soulier de Satin*, Gallimard, 1929.

12. Didier, B., preface to Folio edition, p. 28. Unless, of course (cf. the use of *pondre* for writing), the idea of excreting a text is involved.

13. For more than you may want to know about the whole fascinating subject of puns, across time and space, see my *Puns* (Oxford: Blackwell, 1984).

14. Valéry, P., 'Au sujet d'Adonis', *Variété I* (Gallimard, 1924), p. 53.

15. Ricardou, J., *Problèmes du nouveau roman* (Seuil, 1967), p. 53.

16. Sollers, P., *Ponge* (Seghers, 1963), p. 51.

17. Magny, C.-E., *Littérature et Critique* (Payot, 1971), p. 108.

18. Prévert, J., 'Le Discours sur la paix', *Paroles* (Gallimard, 'Folio', 1984 [1948]), p. 220.

19. I could not pin this down any more than one can Nabokov.

20. Empson, W., *Seven Types of Ambiguity* (Penguin, 1961), p. 101.

21. Bonnefis, P., *Vallès*, p. 41.

22. Barthes, R., *Le Degré zéro de l'écriture* (Seuil, 1972), p. 20.

23. Thoreau, H., *Walden* (New York: New American Library, 1960), p. 215.

24. Lepelletier, E., 'Jules Vallès', *L'Écho de Paris*, 16 février 1888.

25. Daudet, L., 'Jules Vallès', p. 1.

26. Camus, *La Chute*, p. 99.

27. Hubbard, E., *The Philistine*.

28. Strickland, G., 'Maupassant, Zola, Jules Vallès and the Paris Commune of 1871', *Journal of European Studies*, 13 (1983), 301.

29. Flaubert, *Correspondance* (Conard), III, 43.

30. Céline, L.-F., *Bagatelles pour un massacre*, p. 61.

31. Horace, *Art of Poetry*, 471.

32. See Schneider, M., *Voleurs de mots* (Gallimard, 1985), p. 280.

33. Callet, 'Lettres d'exil', *La Revue du Palais* (1 février. 1898), p. 419.

34.   Freud, S., *Beyond the Pleasure Principle* (Hogarth, 1961), p. 17.

35.   Masson, P., *Le Disciple et l'Insurgé* (Presses Universitaires de Lyon, 1987), p. 151.

36.   Pascal, B., *Pensées*, 355 (Brunschvicg); 961 (Lafuma).

37.   Sartre, *Situations II*, pp. 180-84. Maupassant is more ambiguous than Sartre allows, but it is an impoverishing ambiguity.

38.   Strickland, 'Maupassant, Zola, Jules Vallès', p. 303.

39.   Thoreau, *Walden*, p. 341.

40.   Pillu, P., 'L'Autoportrait chez Vallès', *AJV*, 2 (1985), 93.

41.   Camproux, C., 'La Langue et le style des écrivains: Jules Vallès', *Les Lettres françaises*, 22-28 août 1957.

42.   Tournier, preface to *Le Bachelier* (Folio, 1974), reprinted in *Le Vol du vampire* (Gallimard, 'Idées', 1983), pp. 196-204 (p. 199).

43.   Lessing, G.E., *Nathan der Weise*, IV, 4.

44.   Goncourt, E. & J. de, *Manette Salomon* (Charpentier, 1896 [1867]), pp. 28-9.

45.   Fontana, M., 'Jules Vallès et le *Chat Noir*', *AJV*, 11 (1990), 13-18.

46.   Renard, *Journal*, II, 628.

47.   Albalat, A., *L'Art d'écrire: ouvriers et procédés* (Colin, 1913), pp. 195-229.

48   Albalat, *La Formation du style par l'assimilation des auteurs* (Colin, 1901), pp. 134-8.

49.   Montaigne, *Essais* (Garnier, 1958), I, 185.

50.   Masson, *Le Disciple et l'Insurgé*, p. 160.

51.   Roy, C., *Le Commerce des classiques* (Gallimard, 1953), p. 252.

52.   Brombert, V., 'Vallès and the Pathos of Rebellion', *The Intellectual Hero* (Faber, 1962), p. 48.

Postlude

1.   *Corr. A.*, p. 281.

2.   Blake, W., 'London' and 'The School Boy', *Complete Writings* (Oxford University Press, 1972), pp. 216; 124.

3. Brunetière, F., 'La Confession d'un réfractaire', *Histoire et littérature* (Gamber, n.d.), pp. 291-2.

4. Brunetière, *Discours de combat*, Perrin, 1903.

5. Brunetière, 'La Confession d'un réfractaire', p. 294.

6. Bloy, L., 'La Frénésie du médiocre', *Œuvres* (Mercure de France, 1964), II, 92-5; 'Causerie sur quelques charognes', *Le Pal* (Vanves: Thot, 1979), pp. 40-46; and *Journal* (Mercure de France, 1963), p. 227.

7. Daudet, L., 'A propos de Vallès', p. 1.

8. Cf. Ortega y Gasset : 'Man is the novelist of his own life, either original or, mostly, a plagiarist'. Quoted in Marías, J., 'Metaphysics: Existence and Human Life', *Yale French Studies*, 16 (1955-6), 123.

9. Nadeau, M., *Littérature présente* (Corrêa, 1952), p. 67.

10. Rogozinski, D., *postface* to *L'Enfant* (Livre de poche, 1985), p. 378.

11. Rousseau, J.-J., *Confessions* (Garnier, 1946), I, 9.

12. Sabin, M., *English Romanticism and the French Tradition* (Harvard: U.P., 1976), p. 20.

13. Sartre, *Les Mots* (Gallimard, 1964), p. 213.

14. Paulhan, J., 'Jules Vallès', *Œuvres complètes* (Cercle du livre précieux, 1969), IV, 60-61.

15. Queneau, R., *Bâtons, chiffres et lettres* (Gallimard, 1965), p. 54.

16. Goncourt, *Journal*, III, 118.

17. Guilloux, L., 'A propos de Jules Vallès', pp. 438; 440.

18. Veuillot, L., *Les Odeurs de Paris*, pp. 68-9.

Select Bibliography

This is a highly selective bibliography. Many other interesting items are to be found in the endnotes. Place of publication is Paris or London, unless otherwise stated.

Vallès: Editions

Bellet, R. (ed.)	*Jules Vallès: Œuvres.* Gallimard (Pléiade), 1975, 1990, 2 vols.
Gille, G. (ed.)	*L'Œuvre de Jules Vallès.* Le Club Français du Livre, 1968.
Scheler, L. & Bancquart, M.-C.	*Jules Vallès, Œuvres complètes.* Livre Club Diderot, 1969-1970, 4 vols.
Scheler, L. (dir.)	*Les Œuvres complètes de Jules Vallès.* Éditeurs français réunis, 1950-1972, 15 vols, as follows:

L'Enfant, ed. L. Scheler.

Le Bachelier, ed. F. Jourdain.

L'Insurgé, ed. M. Cachin.

Le Proscrit: Correspondance avec Arthur Arnould, ed. L. Scheler.

La Rue à Londres, ed. L. Scheler.

Le Cri du peuple, ed. L. Scheler.

Les Réfractaires, ed. R. Lacôte.

Un Gentilhomme; Les Blouses, eds. L. Scheler, J. Dautry.

Correspondance avec Hector Malot, ed. M.-C. Bancquart.

La Rue, ed. P. Pillu.

Littérature et Révolution, ed. R. Bellet.

La Commune de Paris, eds. M.-C. Bancquart, L. Scheler.

Le Tableau de Paris, eds. M.-C. Bancquart, L. Scheler.

Souvenirs d'un étudiant pauvre; Le Candidat des pauvres; Lettre à Jules Mirès, eds. M.-C. Bancquart, L. Scheler.

Vallès—Séverine: Correspondance, ed. L. Scheler.

Selections

Bellet, R. (ed.)	*Les Francs-parleurs*. Pauvert, 1965.
Bancquart, M.-C. (ed.)	*Jules Vallès*. Seghers, 1971.
Pillu, P. (ed.)	*La Trilogie de Jacques Vingtras*. Bordas, 1974.
Cogny, P. (ed.)	*Jules Vallès et son temps*. Larousse, 1980.

Editions of the Trilogy

Livre de poche	ed. G. Sigaux, 1963-1964; ed. P. Pia, 1972; eds. D. Rogozinski, P. Pillu, R. Bellet, 1985.
Garnier-Flammarion	ed. É. Carassus, 1968-70.
Folio	eds. B. Didier, J.-L. Lalanne, M.-C. Bancquart, 1973-5.

Correspondence

	'Jules Vallès: Lettres à Émile Gautier', *Les Belles Lectures*, 1-14 juin, 1952.
Callet, A. (ed.)	'Lettres d'exil', *La Revue du Palais*, 1 janvier 1898, pp. 1-36, 1 février. 1918, pp. 388-424.
———	'Lettres d'exil de Jules Vallès', *La Nouvelle Revue*, mars-avril 1917, pp. 3-17; sept.-oct. 1918, pp. 45-60, 128-139, 247-58, 299-309; nov.-déc. 1918, pp. 39-47, 97-107, 223-9; 1 janvier 1919, pp. 29-39; 25 janvier 1919, pp. 185-9.

Translation

Petrey, S. (tr.)	*The Insurrectionist* [*L'Insurgé*]. Englewood Cliffs, N.J.: Prentice-Hall, 1971.

Books, Theses, Chapters, Articles

Albalat, A.   'Jules Vallès artiste', in *L'Art d'écrire, ouvriers et procédés* (Colin, 1913), pp. 195-229.

Asholt, W.   *Semantische Strukturen in 'L'Enfant' von Jules Vallès* Rheinfalden: Schäuble Verlag, 1977.

Bellet, R.   *Jules Vallès, Journalisme et Révolution*. Tusson: Du Lérot, 1987-1989, 2 vols.

————   'Les Goncourt et Jules Vallès: une rencontre', *Francofonia*, 19 (1990), 115-31.

————   'Jules Vallès: censure et autocensure', *Revue des Sciences Humaines*, 219 (1990), 53-65.

Bellet, R. (ed.)   *Les Amis de Jules Vallès*, 12 issues so far (1984-June 1991).

Bonnefis, P.   *Vallès: du bon usage de la lame et de l'aiguille*. Lausanne: L'Age d'homme, 1982.

Bourget, P.   'Jules Vallès', *Études et portraits* (Plon, 1903), pp. 139-155.

Brombert, V.   'Vallès and the Pathos of Rebellion', in *The Intellectual Hero* (Faber, 1962), pp. 43-51.

Brunetière, F.   'La Confession d'un réfractaire', *Histoire et littérature* (Calmann-Lévy, n.d.), pp. 291-315.

Brupbacher, F.   *Socialisme et liberté*. Pensée et Action, 1964.

Buckingham, M.E.   *Jules Vallès: A Study in Narrative Technique*. Ph.D. thesis, Indiana University, 1975 (Univ. Microfilms, 1979).

Carassus, É.   'Variations de Vallès sur la Commune', *Richerche sulla Comune*. (Milano: Centro Grafico S), pp. 57-67.

Collectif   *Colloque Jules Vallès*. Presses Universitaires de Lyon, 1975.

Colojanni, G.C.   *Il giornalismo di movimento di Vallès*. Palermo: Annali della Facoltà di Lettere e Filosofia, 1981.

Colombani, H.-G.   *Rhétorique de Jules Vallès*. Genève: Slatkine, 1984.

Delfau, G.   *Jules Vallès: L'Exil à Londres*. Bordas, 1971.

Disegni, S.	'Journalisme et Littérature au XIXe siècle. Deux frères ennemis? Le cas Vallès', *Micromégas*, XV, 3 (1988), 39-68.
Europe	Special number on Vallès, nos. 470-472 (1968).
Feller, H.	'Physionomie d'un quotidien: *Le Cri du peuple* (1883-1889)', *Le Mouvement social*, 53 (1965), 69-97.
Gallina, B.	'Un Journaliste de l'opposition à la fin du siècle dernier: Jules Vallès', *Scuola e Lingue Moderne*, 1-2 (1979), 11-18.
Gallo, M.	*Jules Vallès, ou la révolte d'une vie.* Laffont, 1988.
Gill, A.	*Vingt Ans de Paris.* Marpon & Flammarion, 1883.
Gille, G.	*Jules Vallès, 1832-1885: ses révoltes, sa maîtrise, son prestige.* Flammarion, 1941, 2 vols.
Goncourt, E. & J. de	*Journal.* Fasquelle; Flammarion, 1956, 4 vols.
Green, M.F.	*Jules Vallès and the Social Function of Art.* Ph.D., Columbia University, 1973 (Univ. Microfilms, 1974).
Guillemin, H.	*Précisions.* Gallimard, 1973.
———	*Du Courtisan à l'insurgé: Vallès et l'argent.* Arléa, 1990.
Guilloux, L.	'A propos de Jules Vallès', *NRF*, 35 (1930), 437-44.
Jourdain, F.	*Beaumignon* (J. Lévy, 1886), pp. 223-50.
Lebugle, A.	*Rôle et signification de l'habit chez Jules Vallès.* Ph.D., S.U.N.Y. at Buffalo, 1974.
Lejeune, P	*Je est un autre.* Seuil, 1980.
Lloyd, Caryl	'The Politics of Irony and Alienation. A Study of Jules Vallès's *Le Bachelier*', *Romance Quarterly*, 34 (1987), 25-33.
Lloyd, Christopher	' "L'amour du monstre": Jules Vallès and "Le Bachelier géant" ', *The Monstrous*, Durham French Colloquies, 1 (1987), pp. 26-42.

Lockskin, J. *Jules Vallès romancier: étude de la Trilogie.* Ph.D., University of Rochester, 1974 (Univ. Microfilms, 1975).

Marotin, F. 'Valeur polémique et satirique du thème des saltimbanques dans la pensée vallésienne', in Baader, H. (ed.), *Onze études sur l'esprit de la satire* (Tübingen: G. Narr; Paris: J.-M. Place, 1978), pp. 149-158.

Masson, P. *Le Disciple et l'Insurgé.* Presses Universitaires de Lyon, 1987.

Montanari, F. *Jules Vallès, scrittore libertario.* Fasano: Schena, 1991.

Moores, P.M. *Jules Vallès and the Social Rôle of Literature.* Ph.D. thesis, Leicester University, 1977.

———— *Vallès: 'L'Enfant'.* Grant & Cutler, Critical Guides to French Texts, no. 67, 1987.

Morrissette, L. *L'Expérience intérieure d'un révolté: Jules Vallès, la trilogie et la correspondance.* Ph.D., University of Berkeley, 1970.

Münster, A. *Das Thema der Revolt im Werk von Jules Vallès.* München: Fink, 1974.

Nadeau, M. 'Jules Vallès, écrivain moderne'. *Littérature présente,* Corrêa, 1952.

Nikolov, B. 'Les Néologismes dans l'œuvre de Jules Vallès', *Annuaire de l'Université de Sofia,* LXV, 1 (1971), pp. 5-51.

Paulhan, J. 'Jules Vallès'. *Œuvres complètes.* Cercle du Livre précieux, 1968, vol. 4.

Perrin, J. *Vallès: marges, marques, masques.* Thèse de 3e cycle, Université de Lille III, 1984.

Pillu, P. 'Vallès et Zola', *Europe,* 468-469 (1968), 328-35.

Premuda-Perosa, M.-L. (ed.) *Jules Vallès giornalista.* Perugia: Annali della Facoltà di Scienze Politiche, 1987.

Redfern, W.D. (ed.) *Le Bachelier.* University of London Press, 1972.

Redfern, W.D. 'Vallès and the Existential Pun', *Mosaic,* IX, 3 (1976), 27-39.

Richepin, J. *Les Étapes d'un réfractaire.* Flammarion, 1872.

Rogozinski, D.   'La Parade des monstres: L'Entre-sort', *Revue des Sciences Humaines*, LIX, 188 (1982), 93-115.

Rollin, R.H.   *The Comic Spirit in the Trilogy of Jules Vallès*. Ph.D., Bryn Mawr, 1976 (Univ. Microfilms, 1983).

Rouchon, U.   *La Vie bruyante de Jules Vallès*. Saint-Étienne: Éditions de la Région illustrée, 1935-7, 2 vols.; 3rd vol., chez l'auteur, 1939.

Roy, C.   'Jules Vallès', *Le Commerce des classiques* (Gallimard, 1953).

Stivale, C.J.   *Œuvre de sentiment—Œuvre de combat: La Trilogie de Jacques Vingtras*. Presses Universitaires de Lyon, 1988.

Strickland, G.   'Maupassant, Zola, Jules Vallès and the Paris Commune of 1871', *Journal of European Studies*, 13 (1983), 289-307.

Tholoniat, R.   'La Pauvreté à Londres, à travers *Notes sur l'Angleterre* de Taine et *La Rue à Londres* de Vallès', *Confluents*, 1 (1976), 79-94.

Weller, M.   *Jules Vallès, Counter-Ideologist*. Ph.D. University of Illinois at Urbana-Champaign, 1982.

Secondary Material

Bellet, R.   *Presse et journalisme sous le Second Empire*. Armand Colin, collection 'Kiosque', 1967.

Chombart   *Un Monde autre: l'enfance, de ses représentations*
de Lauwe, M.-J.   *à son mythe*. Payot, 1971.

Edwards, S.   *The Paris Commune 1871*. Eyre & Spottiswoode, 1971.

Fiedler, L.   *Freaks*. Penguin, 1981.

Gerbod, P.   *La Condition universitaire en France au XIXe siècle*. Presses Universitaires de France, 1965.

———   *La Vie quotidienne dans les lycées et collèges au XIXe siècle*. Hachette, 1968.

Horne, A.   *The Fall of Paris: The Siege and the Commune, 1870-1871*. Macmillan, revised edition, 1989.

Hutton, P.H.	*The Cult of the Revolutionary Tradition: The Blanquists in French Politics, 1864-1893.* Berkeley: University of California Press, 1981.
Labracherie, P.	*La Vie quotidienne de la bohème littéraire au XIXᵉ siècle.* Hachette, 1967.
Lidsky, P.	*Les Écrivains contre la Commune.* Maspero, 1970.
Lissagaray, P.-O.	*Histoire de la Commune de 1871.* Maspero, 1982.
Poulot, D.	*Le Sublime, ou le travailleur comme il est en 1870 et ce qu'il peut être.* Maspero, 1980.
Prost, A.	*Histoire de l'enseignement en France (1800-1967).* Colin, 1968.
Queffélec, L.	*Le Roman-feuilleton en France au XIXᵉ siècle.* Presses Universitaires de France, 1989.
Roberts, J.	'The Myth of the Commune'. *History Today,* VII, 5 (1957), 290-300.
Rougerie, J.	*La Commune, 1871.* Presses Universitaires de France, 1988.
Rubin, J.H.	*Realism and Social Vision in Courbet and Proudhon.* Princeton U.P., 1980.
Schama, S.	*Citizens.* Penguin, 1989.
Weber, E.	*Peasants into Frenchmen.* Chatto & Windus, 1976.
Zeldin, T.	*France, 1848-1945.* Oxford : Clarendon Press, 1973-1977, 2 vols.

UNIVERSITY OF GLASGOW
FRENCH AND GERMAN PUBLICATIONS

French Department, The University.   Glasgow G12 8QL, Scotland, G.B.

Works on Zola, Naturalism
and the late 19th century

Henri Marel
'Germinal': une documentation intégrale
Textes réunis et édités par Geoff Woollen; préface de Henri Mitterand
xii + 314 pp., 1989 (réimpression, 1990).
£11 / 110F / $20 U.S. or Canadian
ISBN 0 85261 248 6

Claude Schumacher
Zola: 'Thérèse Raquin' (English text)
Introductory Guides to French Literature **11**. vi + 90 pp., 1990.
£3.50 / 35F / $7 U.S. or Canadian
ISBN 0 85261 263 X

Roger Clark
Zola: 'L'Assommoir' (English text)
Introductory Guides to French Literature **13**. vi + 82 pp., 1990.
£3.50 / 35F / $7 U.S. or Canadian
ISBN 0 85261 268 0

Robert Pickering
Lautréamont: Image, Theme and Self-Identity
iv + 84 pp., 1990.
£4.95 / 50F / $10 U.S. or Canadian
ISBN 0 85261 289 3

La Chauve-Souris et le Papillon:
Correspondance Montesquiou-Whistler
éd. Joy Newton. viii + 246 pp. + 10 pp. d'illustrations., 1990.
£12 / 120F / $22 U.S. or Canadian
ISBN 0 85261 277 X

Zola: 'La Bête humaine': texte et explications
Actes du colloque du centenaire à Glasgow
éd. Geoff Woollen. xiv + 223 pp. + 3 pp. d'illustrations., 1990.
£11 / 110 F / $20 U.S. or Canadian
ISBN 0 85261 279 6

Post paid. Cheques payable to 'University of Glasgow', account 114502